# EL BECKS

## A SEASON IN THE SUN

To Brenda

# EL BECKS
## A SEASON IN THE SUN

### Alex Leith

**VSP**

Vision Sports Publishing
2 Coombe Gardens,
London, SW20 0QU

www.visionsp.co.uk

This First Edition Published by
Vision Sports Publishing in 2004

Design: David Hicks
Editorial: Ian Cranna

Set in Franklin Gothic 9.5pt/13pt
Typeset by Palimpsest Book Production Limited, Polmont, Stirlingshire

Printed and bound in the UK by
Cromwell Press

A CIP catalogue record for this book is available from the British Library

ISBN 0-9546428-0-5

# ACKNOWLEDGEMENTS

This book would not have been possible without the kind co-operation of countless people all over a country which has rightfully gained a reputation for its generosity, honesty and hospitality. Particular thanks are due to Sid Lowe, for his unflagging support; to Roger Gutierrez and Patricia 'La Marquesa'; to Villarreal's César Arzo; to everyone at the Real Madrid peña in L'Hospitalet; to Málaga's Manu; to Ken and Pam of the Tavern in Marbella; to Manolo 'el del Bombo'; to Paco of La Riua in Valencia; to Arximelo and Tato of the Rikitriki in Vigo, to Marcopolo of the Celtarras and to Celta de Vigo's Savo Milosevic; to Sevilla's Jesús and Notario; to everyone at the Real Betis Peña; to Paco the security man at Mallorca; to José Mari, Marisa and Lander in San Sebastian, as well as everyone at the 0-5 peña, to Paco the Real Madrid factotum, as well as to Borja and Cambiasso; to Iñaki and Julio at Valladolid; to Don Manuel and Figo the dog in La Vega; to Albacete's Pablo, as well as Jesús, Luis and Parrita; to Canal Plus' inimitable Michael Robinson; to everyone at the Jai-Ca bar in La Barceloneta; to Rojo and the lads in La Coruña; to Vicente and Baraja of Valencia (for those goals). On the production side, thanks to VSP's visionary duo Jim and Toby, to Dave Hicks for his top design skills; to Brenda for tightening up loose prose and taking fine photos; to José Mari for correcting my idiosyncratic Spanish and to Dave Jackson for his galactic typesetting skills. Also many thanks, of course, for doing his damnedest in trying circumstances to David Beckham, a footballer I admire for his passion, his skill and his ability to take on the sort of challenge that inspired this book to be written.

# CONTENTS

# ONE
# MADRID

GOLFO DE VIZCAYA

OCÉANO ATLÁNTICO

**Real Madrid**

**Mallorca**

MAR MEDITERRÁNEO

**Real Betis**

# ONE
# MADRID

**WEDNESDAY AUGUST 27TH, 2003**

I've heard Catalans calling Madrid 'the arsehole in the desert': it's not the best place to be in August. It's not as hot as it was earlier in the month – they tell me it topped 50 centigrade last week – but it's too hot for comfort. The heat drives the Madrileños out of their city for the month. The many pompous classical buildings that house the government and monarchy of Spain are empty. The great Retiro park, where you can shelter from the sun in the shade of the trees, or get near to some water by boating in the lake, is fairly empty too, save for the odd tourist, killing time waiting for the cooling night. In the city centre most of the shops have metal shutters padlocked over their entrances, and a sign taped up, advising when the owners will be back from their holidays. Traffic is minimal – there are even a few parking spaces. The only people who you see in the city streets are those who can't afford to leave, or the few who have to stay and work. Everybody else is in the cooling mountains to the north, or in one of the beach resorts that fringe the country. It's not just Madrid. Most of Spain takes August off; it's like a school holiday for adults. Newspapers are already talking about the onset of post-August depression. The one consolation? The start of the football season. And this year there's no doubt who's the main attraction.

I've been reading about tonight's match, the second leg of the Supercopa, in *Marca*, Spain's most popular newspaper. The Supercopa is the curtain-raiser of the new Spanish football season, played between the League Champions – currently Real Madrid – and the holders of the Cup – Mallorca. The entire front page of today's edition is taken up by a picture of David Beckham's right ear. The lobe is encircled by a thick diamond ring, there's a swathe of bottle-blond hair brushed behind it. This is Beckham's first home game, but his ear is already the most identifiable in Spain.

2

Judging from the media interest in the England captain over here, it must be burning pretty badly right now. And not much being said is positive. Beckham's first competitive game for Real Madrid, in the first leg against Mallorca the preceding Sunday, was an abject failure. Beckham was substituted ten minutes into the second half, having made little contribution to a match his team lost 2–1. *Marca* is a sports paper which normally dedicates its first eight pages to Real Madrid. An unforgiving judge, it gave him zero points for his performance.

Today is the day of the return leg of the tie. It is Beckham's 'presentation' to his home fans, and the pressure is on. The 75,000 Bernabéu stadium (pronounced 'Bear-nah-bay-oo') is likely to be full; people have even cut short their holidays in order to see the game. *Marca*, a paper which loves to make bad puns, has done well this morning. 'All of Madrid' they say, 'is hanging on Beckham.' In Spanish the word 'pendiente' means both 'hanging' and 'earring'. I'm certainly hanging on Beckham, in more ways than one. I have a ticket for the game in my wallet, and I haven't felt as excited before a match for years.

I don't live in Madrid, I live in Barcelona. I arrived there in the summer of 2003, a year before Beckham made the move to Madrid, to set myself up as a travel and sports writer. I already knew the city, having lived there for a few months before the 1992 Olympics, and loved the place. This time I came with my Irish girlfriend Brenda: a romantic change of life for us both. I gave up my job working on a football magazine, she gave up hers as an intellectual property lawyer. Together we would get to understand the Spanish way of life. But I soon realised that, living in Barcelona, I got a slanted view of the rest of Spain. The Catalans speak their own language, enjoy their own customs, and generally want independence from Madrid. Even after a year there, I realised I didn't understand what Spain was all about, what made it tick. Beckham's arrival at Real Madrid set me thinking. If I could follow him from game to game, from city to city, talking to fans and players and seeking out adventure, I would end the year understanding much better what, if anything, held Spain together. And the idea of this book formed in my mind: a football travel book, using Real Madrid and Beckham as a vehicle in which to visit all the major cities in the country. I would start in Madrid, and then go to all the away games Real Madrid played in the league, occasionally returning to the capital as the season progressed. By getting to know what the Galicians and Andalucians and Castilians thought of Beckham, I would get to understand them better, and work out more about the fabric of this vast and diverse country.

So on the afternoon of Beckham's first game in his new home city, I find myself walking around the semi-deserted streets of Madrid, looking for what first impressions the Madrileños have of the Englishman. I start in the working class district of La Latina, in the city centre, where I'm staying.

"Qué opinas de Beckham?" (What do you think of Beckham?) I ask the guy who sells me vegetables in the Mercado de la Cebada, just off Calle Toledo, which runs south from la Plaza Mayor, Madrid's central square. The market is a typical Spanish affair, a big warehouse with stalls selling fruit and vegetables, poultry products, chorizo sausages, sheets of tripe. There are some skinned lambs' heads. He's a young man in his twenties, wearing a red t-shirt and a gold earring in each ear. "I'm not a merengue, I support Atleti," he replies, placing two red peppers I've bought in a cone of brown paper. Atleti is short for Atlético de Madrid, Real's local rivals, who enjoy most of the support of the working classes in the city; 'los merengues' is the widely-used nickname of the Real supporters, because of the team's all white kit. After a long pause, he continues. "I think they bought the wrong player. Real needed a central defender. They already have enough midfielders." An in-depth discussion ensues. Spanish men love talking football. Wherever you go there's a heated discussion between two or more guys about the current issues of debate: on the metro, in the bar, on the street corner. This week's issue is Beckham. Was he a good buy for Real Madrid? Will he make a big enough contribution to the game to warrant all the fuss that's been made about his arrival in the country?

I order some jamón dulce (sweet ham) from a rotund market stall owner with a big sweeping-brush of a moustache. As he slices it on a large silver machine I ask him about Beckham. "Beckham?" he says. "I am disappointed. He is a mediático (a media star) who was just bought so that Florentino Pérez can make El Real more marketable in Asia. I am a Real fan, and I am not happy. He will sell shirts, but he will not win many games." Florentino Pérez is the club president, the owner of a construction business, who was elected to office in 2000 after promising to buy Luis Figo from Real's traditional rivals Barcelona, a promise he fulfilled.

In a small bar round the corner, a nicotine-tone Hieronymous Bosch vision of hell fills the main wall. As a white-coated barman with a red face and a scruffy short grey hair serves me a caña, (the stock Spanish bar drink, a small glass of lager), I ask him about Beckham. "He's a good player," he says in a gruff black-tobacco-scorched voice, then he walks away to wash a glass. 'Is that it?' I think. He comes back a full thirty seconds later. "But he's better at selling shirts. He was not a good buy for Real."

My host Roger is a lifelong Real Madrid fan who I met while he was enduring an unhappy spell living in Barcelona. He puts the Beckham dilemma more eloquently, as we sit drinking cañas in a bar near his flat, and sharing a bowl of paella, which has come free with the beers.

"Spain has never seen anything like Beckham before," he says, in the excitable manner he has, waving a cigarette for effect. "The hair, the clothes, the ear-rings . . . Pérez has bought one of the world's best players every year for the last four years. They call them 'los galácticos'. First Luis Figo, then Zinedine Zidane, and last year Ronaldo. Each has come to fill a vacant position in the team. Each player has struggled at first, but then proved themselves with their brilliant performances on the pitch. But Beckham's position, wide right in midfield, was already filled by Figo, who has had to move to the left to accommodate him, which he obviously is not happy about. He is not left footed! The Real fans are not happy about this. Figo is their hero, and they suspect that Beckham has been bought simply as a marketing tool. A clothes horse! They have never seen such a media phenomenon as Beckham – and they are wondering what all the fuss is about. I mean, what's the big deal?"

Roger pauses, but not for long enough for me to get a word in. "Pérez has spoken about 'evangelising' new supporters in order to create a kind of world-wide empire of support for the club," he continues, "and Beckham is the spearhead of this process. But if Beckham fails on the pitch – and he has played very poorly in the pre-season matches – and Real start losing games because of this, the 'evangelisation' is unlikely to succeed. And, worse for Real fans, the team will win few matches. The stadium will start to empty! If Beckham is seen as being the reason for this failure, then he is likely to become very unpopular in Madrid. Very unpopular. Among Real fans, anyhow. And most are already suspicious that this might be about to happen."

Like many inveterate talkers, Roger drinks his beer in rare but enormous gulps, and at this point he drains his half-full glass in one.

The Santiago Bernabéu metro exit comes out right in front of the Real Madrid stadium, and it's quite a sight: my first time. A huge modern concrete thing, like an inverted bath-tub, done up by a sci-fi set designer. Now there *are* people around. Thousands of them, dressed in the white shirts of Madrid, carrying banners, even wearing scarves. Around the rim at the bottom of the stadium there are scores of stalls with flags and shirts. It's nine o'clock in the evening now, and the temperature's dropped considerably. Kick-off is at 9.45, relatively late even for this bed-shy country. I feel strange. I haven't been so nervous before a match for a long time, and now I'm excited too; full of little-kid thrill. I realise what it is. I haven't come to support my team: I'm not a Real fan. But I really want David Beckham to do well, to prove his early critics wrong.

I desperately want our lad to come good. I want to be proud of him. It's an odd feeling, which I remember from the days when Gazza played for Lazio.

I'm with Roger. Things start moving fast as we walk towards the stadium. I'm surprised to find stalls selling fake twenty-euro Beckham shirts alongside official versions at 75 euros. Next door someone's trying to sell Union Jack flags – unsuccessfully as far as I can see. I buy a scarf that Roger takes an interest in that says 'Anti-Culé'. Los Culés (Catalan for 'arses') is the nickname for the Barcelona fans, and the scarf shows a boot stomping on the Barcelona FC emblem. It costs seven euros. Roger is delighted, and, despite the temperature still being in the high twenties, he puts it round his neck.

I check out the names on the back of shirts – Beckham apparently sold 10,000 on the first day of trading after his transfer, ten times the equivalent figure for Ronaldo a year before. But it seems that very few of the purchases were made by match-going fans. It's last year's heroes that predominate, the existing 'galácticos' in Pérez' real-life Fantasy Football team: Raúl, Figo, Zidane, Roberto Carlos and, of course, Ronaldo, who scored 23 goals to help the club to a 29th title win. Finally, I see a couple of Beckhams. As I pass them, straining to hear their conversation, I'm disappointed by a very London pronunciation of the name of the team they're about to watch. 'Ray-oo', with full Phil Mitchell glottal stop. The Spanish say 'Ray-al' with the stress on the second syllable. A new phenomenon: Beckham tourists.

I spot a couple of 12-year-old girls, both Beckhamed up, and I ask them the obvious question.

"Who's your favourite player?"

"Beckham," they stereo back, pronouncing it in the Spanish way, 'Bay-kan'. The Spanish find it difficult to pronounce phonemes that don't exist in their language.

"Why Beckham?"

"Because he is so guapo."

"He's very guapo."

'Guapo' means good-looking. They both make vocal swooning noises.

I make my way to a sweaty crowded bar over the road from the stadium – Roger goes in to keep our seats. It's a fight to get a drink. Gruff-voiced men keep getting served in front of me. Finally I have my say.

"Me pones una cerveza?"

By the time I've finished paying for it, I've gulped half of it down. The other half doesn't last long. I take it outside into the street and drink it next to a guy who is mixing hashish and tobacco in his hand. He doesn't seem bothered by the heavy police presence in the vicinity. Hungry, I look for a hamburger stall, or at least something selling bocadillos (hero sandwiches) but all I can find is a trestle table with a selection of nuts and Chupa-Chup lollipops, with their wrapper design by Salvador Dali. The sunflower seeds are selling fast, so I decide to do as the Madrileños do, and put the plastic-wrapped packet in my pocket for later.

I find the relevant gate – 47 – and join the queue behind a bloke in his thirties in a Beckham shirt.

"Why did you choose a Beckham shirt?"

"Because I like Manchester United."

"But you're Spanish."

"I'm not. I'm Catalan. I'm from Barcelona."

"But you support Real Madrid?"

"Believe me, it's difficult. I had to get up at seven o'clock this morning to get here."

I'm amazed, and am about to tell him so, when he nods at the plastic bottle of water in my hand.

"Take the top off, and hide it in your pocket."

"Why?"

"A bottle of water with a top on it is a dangerous weapon. You could throw it at the players. They will confiscate the top as you go in."

I reach the gate and do as the person in front does, putting the end of my ticket in a slot where it is read by an infa-red light. I walk past a security guard (no body search, my bottle top is safe) and follow directions into the brightly lit open air. Madonna is singing *Like a Virgin*. I find my seat. Roger, who is nowhere to be seen, has chosen well: we're on the bottom tier of the stadium, near the pitch, about forty metres from the goal to our right. It's a great sight – four tiers of seats, already half-filled, looming over the pitch. And the Real Madrid players are there, playing a game which involves throwing the ball to one another. I pick out Beckham from the four peroxide blonds in the team, a frail-looking figure, his pony-tail bobbing up and down. He catches the ball, but immediately loses possession. I'm disappointed. I try to gauge his mood. *I'm* nervous enough. The Mallorca team run onto the pitch. They're all dressed in black, and they get the appropriate boos. Roger turns up, too, highly excited. "Florentino Pérez walked into the crowd!" he says. "You missed it! He was shaking hands, and kissing children! Everyone turned to hail him. 'Presi!' they were shouting. They love him!"

A tannoy voice reads out the names of the Mallorca players, whose pictures appear on a huge screen above the South stand. Then come the Real players' names, accompanied each time by cheers. They are in numerical order, so Beckham's name is called last. I want the fans to cheer the loudest, but every player gets the same decibel level.

Perhaps Beckham's cheer is higher in pitch – but that is probably just my imagination. The teams line up for photographs, as the operatic Real Madrid hymn, *Hala Madrid* (Hail Madrid) booms out the tannoy. I check with Roger. Is that Plácido Domingo? It is.

The teams line up and hundreds of camera flashes sparkle in the stands: bound-to-be useless photos of dots in the green. The referee blows the whistle. Raúl and Ronaldo kick off, but immediately lose the ball. Beckham wins it back, dribbles, and passes to feet. A good start. Warm applause.

Beckham's career has just moved up a level. Manchester United were one thing, Real Madrid are quite another. Last year, the 101st of their existence, they won their 29th league title. They have won 17 Spanish Cups, six Spanish Supercopas, one League Cup, two UEFA Cups, one European Supercup, three Intercontinental Cups and, most remarkably of all, nine European Cups. This makes them quite easily the most successful team the world has ever seen. And Beckham has just joined what many rate as being Real Madrid's best-ever team. It's quite a challenge.

We're in great Beckham-watching territory. Playing in his accustomed position on the right, he's trying really hard. In the first ten minutes he does two defensive headers out of his own box. Both times he earns generous applause. The fans are noisy, voicing their emotions, clapping, shouting. Then, on the quarter hour, there's a foul between the touch-line and the far side of the Mallorca box. Figo is nearest, but Beckham moves fast to claim it as his. There is no argument. The wall lines up, and the Englishman starts his run-up, from a peculiar angle. The crowd performs a rhythmic clap, shouting 'ho' on every beat. I find myself joining in. The ball beats the keeper . . . and goes just wide of the far post. An involuntary "ho-ee" sound comes from every chest – the Spanish equivalent of our near-miss 'ooh'.

Mallorca attack and their Cameroon striker, Samuel Eto'o (a former Real player, who is still half-owned by the club) goes down after a challenge from Iván Helguera, just outside the Real Madrid box, in front of the most vocal of the Real Madrid fans, who have been waving flags and singing more than anyone else. Most of them are wearing Real's blue-black away shirts, and are in a neat thousand-strong square behind the penalty box. "Muerto, muerto," they shout as Eto'o writhes on the ground; they are wishing him dead. They chant 'Puto negro, hijo de puta' (fucking negro, son of a whore). The song is whistled down by the rest of the crowd. Mallorca miss the free kick. Roger explains who they are. "The Ultra Sur. Unos hijos de puta racistas" (racist bastards).

Beckham is everywhere, but he looks nervous on the ball, and usually plays the safe option. His tentativeness is rather endearing. Every time there's a free kick he runs over to the spot, and picks up the ball, like he just got it for Christmas, and nobody else is allowed a go on it. He keeps missing the target, though, and finally Zidane has a quiet word in his ear, and takes the next one himself. It goes way over the bar. I'm relieved.

With half-time approaching, Ronaldo runs to the bye-line, draws the goal-keeper, and passes square to Raúl, who side-foots the ball into the empty goal. Everyone around me rises to their feet, cheering and raising their arms in triumph. My reaction is delayed and less exuberant. My man had nothing to do with it. I stand up and cheer for the hell of it. It feels wrong somehow.

The whistle blows for half-time, and almost everyone produces a silver-foil-wrapped sandwich from their bag and starts to eat. Suddenly hungry, I remember the sunflower seeds. It's a fiddly process with little reward. They simply serve to make me thirsty. I've finished my water. I look around me for a refreshment stall, and spot a hastily-made banner hanging on the frieze above. It's in English. 'BECKS: WELCOME TO THE GALAXY THRON' it announces. You can see that they have run out of room for the 'e'. Then: 'FROM RED DEVIL TO WHITE ANGEL. FIGO – ZIZOU – RONIE . . . YOU'RE THE NEXT'. I set off to buy a beer, wondering if they're right. Is Beckham as good as these world class 'galácticos'? I come back with more water. They don't sell alcohol in the ground.

As the second half starts, the Ultra Sur don't appear. This leaves a strange square of empty seats behind the goal. I turn round and ask the bloke behind about it. "They're protesting to the president because he's trying to sell Morientes and Solari," he replies. He's a pleasant guy, smart-casually dressed, who's with two girls. A few minutes later, the match having restarted, I hear him shouting, so I look round. His face is filled with hate. "Indio de mierda," he yells. "Shitty Indian." Then, along with many others around him, he starts chanting "Indio, Indio." Mallorca's diminutive Argentine midfielder, Ibagaza nicknamed 'El Caño' (the nutmeg) for his habit of playing the ball between other players' legs, has just fallen down injured in front of us. 'Los Indios' is the nickname of Real's city rivals Atlético de Madrid (Real are sometimes known as 'Los Vikingos'). This is Ibagaza's last game for Mallorca, which explains the depth of the fans' hatred for him. He's moving to 'Atleti'.

Soon after Figo passes to Ronaldo who scores from a narrow angle. 2–0. Mayhem around me, but again I don't feel moved enough to join in properly. For a while Real start passing the ball round with some assurance, every pass being greeted by an 'olé'. But one Mallorca goal will level the aggregate scores, and it is their turn to start attacking. Real start looking very frail at the back. Iker Casillas, Real's 22-year-old keeper, is playing brilliantly, the best of a string of saves coming from a free-kick by Ibagaza, which looks destined for the top corner.

"Indio, Indio," chant the fans.

To relieve the tension, Madrid get a free-kick at the other end. Beckham is allowed to take it.

"Bey-kan, Bey-kan," chant a minority of the crowd, as he runs up. The net ripples, and the crowd starts a cheer, but there's something wrong – it's hit the roof of the net, and the cheer turns into a near-miss "Oo-ee". Soon after an official comes to the side of the pitch to signal a substitution. The electronic blackboard signals . . . a '7' and for a heart-stopping moment I think that's it for Beckham. Then I remember he wears '23' at Real (apparently an idea of Jorge Valdano, Real's canny Director of Football), and it's Raúl who's going off, replaced by Javier Portillo, a young lean striker with strange hair, spiky at the back, who's come through the ranks of Real's youth teams.

It's just as well Beckham stays on the pitch. Ronaldo gets the ball on the left and launches it across the box. There's a familiar unmarked figure on the far post, who reaches the ball before the slow-off-his-line keeper and heads it gently into the goal. My eyes strain at the far-away figure to see if what I suspect is true. The bobbing pony-tail, the brittle-looking legs. Beckham! He runs to the corner-flag and raises his hands in glee, and everyone in the stadium is up on their feet, cheering. A chant starts up, very loud this time.

"Bey-kan! Bey-kan! Bey-kan!"

I join in, at first pronouncing the name right, then feeling out of place, and changing the 'm' to an 'n'.

"Bey-kan, Bey-kan."

I can't stop myself from jumping up and down this time.

Beckham starts playing like a madman: the goal has clearly helped him shake off his nerves. Suddenly we see what might happen in the months (and years?) to come. He plays a fast-moving 1–2 with Zidane on the edge of the box and lays off a neat little pass to Ronaldo, who has the space for a shot, which he puts into the side netting. The guy to my left shouts 'venga gordito' (go on, fatty) and everyone laughs. The Brazilian looks about a stone overweight.

This is drowned out as fans throughout the stadium launch into a song, the first time, apart from the 'Bey-kan' chants, that anyone in the stadium but the Ultra Sur has done so.

"Así, así, así gana el Madrid" (this is the way that Madrid win). Roger explains: the song is sung by opposing fans after Madrid have won due to the supposed bias of a referee. That it is generally assumed by non-Real fans that the referees consistently favour the Madrid team. The Real fans, however, turn the joke on the opposition by singing the song when Real win with style and panache. The fans are in good humour, and another chant breaks out, which needs no translation.

"Campeones, campeones, Oé, oé, oé'"

The Madrid fans are jolly, but it's not all over yet. Mallorca continue to attack. Because of the away goals rule, 3–2 would give them an aggregate victory, so one goal would mean an extremely nervous endgame for the Real Madrid players and fans. Ibagaza shoots – again Casillas saves brilliantly. The crowd chant his first name 'Iker, Iker'. I'm slightly disappointed. I'm still a neutral, and I want as exciting a finale as possible. The fans start a universally recognisable clap-and-sing number: 'Clap clap – clap clap clap – clap clap clap clap – Madrid!' The final whistle is blown. More mayhem. The hymn comes out of the tannoy again, its operatic pompousness more in tune now with the emotions around me. This is the 80th trophy Real Madrid have won in their 102-year history.

A pull-out players tunnel has been dragged to the edge of the pitch and Raúl, Madrid's captain, runs into it to collect the cup from the directors' box behind me. All the fans around me are standing on their seats trying to see him. I'm looking the other way, watching Beckham, who is kissing all the players on both cheeks: Zidane; Ronaldo; Michel Salgado. I never saw him act in such a way with Gary Neville or Paul Scholes. He keeps blowing kisses into the crowd above me, presumably at his wife Victoria. The other players are chatting amongst themselves: Beckham looks a little isolated. Raúl runs out of the tunnel with a shiny trophy in his hand and the players run into the centre circle and form a huddle, bouncing up and down together. The fans are still singing.

"Así, así, así gana el Madrid."

The players do a lap of honour, passing the cup between them, as they jog round the edge of the pitch. Beckham holds it up to the crowd briefly, then hands it on to Roberto Carlos. There is an odd moment as the players run past the section of empty seats the Ultra Sur were in. I wonder, with so many superstars in the same dressing room, whether the season will end in such high spirits. The players disappear down the tunnel. Beckham is the last in. He is made to pose with the cup in front of the herd of photographers. The cameras flash, he grins a for-the-cameras grin. As if as an afterthought, he rather nonchalantly lifts the trophy to the crowd with one hand. Then he's out of the limelight and into the tunnel to change from his football gear and into his no-doubt-meticulously-planned street attire.

## THURSDAY AUGUST 28TH

I'm sitting in my favourite day-time bar in Madrid, in the immigrant district of Lavapiés (literally 'feetwash') on Calle del Ave María. It's all faded grandeur: baroque corniches, slim Corinthian columns and big mirrors which have long lost their sheen. I've got the daily papers in front of me, bought from a kiosk round the corner, as well as a café con leche, the typical Spanish breakfast drink, a strong coffee topped up with hot milk. There's no froth – I much prefer it to a cappuccino. I pull out what's been burning a hole in my bag. It's time for the moment of truth. What the papers say. And in particular, *Marca*.

Spain's best-selling newspaper is a sports paper which usually devotes most of its front section to Real Madrid. It is open about its favouritism for the team. *Marca* (which means 'score') is a tabloid, printed in the capital, which knows that it can bank on 400,000 people buying it every day, which translates into an estimated 2.6 million readers (newspaper sales in Spain are very low compared with the UK). Those readers can be sure of being privy to strongly-worded views about Real Madrid in particular, Spanish football in general, and then the other sports (which usually get dedicated about 16 of its 48 pages).

It is rare that *Marca* doesn't have a front page featuring Real Madrid, and this morning, again, Beckham is the star. A side-on view of his goal celebration, his head tilted back, his pony-tail dangling down. 'GOZA BECKHAM' reads the headline (Beckham enjoys himself). There follows a quote from the Englishman: 'it was incredible to score from a pass by Ronaldo.' But the really telling information is tucked away on the inside front page: *Marca's* marks.

After every game in La Liga (they are all given at least half a page by the paper) each player is given a mark out of three, and a short (one-to-three word) commentary about his performance. It is a very economical scoring system, which doesn't give much room for fence-sitting. There are no half marks – the system has no nuances like, for example, Italy's more intellectual *Gazzetta dello Sport*, which gives marks out of ten, and awards half marks, too. The Spanish system is more simple, and more brutal. Though I have never seen it explained, the points mean the following.

0 points: the player played badly.
1 point: the player had an average game.
2 points: the player played well.
3 points: the player had a brilliant game.

*Marca* are tough judges: they rarely overmark. Last year Ronaldo, who scored 23 league goals and was widely seen as being the main reason Real won the league, got an average mark throughout the season of 1.46: closer to mediocre than good. Of the other 'galácticos' in the league, Roberto Carlos got 1.21, Figo got 1.41, Raúl got 1.52 and Zidane got 1.57. Poor Steve McManaman, who participated in 15 games, could only manage 0.45.

The marks are qualified by the short comment afterwards. Thus, for the Mallorca game, goalkeeper Casillas is awarded the top marks, a '3' with the comment 'he saved everything'. Four players get a '2': young Raúl Bravo ('he passed the test'); Roberto Carlos ('very concentrated'); Cambiasso ('good game'); and Ronaldo ('goal and playmaking'). And Beckham? Beckham gets a disappointing '1' with the comment 'debut . . . and goal'.

The voice of Real Madrid fans is giving out a clear message: 'we're pleased with Beckham, but not that pleased. He still has to persuade us he is worth all the money, and, more importantly, all the fuss, too.' Thank God for that goal.

The other papers are generally more positive. *As* (Ace), *Marca*'s inferior, more sensationalist rival (80c rather than 90c) gives him two points in the same scoring system. Most of the serious papers carry a picture of Beckham's goal celebration on the front, and a large report inside. *El País*, Spain's left-leaning *Guardian* equivalent, which is the second-most-read daily in Spain, carries a picture of Harrison Ford on its front page. Amazingly, Ford is holding up a red-and-white striped football shirt with his name on the back, over the number 12. Closer inspection shows the shirt to be . . . of Atlético de Madrid. Real's city rivals signed a shirt sponsorship deal with Columbia Tristar in the summer, and will carry an advert for a different film each month. It's a move designed to generate a good deal of publicity, and it's worked: Atlético have managed to steal a little bit of the press limelight from Real Madrid and their new signing's debut goal.

### FRIDAY AUGUST 29TH

It's clear that the pressure is on Beckham to come up with a good performance in the first league game of the season, again in the Bernabéu, against Seville's Real Betis, tough opponents who have the reputation of starting well in the league. In last season's first match they beat then-champions Deportivo de la Coruña 4–2 away, and they're hoping to do the same against current champions Real Madrid.

I want to watch the Real Madrid-Real Betis match in a bar near the Atlético de Madrid stadium to get a better idea of how football is seen in the capital. And I've found just the place, two minutes walk from the elegant Vicente Calderon stadium, which is just south of the city centre, a twenty-minute walk from la Plaza Mayor. But, with tickets in the Bernabéu just about to sell out, my plan is at risk due to a complicated TV rights dispute, which threatens the coverage of the match.

Spanish football is extremely well covered on TV. If you have the right equipment, you can watch any Primera match, simply by pressing a few digits on your phone, and dictating which match you want to watch, though you have to pay 11.99 euros for each game. The system, which the Spanish call 'pay-pair-bue' (written 'pay per view') has been going two years, and complements the one game a week broadcast by *Canal Plus* (which you need to subscribe to), and the one game available for free on terrestrial TV. Most bars now have a TV set on the wall, and show various league games every Saturday and Sunday, plus all the cup and European action in midweek, and the international games. Once the season has got going there's usually a televised game involving a Spanish club every Tuesday, Wednesday, Thursday, Saturday and Sunday.

The TV-rights dispute dominated the Spanish news in the run-up to the season, which looked like it might not start on time as a result. The 12 top Spanish clubs negotiated their own TV rights individually in the summer, the other eight in Primera and 22 in Segunda (having formed a group which called itself G30) were left having to negotiate a separate block deal. With no-one offering the sort of money they were looking for, G30 threatened to use their numerical superiority to vote to suspend the league. This led to a counter-movement from the remaining 12 clubs, including Real Madrid, led by Florentino Pérez, which called itself G12. G12 threatened to form a breakaway league if the G30 clubs took this action.

G30 knew it was in trouble and finally, a week before the start of the new season, signed a deal with Sogecable for 264 million euros over three years. This now just left one club out of the fold – Real Betis, who weren't part of G30, and had yet to sign up a personal agreement. Their outspoken president Manuel Ruiz de Lopera had a strong hand. Betis' first game is against Real Madrid and he knows that half the country wants to watch Beckham's first league game for the League Champions. So, in effect, he is now holding the match to ransom, trying to get as good a deal as possible from Sogecable for Betis' season. By tonight, on the eve of the game, it still hasn't been decided whether or not it will be televised. So I go to bed – feeling rather sick after drinking a very dodgy Bailey's-like chupito (short) in a night club – worried that I'll either have to miss the game entirely, or buy an extremely expensive reventa ticket (from a tout) outside the Bernabéu. If I can get one at all.

### SATURDAY AUGUST 30TH

I get up early, but clearly not early enough to buy a copy of *Marca* in the local newspaper kiosk, so I buy *As* instead. The newspaper tells me that late in the evening, de Lopera agreed to a deal with the TV company, and the match will be shown. I ring up my Atlético de Madrid bar to check that they are definitely showing the match, and they say they have already 'bought' it. I'm relieved. But now I know that I'm going to see the game, I start to get nervous about it. Will Beckham win over the critics? Is he really that good?

I try to take my mind off the match by walking round the centre of Madrid, and pretty soon find myself in la Plaza Mayor, a beautiful grandiose square, and the spiritual centre of the city, where a large proportion of the tourists and pigeons hang out. The Plaza was designed by Felipe II, who founded Madrid on the site of a squalid town of a few thousand inhabitants in 1561. Before then it was customary for the royal court to move from city to city, an expensive and time-consuming business. Felipe wanted to have a single base from which to govern his recently-unified kingdom, and the New World empire. People thought that he was mad. The climate was terrible, near freezing in the winters and suffocatingly hot in the summers; cities such as Valladolid and Toledo seemed much more sensible places to set up. But Felipe insisted, realising that his power would be unquestioned in a newly founded city, and the infrastructure could be built to cater for the needs of his increasingly large court. What's more Madrid, right in the centre of the peninsular, gave easy access to the rest of the kingdom.

Felipe had a lot to do with the strained relationship Britain has had with Spain over the years. English history books remember him as Philip of Spain, the king who launched the Armada in 1588. England was, for a while, virtually part of his realm: he was married to the Catholic Mary I – if they had had children before her death England would probably be a very different place today. She was succeeded by her Protestant half-sister Elizabeth, though, and the war that broke out between the two countries led to a fierce mutual antipathy which was still affecting relations between the two countries nearly 400 years after Felipe's death. In 1996, before England played Spain in the European Championship, the *Daily Mirror* recalled the days of the Armada, and came up with every anti-Spanish joke it could think of, to try to stir passions (and sell copies). An example: 'why do all Spanish men have moustaches? Because they want to look like their mothers.'

Felipe's son, Felipe III, completed the building of la Plaza Mayor, and in the centre of the square there's a statue of him, with a Jimmy Hill-sized chin, sitting proudly on top of a horse. Felipe continued his father's antagonism against the English, sending a 3,000-strong army to Ireland to try and launch an invasion. Looking up at his proud face, I imagine that his countenance might be soured a little by the thought that now an Englishman is now trying to conquer Spain, using Madrid as a base. Then I realise I'm worrying about the match again.

There's hardly anyone in the Bar Casa Ángel when I arrive, nearly an hour before kick-off, so I watch a Chinese guy playing the fruit machine. Within a minute he has won 130 euros, though this fact does nothing to change the serious expression on his face. As he goes up to the bar to exchange his coins for notes, I change my stool for his. A lucky stool. Maybe it will rub off on Beckham. The bar is small, but well equipped with a large TV attached to the wall. The floor is an ashtray, the ashtray is full of prawn shells. My kind of place. I'm absurdly early, there's an hour till kick off. I drink a few cañas. Each is served with an unhealthy tapa: something which looks like chopped up fingers swimming in red grease, which turns out to be chicken; irregularly cut clumps of sweaty cheese with stale bread; a couple of mussels swimming in tomato sauce. Occasionally closing my eyes, and washing everything quickly down with beer, I consume whatever he sends my way. The tapas are free: this is dinner. My budget is limited: I have to take what I can get.

Ten minutes before kick-off a guy sits on the stool next to me. He's wearing a Che Guevara t-shirt, a scruffy little beard and, oddly enough, a David Beckham 2002 World Cup 'faux-hawk' haircut. He's about 30. After a quick chat, during which I ascertain that he is here to watch the game, and that he is an Atleti fan, Enrique accepts my offer of a beer and in return tells me about the less seemly side of Real Madrid's dominance of Spanish football since the '50s.

"Real were Franco's team, when he was dictator of Spain." [Francisco Franco was the commander of the Fascist Nationalist forces which rose against Spain's Republican government in 1936, starting the Spanish Civil War, a bloody affair in which an estimated half a million died. By 1939 he had won the war, and ruled the country as a dictator until his death in 1975.] "And Real Madrid are still the team of the right. Left-wingers in the city tend to support Atleti."

"Don't think," he adds, "that Madrid is a right-wing town. Madrid was still holding out against Franco when Barcelona had surrendered in the Civil War. But Franco's Spain was ruled from Madrid, and Real Madrid were the footballing ambassadors of his regime. He was big Real fan. He used to go to the stadium, and cheer when they scored. When Real won the league, Franco won the league – when they won in Europe, Franco achieved a diplomatic coup."

I wonder if Franco actively helped Real achieve their dominance in the '50s. Enrique looks at me as if I am stupid.

"Of course he did," he says. "The referees were biased in their favour. They had been bought! There were a series of outrageous decisions in crucial matches that gave Madrid a win instead of defeat or a draw. The government still favours Real Madrid. A couple of years ago they were millions of pesetas in debt. They were in real trouble, but the government helped them sell their old training ground for housing and wipe off the debt – it was supposed to always remain a sports facility." It's a story I've heard before: I take a note to look deeper into it.

There's no doubt about the allegiance of the bar we're in. There is an Atlético de Madrid plinth directly under the TV, and pictures of the team, in various eras, all over the walls. I expected the place to be packed with Atlético fans, willing on Betis out of pure hatred for their rivals, but that was naive. With just five minutes remaining till kick off, there are a couple of old men, a bloke in a Real Madrid shirt, a bored-looking woman and her even more bored-looking dog (which is lying in the middle of the doorway with its head pointing away from the TV). Then there's me and Enrique and the barman.

I tell Enrique of my disappointment about the atmosphere in the bar. "Atleti fans hate Real Madrid. But you won't find them watching their matches. They don't care," he explains. "They wouldn't waste their time."

"So why are you here?"

He does not answer, looking intently at the TV. The game starts, and our conversation turns into the sort of grunts you make when a match is on. Within two minutes Beckham, with his first touch of the ball in the Spanish league, scores the first goal of the Spanish season, carefully side-footing a Ronaldo cross into the net.

"Beckham has scored! Beckham has fucking scored! What a genius! What a fantastic thing to happen!" I am thinking, but out of respect for Enrique the only outward sign that betray these emotions is a little clench of the fist. Enrique doesn't notice. He has tilted his head back and put his hands over his eyes, perhaps betraying something with his body language: the real reason why Atlético fans don't watch El Real. The Real-shirted guy is shouting "Venga Beykan" (go on Beckham). The girl still looks bored. The dog hasn't moved.

Around the half hour mark, Betis equalise, through their defender Juanito, provoking the opposite reactions in the same people. Enrique stands up and clenches his fists, then turns round and makes a comment to the Real-shirted guy, who continues looking at the screen as if the ball will go past the post in the slow-motion replay. The barman runs up and down the little area behind his bar. "He's gone too far this time," he shouts, about five times. I imagine he means Pérez with his policy of buying attackers and not defenders, but I can't be sure. The dog doesn't budge.

At half time, I do. I want more atmosphere. I've earmarked a Real-supporting bar with a TV the other side of the centre of town. In the area of town once devoted to the sale of fish, it is called La Taberna del Pez. It's a big place, with azulejo (ceramic-tiled) walls showing rural scenes, and, crucially, a big-screen TV. I have calculated that I can get there in 15 minutes on the metro, so if I'm lucky I won't miss any of the match. Enrique doesn't want to come (I thought I ought to ask him). It's quite a tense journey, with one change of trains. Both trains take several minutes to arrive. When I get out at the Noviciada station, the game has already restarted. I have to run.

The bar has got about 150 people in it, all concentrated on the football. The front of the bar is full of men, the women are all sitting at the back. I glance instinctively at the score in the top left of the screen – still 1–1. I ask a guy if I can use the seat he's got his feet on and he reluctantly agrees.

"Have I missed anything interesting in the second half?"

"Nada," he grunts – nothing. (I later find out that a streaker has run onto the pitch wearing a pair of Xmas tree baubles over his genitals, which for me rates high on the interesting scale, but there you go.)

There's no doubting the allegiance of this bar, either. 100 per cent Real. Everybody pays rapt attention to the screen. There is a tense atmosphere as Beckham starts taking over the game, delivering those beautifully flighted passes of his, getting into scoring opportunities, hitting the bar with a shot on the run. By now most people have empty glasses; nobody is going to the bar to refill them. There is a lot of muttering and cursing; very little conversation. Then, after about 20 minutes, a goal. To Real Madrid. The place erupts. Men hug one another. The tension lifts, and there's a hubbub of relieved conversation. They show the replay and the old guy to my left gives his own commentary along with it.

"The pass was from Beykan, Zizou controls, he passes . . . and Ronie scores."

It's Betis' turn to attack, and they swarm forward. Iker Casillas makes a couple of athletic saves. Beckham's contribution is down to the odd touch. Real Madrid have lost their impetus. The Sevillian side deserve an equaliser. Nobody is speaking now, just smoking and staring up at the screen, willing the minutes away. Betis get a free-kick outside the box in the last minute. Assunçao, their specialist, shoots it wide. The whistle goes . . . and the bar empties in seconds, leaving only about ten of the 150. Real have won, the natural order of the world has been reaffirmed, and, relieved, they are off home for some dinner.

More importantly for me, Beckham has proved himself in Madrid. Two games, two goals, and a very good first league performance on the back of a highly satisfactory home debut. I'm delighted for him – there is a spring in my step. Walking back through the city I see lines of immigrants selling goods on the pavement. One of the most popular items is the number 23 shirt of Beckham. I stop at one 'stall', feel the quality (pretty good; just like the real thing) and ask the price: 20 euros. I think about it for a second or two . . . then decide against it. It's not for me, not now, not yet.

## RESULTS: JORNADA 1

| | | | |
|---|---|---|---|
| ESPANYOL | 1 | REAL SOCIEDAD | 1 |
| **REAL MADRID** | **2** | **BETIS** | **1** |
| MÁLAGA | 0 | VILLARREAL | 0 |
| ALBACETE | 0 | OSASUNA | 2 |
| ATHLETIC | 0 | BARCELONA | 1 |
| VALENCIA | 1 | VALLADOLID | 1 |
| CELTA | 1 | MURCIA | 1 |
| RACING | 2 | MALLORCA | 1 |
| ZARAGOZA | 0 | DEPORTIVO | 1 |
| SEVILLA | 1 | ATLÉTICO | 0 |

## LA CLASIFICACIÓN

| | P | W | D | L | F | A | Pts |
|---|---|---|---|---|---|---|---|
| OSASUNA | 1 | 1 | 0 | 0 | 2 | 0 | 3 |
| **REAL MADRID** | **1** | **1** | **0** | **0** | **2** | **1** | **3** |
| RACING | 1 | 1 | 0 | 0 | 2 | 1 | 3 |
| BARCELONA | 1 | 1 | 0 | 0 | 2 | 1 | 3 |
| DEPORTIVO | 1 | 1 | 0 | 0 | 1 | 0 | 3 |
| SEVILLA | 1 | 1 | 0 | 0 | 1 | 0 | 3 |
| CELTA | 1 | 0 | 1 | 0 | 1 | 1 | 1 |
| ESPANYOL | 1 | 0 | 1 | 0 | 1 | 1 | 1 |
| MURCIA | 1 | 0 | 1 | 0 | 1 | 1 | 1 |
| REAL SOCIEDAD | 1 | 0 | 1 | 0 | 1 | 1 | 1 |
| VALENCIA | 1 | 0 | 1 | 0 | 1 | 1 | 1 |
| VALLADOLID | 1 | 0 | 1 | 0 | 1 | 1 | 1 |
| MÁLAGA | 1 | 0 | 1 | 0 | 0 | 0 | 1 |
| VILLARREAL | 1 | 0 | 1 | 0 | 0 | 0 | 1 |
| BETIS | 1 | 0 | 0 | 1 | 1 | 2 | 0 |
| MALLORCA | 1 | 0 | 0 | 1 | 1 | 2 | 0 |
| ATHLETIC | 1 | 0 | 0 | 1 | 0 | 1 | 0 |
| ATLÉTICO | 1 | 0 | 0 | 1 | 0 | 1 | 0 |
| ZARAGOZA | 1 | 0 | 0 | 1 | 0 | 1 | 0 |
| ALBACETE | 1 | 0 | 0 | 1 | 0 | 2 | 0 |

# TWO
# VILLARREAL

GOLFO DE VIZCAYA

OCÉANO ATLÁNTICO

**Real Madrid**
○

**Villarreal**
○

MAR MEDITERRÁNEO

N
W    E
S

# TWO
# VILLARREAL

## SUNDAY AUGUST 31ST

When I first saw Real Madrid's fixture list for the season I immediately looked for the first away game to see where the Spanish FA's computer had decided I would start my journey. The fact that it was in Villarreal stumped me for a bit. I couldn't find the town on quite a detailed map of Spain, and nobody I talked to could tell me where it was. I looked in the *Rough Guide to Spain*. Its 957 pages didn't include the smallest mention of the place. I went to Waterstones bookshop, and consulted eight guide-books to Spain. Again, no mention. I e-mailed an old Spanish friend, José Mari. He reported back that it was somewhere in the province of Castellón, north of Valencia. I became intrigued. How could a town that is off anything but the most detailed map sustain a top-level football team – a team that had just qualified, through being Intertoto champions, for the UEFA Cup, alongside the likes of Liverpool, Olympique Marseille and Inter Milan?

I finally found details of the place a few days before the game in a District of Valencia guidebook in a bookshop in Madrid. Even they only give the town a couple of pages. Villarreal (or Vila-Real in Valenciano, a dialect of Catalan) was founded in 1274 by Jaume I of Catalonia as a residence for his children, hence its full name, Villarreal de los Infantes. Cervantes once called it a 'beautiful and very pleasant little town'. The main reason for visiting was to see the town's main square, which is 'one of the few in the Valencia district to retain some of its medieval porti-coes.' Don't get me wrong, I love medieval porticoes. But the fact that Real Madrid are coming to town seems a much more compelling pull.

The book also gave the population of the town – 38,000 – and the reason for its relative prosperity. It is an important centre of citri-culture and it has a thriving azulejo (wall-tile) and ceramics industry. I looked up the capacity of the stadium – the Madrigal – in my *Rothmans*-like 500-page annual *Marca Guide* to the season. 23,000. I found out that the club has 17,000 members. Though never a tremendous maths student, I worked out that the team is pretty popular there, with nearly 50 per cent of the inhabitants going to the stadium every other week. And it sets me worrying: that can't leave too many tickets on open sale. So I arrange for a fax to be sent from my publisher to request a ticket in the press box.

I also request an interview with the Villarreal player César Arzo. I chose Arzo, after a careful consultation with the *Marca* guide, because he is the only player in the team to have been born in Villarreal. Just 17, he played a couple of games last season; that is the sum total of his first team experience. I don't think it's going to be a problem getting to talk to him. He's not exactly David Beckham. Later on in the day, a bizarre coincidence. I'm half-watching the TV which is showing the final of the Under 17 World Cup final being played in Helsinki. Spain are 1–0 down to Brazil in the dying seconds. A Spanish player rises to head the ball . . . onto the bar. The camera pans onto the distraught young player. 'A heartbreaking moment for Spain; a heartbreaking moment for César Arzo' says the commentator. Within a minute the final whistle is blown.

The Valencia guidebook also gave me a couple of phone numbers of places to stay. I find a cheap pension in Villarreal itself that will put me up on Monday and Tuesday, the night of the match. But it's full tonight so I have to book a room in Castellón, the capital of the province. Castellón is a thriving port town, with a population of 140,000, just five kilometres from Villarreal.

The Castellón pension is very cheap (16 euros) and when I finally get there I find out why. It's the slummiest little hole I've ever rented, an oven-like musty-smelling cell with one small window that looks out onto an internal courtyard. There's barely room for my ruck-sack, which, granted, is huge, its 80-litre capacity filled-to-bursting with clothes, books and an ever-increasing array of useless souvenirs from my trip. Two men in the room next door are shouting at each other. I've bought a local paper and, trying to block them out, I read the news. Two local people have been killed by rampaging bulls. Many Valencian towns have an annual 'bou al carrer' (bull-in-the-street) fiesta; there are inevitably many casualties.

Rather depressed and worried about tickets, I sound out the hostel owner, a cheerfully plump old man in a white vest. He opens up the bar for me and gives me a much-needed beer. The four-hour train ride from Madrid, followed by a zig-zagging half-hour rucksack shuffle to the pension, has been rather draining in the relentless afternoon sun.

"Well, my son-in-law is a club member of Villarreal. I'm sure he can help you."

"Great."

"But I'm not seeing him till next week."

"Ah. Will you be speaking to him on the phone?"

"No."

"Can you ring him up?"

"I don't want to bother him. I'm sure there'll be lots of people pestering him for tickets, anyway."

Bit of a dead end, then. The Spanish have a habit of wanting to help you even if they can't. Hence the indirect nature of my approach to the hostel: I'm learning to be wary of even the most confidently expressed street directions. I ask him about Villarreal. How come the neighbouring town, much smaller and only five minutes away on the train, is so successful?

"It's because of their chairman, Fernado Roig" (the 'g' is sounded like a 'ch'). "He's the president of the Pamesa ceramic company, and has invested a lot of money into the club. Mucho dinero."

I've seen Roig on the television. The brother of Paco Roig, until recently president of Valencia, Fernando is a jowelly man with thin black hair, known for vociferous outbursts, and running onto the pitch to confront referees. A typical Spanish club president, then.

"Funnily enough," continues the old guy, "he originally wanted to buy Castellón, but they wouldn't let him. So he bought Villarreal instead. Now Castellón, who once came fourth in Primera División, are in the Segunda 'B' and just look at Villarreal." He looks disgusted with this state of affairs.

Spanish football is organised in a very different way from the leagues in the UK. The top division, nicknamed 'División de Honor' is composed of the 20 best clubs in the country, of which a handful realistically harbour ambitions of winning the title, or at least a place in the Champions League: currently Real Madrid, Deportivo de la Coruña, Valencia, Real Sociedad, Barcelona and possibly Atlético de Madrid, Celta de Vigo and Real Betis. For the rest, the season is spent trying to amass enough points to stay in the division (the bottom three are relegated) then, having achieved 'salvation', in hoping to gain a place in the UEFA Cup.

The Second Division (known as 'Segunda') is composed of 22 teams, all of which dream of at least a taste of the top division. Three teams achieve this dream every season; four slip, often excruciatingly slowly, into the abyss below. This is known as 'Segunda B', a collection of four regional leagues, in which a mish-mash of 'B' teams of the top clubs (largely composed of young trainees, or 'canteranos') and other usually provincial teams fight it out. The champion of each division is promoted each year.

Below this melting pot of eighty teams is the Third Division, composed of 17 regional leagues of teams (one from each autonomous region: Catalunya, Andalucia etc) hoping to move from the base of the pyramid. Many of these teams play on dirt pitches, as they can't afford to maintain grass ones. Villarreal have spent most of their existence in the Third Division and the regional leagues below it. They only got into Segunda B in 1992/93, and were promoted immediately into Segunda. They have spent four of the last five years in the 'División de Honor', all of them under Roig's presidency. It's been quite a rise in fortunes.

I've done some homework. The team, trained by the experienced Benito Floro, a former Real Madrid manager, has just fought out a successful Intertoto campaign, a backdoor entry into the UEFA Cup, and will play in midweek European competition for the first time in the club's history this season. This is a long way from dirt pitches. Fernando Roig has been busy over the summer signing high-calibre players to warrant this level of football, including Brazilian international forward Sonny Anderson, bought from French club Olympique Lyonnais, former AC Milan striker José Mari (from Atlético de Madrid) and Juan Román Riquelme, the Argentine international playmaker, Barcelona's great hope and big disappointment last season.

Villarreal play in yellow and the club makes a lot of its association with the colour. The fans sing the Beatles' *Yellow Submarine* and the club's mascot isn't a tiger or a bear, but a strange creature with a submarine for a head. This season the club's nickname has been updated from 'the Submarines' to 'the Atomic Submarines' to signify their change in status. There is a lot expected of them: they have been cited by many as this season's potential 'equipo revelación' (surprise package). A 0–0 draw in Málaga, with scarcely a shot on target, in their first game, disappointed the optimists, but many fancy that a surprise is on the cards against Real Madrid.

## MONDAY SEPTEMBER 1ST

My first sight of Villarreal, from the window of an inter-regional bus the next morning, makes me think that things have changed since Cervantes' day; 'beautiful' and 'very pleasant' don't come to mind. The town's outskirts are filled with large factories: dusty trucks seem to make up half of the traffic. I am dropped off the bus on a characterless main road; I have to ask directions about five times before I find my hostel. There's a bar downstairs which is packed with workers in overalls eating sausage sandwiches and shouting about football: this is the primer almuerzo (brunch). It takes me ten minutes to get my key, the staff are so busy.

They are precious minutes. I have no time to shower. I have to arrange my accreditation and do the interview as soon as possible. The club's training ground turns out to be a fifteen-minute walk from the hostel, on the outskirts of town. I walk fast, even though it's hot. The establishment, grandly known as 'La Ciudad Deportiva' (sporting city) is an impressive sight, a big modern square building set within a series of fenced-off playing fields. I try to take a short cut through a field, but realise it's a dead end. My navy-blue suede shoes get covered in red dust. I'm sweating. I eventually find a waiting room flanked by a couple of offices, containing 20 well-dressed people queuing at a window: club members picking up their tickets.

It's 11am. I ask for the press secretary, and am led towards a room. A big stressed-looking grey-haired man straining the buttons of a light blue shirt confronts me, looking me up and down. It's a couple of days since I last shaved. I explain about the accreditation request, and the interview with César Arzo. He leads me into the ticket office, and starts leafing through a deep pile of faxes. He goes through them twice. I can see some familiar letter headings: the *Daily Mail*, *The Independent, The Guardian, The Sun*. There are some with Japanese script on the headings. Villarreal have gone international. But not international enough. There is no fax from my publisher. It hasn't come through.

"There's no room in the press box. It's too late to arrange accreditation for you now."

I stand around for him to suggest a solution, but I can see in his eyes that he isn't going to come up with one, and wants rid of me.

"Can I buy a ticket here?"

"You have to go to the stadium."

"Are there tickets left?"

"4,000 go on sale this morning."

"How far is the stadium?"

"Twenty minutes walk."

"How about my interview with César Arzo?"

He picks up his mobile, tiny in his hand, and rings a number.

"There's an English journalist here who wants to talk to Arzo," he says. He listens to the reply. "Come back at 12. He will be here."

I'm off down the road back under the hot sun walking as fast as I can. It is easy to find from its floodlights and yellow roof. I see a queue of people outside a series of small barred windows under a sign saying 'Taquilla' (ticket office). There are 10 people in the queue. Only one window is open. You can see the round face of a bored middle-aged woman behind.

4,000 tickets on sale, 10 people in the queue. I sense something is wrong.

"Is this the queue for tickets?" I ask a bearded young guy in front of me.

"I hope so," he replies.

I ask him which is the stand with the most atmosphere. He points at the ticket prices, which range from 55 euros to 130 euros.

"At those prices every stand will have a good atmosphere," he says.

Spanish teams can double their prices for big games, and this is Villarreal's biggest league game of the season.

After about 20 minutes (I suspect one guy must have been negotiating to buy one of the players) I get to the window, and ask for a 55 euro ticket in the North Stand. I hand over the exact money. The woman gives me a ticket. A ticket! For the big game! I feel a surge of excitement. I carefully put it into my wallet.

But I'm still in a hurry. I adopt my fastest walking pace back to the training ground, arms swinging. Lorries thunder past. I pass an electronic thermometer: 32 degrees. I make it there by ten to 12. The waiting room is full of another group of well-dressed club members queuing for tickets. The press manager keeps walking from office to office, still looking stressed. He won't catch my eye. But pretty soon he shepherds a young man towards me. I recognise César Arzo from the TV and the *Marca Guide*. A nice-looking kid, with a friendly manner. He's wearing a blue t-shirt, white shorts and flip flops. Slight acne gives away his age. A nervous smile . . . an outstretched hand. He ushers me upstairs to a spotless cafeteria for the interview.

I tell him that I want to talk to him because he's the only player in the squad who was born in Villarreal itself. I get the impression that he thinks that I might have got the wrong person.

"You know that I've hardly played a game yet, don't you?"

I assure him I know exactly who he is. That I saw him on the TV, nearly scoring a goal a couple of days back. He doesn't enjoy the reminder.

"I'm still getting over it," he says. Then he continues, in that sage manner bright teenagers have, that football moves quickly, and he has to move on, too. That he is now concentrated on the forthcoming match against Real Madrid. I'm slightly surprised by his last comment. I'm not expecting him to have a chance of playing.

"What? Are you playing?"

"I'll be on the bench," he says. "I hope I'll be called on to play, because I want to convince the manager I'm good enough for the starting eleven."

"I bet you'd love to play against Beckham?" He lightens up.

"I'd love to play against Real Madrid!" I lighten up, too.

"But Beckham is a great player," he continues. "One of the best set-piece takers in the world. I've watched him play for Manchester United and England. It would be very interesting to play against him."

I think back to when I was a teenager, and envy the kid the opportunities his skill gives him. I delve deeper into his career. It turns out that César arrived at exactly the same time as the president, Fernando Roig. I comment that the club has grown up with him.

"And I've grown up with the club," he smiles. He's all smiles, now.

"It's changed enormously since I arrived. The club was in the second division, and the facilities were terrible. We trained on dirt pitches – none of this was here."

He waves his hand around the brand-new-looking cafeteria.

"Now we have amongst the best training facilities in the country; we have had for the last three or four years."

Before he joined the club he was a fan – he was taken by his father to see the Villarreal-Castellón derby when he was seven, and always wanted to play for his local team – an ambition that was finally fulfilled last year. César was brought on for the last 30 minutes against then-league-leaders Real Sociedad in San Sebastian, his team 2–0 down. The score remained the same until the 93rd minute, when Villarreal scored a goal. Then, almost straight from the kick-off, having won the ball back, they hit a second to level the scores.

"It was a dream debut," comments César, still smiling at the memory. "Though I don't remember much about the atmosphere. When you play you are so concentrated on your game you hardly notice what is going on around you."

To finish off, I ask him what it means to his hometown town to have a Primera División club, to have teams like Real Madrid coming to visit.

"We are such a small town, but we have such a big club. And we have such good supporters. They know a lot about football in this town. And imagine how proud they are. How proud we are." He looks at me, and I signal that that's all I need. But he's not finished yet.

"You know, tomorrow night, I think we can beat Real Madrid," he says. "Don't you think we can beat them?"

I say that I do.

I eat a four-course lunch in the restaurant of my pension. One of the biggest culinary bargains in Europe is the Spanish lunchtime 'menu del día'. There are usually no written menus – the waiter rattles off what's on offer that day. I have a salad, paella, fried squid and chips and a huge slice of watermelon, washed down with all I can manage of a bottle of red wine (three quarters of it) and a bottle of mineral water (a couple of glasses), followed by coffee. I decline a brandy. The bill comes to 11 euros. Then I wander happily into town, almost alone.

Spanish provincial towns empty between 2pm and 5pm. I see the famous medieval porticoes in the otherwise modern-looking main square (definitely not a reason to go out of your way), and a big limestone baroque church, destroyed in the Spanish Civil War, and not restored until 1970. I yearn for the coolness of its interior, but the door is locked. Some Italians approach me to ask me directions. They're looking for the porticoes. I help them with my map.

"What the hell are you doing here?" I ask them.

They laugh.

"We made a mistake," one of them says.

I wander back to my pension.

The Real Madrid players are staying in the best accommodation the town can offer: the four-star Hotel Palacio, just up the road from my place. I know that Carlos Quieroz is giving a press conference at 8.30, and the team is due to arrive at 7.30. I decide to witness their arrival. In a one-horse town, the coach coming in provides a good deal of entertainment, so when I get there, I shouldn't be so surprised to see that about 300 other people have had the same idea. There are all sorts there, but about half are teenage girls. Many are holding open notebooks and pens, for autographs. The four-storey building is built on the fork of two main roads, opposite a Carrefour hypermarket. This, and the coach ride to and from the stadium, will be all the Real Madrid players will see of Villarreal.

The Real squad which is arriving is short of players. Three South Americans: Ronaldo, Roberto Carlos and Cambiasso, are away on inter-national duty. They have to play in World Cup qualifiers across the Atlantic. This leaves an already small squad very short. Zinedine Zidane and Raúl, two of the team's 'galácticos' will be playing, but there's little doubt who is the main attraction tonight.

The word 'Bey-kan' punctuates most conversations. The crowd, which is increasing by the minute and cordoned off by barriers either side of the large rotating door of the hotel, is patient. They know that the Real coach will be late. Traffic is heavy and slow. I keep seeing phantom coaches in the distance that turn out to be yet more lorries. They take at least ten minutes to reach us. There are about twenty journalists inside the barriers in front of the hotel; half of them carry TV cameras. I decide to cross over, and show my press card to a security guard. He doesn't question me. Some kids behind the barrier to my right ask me when the coach will arrive.

"Tell me that they're near," says a 12-year-old girl.

I ask her who her favourite player is, already knowing the answer.

"Bey-kan," she says. "Because he is so guapo."

A little boy with gap teeth, possibly her brother, tells me the girl's name: Victoria. Four of them start up a chant.

"Se llama Victoria, y es su novia" (she's called Victoria, and she's his girlfriend).

The girl asks me if 'Spice Girl Victoria' will be on the coach. I tell her I think not. She looks disappointed.

It's getting dark. TV cameramen start flashing their lights into the crowd of kids. Another chant starts up from the kids.

"Viva Victoria Beykan."

Like the girls, I have a notebook open on a fresh page. I quickly write a nonsensical note to make sure everyone knows I'm a journalist. Then I wander into the hotel to try and find a toilet, so I can gulp some water. It's still hot and I'm thirsty. But a rumpus draws me out again. The TV guys have rushed up to the crowd on our left, and are pointing their cameras down into it. Three security guards rush round; one runs into the hotel and comes back with a bottle of water. A teenage girl has fainted; she is escorted over the road. I know how she feels. Beatlemania comes to mind.

At 8.45 the other journalists clearly get word that the coach is arriving, and line up in an arc, completely cutting off half of the spectators from a chance of seeing the players. A black Mercedes pulls onto the kerb, and two black-suited men, one of them looking remarkably like French film star Jean Reneau, get out of the car, talking into mobiles. They are wearing little Real Madrid pin badges: the club's heavies. There is a rise in the pitch of excitement – then a big blue coach, with the club logo painted on the side, pulls up to the kerb. A hubbub of clapping and screaming.

Raúl gets out first, wearing the club's official dark suit. His name is called by a handful of fans. He hurries into the hotel, head down, followed by youngsters Pavón, Rubén and Núñez, who are hardly noticed. Beckham is visible through a window. The crowd start chanting his name.

"Bey-kan, Bey-kan."

Zinedine Zidane comes out, then Figo, then Javier Portillo. They are virtually ignored.

There is pandemonium as Beckham steps off the coach, and the semi-darkness is lit by hundreds of camera flashes. The girls are screaming. Beckham, who has individualised his appearance by fattening the knot of his stripy club tie, looks calm. He has a slight smile on his lips, pointy Italian-looking shoes, a Louis Vuitton bag. He walks directly into the hotel. I follow him in.

There is a jam of Real Madrid players, waiting for one of the two lifts. One of the players gently play-punches Beckham on the pony-tail. The crowd outside starts to disperse. A TV cameraman jumps into the last lift-load of players just as the silver steel doors are closing. One of the Real heavies vaults over a barrier and tries to pry them open. He fails. The lift moves up. He looks angry. He is joined by his colleague.

"The press cannot go upstairs," he shouts. The two men are surrounded by angry pressmen. An argument ensues.

"We have been promised a press conference by Carlos Queiroz."

"You cannot go upstairs."

"We have been promised a press conference."

There's a lot of shouting, though little substance is added to develop either point of view. Finally the heavies give in, and the pressmen head for the lift. I slip in with them.

I'm looking forward to seeing Carlos Queiroz up close. Until a couple of months ago his name had hardly registered on my consciousness – and suddenly he was manager of Real Madrid. A day after winning the championship, on June 23rd, Florentino Pérez sacked the manager who won it, Vicente del Bosque, stating that the club needed a more modern, forward-looking man at the helm. One, presumably, without a sweeping-brush moustache. The choice of Carlos Queiroz was a surprise. Carlos who? Queiroz had an interesting CV – he'd managed in the United States and Japan, had been national manager with Portugal and South Africa, and had just completed a successful year as assistant to Alex Ferguson at Manchester United. But he was hardly the big name that was expected.

This was, however, just what was needed. The manager in Spain is referred to as 'el mister' (from the early days of Spanish football when Englishmen used to run the teams) or 'el entrenador' (the trainer) or even 'el tecnico' and is very much a coach rather than a manager. He picks the team but, crucially, he does not generally choose which players are bought, or deal with their salary negotiations. This is the responsibility of the president and/or the Director de Futbol. In Real's case the latter position is held by the suave Argentinian Jorge Valdano, former Real Madrid player and manager, a sharp dresser with a sharp intellect, who used to be known in his playing days as 'El Filosofo' (the philosopher). Valdano was a fine player, Argentina's captain, who was on hand unmarked to receive the ball that never came when Maradona ran through England's defence to score Argentina's second goal in their 1986 World Cup win over England. He has written regularly for *El Pais*, showing a poetic turn of phrase, and has published several books. In one, *El Miedo Escénico* (Stage Fright) he compares the off-field Beckham to 'a Patagonian duck, shitting idiocies at every step'. For a young manager like Carlos Queiroz, this is quite an imposing figure to have as your immediate boss, and the rumours that Valdano is responsible for picking the team have already started circulating.

There are 20 or so seats lined up in rows facing a wide table with advertising slogans for the theme park Terra Mítica, Villarreal's sponsors, behind, on a white board. The cameramen line up. I sit in the second row. Carlos Queiroz arrives, flanked by a fat man in a suit, who looks unfriendly. Queiroz is wearing a brown suit that could have been tailored in the 1960s. He sits down. There's an awkward silence.

"Well, have you got any questions?" says the sidekick.

A series of serious questions about the match are asked, and Queiroz answers them, in the way that Portuguese-speakers speak Spanish before they learn it properly. He's very quietly spoken, and I hear people behind complaining that they don't understand him. The gist is that Villarreal are a very good side, and that Real will have to play well to win, especially with the absence of their star players. Beckham is not mentioned. If Queiroz has got any charisma, it is definitely of the dead-pan kind. I don't dare test my Spanish out on a question. After all the excitement, the press conference is a let-down. After five minutes it's over.

I wander into town to see if it is in a state of high excitement the night before the big match, but apart from a few yellow flags draped over balconies, it's just a typical provincial Spanish town on a Monday night. There's nothing going on. On my way back to the pension I see that the old folks seem to be enjoying themselves the most. The flats obviously have no gardens; the pavements are lined by pensioners sitting on easy-chairs having a chat. I enjoy myself by trying out the local dialect. "Bona nit" (goodnight) I say to each group as I pass. Without fail they reply "Bona nit" and continue their conversations. Before falling asleep, I watch on one of those hotel TV's attached to the wall above your bed, a fascinating documentary by a journalist (whose pseudonym is Antonio Salas) who infiltrated Real Madrid's Ultra Sur in 2001 and 2002 with a hidden camera. The result was a book (*Diary of a Skin*) and this programme. He finds out, to his surprise, that they are often well educated young men and women (their leader is a lawyer) with deep-seated fascist views who indulge in man-hunts in the streets around the Bernabéu after games. The journalist, shown in silhouette, says that he feared for his life on several occasions whilst making the film, especially when he thought that someone in their secret, swastika-decorated bar on the outskirts of the city seemed to have discovered his camera. The menace of Madrid seems a long way from Villarreal.

**TUESDAY SEPTEMBER 2ND**

Real Madrid are deemed by the local press to be in trouble. There is a big story in the paper about the non-transfer of Argentinian central defender Ayala from nearby Valencia, after negotiations which had been ongoing for nearly a year. The 'transfer window' closed shut at midnight on Sunday, meaning that no more signings could be made until Christmas, when it is briefly to open again. Negotiations finally broke down at 8pm, when Real matched Valencia's demands, only for Valencia to move the goalposts again. As well as 24 million euros, they wanted Real to hand over their half-share in Mallorca's brilliant striker Samuel

Eto'o. The Spanish transfer market is a complicated business. Florentino Pérez, through his director of football Jorge Valdano, refused, and the transfer fell flat. This left El Real, who were already deemed to have too much in attack and too little in defence, with no centrales (central defenders) with more than a couple of seasons' experience.

Last year Real's vastly experienced captain, Hierro, had played in central defence alongside Helguera, who had moved back from midfield to help out. Youngster Francisco Pavón had filled in when necessary. But Hierro, alongside manager Vicente del Bosque, had been sacked the day after Real celebrated their championship win, and nobody had been bought to replace him, Real's only signing being Beckham, an attacking midfielder.

To make matters worse, French defensive midfielder Claude Makelele, seen as being key to Real's success last season for his ability to protect the defence and start up the team's attacks, had decided that he wasn't earning enough money at the club, and opted to go to play for Chelsea in London, another deal which went to the wire. Madrid tried to stymie the deal by refusing to pay the player his 15 per cent commission on the 24 million euros they were to receive. Makelele said that if he had to stay under contract at Madrid, he would refuse to play; he would give up football entirely if necessary. Eventually he relented and signed the contract to move to London. The Argentinian Esteban Cambiasso, his understudy last season, is for the moment filling in.

The absence from the Villarreal match of three South Americans on international duty, Cambiasso, Roberto Carlos and Ronaldo, complicates matters even further. Helguera has to move out of defence and into the defensive midfield position he used to play in. Roberto Carlos is to be replaced at left back by young Raúl Bravo, who has played in central defence for the last two games alongside Helguera. That means that young Pavón, so far ignored this season, is to be partnered for the Villarreal game by the even younger Rubén, who has only started two league games in his three-year career at the club. The Real defence looks like this:

Portero (goalkeeper): Iker Casillas (former youth teamer, 22)
Lateral izquierdo (left back): Raúl Bravo (former youth teamer, 21)
Central (centre back): Pavón (former youth teamer, 23)
Central (centre back): Rubén (former youth teamer, 21)
Lateral derecho (right back): Michel Salgado (Spanish international, 27)
And no Ronaldo, to boot, replaced by youngster Javier Portillo up front. No wonder the local journalists are licking their lips.

The inexperience of the team shows up the weaknesses in Pérez's player-signing policy. Whatever financial jiggery-pokery Pérez has achieved to make Real Madrid solvent, he has had to make sacrifices in order to be able to afford the transfer fees and wages of their 'galácticos'. This has led to a situation Pérez has dubbed his 'Zidanes and Pavones' policy, a virtual class system that divides the squad in terms of wealth and prestige. 'Zidanes' refers to the well-paid superstars – Zidane himself, Ronaldo, Figo, Raúl, Roberto Carlos and, of course, Beckham – who earn up to 200,000 euros a week. 'Pavones' refers to the relatively poorly-paid youngsters up from the youth team, who are happy to play for the honour and experience and a tiny fraction of the money – Pavón himself, Rubén, Casillas, Núñez, Portillo etc. There are a handful of players who do not fall into either of these categories; these – Guti, Solari, Michel Salgado – are known as the 'clase media' (middle class).

Spanish squads tend to be better organised than their British equivalents. 'La plantilla' usually contains exactly 22 players, with a starting eleven (los titulares) and a back-up for each position. Most top clubs (such as Valencia and Deportivo de la Coruña) have two experienced men fighting for each position, with a handful of youngsters coming through. Pérez puts more emphasis on the youngsters, who he pays less wages, so he can afford to pay top whack for the world's best players. The problem is that if Real lose a couple of 'galácticos' to injury, suspension or (like today) international duty, there are very few tried-and-trusted replacements to come into the side. In fact Real only have 21 players in their squad. Like all Pérez's policies it is a risky one. And an exciting one, of course.

I walk from my pension to the stadium, arriving an hour before kick-off, time for a couple of beers in the many bars outside the stadium. Then I make my way inside, and am soon sitting down in my seat. This time I'm prepared. I've bought a bocadillo sandwich wrapped in silver paper for half-time. El Madrigal is like an English stadium, a rectangle with the seats going straight down onto the pitch. Even the floodlights are square: like the ones I am used to at home. There's a fat chatty guy to my right, who tells me lots of stuff about his team when he realises I'm a forastero (foreigner).

"Will there be a lot of celebration in the town square if Villarreal win?" I ask him, hoping for a party.

"Not on a Tuesday night," he says. "People have to work tomorrow."

To my left there's a lean middle-aged man who is silent, totally absorbed in what the radio is transmitting through the tiny speakers he wears in his ears. The players warm up and go back into the changing room. The tannoy announces their names, out of synch with the pictures on the big screen behind me. I hear César Arzo's name amongst the substitutes, and imagine his surge of pride. The submarine-headed mascot dances round the touch-line. There are still several thousand empty seats: the 'galactic' price-policy has kept people away. Torn up bits of paper are thrown into the air as the players run onto the pitch to the Villarreal hymn, its words in the Valenciano dialect.

*The hope of the whole town,*
*Industrial and hard-working,*
*Lies with a club which all the fans*
*Support with all their force.*
*The people of our town*
*From La Plana, from Millars*
*Carry in their heart their respect*
*For the most exemplary of teams.*

*Our colours are blue and yellow,*
*And our love is for Villarreal,*
*In the Madrigal stadium we will always strive,*
*All together we will always cheer you on . . .*

*Sing up fans! Sing up supporters' clubs!*
*Onwards, to triumph,*
*Villarreal will win!*

The beginning of the match suggests that this might well be the case. Riquelme, this year wearing his middle name 'Román' on the back of his shirt (hoping for a change of luck), starts running the game from his attacking midfield position, pushing probing passes into the path of attackers Victor and José Mari, trying to get behind the Real defence. The crowd start getting frustrated, directing their anger against the referee, especially after he doesn't act when José Mari goes down after an elbow in the face. Hundreds bring out white paper kitchen towels, and start waving them in the air. A disposable version of a Spanish custom, originating in the bullring, la pañolada, a waving of white handkerchiefs, to show dissatisfaction with the team, a player, the management, or in this case the referee. The paper towels must have been brought specifically for this purpose, as necessary equipment for the game: unless the supporters' mums and wives pack them with that other football fan prerequisite, the silver bocadillo.

The formerly quiet guy to my left keeps standing up and delivering a series of the sort of expletives that Hemingway used to love to transcribe. Every time he does so, he pulls the earphones out of his ears, as if to hear himself better.

"You are a son of a whore, referee."

"That you should kiss it."

"I shit on your mother's milk."

He is obviously nervous of Beckham, whose free kicks and corners are the only dangerous thing about this Real Madrid side today. He starts calling him 'La Rubia' (Blondie, in the female form).

"Can't you do better than that, Blondie?"

"You donkey."

On 40 minutes Beckham is booked for a studs-up tackle from behind on the Argentinian defender Arruabarrena. My man is furious.

"Go and fuck the Queen, Blondie," he splutters.

Meanwhile Villarreal continue to make most of the running, without coming close to scoring. When his team attack he nervously picks at his nose. At half time he unwraps his sandwich from its silver paper. I do the same.

The second half continues much like the first, with a toothless Villarreal attacking but rarely threatening a goal. Late on they bring on their Brazilian international substitute, Sonny Anderson. Within a minute he has scored a brilliant goal, a left-foot volley from outside the box that scuds in over the keeper. The crowd go mad. My guy stands up, and raises his arms in silent triumph. There are 17 minutes to play. The first song starts up from the fans around me, but it's half-hearted.

"Amarillos (yellows) oé, Amarillos, oé Amarillos oé, oé."

I was expecting a much better atmosphere.

Villarreal start defending deep. Beckham, playing on the right, but often drifting into the centre, starts taking over the game. Real get a series of free kicks and corners which 'La Rubia' takes. He stands for a few seconds, a picture of concentration before each free-kick, like a bullfighter timing the kill. Every time a guy behind starts up a nervous mantra. "Ay-ay-ay. Ay-ay-ay. Ay-ay-ay-ay-ay." My man continues with his insults.

"Go and suck my cock."

"I shit on God."

"Cuckold."

"Whorish pansy."

An umpteenth Beckham corner curls into the box.

"Ay-ay-ay-ay."

This time the net ripples. The ball has been headed in. It's one of the substitutes, the 21-year-old Núñez. Then a remarkable thing happens. About a third of the crowd, interspersed around the stadium, including several people directly behind me, stand up and cheer. Some of them are wearing yellow shirts. My man puts his head in his hands. He is lost for words.

One-all is the final score, though Beckham nearly wins the game with a late, late free-kick, which is brilliantly saved by keeper Reina. In the 89th minute, the Villarreal manager makes a nervous substitution, bringing on a defender for a midfielder. When I see his number – 28 – I'm pleased. It's César Arzo. The only thing he does of note is to kick Beckham, which delights my man, who finds his voice again.

"Kick him back to England," he shouts.

It's an apt phrase, as that is where Beckham is off to next, to train before a couple of matches for the national team. Spain are playing twice too – there is a ten-day break before the next Real Madrid match. Beckham gets another '2' from *Marca* the next day.

## RESULTS: JORNADA 2

| VILLARREAL | 1 | REAL MADRID | 1 |
|---|---|---|---|
| OSASUNA | 0 | VALENCIA | 1 |
| REAL SOCIEDAD | 1 | CELTA | 1 |
| BARCELONA | 1 | SEVILLA | 1 |
| VALLADOLID | 1 | MÁLAGA | 0 |
| MURCIA | 1 | RACING | 1 |
| BETIS | 2 | ESPANYOL | 2 |
| DEPORTIVO | 2 | ATHLETIC | 0 |
| MALLORCA | 2 | ZARAGOZA | 0 |
| ATLÉTICO | 1 | ALBACETE | 0 |

**SATURDAY SEPTEMBER 13TH**

The days pass quickly. I decide to try and watch Real's second home game of the season against Real Valladolid in one of the Real Madrid supporters clubs in Barcelona. After asking round, I find myself in Bellvitge, in the working class district of L'Hospitalet on the outskirts of Barcelona. I've been told there's one around here. It's the Peckham Estate of Barcelona, a rough area comprised of countless blocks of fifteen-storey flats, with a municipal area in the middle with a few shops and bars in the middle.

This is real Barça territory, where the infamous neo-Nazi ultra group the 'Boixos Nois' are from. The Boixos were in the news earlier in the season for attacking a couple of North African Barça fans in the stadium. In 1991 five members of the group attacked and killed Espanyol fan Frederic Rouquier outside the stadium after a Catalan derby. In 1986, after the Heysel disaster, the Boixos raised a banner reading 'Thank you Liverpool.' A nasty bunch, and I have no desire to come into contact with them. I walk into a fairly crowded bar. There are a few short-haired lads wearing Barça shirts drinking beer in the corner. I approach the barman, and practically whisper in his ear . . .

"I hear there's a Real Madrid supporters club around here. Do you know whereabouts?" The guy doesn't hear me, and asks me to repeat myself. I do, more slowly, but keeping my voice down. He finally understands.

"HEY PACO, THIS GUY WANTS TO KNOW WHERE THERE'S A REAL MADRID CLUB ROUND HERE!"

His colleague comes round. Everyone's looking at me.

"A REAL MADRID CLUB? YEAH, THEY'RE SETTING UP ROUND THE CORNER!"

He gives me very loud directions, and I sidle out. Thank God, nobody seems to be following me.

It's the barrio's fiesta tonight, and there are countless stalls setting up: hamburger stands, a fairground, a win-the-cuddly-toy shooting range. At the end I spot . . . 'Peña del Real Madrid'. I'm amazed. I walk up to a bunch of guys, ask if they're showing the match later. They point to a TV in the corner of the marquee, its screen turned to the wall.

"It doesn't work. We can't get a reception on it. We're going to listen to the game on the radio. It'll be great." He points to a bell hung up by the bar. "We're going to ring that every time there's a goal."

One of the guys gives me the address of another peña in L'Hospitalet, and directions how to get there.

"It'll be packed tonight," he says.

All eyes will be on Beckham, who has been busy over the past week on international duty in the vital European qualifiers against Macedonia and Liechtenstein, which have meant a nerve-wracking week for England fans. The Macedonia match, which I watched in the packed 'Black Horse' pub in central Barcelona, was a potential nightmare, with England going down to a Hristov goal in the first half and Beckham getting booked for a shirt-pull on the former Barnsley player. The pub was full of ex-pat lads moaning in their pints and shouting 'Come on England!' in an aggressive manner. Then Beckham scored a penalty and produced a deft chip which Heskey laid on for Wayne Rooney to score his first goal for England. The place erupted. Beer was spilt. The English really know how to celebrate a goal in a pub.

*Marca*, starved of news about Real Madrid (which is all most of their readers want to hear about), did a big spread on the match the following Monday, with the headline 'Top Scoring Beckham'. They had a picture of Beckham celebrating his penalty with the sort of understatement with which you do such things when you've been spat at and intimidated all game and told by an opponent that you won't get out of the country alive. The article produced a big chart showing Beckham's goalscoring record in the first six games of every season of his career, going back to 1994/95, including one for 'Preston North' in 1995. This season's total of four, they noted, was the most he had ever scored in the first six matches of a season. They produced a pie-chart showing in which competitions he had scored the goals. Vital information for its 2.6 million readers . . . and an indication of the country's growing obsession with the England captain.

I watched Beckham's Old Trafford comeback, as England faced Liechtenstein in Manchester, in the 'Fastnet', another ex-pat pub, this time round the corner from my flat in Barceloneta. The city is full of such places, where you can watch British football all through the week, ordering your pints in English and listening to the commentaries of John Motson or Martin Tyler. Apparently at Beckham's request, as if to rub it into Alex Ferguson that he was now a Real Madrid player, England turned out in an all-white strip. A win would mean that a draw in Turkey would be enough for qualification . . . Beckham was desperate not to get a yellow card, which would have meant him missing that match. There was a group of Asian lads from Birmingham in the pub, behaving the way England fans always do when England don't do well immediately.

"Get stuck in."

"This is fucking Liechtenstein. Come on!"

"For fuck's sake, England."

Finally, early in the second half, Owen scored a much-needed opener. The lads went mental, then started clapping the TV, hands over head. Beckham set up England's second – from young Wayne Rooney, and was taken off to warm applause from his former public, presumably to avoid getting that yellow card. Out of the frying pan and into the paellera. Just three days later, Beckham is lining up for his second league game in front of his new home fans, and another good performance is vital to continue to enhance his increasing prestige in the country.

I reach the Real Madrid peña an hour before kick off. Though it's less than a mile away from Barcelona's Camp Nou stadium, it is hardly trying to disguise its allegiance to the Catalan club's arch enemies with a big sign reading 'REAL MADRID PEÑA' and the club badge moulded into the window.

"Have you ever had a brick through the window? Or a pig's head?" I ask the club president, an old fellow of 80 or so, who is called Luis.

"No," he laughs. "Though we have had some trouble on derby days. Eggs, mostly."

Peñas are very important facet of Spanish society, reflecting the Spaniards' love of being part of an organised group. There are peñas of bullfighting enthusiasts, peñas of musicians, peñas formed to organise the city's annual fiesta. But above all there are football peñas. They are official supporters' clubs par excellence, usually based in a bar, which have paid-up members who collect to watch matches on the TV, or just to talk about their team. The bar has paraphernalia of the club adorning its walls: signed photographs; signed shirts; trophies won by the foot-ball teams they run. They arrange trips to away games. They often hold fund-raising events to help subsidise such trips. Real Madrid realises the importance of its peñas – Florentino Pérez often has dinners in them on the eve of matches. Most peñas are in the city or area of the team in question, though more important teams have them all over the country, and indeed the world. Real Madrid has a peña in Fairfield, Australia 'Los Canguros Blancos' (the White Kangaroos), one in Beijing, one in Dubai, one in Miami, a score or so in Europe (though none as yet in the UK) and one or more in 44 different provinces of Spain. Remarkably there are 66 official Real Madrid peñas in the province of Barcelona. La Peña Madridista de Hospitalet is one of the longest-standing, founded back in 1982. There are pictures of former Real Madrid president Luis de Carlos on the walls, inaugurating the club, among scores of team pictures, signed pictures of players, newspaper articles.

"Where are your members from?" I ask Luis.

"Andalucia, Extremadura, Galicia. Most came over in the '50s and '60s to work, or are sons of those who did."

"What do you think of the current team?"

"I think it is better than any team since the Di Stéfano team of the '50s. Better than 'Los Yeyes' [the team that won five consecutive titles in the '60s, nicknamed after the 'yeah yeah' Beatles], better than 'La quinta del Buitre' [the 'vulture gang' of the '80s, starring Butragueño, Sanchís, Martín Vázquez, Michel and Pardeza], better than the European Cup team of 2000."

"And Beckham?"

"He seems like a good player. But he has a lot to prove."

I am led into the spacious 'members only' section of the club, where there is a big-screen TV under a flag of Spain (non-members can watch the game on a smaller TV in the cramped bar). I read the build-up for the game in *El Mundo Deportivo*, the Barcelona FC-oriented sporting paper. There is an article denouncing the inefficiency of Carlos Queiroz, which claims he has little to no support within the club. They go big on a gaffe of his in last night's pre-match conference, in which he seemed not to know who his opposite number at Valladolid, Fernando Vázquez, was. They claim that, before sending young Antonio Núñez onto the pitch against Villarreal, he asked the lad 'whereabouts do you play?' His days are numbered, they imply, having only just begun. The news-paper has a schoolboy passion for slagging off all things Real Madrid.

As I read, with kick-off looming, the place fills up, largely with old men, who have presumably lived with such nastiness for most of their lives. The room becomes incredibly smoky. What happens next is a complete vindication of Queiroz, and his tactics. He has made an important tactical change. Beckham is playing in the centre of midfield, alongside Cambiasso, with Zidane, Figo, Raúl and Ronaldo up front. Salgado and Roberto Carlos, ostensibly full-backs, join the attack whenever they can. Real's interpassing is superb, with Beckham an ever-present, full of give-and-go, always wanting the ball. Valladolid, a young team playing in their red away strip, don't know where to hide.

The scoring is opened with an own goal by Brazilian defender Julio Cesar on 20 minutes. By half-time, the score is 3–0, with Raúl scoring twice, the second a sublime chip (in Spanish 'una vaselina') over the head of Argentinian 'keeper Bizzarri. Remarkably the old men in the bar greet each goal with little more than a clap or two. They don't even rise out of their seats. Are they, I wonder, over-used to success? They have seen little but, after all, in the last 50 years. Maybe they're used to not being very vocal about their fifth-column support for Real Madrid. The best is still to come. Ten minutes into the second half Beckham receives the ball just inside his opponents' half, having drifted wide. He plays a 40-yard lofted diagonal ball into the box, and into the path of Zinedine Zidane, who volleys it into the goal without breaking stride. It is a fabulous pass, and a fabulous strike.

"Was that Beykan?" asks one old guy.

"That was Beykan," replies his mate.

"That was good."

Within three minutes Valladolid have replied (a penalty by Losada after a handball by Beckham); within five, Real have scored again, another penalty put away by Figo after a foul by the unfortunate Julio Cesar. On the hour Chema heads in a second for Valladolid, on 69, Ronaldo receives an accurate Beckham pass into his path from which gives him room to left-foot it first time into the net. Raúl finishes proceedings off with a cheeky backheel, to complete a hat-trick. 7–2! On the final whistle, the bar completely and immediately empties. I look around for Luis, the president of the peña, for comment, but even he is gone.

## SUNDAY SEPTEMBER 14TH

There is plenty of positive comment from *Marca* the next morning, which I read on Barceloneta's crowded and dirty beach. My first move is to see Beckham's mark. Along with Zidane and Raúl, he's awarded a '3', his first of the season, with the comment 'he shines and he works'. Julian Ruiz, in his hard-hitting 'The Lawnmower' column, states that Beckham 'gave a powerful recital with his silken glove'. Roberto Palomar writes 'we were expecting a pretty boy, but we have found ourselves with a guy that could lead a team of brickies'. Beckham, it seems, the bricklayer with the velvet glove, is settling in rather well in his new position, his new club and his new country.

## RESULTS: JORNADA 3

| REAL MADRID | 7 | VALLADOLID | 2 |
|---|---|---|---|
| CELTA | 0 | BETIS | 2 |
| RACING | 0 | REAL SOCIEDAD | 1 |
| SEVILLA | 1 | DEPORTIVO | 2 |
| OSASUNA | 1 | ATLÉTICO | 0 |
| ESPANYOL | 1 | VILLARREAL | 2 |
| VALENCIA | 1 | MÁLAGA | 0 |
| ZARAGOZA | 3 | MURCIA | 0 |
| ATHLETIC | 4 | MALLORCA | 0 |
| ALBACETE | 1 | BARCELONA | 2 |

## LA CLASIFICACIÓN

| | P | W | D | L | F | A | Pts |
|---|---|---|---|---|---|---|---|
| DEPORTIVO | 3 | 3 | 0 | 0 | 5 | 1 | 9 |
| **REAL MADRID** | **3** | **2** | **1** | **0** | **10** | **1** | **7** |
| BARCELONA | 3 | 2 | 1 | 0 | 4 | 2 | 7 |
| VALENCIA | 3 | 2 | 1 | 0 | 3 | 1 | 7 |
| OSASUNA | 3 | 2 | 0 | 1 | 3 | 1 | 6 |
| REAL SOCIEDAD | 3 | 1 | 2 | 0 | 3 | 2 | 5 |
| VILLARREAL | 3 | 1 | 1 | 1 | 3 | 2 | 4 |
| SEVILLA | 3 | 1 | 1 | 1 | 3 | 3 | 4 |
| RACING | 3 | 1 | 1 | 1 | 3 | 3 | 4 |
| VALLADOLID | 3 | 1 | 1 | 1 | 4 | 8 | 4 |
| BETIS | 3 | 1 | 1 | 1 | 5 | 4 | 3 |
| ATHLETIC DE BILBAO | 3 | 1 | 0 | 2 | 4 | 3 | 3 |
| ZARAGOZA | 3 | 1 | 0 | 2 | 3 | 3 | 3 |
| MALLORCA | 3 | 1 | 0 | 3 | 3 | 6 | 3 |
| ATLÉTICO DE MADRID | 3 | 1 | 0 | 2 | 1 | 3 | 3 |
| ESPANYOL | 3 | 0 | 2 | 1 | 4 | 5 | 2 |
| CELTA | 3 | 0 | 2 | 1 | 2 | 4 | 2 |
| MURCIA | 3 | 0 | 2 | 1 | 2 | 5 | 2 |
| MÁLAGA | 3 | 0 | 1 | 2 | 0 | 2 | 1 |
| ALBACETE | 3 | 0 | 0 | 3 | 1 | 4 | 0 |

# THREE
# MÁLAGA

GOLFO DE VIZCAYA

OCÉANO ATLÁNTICO

**Real Madrid**
○

MAR MEDITERRÁNEO

**Málaga**
○

N
W E
S

# THREE
# MÁLAGA

**TUESDAY SEPTEMBER 16TH**

The 13-hour train journey from Barcelona in the north east of Spain to Málaga on the south coast is a lesson in just how big this country is. I leave just as the sun is rising, saturating the huge yellow blocks of flats in L'Hospitalet, their brief daily moment of beauty. Then we're out of the city, off down the coast, through tunnels in the limestone rocks, so close to the sea that at times you could jump out into it. A Jean-Claude Van Damme film comes on the video screens. We go through Sitges, the gay capital of Spain, and Tarragona, with its old Roman ruins enjoying their third millennium of sun, then through Castellón and Villarreal, from the train just an ugly jumble of factories which we flash through in seconds.

We stop for half an hour in Valencia, then cut across Don Quixote country: it's flat and dry, with the odd windmill breaking the monotony of vast tracts of virtually barren land, sparsely dotted with brave green trees adding a flash of colour and a rare drop of shadow: all this under the brilliant blue of a huge sky. It's hot out there but cold in here; they've got the air conditioning up so high I have to grope in my rucksack for a pullover. We stop in Albacete, where Real are to play in April. In Alcázar de San Juan the train stops for half an hour. No-one seems to mind; the old men get off and smoke cigarettes on the platform. I wonder how come we're over half way there and there are still nine hours to go.

The train starts going more slowly, and stopping at every stop. The people have changed their behaviour – they're chatting and laughing, making friends, as if something in the air has altered the way they behave. We are now in Andalucía, a huge region that incorporates the whole of the south of Spain. We're through the Meseta plateau – the land is still barren, but rocky now, and rather beautiful, with deserted roofless hovels showing how inhospitable this area is to man; I see several deer running through a valley, and a herd of goats on a mountainside. Then the ground flattens out again and there are vast groves of olive trees, enjoying the water from a complicated irrigation system that has performed the miracle of making this edge of the desert fertile.

The next film stars Adam Sandler. I put in my freebie earplugs, but within five minutes I've stomached enough. I get back into the book I'm reading, a biography of Picasso, occasionally popping off to the bar for beer or a whisky. Reading about this womanising genius makes such indulgences seem trivial.

Picasso was born in Málaga, and spent his first ten years there. The city is opening a permanent collection of the artist's work, hoping to draw discerning tourists to the place. The Costa del Sol lot fly into the city's airport, but don't bother the place much. They head straight off to Marbella, Torremolinos and Fuengirola, only returning to the provincial capital to go to its vast department store, El Corte Ingles, to stock up on electronic goods and underwear. An increasing number of them, however, are starting to head into town once a fortnight to watch the local football team – Málaga CF. It's been rumoured that more than 4,000 Brits will be at the Málaga v Real Madrid game this Saturday.

I finally arrive in Málaga at 11.20pm, earlier than scheduled, which gives me the chance to catch the last ten minutes of Real's Champions League game against Marseille, alongside Gunther, a forensic policeman from Salzburg I've met on the train. It's already 4–2 to Real when we get to the bar, and a grumpy man tells me that, no, Beckham didn't score. The final whistle is blown. I check into my pension, sharing a room with Gunther, who insists that we do this to save money. He asks me how many times I have been to Spain, what interesting sites I have visited, and how long does the train take from Barcelona to Valencia. I escape him and watch the highlights of the Champions League game with Juanjo, the night porter, a young biologist who says he doesn't like football, but nevertheless purrs with pleasure every time Real score. Beckham is great, playing again in a central role – his long diagonal pass to Zidane for the third goal is magnificent.

"My father," says Juanjo, "is a Real fan. He will have been shouting and jumping around all night. Four times he will have made the dogs bark."

Juanjo has the lovely soft sing-song accent common to Andalucians. He is a birdwatcher, who has been to Cornwall but never to Barcelona. When Beckham's pass is shown, he asks me what Manchester is like. I tell him he probably wouldn't appreciate the place.

## WEDNESDAY SEPTEMBER 17TH

Málaga are a curious team, with a patchy history. They played their first matches in the local bullring in 1904 then moved to a ground so near to the beach that they had to hire a man in a boat to fish out any balls that were kicked into the sea. They first reached the División de Honor in 1949, but could never stay there for long. In 1988 they won their 11th promotion to the top flight. In 1992 the club went out of business for financial irregularities. The 'B' team, with a slight change of name, became the city's major club. They had to fight their way up from the Third Division, finally reaching Primera again in 1999, where they have been ever since. They enjoyed a season in the UEFA Cup in 2002/3, beating Leeds before going out to Boavista in the quarter finals. Their bouffant-haired president, Serafín Roldán Freire, has a house in Barcelona and admits being a Barça supporter. "My heart is with Barcelona, but my money is with Málaga," he once said. He is, needless to say, unpopular with many of the fans. Some of the best players from last season – the Panamanian Dely Valdés, the Uruguayan Darío Silva, and the Cameroon Kizito Musampa – moved on in the summer, leaving a squad made up largely of young local players. Having not scored a goal in their first two games, their chances of beating Real Madrid look fairly slim.

Freire has taken a risk with the pricing policy of this match. Málaga v Real Madrid will be the most expensive show ever staged in Spain. The cheapest tickets are 90 euros, the most expensive cost 200. This is more expensive than any Plácido Domingo opera has ever been, and twice the price of the recent Rolling Stones concerts in the country. This means that I have to try to get press accreditation – there's no way I'm paying 60 quid. I get my publisher to send a fax requesting a place in the press box, and also ask for an interview with the Málaga right winger Manu – a local lad (from Fuengirola) who played in the Real Madrid 'cantera' (youth team) but never made it into the first team, and moved back home for some first-team action.

I make the phone calls from my mobile in my hotel room, watched by Gunther. I am told to ring the club again later. Gunther tells me that he can tell that I like my job, then he asks me if I believe in God. It takes me 20 minutes to extricate myself from the conversation. Gunther is off back to Salzburg that afternoon, so I say goodbye, and flee into the city.

It's a good city, built on the sea, with a port, a beach and a mazy old town dominated by two Moorish hilltop castles. I lunch in a cheap fish place near the market: seafood soup followed by a mixed fried seafood platter and a bottle of wine, all for eight euros. The TV in the corner is showing the Davis Cup tennis match between Spain and Argentina, which is also taking place in Málaga. The crowd is fun – there are hundreds of Argentinians wearing football shirts and waving flags. The Spanish fans are doing the same. The atmosphere is great: every point scored is like a goal, every game-winning point like a match-winning goal. I finally get through to the press office, who tell me to turn up at training at 11 o'clock tomorrow. I dedicate the rest of the day looking round town and find out the following things.

1) The port of Málaga was occupied by the Phoenicians, the Carthaginians, the Romans, the Visigoths, the Byzantines and the Moors, but has largely been left alone by the ex-pat Brits.

2) The best snack to have is churros con chocolate. Churros are long thin doughnuts cut into strips which you dunk into your drinking chocolate. In just half an hour you can sort out your calorific needs for the whole day.

3) You can visit the room Picasso was born in. He was born dead, but his uncle blew cigar smoke into his lungs and he spluttered into life.

4) If you walk up the Gibralfaro castle and look from the platform at the town below, you can see right into Málaga's famous bullring. I watched a matador practising his cape movements: it looked easier without the bull.

5) Don't ever bother trying to eat prickly pears from the old fellow who sells them outside the market. They are full of pips and when they slip out of your hands and onto your white t-shirt they stain it yellow.

6) The local wine, moscatel, comes in many different varieties from the sickly sweet joven dulce to the dry and eminently drinkable trasañejo seco. At 80c a glass, trying them all out in a bar full of barrels is a pleasant way to spend the evening.


**THURSDAY SEPTEMBER 18TH**

I walk from my pension along the side of the dry bed of the Guadalmedina river. It's hot and the sky is clear. The local tourist board say that Málaga enjoys 360 days of sun, which is an exaggeration but can't be off by much. The stadium – La Rosaleda – is about half an hour away. On the way up I stop in a small bar for a breakfast and a read. Beckham, again, is on the front page of *Marca*.

'BECKHAM: UN TÍO BUENO' reads the headline (literally 'a good guy'). The sub-heading reads: 'The unbelievers have already surrendered to his game and his numbers.'

Then another: 'He is the most active player in the league who has participated in the most moves, given the most passes and taken the most dead-ball kicks.' There is a picture of Beckham standing in the Bernabéu, his arms raised in the air, the crowd behind smiling and clapping (taken after his goal against Betis). On the inside front page there is a column by Paco García Caridad, in which the journalist recognises that he was wrong to previously doubt the England captain's ability. That despite being pretty, despite being married to Victoria Adams and despite selling 'a million' shirts, Beckham is a good player 'who runs more than anyone in the team, shoots banana-kicks that make people go crazy and has the physique of an animal'.

It is not an unequivocal thumbs-up for Beckham. 'It is debatable whether Beckham is a mega-star, or if he is necessary for Real Madrid,' comments Caridad. But it is certainly a thumbs-up for Pérez (*Marca* rarely stray from a policy of complete support of the Madrid president). 'There is an unwritten rule in the offices of the Bernabéu that Real Madrid don't spend, they invest. Beckham is an investment, just like Figo, Zidane and Ronaldo. And no-one says they were bought to sell shirts.'

The stadium is a big, square, grey thing, looped by busy roads. Having introduced myself to the press officer, a friendly small man with a carefully trimmed beard, I walk inside to watch training. The players are standing and stretching, flamingo-like, in the only sliver of shadow on the far side of the pitch. A guy sees my notebook and asks me if I'm press. I introduce myself, and ask him what he does. We switch from Spanish to English – his is excellent. He's about 30, with a thin beard. He's with a couple of other guys and a television camera.

"Have you ever watched the Spanish football on Sky?" he asks.

"No, I haven't, I'm afraid."

"Oh."

"Why?"

"Well, you know the Spanish expert who does the colour commentary?"

"No, obviously."

"That's me."

His name is Guillem Balagué, and he is from Barcelona. He supports Espanyol because his parents moved to the city in the '60s and he hates Catalan nationalism – he doesn't speak Catalan. He says something controversial about FC Barcelona, which he asks me not to print. He speaks English in the manner of enthusiasts who love using out-of-the-ordinary expressions.

"I am a closet Liverpool fan," he says, and I notice a slight Mersey twang to his accent. He talks about the Málaga team as the training drills start up.

"The new chap (manager Juande Ramos) is using youngsters who hardly have any experience," he says. "Every year it's the same: they have to build from zero, because they have sold their best players. But they have pacy forwards, and they should survive – there are other teams in worse shape. Valladolid, Albacete, Murcia, Racing. And every year a big club goes down. Maybe this year it will be Espanyol."

We move from our position in the press box to a place behind the goal, as Guillem has to introduce a short piece about the Málaga v Real game for Sky Sports. The team is perfecting a counter-attack drill whereby two attackers run at the goal, defended by one defender and the goalkeeper. Guillem does three or four takes of his introduction.

"Welcome to Málaga Club de Futbol, or rather Málaga Football Club. They have 1,600 British season ticket holders, and they are expecting 3,000 more Brits this weekend."

I check out Manu, who I'm to interview later. He's wiry like Beckham, and slightly bandy-legged. He shoots the ball terribly off target and his body language shows his disgust with himself. Maybe he's nervous. Today's local newspaper is talking about a change in tactics which will see him relegated to the substitute's bench. Another mis-hit ball comes screaming past the post and straight for me. I block it instinctively with a raised foot. 'Not bad' I think. Every football writer has a frustrated player somewhere inside.

Spanish names are such a mouthful (each person takes on the surname of their father, and the paternal surname of their mother) so players have to choose a 'playing name' which is put on their shirt. Usually it is just their paternal surname: (so Iker Casillas Fernández becomes 'Casillas'). Some players, especially those with common surnames, like using their Christian name (thus Raúl González Blanco is known as 'Raúl'). Some like to make a Christian-and-surname combination (Michel Salgado Fernandez). Others like to use a nickname, often part of their surname. 'Guti', for example, is short for José María Gutierrez Hernández. Others opt for a nickname completely unconnected with their real name (like Valencia's Miguel Ángel Ferrer Martínez, known as 'Mista').

Antonio Manuel Sánchez Gómez uses Manu as his playing name, and has done since he was a Real Madrid hopeful a few years back. Half an hour after the end of training I'm shaking his hand outside the changing rooms. He's got mid-length wet-look hair which smells of gel. We sit on a couple of plastic chairs. I tell him I want to talk to him because he used to play for Real Madrid. "Well, I never played for the first team, apart from in a few friendlies," he says. "I was there for four years in total. It is the best place that you can go for a football education."

"It must have been difficult to leave."

"It was a very difficult decision, because I was leaving the best club in the world. But I wasn't in the team. An offer came in from Málaga – my local team, the team I have supported all my life: my dad took me to my first game when I was eight years old – and I decided that it was better for my career. So I moved."

"Was it hard to accept that you wouldn't make it at Real Madrid?"

"Yes. It is hard to accept that you have failed in something you have set out to do. For a young man it is a difficult lesson. But I look back on it as a good experience and I am happy with my choice."

"What was it like to play against Real Madrid in the Bernabéu last year?"

"Incredible. I know all the young players in the Real team because I played with them. Portillo, Rubén, Pavón, Casillas, Raúl Bravo, they are all my friends. And then, I scored a goal! That was amazing. To score a goal in the Bernabéu. Against Real Madrid. We lost 5–1, I think, but at least I scored. I scored!" Talking about the goal puts a light on behind his eyes.

I ask Manu about Beckham, who although he was moved into central midfield against Valladolid, usually plays in Manu's position, wide on the right. What does he think of him?

"I have studied Beckham a lot and I think he is the best right-sided midfielder in the world. His corners and free-kicks are incredible."

"What have you learnt from him?

"I have learnt that it is important to work hard, to run back and defend, to play for the full 90 minutes. I'm looking forward to playing against him . . . if I play."

And what about Málaga's British fans. Are you aware of them?

"Ah, the Frente Inglés. Yes, I have met these people. They sing in English. Sometimes you can hear them."

## SATURDAY SEPTEMBER 20TH

I take a bus to in Marbella, 30km down the coast. Marbella is the epicentre of the British ex-pat community in the Costa del Sol, a pretty, if rather twee town where white-painted buildings flank narrow pedestrian streets. The main square, Plaza de las Naranjas, is full of orange trees.

Not far from that square, in a bar called 'The Tavern' is the base of the 'Peña Internacional', the Málaga supporters' club representing the British ex-pats. Chelsea are playing Wolves on the TV, but it's Málaga paraphernalia which dominates the room. There are pennants, flags, shirts, photos of grinning players and a big poster of Manu with the legend 'Yo no soy de Manchester, yo soy de Fuengirola' (I'm not from Manchester, I'm from Fuengirola), a club-produced advertisement urging locals to buy a season ticket.

Ken, the owner of the bar and director of the peña, is clearly excited that he is currently the centre of national attention. The English connection in Málaga, coupled with Beckham's arrival in town, makes this a hot news item, and I'm not the only journalist to have been round these parts. He shows me today's edition of *As*, which dedicates a page to the story. They have written up an interview with Ken. 'I WONT CHANGE MY COLOURS FOR BECKHAM' reads the headline. There's a big picture of a group of grinning fans holding up a Málaga flag in the bar.

"I had to go looking for them, you know how it is," he tells me, his Scouse accent still detectable despite 10 years in the sun. "They were actually a bunch of Bolton fans I found drinking in a bar down the road."

Ken is an Everton fan, but when he arrived in Málaga he wanted to go on watching live football, so he started going to El Madrigal. He realised he wasn't alone, and in 2000 he decided, along with his wife, Pam, to start up the Peña Internacional to organise trips to home and away games for British ex-pats. "It's been a rollercoaster since then," he says. "The highlight was all the European trips last year. Have you ever tried doing a Mexican wave on an aeroplane?" He took a banner saying 'Manu the Man' to all the European games last season – to Sarajevo, Wronki, Leeds, Athens and Porto. "We get along with the other Málaga peñas," he says. "They call us 'la peña guiri'." 'Guiri' is a pejorative Spanish term for 'foreigner'.

For all the euphoria last season, he has never seen anything like the interest in the Real Madrid game.

"I could have sold 500 tickets for the match," he says, "even at the prices they are charging."

He admits most of the English fans are there to see Beckham, though he is adamant that the peña will be supporting the other team.

"Our allegiance is to Málaga – we are Malaguistas, it's as simple as that." Though he doesn't hold out much hope for a result tomorrow.

"We got rid of three our forwards in the close season," he says. "I really fear for the lads tomorrow. We could get turned over and, at this stage in the season, that wouldn't do the confidence much good."

A young guy with a southern English accent comes into the bar and orders a pint. "Do you know how Portsmouth did last week, Ken?" he asks. "I've been out the country."


**SUNDAY 21ST SEPTEMBER**
Waiting in line to pick up my ticket, I see the Real Madrid bus arrive, through a corridor of Málaga fans who have been waiting for it. But this isn't the friendly reception the players got in Villarreal. Fans are doing

the 'corte de mangas' (a violent arm gesture where you clench your fist, jab it upwards, and hit your biceps with your other hand).

"Puta Madrid, puta Madrid, puta, puta puta Madrid," is chanted.

The players hurry into the stadium, protected by a cordon of stewards.

There is a cluster of bars over the road from the stadium and a good half of those drinking in them are speaking English. Many are wearing Málaga shirts. I buy a beer and start chatting to Mark, who tells me he owns a bar called Slammers, in Fuengirola.

"It's funny, but I really feel like I support Málaga now," he says. "At first I just started to watch them, then I started getting to know all the nuances of all the players. Now I get a real emotional reaction to the games. It takes a while, but it's just like supporting a team at home."

An older man, who says he owns a tennis club in Marbella, keeps butting in. He tells a boring story about how terrible the traffic is on match-days, and how they should widen a certain stretch of road to alleviate the problem. I ask Mark what he thinks about Beckham, playing today. Will the England captain's playing for the other team temper his allegiance to Málaga?

"I'd like to see him do well, because I'd like to see him succeed over here. As an Englishman living in Spain, I can empathise with his situation, like. But I don't want him to do too well. I still want Málaga to win. I'd allow him a consolation goal, maybe from a free-kick."

I move over to Delia, who has a rolled up Union Jack flag. I ask her to unfurl it. It simply says 'Málaga,' on it. I ask her if she sings in English.

"Not really," she says. "But we did in Leeds in the UEFA Cup last season. We were winning 2–1 and Elland Road was silent. We started singing: 'Jingle bells, jingle bells, jingle all the way, oh what fun it is to see Málaga win away.' It was just before Christmas. You should have seen their faces."

It's difficult to find my seat in the press box. It's a little concrete cubicle with room for 12 people, about halfway between the halfway line and the penalty box. There is a good view of the singing end of the Málaga fans behind the goal. The stadium, which was renovated about ten years ago, has already started falling down. There is a cable hanging loose above my head, and the concrete pillar in front of me is crumbling. It looks like it's been built on the cheap, like much of the construction work in the Costa del Sol.

The fans start chanting when the players run onto the pitch. There may be a few thousand Brits here, but you wouldn't know it. Blue-and-white polythene strips cover the whole of the lower tier behind the goal to my right. In one section to my right there are at least 50 big flags waving. There is a banner there, reading 'La Galaxia es Nuestra' (the galaxy is ours). Behind the goal to my left stands a group of about 500 fans who are on their feet, constantly singing. Most of the songs are frequently punctuated with the word 'puta'. A guy with a megaphone, his back to the pitch, directs the chorus. Opposite me there is a stream of fans risking death by jumping over a precipice from one stand to the other. A big plastic poster unfurls behind the goal: a head-and-shoulders picture of a young man and the legend 'Manuel, no te olvideremos' (we will not forget you). A Málaga fan has clearly died. Fernando Sanz, Málaga captain (and son of former Real Madrid president Lorenzo Sanz) runs down the pitch and places a bouquet of flowers behind the goal, to great acclaim. It's a terrific atmosphere – only a number of the expensive 200 euro seats opposite me are empty. The chant goes up . . . "Malagueño, oé, oé, oé" (A 'Malagueño' is a resident of Málaga). The whistle blows and the air is filled with ticker tape. The most expensive show in the history of the Spanish entertainment industry has just kicked off.

Being in the press box, I get a good view of the match despite the hanging cable. Málaga start on the attack, hitting several hopeful long shots at Casillas, who isn't too bothered by them. Then, on 12 minutes, Madrid, who have been going through the motions, get a corner. Beckham, dodging a toilet roll, takes it. Zidane flicks the ball on and Ronaldo, on the far post, puts it into an empty net. Easy. Too easy. In the stand opposite me, the expensive one, a few fans celebrate.

The game goes to sleep again – only the constant singing of the Málaga fans behind the goal livening things up. That and the outrage of the rest of the stadium when any decision goes against them.

Ronaldo goes down injured, even though it looks like he hasn't been touched – TOTAL OUTRAGE!

The Brazilian, who has been taken off the pitch behind the goal, cheekily cuts across the corner of the pitch before being allowed back on by the referee from the sideline – WHOLESALE INFURIATION!

Ronaldo is tackled on the edge of the box and a foul is given against Málaga – ABSOLUTE INDIGNATION!

The referee plays a good advantage in favour of Málaga, who then lose the ball – HE IS THE 'SON OF A WHORE'!

Just before half time Manu is brought on in place of the injured Gerardo. Immediately, he is easily beaten to the ball by Beckham, as if he wasn't there. It sums up a lacklustre Málaga first half performance, with Real Madrid doing just enough to keep their noses in front. It's not been much of a spectacle.

The second half is much better. Málaga, with Manu injecting pace on the right, start attacking Real Madrid in waves. A middle-aged guy in a white shirt and black slacks stands in front of a section of the Málaga crowd in the end behind the goal and exhorts them to sing.

"Oé, oé, Malagueño oé, oé" spreads round the ground. The atmosphere moves up a notch and the players catch the bug. Málaga hit the crossbar, then a spectacular diving header goes just wide. El Real are on the back foot.

Then, on 72 minutes, it's all over. A cleverly worked free-kick routine involving Beckham, Figo and Roberto Carlos ends with Beckham gently lofting the ball over the wall into an unguarded corner of the net. It's a delicate kick, a wonderful moment. Beckham's joy is clear to see: he runs towards the dug-out, with his arms pointing towards the ground and a big grin on his face. Figo is the first to catch up with him and celebrate. I'm delighted for him, but slightly disappointed, too. It's the end of the match as a contest.

Or is it? The ebullient bald-headed Portuguese attacker Edgar has come on for Málaga. He was once on Real Madrid's books, but never got a first-team game and has a point to prove. He makes a mazy run at high speed and shoots just wide. Then he launches himself at a cross, and performs a perfect 'chilena' (overhead kick) into the net. It's a superb goal that puts Málaga back in the game, the team's first of the season, and Edgar's first for two years. The Málaga fans start acting like they've won not just the match, but the League and Cup double, to boot. The whole stadium starts up the song:

"Malagueño oé, oé, oé . . ."

The fans behind the goal to my right start to perform a conga. The team might be losing to Real Madrid, but hey, what a goal! The whole crowd is buzzing with excitement. And Málaga are pressing for an equaliser . . .

Seven minutes later Guti, who has come on for the injured Raúl, scores a third goal for Real, to put the game beyond Málaga, and the home fans quieten a little. They liven up when the referee declines to give them a late penalty (more outrage) and at one point plastic water bottles rain down towards Real's goalkeeper Casillas. He takes a drink from one, and throws it coolly back into touch. Somehow it sums up the evening.

After the game, with the help of my press card, I watch Queiroz give another low-key press conference, and end up in the mixed zone, a room by the players' exit where a gaggle of journalists and cameramen try to accost the players for interviews before they leave the stadium and get onto the bus. When Beckham comes out there is mayhem. I jostle my way to the front, and for a split second I find myself face to face with him, with just a barrier between us. I can see the dark roots in his hair. I can see the light in his eyes. I've been interviewing football stars for a decade, but I am unexpectedly overwhelmed by this occasion. I try to think of a question to ask him, but am too slow, and he's moved on. Face to face with the man himself! He looked at me! It's quite a moment.

As I leave the stadium (by the same exit as the players) I stop to watch a group of 15 or so drunken Málaga fans who are jumping up and down on a generator trailer singing, to the tune of 'Johnny Comes Marching Home' "Beckham maricón, Beckham maricón, Beckham, Beckham, Beckham maricón" ('maricón' means 'pansy'). The trailer, balanced on a single axle, suddenly see-saws and they all fall off. Nobody is hurt, they all laugh, get back on the trailer, and continue with their song.

I check out the bars but the British fans are nowhere to be seen. They have all gone home; to Torremolinos, to Fuengirola, to Marbella. They outnumbered the Spanish before the game in the bars around the stadium – but that's just because they were recreating the British football culture of going to the pub before the match. They were big news before the game, but they were unable to make themselves heard during it, unable to Anglicise a very Spanish occasion: Real Madrid coming to town. There was one Brit, however, who did make his mark on the game, and he was playing for the other team. David Beckham was involved in all the goals, and ran the game from the central midfield.

## RESULTS: JORNADA 4

| | | | |
|---|---|---|---|
| BARCELONA | 1 | OSASUNA | 1 |
| ATLÉTICO | 0 | VALENCIA | 3 |
| DEPORTIVO | 3 | ALABACETE | 0 |
| MALLORCA | 1 | SEVILLA | 1 |
| VILLARREAL | 1 | CELTA | 1 |
| VALLADOLID | 3 | ESPANYOL | 1 |
| REAL SOCIEDAD | 3 | ZARAGOZA | 0 |
| BETIS | 0 | RACING | 0 |
| MURCIA | 2 | ATHLETIC | 2 |
| **MÁLAGA** | **1** | **REAL MADRID** | **3** |

## LA CLASIFICACIÓN

|  | P | W | D | L | F | A | Pts |
|---|---|---|---|---|---|---|---|
| DEPORTIVO | 4 | 4 | 0 | 0 | 8 | 1 | 12 |
| **REAL MADRID** | **4** | **3** | **1** | **0** | **13** | **5** | **10** |
| VALENCIA | 4 | 3 | 1 | 0 | 6 | 1 | 10 |
| REAL SOCIEDAD | 4 | 2 | 2 | 0 | 6 | 2 | 8 |
| BARCELONA | 4 | 2 | 2 | 0 | 5 | 3 | 8 |
| OSASUNA | 4 | 2 | 1 | 1 | 4 | 2 | 7 |
| VALLADOLID | 4 | 2 | 1 | 1 | 7 | 9 | 7 |
| VILLARREAL | 4 | 1 | 3 | 0 | 4 | 3 | 6 |
| BETIS | 4 | 1 | 2 | 1 | 5 | 4 | 5 |
| SEVILLA | 4 | 1 | 2 | 1 | 4 | 4 | 5 |
| RACING | 4 | 1 | 2 | 1 | 3 | 3 | 5 |
| ATHLETIC | 4 | 1 | 1 | 2 | 6 | 5 | 4 |
| MALLORCA | 4 | 1 | 1 | 2 | 4 | 7 | 4 |
| CELTA DE VIGO | 4 | 0 | 3 | 1 | 3 | 5 | 3 |
| MURCIA | 4 | 0 | 3 | 1 | 4 | 7 | 3 |
| ZARAGOZA | 4 | 1 | 0 | 3 | 3 | 6 | 3 |
| ATLÉTICO | 4 | 1 | 0 | 3 | 1 | 5 | 3 |
| ESPANYOL | 4 | 0 | 2 | 2 | 5 | 8 | 2 |
| MÁLAGA | 4 | 0 | 1 | 3 | 1 | 5 | 1 |
| ALBACETE | 4 | 0 | 0 | 4 | 1 | 8 | 0 |

# FOUR
# VALENCIA

GOLFO DE VIZCAYA

OCEANO ATLÁNTICO

**Real Madrid**

Valencia

MAR MEDITERRÁNEO

N
W E
S

# FOUR
# VALENCIA

**TUESDAY SEPTEMBER 23RD**

The first thing that I do after finding my pension in Valencia (I've come directly from Málaga, a nine-hour train journey) is to go and get a haircut, in a trendy-looking hairdresser near the Moorish-looking food market in the centre of town. My barber, a young man in his twenties (with an '80s flick haircut) has a high voice and a bad cold – every sentence is topped and tailed by a long sniff. I want to give him a handkerchief and tell him to have a good blow. Instead I ask him about the football.

"Are you going to the match on Saturday?"

"No, I'm working. I'll miss it."

"But you support Valencia?"

"Of course. I'm from here."

"What do you think of Beckham?"

"Good player. Sniff. Bad hair."

He goes on to have a go at Ayala, Valencia's Argentinian defender, who seems to be feigning injury so he doesn't have to play for the club until he has renegotiated his contract, a story which is dominating the pages of the football papers.

Spain's 'prensa rosa' (tabloid magazines) are interested in a different matter. In the face of mounting speculation about the state of his marriage, Beckham has just given out a statement, jointly with his wife, through his management company, that everything is alright between them. 'Contrary to newspaper reports our marriage is not in crisis' it reads. 'We are extremely happy together as a family. Our only difficulty has been finding a house in Madrid that meets our needs. Since we first met our careers have always meant we have spent time apart. This is not a reflection on the strength of our marriage and we are very much enjoying our new life in Spain.' It's a curious move by the Beckhams, and one which seems as likely to add fuel to any flames of speculation than to douse them. As I stroll through the traffic-heavy centre of the city, I wonder whether the speculation and estrangement from his family is likely to affect his game. It doesn't seem to have so far: quite the opposite, in fact. Perhaps, I muse, he's a better player without the distractions of family life. Then I dwell on the similarities between Beckham's position and my own. I spent a month of the summer in Dublin with Brenda, but as I've had so much travelling to do, she has decided to stay in Ireland until the beginning of October. This has given me space and time to fully follow my adventure.

## WEDNESDAY SEPTEMBER 24TH

Valencia's stadium, known as 'Mestalla' is a large, square grey affair surrounded by main roads and high-rise residential buildings. It holds 55,000 fans, and looks from the outside as though it could happily double up as a prison. Valencia is Spain's third-largest city, with a popu-lation of around 740,000, a busy, self-important place full of churches with tiled blue roofs and heavy traffic. Valencia CF is the only Primera División club in the city, and is very well-supported. Valencia was once a province of Catalunya, and though not as fiercely independent as Catalans or Basques, locals are proud of their heritage. The annual arrival of Real Madrid is eagerly awaited, as the Valencianos like nothing better than putting one over the establishment team. Some fans' passion got too much for them last night. According to this morning's local sports paper *Super Deportes* some hooligans broke into the stadium last night and set fire to the visitors' dug-out. It needs to be replaced before the game. A threatening gesture to the Real Madrid team. The police have placed the game in the 'high risk' category. Looking at the foreboding walls of this fortress of a stadium I wonder how the hell they got in.

The most famous of Valencia's fans is Manolo 'el del Bombo' (the one with the drum) who you may well have seen at the World Cup on TV, bashing a big drum, wearing an oversized beret. Manolo owns a bar opposite Mestalla stadium. In it there are scores of little drums hanging from the walls, and hundreds of pictures of Manolo on his travels with 'la selección' (the Spanish national team) around the world, usually attached to his big drum. The drum itself is on display in the corner of the bar, with its admirable slogan 'Violencia – no, fútbol, sí' which needs no translation. I ask Manolo if he is up for doing an interview. He tells me to come back for Valencia's televised UEFA game aginst AIK Solna, being played in Sweden tonight. He'll talk to me after that.

I watch the game next to an old man who is chain-smoking while hawking loudly and from very deep in his chest after every drag. He isn't long for this world, I fear. At one point he puts an entire tissue in his mouth to mop up some disorder or other in there – I don't see him take it out again. I order some patatas bravas (fancy Spanish chips) and some meat stew, but I don't have much appetite for my food when it comes.

The most entertaining moment of the game is its only goal – a crisp volley by the Brazilian Oliveira – and the commentary that succeeds it. 'Gol, Goooooooool de Oliveira. Gol, gol, gol, gol, gol. Un golazo!' (great goal). It's a long way from John Motson.

After the game Manolo shows me round the photos on the walls, in which he gets increasingly old and more, well, drum-shaped. He is a well-meaning man from Huesca, Aragón, who was given a big drum in 1970/71 and started bashing it at Real Zaragoza games. In 1982 he decided to follow Spain round the country during the World Cup. He became a symbol of the tournament, as the cameras inevitably focussed in on his eccentric and noisy behaviour.

"I travelled a total of 15,800 kilometres that summer, hitch-hiking all the way. With my drum I was very recognisable, so I never had to wait long. It was a dream month . . . but when I got back home I found I had lost my job and my wife had left me with the three kids," he says. Warning: football can severely damage your marriage.

He moved on to Valencia, where he got work as a PR man for a bar/restaurant chain before starting up his own bar – where we are – near the Mestalla. In the bar you can buy booze, hot food, and paraphernalia with Manolo's image on it – bottles of wine, footballs, drums.

"People love it here, it's always full. Everyone wants to take my picture, have a little chat." I ask him if his fame has changed him – Manolo even appeared in a popular TV ad in the '90s.

"No, I'm still the same person. And I'm happy. I have a girlfriend now, and another child of three years."

"Do your children like football?"

"No, they hate it. I don't know why . . ."

Manolo has an injury at the moment (a hernia problem, caused by carrying his drum around) so he's not going to the match tomorrow (he normally animates the Valencia end, too). He carried his injury a couple of weeks before to the Ukraine, to watch Spain in the Euro 2004 qualifiers.

"I went without my drum because my doctor told me it would make my injury worse, but someone recognised me in the crowd and I was given a drum. I couldn't resist it, so I started hitting it, and of course the cameras focused in on me. When I got back to Spain my doctor, who had been watching, gave me hell."

I ask him how he thinks Beckham and co. will fare tomorrow against his Valencia.

"Beckham is a good player, but like all Madrid players he needs too much time on the ball. Valencia play very quick football. He will not get the time he needs. Real Madrid will not get the time they need. We will win. Maybe 2–0. Maybe 3–1."

There are pictures behind the bar of Manolo with King Juan Carlos, and with Spain's right-wing prime minister José María Aznar. Although a humble bar owner (and it's him who serves you the drinks in his bar) Manolo is one of the most recognisable figures in the country, the David Beckham of drummers. I ask him what he has learnt out of the whole experience. He's been asked the question before, because he doesn't reflect on the answer.

"Football is a universal language and can be used to make friends in the world. My message is clear. Football yes, violence no."


## THURSDAY SEPTEMBER 25TH

Having queued for an hour and a half to get a ticket (there was an orderly line until the windows opened, after which it was a bit of a scrap) I'm interested in finding out more about Valencia's history, so I wander to the nearby Club de Veteranos del Valencia CF, the veterans' club, which has a black glass front like a casino or a porn shop. Manolo has told me that if I use his name I will be able to look round the various artefacts there, and that it will be a good history lesson. I ring on the bell and the door buzzes open. At the end of a long corridor lined with photographs is a bar, with a table in front of it, at which five old men sit. One of them has only one arm, one is wearing shades. They are nearly all smoking ciga-rettes and have empty coffee cups in front of them.

"Manolo el del Bombo sent me here. I'm a journalist."

"Manolo el del Bombo's bar is round the corner."

"No, idiot, he said that Manolo el del Bombo sent him."

"Why did Manolo el del Bombo send you?"

"I'm interested in looking at the pictures and learning more about the club." I explain my mission.

"Feel free to."

They return to their conversation, which is punctuated by the words 'Madrid' and 'Bey-kan'.

The walls tell their story. The club reached one cup final before the Spanish Civil War – but after the fighting ceased they became the best team in the land with a famous attack known as 'la delantera eléctrica' (the electric front line). In 1941 they won the cup, in 1942 their first ever league title. In 1944 they won a second championship, and in 1947 a third, losing the cup final. There is a picture of the losing cup final team (the trophy, now known as the Copa del Rey, was then called the Copa de Generalísimo, after Franco): the goalkeeper is wearing a woolly jumper and thick kneepads, and from one look at the gravelly pitch the players are standing on, you can see why). Valencia were again losing cup finalists in 1948, but won the trophy in 1949, beating Barcelona in the Chamartín, to finish off a fantastic decade.

Valencia won the league again in 1970/71 (managed by Alfredo Di Stéfano) and the European Cup Winners Cup in 1980, against Arsenal, with the Argentinian striker Mario Kempes in the side. But today's squad is the first that looks like emulating that great side of the '40s. The man who started the revival, well known to British fans, is Claudio Ranieri. I know Claudio – I was his occasional interpreter when I lived in London (my home was Italy for four years and I speak the language fairly fluently), and he is a great hero over in these parts. Ranieri built a young fast team which qualified for the Champions League in 1999 by finishing fourth, then he moved on to Atlético de Madrid. A year later he was out of a job, and Valencia, under Héctor Cúper, were in the European Cup final (they lost 3–0 to Real Madrid). The year after that (2000/01), having come third in the league, they again reached the final of the competition, this time going out on penalties to Bayern Munich. Finally in 2001/02 some fruit was born of Claudio's spade-work – Valencia won La Liga again, under current manager Rafa Benítez, their first for 31 years, finishing a full seven points ahead of second-placed Deportivo de la Coruña and nine ahead of Real Madrid. Benítez based his game on a tight defence, and a quick counter-attack: last season he put out a more attacking formation, and Valencia did relatively poorly, failing to qualify for the Champions League. This year he has returned to his original format. And, though it's still early in the season, Valencia look like one of the few sides capable of keeping up with Real Madrid.

The most amazing thing I see in the bar is a photo of a little van-come-bus, with the whole team posed in front of it in their club suits. The date (1953) and the names of the players is written in pen at the bottom. There's a Tardis-effect; it doesn't look possible that they could all fit in. As I say goodbye to the old fellows, still sitting in front of the same empty cups, I ask them about the old team bus. No doubt some of them travelled on it?

"It's just outside on the right, the number 11 will take you into town."

"He's talking about the photo of the bus on the wall."

"Is that how the players had to travel to away games?"

"Yes, it was," says the one in shades. "I spent many an hour in that old bus. Twenty hours to Vigo, 15 to Málaga."

"Did it not affect your performances?"

"Of course it did!" (Shades again). "One year we beat Alavés (in the Basque country) 8–0 at home, but after travelling all the way there, we got beaten 6–1 by the same team . . ."

## FRIDAY SEPTEMBER 26TH

On the eve of the match I ring the tourist office to ask where I can get a good paella. Valencia is a rice-growing region (a legacy of the Moorish irrigation systems and saffron-growing trade) and paella is a local dish – though properly served with snails, rabbit and chicken in the city (seafood paella being a more modern invention). The choice they make for me – La Riua, in Calle del Mar, is a fortuitous one.

It's a little family run place and when I get there at five to nine there's a queue waiting to get in. I get a table on the first floor overlooking the kitchen. The patron, a fellow of 60 or so, does the rounds of the tables, greeting all his guests. At the table in front of me there's an Italian couple with their little girl, and when he reaches their table I hear them talking about Claudio Ranieri. When he approaches me I tell him that I know Claudio. His face lights up. "When Claudio first came to manage Valencia, before he found a house, he ate here every night for three months. With his goalkeeping coach, the one with the hair, and two others. A little guy – the fitness coach."

"I know all these guys! Giorgio, Angelo, Antonio!"

"Out of them all Claudio stood out as a real gentleman. He loved paella, and tried everything else on the menu. He said 'Paco, I need pasta.' I told him I was not an expert. He said 'don't worry, I will organise' and told us he would arrive early the next day. So he arrived with a bag full of food, and he cooked us all a plate of spaghetti in a tomato sauce! He was an excellent cook!"

"And very popular, here, too . . ."

"In the end he was very popular, but in the beginning . . . When he first arrived Valencia couldn't win. They would draw and lose, draw and lose. It looked really serious. I think the only reason he wasn't sacked is that it would have cost the club so much money to terminate his contract. So they kept him on, and in the end he turned it round. And now look at the club!"

Paco's chef isn't too bad either. When my paella arrives it's done just right, with 'socorrat' (a thin crispy layer at the bottom), the rice having absorbed most of the flavour of the chicken and rabbit, but leaving enough for the meat to be tasty, too.

## SATURDAY SEPTEMBER 26TH

Valencia's city centre is flanked by the dried out river Turia (diverted after a disastrous flood in the '50s), which has been turned into a park, patch-worked with football fields, overlooked by medieval bridges. On the way to the game I look down to watch an amateur game on one of the gravelly pitches in the river bed. The manager of the blues is standing in front of a little concrete bench just below me – a middle-aged man in a leather jacket with dark hair and a large moustache. There are two substitutes on the bench. He is keeping up a barrage of shouting, full of Spanish outrage. The referee gives an offside decision against his team (there are no linesmen) and he starts abusing the official, though to me the decision looked perfectly fair. "You cuckold!" he shouts. "You son of a whore!"

This is interesting – he does not enjoy the anonymity of the crowd, the referee is well aware who is abusing him.

He continues with a torrent of abuse, then pauses, as if he has run out of insults.

"You are . . ." he splutters . . . "you are . . . you are . . . very bad."

This is one insult too much for the ref, who blows his whistle, and runs up to the touch-line, then brandishes the red card at the manager. Then he restarts the match.

The manager looks around him, wondering what to do. Where do you go on a dry riverbed of a pitch when you have been sent off? Instead of standing in front of the bench he stands behind it. The referee looks over, and seems happy with that. But the manager isn't. He keeps edging forward, like a defender in a wall. For a while he is level with the bench. Then he shuffles even further forward, so he is just in front of it again, though to the side of it. The referee blows his whistle, runs to the ball, and picks it up, then runs over to the manager again. He is bristling with anger. The blue players are looking over, with 'here we go again' expressions on their faces. The ref gives an angry peep, pointing off the pitch, and makes it clear that he won't start the game again until the manager complies. The manager steps back behind the bench again, a matter of two yards, and the game continues.

I move on down to Manolo's bar and sit at the terrace outside. There are 30 or so Valencia ultras next to me, shouting instead of talking and occasionally pissing against a wheelie-bin. I read in *Super Deportes*, the local version of *Marca*, an article about the Valencia striker, Mista. He doesn't know why he's called Mista, he says, everyone in his family has been nicknamed Mista for generations. He was in the Real Madrid cantera, and caused quite a stir when he decided to leave it in 1999 to go to Tenerife, because he didn't think he'd get a chance in the first team. This was considered to be a dangerous precedent, at a time when Real Madrid were not in the financial position they are currently enjoying. On hearing the news, then-president Lorenzo Sanz threatened to scrap the whole of the youth system. What was the point in paying for the education of a player if they can just up and leave at the slightest opportunity? Mista scored 22 goals in two and a half seasons in the Canaries, then moved onto Valencia.

There's now an hour and a half before kick-off and a raucous crowd of several thousand Valencia fans is developing in the main road in front of the stadium, so I join it. They are waiting for the team buses to arrive. Several police horses are keeping the road clear, so the mob are in two sections. Those opposite me, away from the stadium, are the noisier half.

"Madridista el que no salte," they are singing, jumping up and down ('whoever isn't jumping up and down is a Madrid fan'). Someone sets off a machine-gun of bangers and one of the horses gets scared, charging down the road. Its rider, a policeman with a grey moustache, barely manages to control it.

"Puto Madrid, puta capital!"

"Puto Madrid, puto Madrid, puto, puto, puto Madrid."

The Valencia coach comes in, and the players rush into the stadium, scared-looking, despite the huge acclaim they are getting from the fans. Once they're in, the acclaim turns again to hate. God knows how the Real players are going to be received. This is not Beckham-mania.

"Puto Madrid, puta capital."

"Madrid, Madrid, hijos de puta."

Then the policemen ride off, and the road is allowed to fill with people. What the . . . ? General bewilderment. Where is the enemy?

"Where are the Madrid players?" I ask a guy.

"They must have gone into the back entrance," he says. A trick!

Next I queue to see if there is a press ticket for me. I have arranged press accreditation, but I am not sure it will have come through. At the window I am greeted with a smile and an envelope, and I now have two tickets, and a dilemma. Do I go try and sell my genuine ticket and sacrifice the better atmosphere for a better view and the chance to access the press conferences afterwards? I decide that yes, I will. I want to see the English Beckham correspondents at work. I am now a ticket tout.

I wander over to Manolo's bar to see if he has any advice. Perhaps he can help me sell it? He is doing a TV interview, wearing his oversized Basque beret and holding his drum. I leave.

I decide to go for the English-speaking market. There is a Japanese couple by the entrance to the bar.

"Do you need a ticket?"

"Solly?"

"Do you need a ticket. Face value?"

"Ah! We have ticket! Ha ha, we have ticket!" They think this is very funny. I wander over towards the ticket windows at the stadium wall. On the way I see some policemen.

"Excuse me officer," I say. I explain my situation. That I don't want to make a profit. What does he advise that I do? He looks at me as if I am slightly mad. "Well, go and sell it!" he says.

It has started raining. There is now half an hour before kick off. There are loads of touts around, and very few buyers. For the biggest game of the season! I can't believe it. I find three German guys who have two tickets and are looking for a third.

"Forty euros," I say, showing them the price on the ticket.

"Twenty," says one of them.

"This is Real Madrid."

"Twenty."

"OK, 30." I'm getting a little desperate.

"Twenty."

I wander off, and take a walk around. There are still many sellers, very few buyers. It's still drizzling.

"Quién quiere entrada?" I say, too quietly. ('who wants a ticket?'). I feel self-conscious. I walk around, saying my mantra. Who wants a ticket? Who wants a ticket? Twenty minutes to kick off. It's still raining. I walk back to the Germans.

"Thirty."

"Twenty."

"OK, 25."

"Twenty."

"Go on then, 20." We do a hurried swap, note for ticket. He high-fives one of his mates. "Enjoy the game," I muster, mournfully, stuffing the note into my pocket. Half of what I paid. Mr Beckham is not quite the draw I'd imagined him to be.

Never mind. I start getting excited by the match in prospect. I find my way to my seat, in amongst a number of journalists. The seats have plenty of leg-room, but there's one problem. The view. I am perfectly placed on the halfway line and I can see the whole of the field, but the stand above juts out in front of my field of vision, so I can see nothing of the fans in front of me, and I realise that if anyone kicks the ball into the air, I won't be able to see it. I can, however, see the Valencia ultras, who are already singing. They have been divided into two fenced-off pens, placed at either side of the long touch-line stand that I am in. "Madridista el que no salte" they are singing, jumping up and down. They look like they're having a great time.

I've noticed that the bloke next from me is from the *Daily Telegraph*, so I introduce myself.

"I also work for *The Guardian* web-site," he says.

"You must be Sid."

It's Sid Lowe, who for several years has been writing clever pun-filled round-ups of the Spanish Primera División for the *Guardian* website. We get chatting, and laugh about the anachronistic brass band marching on the pitch below, followed by a surreal cartoon figure with a bat's head. The Ultras are drowning out their noise, to the tune of 'Enola Gay' . . .

"Lo lo lo, lolololo-lo lo lo-lo, Forza Valencia-ale, lo lo lololo lo lolo."

Then the players run out onto the pitch – both sets of ultras have prepared a snowstorm of ticker-tape, which leaves a light covering of white on the pitch in front of them. The referee's whistle pierces the wall of sound, and Valencia kick off, to the accompaniment of the Scotland 1978 World Cup anthem ('We're on the march wi' Ally's Army').

*Som la forca del Valencia*
*i ningu mos parara,*
*viatjarem per tot el mon,*
*orgullosos del teu nom,*
*el Valencia es el nostre campeo!*

(We are the fans of Valencia,
no-one will stop us,
we'll travel the whole wide world,
proud of your name,
Valencia are our champions).

Valencia respond to their fans with a couple of whirlwind attacks, playing short passes to feet and pushing quickly up front. I realise that Manolo was right. Beckham, who likes to ponder over his passes to make them perfect, would find it difficult to fit into the home team's style of play. And he's being virtually bypassed tonight. The curly-haired little Argentinian Pablo Aimar, a much more pushy, naggy, tricky player, is in Valencia's play-making role and he is brilliant, getting the ball, occasionally dribbling a little, always moving it up the field, pushing his team forward. After five minutes an attack penetrates down the left, a cross comes in, and the net ripples. The tannoy guy goes mad.

"Gol gol gol!" he shouts. "Golgolgolgolgolgolgolgol,golgolgolgolgolgol-golgolgolgol! Gol! Goooooooooooooooooooooool! Mista! Gol de Mista!"

Valencia are 1–0 up, and the match has hardly started.

Real Madrid reply with a couple of attacks of their own which lead to Beckham corners. Both are taken to my left, right in front of one section of the ultras. Despite the abuse, the empty plastic bottles and the two toilet rolls that are flung at him, he puts in a couple of viciously curling in-swingers, which Valencia manage to clear. But it's the home team that is making all the running. Aimar continues to be brilliant, passing perfectly and running onto the return ball, driving his team forward in waves. Beckham is all over the pitch, but without the ball, unable to find a place to settle in a match in which Real Madrid find it hard to keep possession. Then on the half-hour the referee's assistant holds up a board, and Aimar goes off. A slight limp. "Damn it," I hear myself thinking. "Damn it!" I say to Sid. "Damn it," he replies. He's been the star of the show . . . and now Real Madrid are much more likely to win. I realise that this is something I do not want to happen. I don't want them to run away with the league. Valencia look like being their closest rivals – if they win tonight, it will set things up really nicely.

Towards the end of the first half Ayala starts warming up on the touchline. Pointedly, he starts stretching in front of the group of ultras to my right. I'm expecting whistles and abuse, but the crowd are too happy to care. Instead they are happily humming the music to *The Waltons*. The half-time whistle blows, and the brass band marches back onto the pitch, followed by the bat mascot, clapping at the fans. I already can't wait for the second half.

It starts like the first half ended. Valencia are nowhere near as fluid without Aimar, but in Albelda and Baraja they have a formidable defensive midfield which smothers anything that Real can get going, and quickly moves it into attack. They are playing as a pair in front of the defence, the classic Spanish 'doble pivote'. The Valencia midfielders are a first line of defence, but as soon as they get the ball they move it forward quickly. Real Madrid are thus snuffed out as an attacking force. In the centre, Beckham can't get enough of the ball and Cambiasso can't get the ball at all. Wide right, Figo is trying hard but is cut off from the action. On the left, Zidane is outmuscled. Guti looks tired in Raúl's role. Ronaldo is marked out of the game by Ayala's replacement David Navarro.

Then, with 20 minutes left another Valencia attack, a shot is saved, Oliveira pounds in the rebound. 2–0. The tannoy guy starts his 'gol' stuff and the fans, having gone through their first cycle of joyous celebration, start all over again.

"Lo-lo-lo lololo Valencia Club de fu fútbol," they sing, again to Enola Gay. They are rolling around, bouncing off one another, jumping, falling over, everyone grinning, starting up another song. I don't think I've ever seen a group of people having such a good time. 2–0 up against Real Madrid, 20 minutes to go.

Madrid finally start enjoying most of the possession, and Figo has a shot tipped over the bar by Cañizares, Valencia's imposing blond keeper. And the referee starts giving all the decisions Real's way. But Valencia are quick on the break, and always look the more likely team to score. Their fans continue celebrating, seemingly oblivious to the fact that Real Madrid pose any danger to their victory celebrations, singing a Valenciano version of the 'Chipmunks are go' US Marines' marching song. A guy with a megaphone solos the lines, which are then repeated by the rest of the fans.

*Blanc i negre els teus colors,*
*blanc i negre tenim el cor,*
*i Mestalla vibrara,*
*el Valencia guanyara*

(Black and white are our colours,
our hearts are black and white,
the Mestalla will vibrate,
Valencia will win.)

Late on, Beckham steps up to take a free kick, and for the first time since he has arrived in Spain, I don't want him to score it. I desperately want this hard-working Valencia side to win the game. He stands to the side of the ball, concentrates his mind, takes a run up . . . and puts the ball straight into the wall. I needn't have worried. It is virtually the last kick of the match. Game over.

Afterwards I watch Carlos Queiroz' press conference. He evidently deals with defeat in the same deadpan manner with which he greets victory. 'Ni respiración ni inspiración' are his opening words ('neither breath nor inspiration'). He doesn't understand it, but his team decided not to play. He doesn't stay for long. Neither do I. I rush down into the 'mixed zone' where the players have to filter past the press before they can get onto their buses. There is a mob waiting. I see Sid, who is on the edge of a group of English-speaking journalists, who seem to be having rather a violent row. I eavesdrop. One of them is claiming that their questions should only be about football. Others are arguing that this should not be the case. Beckham has been photographed in a nightclub next to a woman who is not Victoria Beckham (it's his SFX agent Rebecca Loos): the Spanish press is full of rumours concerning the alleged crisis in his marriage. Suddenly Beckham appears, and the rat pack moves in, muscling their way to the front of the crash barrier all shouting "David, David, David" hoping that their obvious English accents, their by-now-familiar faces, will stop him. They are led by a blond guy who jabs a microphone into his face and starts asking questions . . . about his personal life. Beckham stops, politely answers, stays there several minutes, moves on. "Cheers David, thanks a lot" says the guy. Another of the journalists is waiting at the end of the row, an unshaven but smart fellow in a leather jacket. "David, David" he shouts, as Beckham nears the salvation of the exit. His trick has worked. Beckham stops. He's got an exclusive. I muscle in beside him. This guy's asking about the football, how the game went. Beckham makes his excuses. Valencia were very good, they stopped Madrid from playing, it's very disappointing to lose such a big game, the important thing is to win the next one. That sort of thing. It's the first time I've heard his voice so clearly, so live. A slight voice, high, not hesitant, but not confident, either. I can't resist handing my notebook and pen to him over the barrier. Without looking at me he scrawls his autograph and hands it back. As it does, our fingers touch. It's an odd sensation, actually touching the guy I've been following over Spain. He finishes his conversation, heads to the exit, to the safety of the team coach. Outside there are fans waiting, not to greet him, but to hurl abuse.

"Puto Madrid, puta capital."

"Beckham maricón."

Inside the English journalists are still arguing about the same thing. One of them wants all of them to do the same interview, and that it should be about the football. Another reckons it should be each for his own. The first counters that the other is destroying their reputation. It goes round and round in circles. I say my goodbyes to Sid, and head off.

I have a beer in Manolo's place. There is a Real Madrid fan there, wearing the white club shirt, carrying an umbrella. I suspect he is a tourist. But he has been spotted and a group of Valencia ultras is collecting outside the bar, pointing in. The mood starts to get ugly. The guy with the umbrella doesn't seem to read this mood. He saunters out, and walks straight past the group, by now about 20 strong, crossing the road behind them, walking past an open bar.

The Valencia fans don't know what to do. He's more bold than they have expected, probably because he is unaware of the danger. The smallest amongst them sprints across the road, and pushes the Real Madrid fan in the back. He takes refuge in the bar. Manolo comes to his doorway. He is trying to calm things down. One of the ultras goes up to him. "If I did that in the centre of Madrid in my Valencia shirt I would be dead." Manolo has a word. I remember his philosophy – 'fútbol sí, violencia no'. The ugly mood abates, the crowd disperse. There is no sign of the Real Madrid fan. Perhaps he has wisely taken off his shirt.

Ten minutes later I am sitting on a bridge over the riverbed, contemplating the match. A homeless-looking bloke walks past pushing a shopping trolley with two dogs attached to it. He asks me for money. I give him a euro; I'm feeling good. He sees this as a signal to sit down and join me. I've spent much of the last two weeks on my own, but I'm not sure if I appreciate the company. Not him, not now. I make out a familiar figure walking towards me. It's Sid Lowe from *The Guardian*.

"Made a friend?" he says, as he reaches me. He invites me for a drink in another part of town. We hail a cab, and pretty soon I'm sitting at a pavement terrace drinking a beer with the same English journalists I've seen in the mixed zone. I study them with some interest; these are the seven-day a week Beckham correspondents, the tabloid journalists who follow his every move. The one from *The Sun*, in his early twenties, has blond Beckham-like hair, half-covered by a baseball cap; The *Daily Mail* have sent out a chirpy Geordie in his thirties, a big guy with very short hair; the *News of the World's* correspondent is a Greek with clipped faux-posh English, smart, in a leather jacket, an outsider. Sitting rather sheepishly beside them is the *Sunday Times* correspondent, a quieter chap with serious glasses. The *Mirror* guy is on the other table. The conversation is Beckham, Beckham, Beckham. They are still arguing about their modus operandi; whether they should be talking about the rumours about his marriage or staying on the subject of the football. Whether they should stay in one group and share their quotes, or split up and each to their own. It's not a constructive debate, moving to a conclusion through give and take. It is a circular shouting match, with the *News of the World* guy taking a lone stance against the others. They are a curious bunch, strange figures sticking together in an alien environment; deadly rivals for an exclusive quote from Beckham, but dependent on one another, too, for a beer after the game, a friendly face, a fellow ex-pat in the same queer boat.

### RESULTS: JORNADA 5

| | | | |
|---|---|---|---|
| ALBACETE | 2 | MALLORCA | 0 |
| OSASUNA | 3 | DEPORTIVO | 2 |
| ATLÉTICO | 0 | BARCELONA | 0 |
| ESPANYOL | 1 | MÁLAGA | 2 |
| CELTA | 3 | VALLADOLID | 2 |
| RACING | 0 | VILLARREAL | 2 |
| ZARAGOZA | 0 | BETIS | 1 |
| ATHLETIC | 1 | REAL SOCIEDAD | 0 |
| SEVILLA | 1 | MURCIA | 0 |
| **VALENCIA** | **2** | **REAL MADRID** | **0** |

**SUNDAY 5TH OCTOBER**

I ring on the bell of the Espanyol central peña just off the Ramblas in the old part of Barcelona, and walk up the concrete stairs to the first floor. Real Madrid are about to play the other team from Barcelona in the Bernabéu, and I've decided to watch the game with the Espanyol fans. It's a crucial match – after losing to Valencia, Real desperately need the points to keep up with Deportivo, who thrashed Atlético 5–1 yesterday, and Valencia, due to play Barcelona in the Nou Camp up the road later on today. I walk into a packed room with the usual club paraphernalia on the walls, and order a beer at the bar.

I've expected only Espanyol fans in the bar, but I'm disappointed. There's a group of Northern English lads, a couple of whom are in that menacing state of drunkenness where one wrong look could lead to a violent confrontation. There's a table free in front of the TV, so I quietly settle myself there, trying to give no signal as to my nationality. The TV is off, so I settle into my papers.

The good news is that Beckham is playing. He bruised the instep of his foot taking a free-kick against Valencia, and looked to be doubtful for both this game and the forthcoming England game against Turkey. The injury forced him out of Wednesday's Champions League clash in Porto. Real won 3–1 but put in an unconvincing display without him.

A lot of the talk is of Espanyol coach Javier Clemente and the negative tactics he is to take to the Bernabéu. You might remember Clemente from his six years as coach of 'la selección', the Spanish national team. He was an extremely talented inventive forward for Athletic de Bilbao until his career was ended at the age of 21 by a savage kick in the knee by a Sabadell defender. He became a coach, and in his early thirties masterminded two consecutive championships (1983 and 84) for the Basque team: a remarkable achievement for the team which only included local players in an era when the likes of Diego Maradona, Hugo Sánchez and Mario Kempes were playing in La Liga.

His career since then, however, has been spectacularly devoid of success, and Clemente's tactics, perhaps as a result of this, have become increasingly, almost freakishly, defensive. He has become something of a specialist at avoiding relegation; it looks like his Espanyol side this season (it is almost entirely new) has been designed with a flirtation with the drop to Segunda in mind. Before kick off Espanyol are 'los colistas' (the tail-enders; bottom of the table) with two draws and three defeats from their five games. Clemente's formation for the Real Madrid game is his famous 'autobús' formation of 5-4-1, with three centre-backs, two non-attacking full-backs, and a pair of defensive central midfielders sitting in front, for added security. It is called 'el autobús' because it is akin to parking a bus in front of the goal.

As if to compensate for his crushingly boring tactics, Clemente is hugely entertaining in interviews, an outspoken man who peppers his phrases with startling analogies. I'm delighted to find an interview with him in

*El País*, the intellectual left-leaning national daily which vies with *Marca* as being the most-read newspaper in Spain. In the interview he talks about the importance of Beckham to the Real Madrid side, bemoaning the fact that Real Madrid are the only club that could afford his talents.

"I could buy 20 players for Espanyol for what Beckham cost Madrid," he says. "Valdano goes to the market and buys the freshest lobster."

"Beckham is the difference between last year's side and this one," he continues. "Many people thought that he was only good at crossing, but if you can cross well, you can pass well, and if you know how to pass, you know how to play football."

If you watch football in a Spanish bar don't be surprised if the barman doesn't get round to turning the TV on after the match has actually started. There are 50 or so people here to watch the game – the English lads don't seem bothered – but by the time the guy manages to tune in (he has to go through the complicated process of 'buying the match' with his remote control) five minutes have elapsed. All eyes jump to the top left of the screen. Still 0–0.

That's the way it remains for the first half, with Espanyol hustling a patient Real Madrid and allowing no space for them to get through. Chances are few and far between. Halfway through the half, Beckham lines up for a free kick. His trademark pause for reflection, body bent slightly back, looking at his target, perhaps visualising a goal.

"Look, there's Beckham," says one of the English lads, perhaps noticing the game for the first time. They all look over.

"Wanker!"

"He must be playing away."

Beckham shoots the ball straight into the wall. They all shout 'aaaaah' and get back into their drinking, cementing in the mind of those around them the stereotype of the Englishman abroad Beckham has been striving so hard to break.

Real finally break through early in the second half, Ronaldo poking home into an empty net after some brilliant work by Raúl down the left of the box. But the goal does not open the game up. Espanyol continue parking in front of the goal, devoid of much ambition, hoping for an unlikely breakaway equaliser. Zidane is impressive, probing for a way through the wall. Beckham, further back, starts things off for Real when one of Espanyol's rare attacks break down. On 67 minutes, Lemmens keeps the Catalan side in the game with a penalty save from Figo. Then on 81, Beckham strays into his old position down the right, negotiates his way into the box, and delivers a delicate centimetre-perfect ball onto the head of Ronaldo, who makes no mistake. 2–0, and game over.

In injury time Alex Fernández beats Cambiasso and Helguera, and hits a cross-shot past Casillas. A guy sitting behind me stands up and starts shouting "Espanyol, Espanyol, Espanyol" while jabbing a flurry of Nazi salutes. Espanyol has a number of ultra-right-wing fans. The English lads cheer him. Soon after the final whistle they pose for a picture. The smallest and most dangerous-looking, standing in the middle, pulls his trousers down for it. I leave.

## RESULTS: JORNADA 6

| | | | |
|---|---|---|---|
| DEPORTIVO | 5 | ATLÉTICO | 1 |
| VILLARREAL | 1 | ZARAGOZA | 1 |
| BETIS | 1 | ATHLETIC | 1 |
| REAL SOCIEDAD | 1 | SEVILLA | 1 |
| VALLADOLID | 0 | RACING | 4 |
| MALLORCA | 1 | OSASUNA | 1 |
| MURCIA | 1 | ALBACETE | 0 |
| MÁLAGA | 2 | CELTA | 1 |
| **REAL MADRID** | **2** | **ESPANYOL** | **1** |
| BARCELONA | 0 | VALENCIA | 1 |

## LA CLASIFICACIÓN

| | P | W | D | L | F | A | Pts |
|---|---|---|---|---|---|---|---|
| VALENCIA | 6 | 5 | 1 | 0 | 9 | 1 | 16 |
| DEPORTIVO | 6 | 5 | 0 | 1 | 15 | 5 | 15 |
| **REAL MADRID** | **6** | **4** | **1** | **1** | **15** | **8** | **13** |
| OSASUNA | 6 | 3 | 2 | 1 | 8 | 5 | 11 |
| VILLARREAL | 6 | 2 | 4 | 0 | 7 | 4 | 10 |
| REAL SOCIEDAD | 6 | 2 | 3 | 1 | 7 | 4 | 9 |
| BETIS | 6 | 2 | 3 | 1 | 7 | 5 | 9 |
| SEVILLA | 6 | 2 | 3 | 1 | 6 | 5 | 9 |
| BARCELONA | 6 | 2 | 3 | 1 | 5 | 4 | 9 |
| ATHLETIC | 6 | 2 | 2 | 2 | 8 | 6 | 8 |
| RACING | 6 | 2 | 2 | 2 | 7 | 5 | 8 |
| MÁLAGA | 6 | 2 | 1 | 3 | 5 | 7 | 7 |
| VALLADOLID | 6 | 2 | 1 | 3 | 9 | 16 | 7 |
| CELTA VIGO | 6 | 1 | 3 | 2 | 7 | 9 | 6 |
| MURCIA | 6 | 1 | 3 | 2 | 5 | 8 | 6 |
| MALLORCA | 6 | 1 | 2 | 3 | 5 | 10 | 5 |
| ZARAGOZA | 6 | 1 | 1 | 4 | 4 | 8 | 4 |
| ATLÉTICO | 6 | 1 | 1 | 4 | 2 | 10 | 4 |
| ALBACETE | 6 | 1 | 0 | 5 | 3 | 9 | 3 |
| ESPANYOL | 6 | 0 | 2 | 4 | 7 | 12 | 2 |

# FIVE
# VIGO

# FIVE
# VIGO

## TUESDAY 14TH OCTOBER

When I wake up I am in Galicia. I've slept fitfully in a top bunk bed on the night train from Barcelona, in a compartment with five other men. From their looks when I sit up and drop lithely down into my shoes on the floor I'm the snorer with the smelly feet. And I was lying about the 'lithely'. I decide to get a coffee in the bar carriage and it's still dark outside. The sky lightens a little and I watch Galicia develop through the window. I can see a land of fog and forest, very green, very wet. There are melons growing in allotments, and many low houses with small granaries on stilts. Men in flat caps and tweed jackets with patches on their sleeves, and dogs.

A river appears to my left. Not one of those dried-up things I've seen in Valencia or Málaga, but a wide expanse of green water gushing plentifully along, bordered by deep green pine trees, the odd colourful rowing-boat moored in the middle. It is the river Minho, and it separates Portugal from Spain. My mobile phone sends me a message. It is confused. It welcomes me to Vodafone Portugal. The train stops in a small town. A group of drunken Portuguese, who I suspect have been in the bar carriage all night, get off. We are within a bridge-width of their country.

Officially, Galicia is in Spain, but it doesn't look like it. Vigo is on the west coast of the peninsula. Due south is Portugal, due north is the south coast of Ireland. Due west, a long way due west, is New England. Until 1492, this was the edge of the known world, a barren, rocky place that looked into the abyss of nothingness. It was in Padrón, just down the coast, that Columbus landed with the biggest news of the century. There is more land out there! This isn't, in fact, the end of the world! The news didn't, however, change the look of the place. It's so rugged, rocky and rainy it might have been torn off the west coast of Ireland and welded onto the rest of Spain, weather and all. They even play the bagpipes . . .

Vigo was a small fishing port of 15,000 inhabitants until the beginning of the 20th century when a number of canning factories were set up. Now it has a population of 400,000 and is the second biggest fishing port in the world next to Tokyo. A rough place in a rough part of the world, and the next destination for the Real Madrid roadshow.

I book into a one-star hotel next to the port. It's the best value place I've stayed so far. I make myself at home, unpack my rucksack, throw a few things around, make a bit of a mess. I'm going to be here a few days. I'm happy. Despite a slapstick Beckham penalty miss, England have just qualified for the European Championships, by drawing 0–0 with Turkey. They'll be playing just over the border this summer. I go for a walk round the port. The bit by the town centre looks busy but not too industrial. There is a marina and a few official buildings, and a couple of ferries which regularly chug back and forth across the ría. This is the local word for a large estuary akin to a fjord – there are several of these wide estuaries penetrating the west coast of Galicia, and Vigo is built on one. From the port you can see across the ría to the towns on the other side – in between are hundreds of flat barges: platforms for mussel fishing.

There is a curious statue on the portside, in two halves. An iron torso has seemingly fallen from a pair of wooden legs, five metres high. The torso is armless, and has landed on its big nose, which is squashed into the concrete ground. It looks like a warning: 'don't be too proud'. I think of Real Madrid and Beckham. Are they heading for a fall? Celta de Vigo qualified for the Champions League last season, but they have made a poor start to the season. Defeat for Madrid would be quite a shock.

Behind the hotel is the centre of town – a few grand buildings, a few shopping streets and a hill with a mossy castle on the top. On the way to the centre, looking for lunch, on a narrow stepped street leading down towards the centre, I pass a small poorly lit bar which is full of young women, sat at a table. 'How strange', I think. Then there is another, also full of young women. One shouts something lewd to me, and I cotton on. From another doorway another woman, middle-aged, dressed in black lace, comes out and beckons me to join her.

"Joven," (young man) she shouts. "Joven, come here." I don't stop to tell her I am actually not so 'joven', being just a few months shy of my 40th birthday. Instead I put my head down in the way you do when you don't want to give money to a beggar, and walk on. I am grateful to reach the main road. I cross it, and walk into a street lined with restaurants where there are several old women standing by big trestle tables full of boxes of fresh oysters. They beckon me over.

"Joven! Would you like some? They are good!"

I shake my head. They are insistent.

"They are very good. The best in town." I hurry past them, too, though I'm tempted this time. And hungry.

After a more modest lunch (I should have gone for the damn oysters, but I'm on a tight budget) I decide to wander down to the stadium. I've been told that there is a 'fundación de peñas' (supporters club head-quarters) there and I want to watch the match with the Celta de Vigo ultras, the passionate fans who stand behind the goal and sing throughout the match. I skirt round the red-light district and head up to the castle that overlooks the city. Vigo's not a pretty sight. You can see just how industrial the place is, with dockyards and cranes lining the coast as far as the eye can see in either direction. The stadium is on the other side of the hill, through an extensive district of '60s and '70s blocks of flats, and a modern and very busy shopping district. The streets are grey and unappealing, filled with the bustle of bars and shops and of people having to shout over the roar of the traffic. It starts to rain. The fact that every-body is already carrying an umbrella confirms the area's reputation of the rainiest in Spain. Forget that stuff about the plain.

It's always exciting to come across a new stadium, and despite its surroundings, the oblong El Balaídos is no exception. I've read about it – when it was first built in 1923 it was out in the middle of nowhere, a couple of miles from town. The city has since caught up with and surrounded the ground with busy main road. The bottom tier of it houses a line of offices; one has a hand-painted sign above it 'Fundación de Peñas del Celta de Vigo'. I walk in and ask for Begoña, who is the pres-ident of the fundación, which is the collective body for all the supporters clubs of Celta de Vigo (mostly located in Galicia, though there are a couple in Madrid and one in Barcelona). I introduce myself.

"I want to watch the game with the Celta ultras."

Begoña smiles; a chubby young woman who looks busy.

"We represent all the supporters clubs of Celta Vigo, but not the ultras. We have no contact with them."

"How can I find them?"

"Are you sure you want to?"

"I am sure."

"You have to go through the head of security of the club."

She gives me a name and number. I don't like the sound of this.

"Is there anyone who would be willing to chat to me about the history of the club?" I ask. "Over a drink or two maybe?"

I'm fishing for a date, to fill up the lonely evening. I'm a long way from home.

There's a middle-aged guy there with a big moustache of the type only sported in Spain, some Arab countries and English period dramas set in the 19th century. He puts his hand out. His name is Arximelo.

"I finish here at 6.45. I'll be in my bar at about 7.30. The Rikitriki on Rua María Berdiales. Why don't you come on up?"

To fill in the time Arximelo gives me a book to look at which contains a season-by-season guide to the club from its foundation in 1929 to 1996. I also need to get a ticket for the match.

The ticket office, a couple of holes in the wall, is just up the way. I ask the girl at the counter which section the ultras go in.

"That's the fondo."

"Which bit of the fondo?"

"Once you're in the fondo, you can go where you want. Nobody sits in the fondo."

"How much."

"30 euros. It's the cheapest. But be warned. You can hardly see anything from there."

"It's alright. I'm here for the atmosphere."

"There'll be atmosphere all right."

For the first time I haven't been nervous about getting a ticket. I'm starting to sense how things work in Spain. There is not a big rush when tickets go on sale. People buy them in their own good time: there is rarely more than a trickle of customers queuing. If you get there early, a ticket is yours, even when Real Madrid come to town.

I try to find the head of security. I am able to walk into his empty office unchallenged, so he can't be that good at his job. Anyway, he isn't there. I wander into a bar opposite the Balaídos, and read about the history of the club over a couple of cañas. The book goes into some detail about the original foundation of the Spanish football league, which is interesting. Football was brought to Spain by British sailors and students at the end of the 19th century, and proved so popular that clubs soon started forming (the oldest of which have already celebrated their centenary). A cup competition – the Copa del Rey – was organised in 1902. Basque team Vizcaya were the first winners, beating Barcelona 2–1. The teams also played in regional leagues. In Vigo there were two teams, Vigo and Fortuna. Vigo got to the Copa del Rey final in 1908 (beaten 2–1 by Real Madrid), but it was decided that the town could not sustain two teams successfully and they merged in 1923.

In 1927 the idea of a Spanish league was mooted, which led to heated debate. One small group of more successful clubs, nicknamed 'los minimalistas' wanted to play in a small league composed just of themselves (the first superleague breakaway?). Many of the elitist clubs in question have a familiar ring to them: Athletic de Bilbao, Barcelona, Real Madrid, Atlético de Madrid. Other clubs, 'los maximalistas' favoured a bigger two-tiered league with promotion and relegation. These included Real Club Celta de Vigo. The smaller clubs persuaded the FA to arrange a fixture list for 1928.

Those fixtures were never played, but on 23rd November 1928, the teams finally agreed terms. The First Division was to be formed by the nine teams which had reached the cup final over the years, and a 10th team which was to be decided in a knock-out play-off between other contenders. The nine teams were Athletic de Bilbao, Real Madrid, Barcelona, Racing Irún, Real Sociedad, Español, Europa, Atlético de Madrid and Arenas. Vigo's cup win was not deemed to be valid for qualification into the elite as it was pre-merger.

The knock-out play-off was eventually won by Racing de Santander. Celta were knocked out in the second round. Racing were relegated after the end of the first season – Celta also dropped from the second to the third division.

The club's history has been patchy since then, and included a startling run in the '70s and '80s which must be a world record. In 1975 they were relegated to the second division, in 1976 they were promoted again. In 1977 they were relegated, in 1978 they were promoted again. In 1979 they were relegated and in 1980 they dropped down to the Third Division. Not for long. In 1981 they went up to the Second, in 1982 straight up to the First. Of course, they went straight down again to the second in 1983. In 1984 they stayed where they were (missing out on promotion by a single point). In 1985 they were promoted, in 1986 they were relegated, in 1987, under the management of West Countryman Colin Addison, they were promoted again. They managed to stay there for three seasons, a remarkable period of stability. They call them los años de ascensor (the lift years).

The current period is the best the club has ever enjoyed. They have been in Primera since 1992, finishing in the top seven in the last six years, and finally making it to the Champions League, after a long apprenticeship in the UEFA Cup, at the end of 2002/03. The game against Real Madrid is followed three days later by a trip to Amsterdam to play against Ajax.

Arximelo's bar, El Rikitriki, is a shrine to Celta's European adventures. The ceiling and walls are decorated with the scarves of every club the Galician side has played in their six seasons of competition, including those of Aston Villa and Liverpool, both of whom they beat on their way to the quarter-finals of the UEFA Cup in 1999, a feat they equalled in the two subsequent years. In 2002/03 they were knocked out of the competition on away goals by Glasgow Celtic, a tie that was much enjoyed by fans of both teams, who liked the coincidence of names (Celta v Celtic!) and made a lot about their common Celtic heritage (Galicia is a land of bagpipes and mystic crosses, though there are no traces of the Celtic language).

I've noticed an interesting correlation on my travels: the more it rains, the more interesting the bar-life. And there is something very surreal about the conversation in the Rikitriki, a small place with no tables or chairs, where people wander in for a half hour or so, chew the fat a bit, drink a few glasses of wine, eat vast quantities of shelled peanuts, which are liberally distributed periodically by Arximelo into little piles on the bar, and then wander out again. I've envisaged a stiff, formal interview with Arximelo. What I get over the next couple of hours is much better: a free-for-all with everyone in the bar contributing.

"I'm not a merengue," I announce, on arriving in the bar. This proves to be a popular statement and encourages a debate.

"If you live in Vigo, you support Celta," says one guy, who looks like he's been enjoying Arximelo's wine for a while. "But you also support Real Madrid or Barcelona. I chose Barcelona. That means that I hate Real Madrid. It's like the law of the Bedouin. My friend's enemy is my enemy."

"But that's not true. I support Celta, but I don't support Barcelona or Real Madrid," says Arximelo.

"Anyway, what is the point of your English pounds?" says the guy, finally changing the subject.

"Pounds weight or pounds sterling?"

"Start with the weight."

"It's imperial. Like we have inches and yards. From Roman times."

"It's illogical. I mean a metre is a thousandth of a kilometre. What's a yard a thousandth of?"

"Nothing. But that's not the point. Anyway, it is the pace of a man. You can measure it with your body. Just like a foot is the size of a foot."

"But people have different-sized feet! What good is a common measurement when you can have size 35 feet and size 46?"

"You just kind of estimate up or down . . ."

"And how can you drive on the left? It's a good job you don't have borders with other countries. What would they do?"

A corpulent well-dressed guy has come in.

"This is Celta's number one fan, Tato. He's travelled all over the continent following Celta Vigo," says Arximelo.

"Hi Tato," I say. Then, for some reason, "Can you estimate the distance you've travelled following Celta, in miles?"

He starts counting all the scarves on the ceiling and doing a mental calculation.

I ask Arximelo about Vigo's qualification for the Champions League.

"What a party!" he replies, a smile pushing up the edges of his moustache. "It was the penultimate day of the season. We had to beat Real Sociedad, who were league leaders, and hope that Valencia lost at home to Barcelona. We didn't think that all that would happen."

"At half time we were 1–0 up, and so were Barcelona!" interrupts another guy, who points to his empty glass, and then to mine.

Arximelo pours Ribeiro, a highly palatable local wine, into our glasses, and takes up the story again.

"Mostovoi scored a second goal, then Nihat pulled one back. 2–1. Then Mido, the Egyptian lad, scored a third for us, and almost immediately Barcelona scored two more in Valencia. All we had to do was to win! Everyone started celebrating. Then, with about ten minutes to go, Nihat scored for Real Sociedad, to make it 3–2. The next ten minutes seemed like ten hours. Finally the referee blew the whistle. We were there! In the Champions League!

"Everybody went out on the streets, celebrating. The whole town came out, everyone who had a car or a scooter drove round, tooting their horns, every fountain was full of people.

"Even the Real Sociedad fans joined in, even though their defeat knocked them off the top of the table. They joined in singing the Rianxeira, which is our victory song. It is about a girl who emigrates across the Atlantic. We only sing it when we are very, very happy."

Tato has finished his estimation. "Approximately 30,000 kilometres," he says. "Which works out to about 20,000 of your miles. It would have been more, but I was working abroad sometimes. Once I was in Nicaragua, and I had to phone Arximelo to see how the game was going in Stuttgart. He gave me a live commentary down his mobile, from Germany. That was quite a phone bill."

After a couple of hours in the bar I feel it is time to go off and eat. I have drunk five glasses of wine – but every one of them has been paid for by someone else in the bar. I try to complain, but to no avail. I am not allowed to pay, full stop.

In the restaurant I have a Galician speciality – octopus and potatoes sprinkled with paprika, washed down by a bottle of red wine, and accompanied by a salad. The octopus it's a lovely mixture between chewy in the middle and squidgy at the sides. It is delicious. The bill comes to less than ten euros. I'm enjoying this place a lot.


**WEDNESDAY OCTOBER 15TH**

The next morning I find myself up in the hills behind the town, waiting to do an interview with Celta striker Savo Milosevic. It's a sunny hot day, with no hint of yesterday's poor weather. There are a handful of other journalists hanging round next to an empty artificial pitch, and a car-park which is jigsawed with BMW's. Mercedes, Volvos and VW jeeps. I am told that the players have finished training, that they are now in the gym.

Suddenly Milosovic walks out, wearing a crumpled black silk shirt and a pair of fake-faded jeans. He is one of the few Celta players I would have recognised, from his days at Aston Villa where he was nicknamed Missalotovic after a poor goals-games ratio in his final year. But I have studied his career in my *Marca Guide*, and the Bosnian Serb has done pretty well for himself since, especially in Spain, where he has scored with some regularity for Zaragoza and Espanyol. And he's already got four Liga goals this season, using his guile rather than his speed to find the space to create scoring opportunities for himself. He's currently using the same guile to attempt an escape from a journalist eager for an interview.

"Savo, Savo," I shout, to attract his attention. I decide to carry on in English. "Atilo, the press officer, arranged for me to come here to interview you. I've come from England."

It's an exaggeration, but there you go. Milosovic looks crestfallen. "Look, I'm in a hurry," he says, betraying the fact that his English is still in fine nick. "Will it take long?"

"Ten minutes," I lie.

"OK, then."

He shuts his car door again, and leads me into the waiting room of the 'vestuarios' (changing rooms). We sit down at a little table. He looks older up close, very Slavic, with short mousy hair, brown eyes and a long, serious, seen-a-lot-of-life face. I ask him how special it is to be playing against Real Madrid at the weekend.

"I would be lying," he replies, "if I pretended that playing against Real Madrid wasn't something special. You only have to look at their players – Ronaldo, Zidane, Raúl, Beckham – to know that we will have to do something special to beat them. And of course that makes the team motivated. Because we know that if we do not play our best game, we will not win."

"How is your personal record against Real Madrid?"

In eight or nine games I have scored five goals, so it is fairly good. Even though all goals are worth the same they feel important against Real Madrid, because it is always an important game."

"How about David Beckham. You've played against him, of course."

"Yes, we had a sort of a fight seven or eight years ago, in Manchester. It was nothing serious. [In fact the two got into a scrap after the Serb allegedly spat at the 20-year-old Beckham]. I have great respect for him, even though I think it must be difficult for him to hold onto everything that is going on around him. He has had his problems with the England supporters, but he has shown character to come through that. He is one of the best five or six English players ever, and England are a much improved side because of him."

I wonder about the differences that Savo finds between the English and the Spanish games.

"Both are exciting in different ways. It's no secret that the Spanish game is more technically skilful, but I think the English players score higher in terms of character and mentality. The players always go out and try to win games: they rarely go away just to defend. That's why Beckham is doing so well here. That and the fact that the English are more fond of longer balls to move from defence to attack, a Beckham speciality, which he is starting to apply to his game here. People are trying to change the English game, but I think they play in a way that they are naturally suited to playing. It's been like that for 100 years. Why change it now?"

He smiles a pleasant, slightly crooked-tooth smile. I try to maintain eye-contact with him, but his eyes remain on my notebook throughout our talk. This is rather off-putting – I have no short-hand, and have developed a doctor's scrawl only I can understand. I worry that he thinks I'm not a real reporter.

"In a way," I propose, "a striker's life is easy . . . if you're scoring you know you are doing well, if not, you know you are doing badly . . ."

He looks at me as if I am mad.

"As defenders are getting better, it's getting even more difficult every year," he says.

I wonder how come.

"They are more and more prepared, they are fitter and fitter. And do I need to tell you why it is easier for them?"

I say that maybe he could just remind me.

"It is easier for them because we need to put the ball between the posts, and they just need to kick it away."

In the afternoon I ring Celta's security officer.

"I have no contact with the ultras," he tells me. "I can't help you contact them. But before the match they go to the Bar Luar, near the stadium. You might find them there."

The only people in the Bar Luar are several old fellows noisily playing dominoes. I go to the bar, and buy a beer. I feel slightly seedy, like a private dick on a case. A young guy with a pony tail serves me.

"Where can I find the Celta ultras?"

"Why do you want to find them?"

I explain, and he writes down the name of another bar, La Revolta, in Rua Real, in the old part of town.

"They come here before matches. But that is where they spend their evenings. They will be there tonight, I think. Oh . . . and good luck."

Every major Spanish team has a group of ultras who usually stand directly behind one of the goals. The ultras can be usually relied upon to give unstinting support for the team throughout the match, and are often given tickets and a place in the stadium to store their paraphernalia (flags, banners, megaphones, flares). Most groups of ultras are of extreme-right political persuasion. They are often actively racist, chanting insults throughout the match at non-white players. And they are often violent, well known in some cases for going on 'man-hunts' after games for opposing fans. It's quite a problem; earlier this season a fan from nearby Deportivo de la Coruña was killed after a game. Ultras are not the type of people I would usually seek out. Yet here I am, standing, nervous and confused, outside a bar in the dingy narrow streets of the old part of town.

I am confused because there is a serious talk going on in the bar, with a man and a woman set up with microphones on a trestle table. Behind them are two posters, black and white portraits, one of a young woman, the other a young man. I read that they are 'martyrs for the Galician cause'. I can see the national flag of Galicia, and several posters reading 'Nunca Mais' (never again) referring to the *Prestige* oil tanker disaster, which took place a year before just off the Galician coast. Everybody in the bar is maintaining a respectful silence, listening to the talkers. All the chairs are taken up. It doesn't look like a Nazi-skin hangout.

I keep wandering off and coming back to the bar, but the speech keeps going on. Finally, when I return for the fifth time, it's over. There are about ten young lads left in the bar.

"Can I find the Celta de Vigo ultras here?" I ask the barman, a young guy with gap teeth.

He laughs.

"Well, here they are . . ." he says, gesturing to three blokes sitting right next to where I am.

"Who's asking?" says one, a skinhead with large sideburns. I explain who I am.

"We are the Celtarras," says the guy. "We stand behind the goal and we sing. But don't call us ultras. Ultras are right wing. Ultras are Fascists. We hate ultras."

I take a closer look at his t-shirt. On it is the symbol of the hammer and sickle, and the date 1917, the year of the Russian revolution.

The guy is called Marcopolo, and he stands me a beer. He tells me that the Celtarras are Anti-Fascists and Galician nationalists. He tells me that 'castellano' (the Spanish language) is normally banned in the bar, that everyone has to speak in Galician, but they'll make an exception for me. He takes me to the library in a room behind the stage, with a wall full of books on Lenin, Marx and Castro, and he tells me that he will give me an interview tomorrow.

**THURSDAY OCTOBER 16TH**

I arrive at the bar at about 8pm, and am told to sit at the table, that Marcopolo will be right out. When he arrives he has a sheet of A4 maths paper in his hand. He has filled it with notes written in pencil. He sits down and several other lads, and one girl, sit down beside us.

"The first thing I want to say is that we are predominantly a political group and that I am not here to talk about the football players," he says. "We support a free Galicia. We believe that is a separate country from Spain and should be recognised as such."

He continues with a monologue about the repression of Galician culture by the Spanish in the Franco regime, and about how the Spanish government is responsible for the economic problems the country has suffered. The other guys gravely nod their approval of his every point. I do the same.

"How many members are in your group?"

"Not many. 100–150. We are very loosely structured – we have no leadership and no strict membership."

"Do you have any links with the club?"

"We used to, but four or five years ago we had some problems, and we cut all links. We get no free tickets, and no support from the club."

"Do you use the football match to make political points?"

"Yes, we do. We have called for Galician freedom, and for Palestinian freedom, too. We have held up banners against the war in Iraq. And look at what we did when the *Prestige* sank."

He pulls out a fanzine which has a picture of scores of fans holding up placards reading 'Nunca Máis' ('Never again' in Gallego, the Galician language).

"We hate the Dépor fans. But we were united when the *Prestige* sank, because it had a devastating effect on the whole of Galicia. And instead of shouting abuse at each other, we shouted abuse at the government, calling for them to resign. We know that if the ship had sunk in the Mediterranean, the government would have acted in a very different way. But they didn't care, because we are from Galicia, we are on the edge of the country."

I ask him what he thinks about Beckham.

"What are his politics?" I say that I have never heard him express any political views.

"Let's say that we don't approve of him. But having said that, we wouldn't mind it if he came to play for Celta."

As the meeting winds down, someone brings a tray of drinks to the table which have a similar colour and texture as oil.

"A local speciality," says Marcopolo. "Coffee liqueur and grappa. Sip, don't gulp."

I sip, and am glad. It's throat-rasping stuff.


## SUNDAY OCTOBER 19TH

I'm back in Arximelo's bar, the day of the game, looking at a picture of the Balaídos stadium on the wall. I get out my ticket, to explain where I'm going.

"In the fondo. You won't be able to see anything!"

I'm talking to Fernando González Amadios, who knows the stadium well. He is member number 13 of Celta de Vigo, one of the oldest living fans of the club.

"I was at the first ever game in the Balaídos in 1929, on my third birthday. I still remember it – I was put on the steps by my father," he claims. I've seen pictures of the game in the Celta museum, in the stadium. It's an old fashioned museum, with old balls, shirts, medals and photos. On that day Celta beat Real Irún 2–1.

"In the old days there were only rabbits between here and the stadium. It was right outside town. There was a tram that went out on match-days, though a lot of people walked. I used to get the tram, if I could. You had to hang on for dear life."

I ask him his favourite player of all time.

"Antonio Fuentes. A Canarian, who played in the '40s. He was a medio central, in the old system (the equivalent of a centre-half in the old 2-3-5 system). He was a good dribbler. We were losing 1–0 to Racing Santander, and they injured him. They smashed his face. But it was in the days before substitutes. It wouldn't be allowed now but he just got a handkerchief and played on. Pretty soon it was covered in blood. But we won 2–1, and he scored both of the goals."

I wonder if any of today's players compare. Zidane, perhaps. Or Beckham?

"It's a different game, and players were different then. They had more skill then. Or perhaps they just seemed to, as the game was so much slower."

Fernando wanders off home and it's just Tato and Arximelo and me. I look up on the TV screen, and there's Arximelo again. It's quite a shock.

It's a round-table discussion about football. The other guy is the security chief of Celta. They are talking about football violence.

"Did he put you in touch with the ultras?" asks Tato.

"He said he had no contact with them."

"He wouldn't have said that if we'd come with you."

"Will there be any violence tonight?"

"Of course not."

I try to pay for Tato's drink and my own. Mysteriously it's already been accounted for.

Before the game I go to the Bar Luar, and sure enough the ultras have collected there. Well, they look like ultras. Most of the boys are skinheads, wearing bomber jackets and black boots. There are quite a few girls – many of them have the girl-skin cut, shaved at the top with long bits left at the fringe and behind. Up close you can see, from the fans' t-shirts, their badges and the banners they are carrying, that they might be dressed right wing, but they are actually left. There are Che Guevara t-shirts and Basque and Galician national flags. I recognise a couple from the other bar, and they nod, but don't greet me. My hair is too long, my clothes are wrong. I am nearly 40. I am obviously not the coolest person to talk to.

The bar is heaving. I order a coffee liqueur with grappa. It comes in a large wineglass. A guy walks past with an Irish flag draped round his shoulders. Everybody is drinking heavily. People are knocking back litre plastic glasses of beer, and litres of vodka and coke. A huge rolled-up banner is carried by two skinheads through from the back of the bar (where it must have been kept). I get talking to one of the Celtarras who was at the meeting with Marcopolo. Does he think Celta will win?

"Not a chance. We've made a terrible start to the season. We've only won once. The team is playing with no passion. How can we expect to beat the galácticos?"

"But you'll be singing . . ."

"I will, but not in the stadium. I'll be watching in the bar."

"In the bar? How come?"

"I can't afford 30 euros. Normally it only costs five to stand in the fondo. There will be less than normal there, it won't be full. The bar will be full, though. We'll watch it on the TV. We'll see you afterwards."

I find Marcopolo who walks with me into the stadium. I ask him if there will be any violence.

"I shouldn't think there will. I don't think there are many from Madrid."

"But if there were, you're not violent anyway, are you?"

"Let's not make out that we're a bunch of angels, huh?"

We walk through the ticket check and straight through to the fondo section. There are plastic seats, but everyone is standing on them. The view of the pitch is terrible. There's a big space with advertising hoardings between us and the goal. The rest of the place is full. The Celtarras are already singing.

"Puto Madrid, puta España."

One guy next to me is holding out a version of the Galician flag, a sky blue cross on a white background, with a red star in the middle. Another fan is holding a Basque flag. The Celta hymn comes on the tannoy.

Hail Celta we shout,
Hail Celta the champions
Celta, Celta, ra ra ra.

The Celtarras don't join in. They are busy pointing up to where the Real Madrid fans must be sitting, though I can't see any.

"They're not Galician, they are the sons of whores," they chant.

The singing is continuous among the 150 or so collected behind the goal. When one song stops, another starts up.

Celta attack: "Come on Celta, give us a goal"

A foul is given to Real: "That's how Madrid win."

The ball goes off for a throw: "Whorish Spain and whorish Madrid."

Celta go on the attack again: "Come on Celta. La la la."

Michel Salgado, who used to be a hero at Celta before moving to Real Madrid in 1999, is hardly given a welcome.

"Michel Salgado, son of a whore."

It's not much of a match. Celta can't keep the ball for long, Real don't seem to want to play. The fans don't mind. They're happy singing.

"Ale, ale-ale-ale, Celta, Celta."

Then Real Madrid start moving the ball around. It comes to Ronaldo inside the box, he makes some space for himself, and shoots the ball into the net. Right in front of our eyes. There is an eerie silence. If there are some Real Madrid fans, they are keeping their whereabouts a secret.

"They're not from Galicia, they are sons of whores," sing the fans, pointing to where they imagine the opposite fans to be. Then, as if nothing has happened on the pitch, they go back to singing the same song that was interrupted by the Brazilian's goal.

"Ale, ale-ale-ale, Celta, Celta."

Beckham runs up to take a corner, and gets some especially vitriolic treatment.

"Fuck yourself, fuck yourself, fuck yourself."

"Son of a whore, fuck yourself."

It's a good corner, a heart-in-the-mouth one, but the ball is cleared. The fans start getting louder, as if their anti-Beckham vitriol has cheered them up.

"We are with you Celta, we will always be with you."

The rest of the stadium joins in the song. Possibly fired up by the noise Celta start stringing a few passes together, pushing forward down the left. They get a corner, their first of the match.

"Come on Celta, give us a goal," continue the Celtarras, though "give us a shot" would be more apt. Then Mostovoi finds space outside the box and hits the ball . . . over the bar.

"Ooooh! Go on Celta, give us a goal."

Celta get a free kick at the other end. It must be just outside the box, but from where I'm standing it looks like it's two inches out from the goal. High excitement, big disappointment. Straight into the wall. At our end Beckham, who has been a ubiquitous, scurrying figure, playing again in central midfield, hits the crossbar. It's nearly game over, but not quite. The fans sing a song to the tune of 'Johnny comes marching home' which alleges that Real Madrid are all whores, and the half-time whistle blows.

The second half starts with a Celta attack going out for a goal kick. As Casillas takes his run up to kick the ball the Celtarras, and the whole tier of fans above, chant "oooooh" increasing the chant in volume as he gets nearer the ball. Then when he kicks it they all shout, in unison, "hijo de puta maricón español" (queer Spanish son of a whore). "You're not a goalkeeper, you're a cabaret whore" shouts a guy in front of me. Then the rain starts.

At first it's a light drizzle. Then it really starts sheeting down. Where we are standing there is no cover. Most of the fans, including myself and Marcopolo, move back further away from the goal to where there is shelter. A group of about ten guys stay where they are, despite the rain. They are disgusted with the rest of the fans who have retreated, and start making hand-gestures at them (us) to return. Nobody makes a move. The rain starts coming down about as hard as rain can come down, but the guys have made their stand. As if to reward them the blues start pouring forward towards them. They get a corner. High excitement. But from where we are we can see how good Real Madrid are at defending – how little space they allow the opposition. There looks to be no way through. And there isn't.

Beckham is seeing quite a lot of the ball. He is particularly unpopular.

"Beckham capullo, te voy a romper el culo" (you bastard Beckham, I'm going to break your arse). He starts off a move which ends up with a galloping Roberto Carlos thumping the ball into the far net. 2–0 to Real Madrid. Celta start attacking again. The singing in the rain doesn't abate.

"Come on Celta, give us a goal," is sung again and again and again. An eccentric in a transparent raincoat who has spent the entire second half standing on his own in the rain is shouting "Gol! Gol! Gol! Gol!" All the fans want is a goal against Real Madrid. But it never comes, and it never looks like coming. The whistle blows on a dire home perform- ance. I head back to the Bar Luar.

The fans who have been watching the game there are absolutely hammered – they must have carried on with their pints of vodka and coke. I get a beer and am approached by the guy with the Irish flag round his shoulders. He is swaying dangerously from side to side. He approaches me, and shows me that he's wearing an IRA badge. But somehow the action of showing me disrupts his balance and he falls flat on his back and passes out. His friends pick him up, slap him round the face a bit, and he comes to. He's still grinning, an amiable drunk – he's probably already forgotten the score.

Afterwards I wander over to Arximelo's bar. It's just him and his wife there. He hasn't forgotten the score.

"Nobody comes to celebrate a defeat," he says. You can see that all he wants to do is close up and go to bed, but he serves me a drink.

"I'm depressed. We have no rhythm, we have no drive. I can't see where the goals are going to come from. Milosevic wasn't there today! It's like he wasn't playing!"

"There was no Rianxeira tonight," I say, attempting to pay for my drink, to leave. Arximelo won't hear of such a thing. He doesn't want any money, he just wants to have his say.

"Lotina hasn't heard the Rianxeira all season. And you know what . . . I doubt that he will."

## RESULTS: JOURNADA 7

| ALBACETE | 3 | REAL SOCIEDAD | 1 |
|----------|---|---------------|---|
| OSASUNA | 2 | MURCIA | 1 |
| ATLÉTICO | 2 | MALLORCA | 1 |
| BARCELONA | 0 | DEPORTIVO | 2 |
| **CELTA** | **0** | **REAL MADRID** | **2** |
| RACING | 4 | MÁLAGA | 2 |
| ZARAGOZA | 1 | VALLADOLID | 0 |
| ATHLETIC | 2 | VILLARREAL | 0 |
| SEVILLA | 2 | BETIS | 2 |
| VALENCIA | 4 | ESPANYOL | 0 |

## LA CLASIFICACIÓN

| | P | W | D | L | F | A | Pts |
|---|---|---|---|---|---|---|---|
| VALENCIA | 7 | 6 | 1 | 0 | 13 | 1 | 19 |
| DEPORTIVO | 7 | 6 | 0 | 1 | 17 | 5 | 18 |
| **REAL MADRID** | **7** | **5** | **1** | **1** | **17** | **8** | **16** |
| OSASUNA | 7 | 4 | 2 | 1 | 10 | 8 | 14 |
| RACING | 7 | 3 | 2 | 2 | 11 | 7 | 11 |
| ATHLETIC | 7 | 3 | 2 | 2 | 10 | 6 | 11 |
| BETIS | 7 | 2 | 4 | 1 | 9 | 7 | 10 |
| SEVILLA | 7 | 2 | 4 | 1 | 8 | 7 | 10 |
| VILLARREAL | 7 | 2 | 4 | 1 | 7 | 6 | 10 |
| REAL SOCIEDAD | 7 | 2 | 3 | 2 | 8 | 7 | 9 |
| BARCELONA | 7 | 2 | 3 | 2 | 5 | 6 | 9 |
| ZARAGOZA | 7 | 2 | 1 | 4 | 5 | 8 | 7 |
| MÁLAGA | 7 | 2 | 1 | 4 | 7 | 11 | 7 |
| VALLADOLID | 7 | 2 | 1 | 4 | 9 | 17 | 7 |
| ATLÉTICO | 7 | 2 | 1 | 4 | 4 | 11 | 7 |
| CELTA | 7 | 1 | 3 | 3 | 7 | 11 | 6 |
| MURCIA | 7 | 1 | 3 | 3 | 6 | 10 | 6 |
| ALBACETE | 7 | 2 | 0 | 5 | 6 | 10 | 6 |
| MALLORCA | 7 | 1 | 2 | 3 | 6 | 11 | 5 |
| ESPANYOL | 7 | 0 | 2 | 5 | 7 | 16 | 2 |

# SIX
# ZARAGOZA

GOLFO DE VIZCAYA

OCÉANO ATLÁNTICO

Real Zaragoza

Real Madrid

MAR MEDITERRÁNEO

N
W        E
S

# SIX
# ZARAGOZA

## MONDAY OCTOBER 27TH

The pre-match talk before the midweek game between Real Zaragoza and Real Madrid is about who will be playing, who won't be playing, and how the Real Madrid squad will be travelling to the game.

Beckham injured the hamstring of his right leg during Real Madrid's laboured 1–0 Champions League win over Partizan Belgrade in the Bernabéu in midweek, and missed the even more laboured 3–1 win over Racing de Santander in the league on Saturday, in the same stadium. His replacement in the league game was Spanish international Guti. It is touch and go, when I travel to Zaragoza, whether Beckham will be doing the same.

Beckham or no Beckham, Real Madrid are planning to give some much-needed publicity to the new high-speed AVE train line by using it to travel up to Zaragoza, instead of chartering a flight. The AVE, a sleek-nosed arrow of a train, will eventually join Barcelona to the capital, and help forge a high-speed link from London to Seville. The train takes just two hours from Madrid to Zaragoza, which lies roughly half way between Spain's two major cities.

The trouble is, there has been much talk of a chasm appearing in a hill over which the AVE line travels, which has been terrible publicity for the new service. Scary pictures have appeared in newspapers – it's made me wonder whether I'll ever use the service. Beckham and co. arriving in the city's bright new station with hordes of fans greeting them is just the sort of counter-publicity that the AVE needs. But, you've been made to wonder, will they survive the journey?

I arrive in the big, brash, bright Zaragoza Las Delicias station at 12 o'clock on the Monday morning, the day before the match. There is a whole fixture list scheduled midweek. The forthcoming European Championships in Portugal have shortened the Spanish season, which normally runs from September through to the end of June, but will this time be wrapped up by May 23rd, hence the squeeze.

On the train I've been reading about Zaragoza's 22-year-old Argentinian central defender Gabriel Milito. In July, Milito, an international from the Buenos Aires club Independiente, was destined to become the answer to Real Madrid's defensive problems. Only a medical stood between him and a place in the squad. Unfortunately the test purportedly showed that Milito had not recovered sufficiently from an injury to his right knee which kept him out of most of the 2001/02 season. Real Madrid procrastinated about buying him – probably simply trying to move his price down. Zaragoza came in with a concrete offer, and he decided to go instead to the newly-promoted Aragonés side. Real Madrid turned their attention onto his compatriot Ayala instead.

This is the main morbo of the pre-match coverage of the game. Morbo literally means 'disease' but in a football context is roughly the Spanish equivalent of 'needle'. Morbo adds spice to an occasion. In football terms, if a player is playing against his old team, and he has a point to prove, there is said to be morbo. For Milito there is plenty of morbo in his encounter with the club he so nearly played for. He has a big point to prove.

I get a bus from the train station straight to the stadium through busy Monday-morning streets. The clocks have just gone back, this is the first day of winter, and you can really feel it. Jackets, first donned in early October, have been replaced by coats. I see a thermometer reading 4 degrees centigrade. When I get off the bus I can see my breath. The stadium, known as La Romareda, is a low, round affair built in a modern high-rise area, with its floodlights on square blue pillars constructed outside the building. There are a few fat guys, with cigars, hanging outside the ticket office, but they're not queuing. I order one of the cheapest (60 euro) tickets.

"Are there many left?"

"That's just about the last one."

I've been lucky. The fat guys are touts, and they're hovering.

I get a bus into town and find myself a cheap and rather nasty pension room in the main square, which is one of the most beautiful in Spain, with a basilica, a cathedral, a statue of local artist Francisco Goya, and a modern fountain in the shape of South America. All I get from my sock of a room, though, is a view of the internal courtyard, so I hurry out. Laziness isn't so appealing in a cell just bigger than the bed.

Pretty soon I'm in the basilica across the square. It's famous for a pillar down which the Virgin Mary is said to have travelled from heaven before appearing on earth in central Zaragoza in medieval times. All you can see of the pillar is a little round circle inside a panel about a yard up from the ground, circled by bronze. People queue, kneel, kiss this little section of stone and go off, having made a wish. I've just recovered from a bout of gastric 'flu I picked up on the train back from Galicia, so don't indulge. But I touch it, just in case.

It's because of this pillar, by the way, that one of the most popular girls' names in Spain is 'Pilar' (as in the Minister for Education, Culture and Sport, Pilar del Castillo). Spanish girls have to put up with very odd religious names: they get called Dolores (pains), Inmaculada Concepción (Immaculate Conception), Consuelo (Consolation), even Cesaria (Cesarian). Pilar isn't that bad, on reflection.

Zaragoza is a fine city to spend a couple of days in, with a rich history visible in its buildings. It was a Roman settlement (its strange name derives from 'Caesar Augustus') an important Visigoth centre and a thriving Moorish outpost, near the north-western border of the vast Islamic territories which spread east as far as India. The Albarracín Palace is the biggest Islamic monument in Spain outside Andalucia, but was also the base of the Reyes Católicos (Catholic Kings) who ruled Aragon in medieval times. Afterwards, when Aragón allied with Castilla, the Albarracín became the seat of the Spanish Inquisition. Since those times the city has declined in importance, and now is merely a provincial capital (inhabited by 750,000 of Aragón's million and a half inhabitants) albeit one with a strong sense of its former importance.

I get a sense of this in the evening when I take a bus up to the Fuji-Jama Real Zaragoza FC Peña in the modern shopping district of the city just outside the historic centre. I'm expecting a Japanese restaurant, but when I arrive I find a standard Spanish bar with hams hanging from the ceiling and old men smoking and drinking beer. I've arranged an interview with the President of the peña. I'm led through the bar to a separate room at the back, where a serious old man is sitting behind a desk. There is the usual paraphernalia – pennants, signed photos of players, team photos – on the wall.

I've worked out my opening question on the bus on the way up. "I used to live in North London which is divided in its opinion of one former Real Zaragoza player. Half of the area, those who support Arsenal, hate him, half of them, who support Tottenham, love him. I'm talking about . . ."

"Nayim." Fernando finishes my sentence with a smile. The seriousness abandons his eyes for a moment.

Real Zaragoza have had two great periods in their history, one in the mid-'60s, and one in the mid-'90s. They won the Spanish cup twice, in 1964 and 1966, and the Fairs Cup (in 1964, beating Valencia in the final in Barcelona after beating Juventus in the quarters). Then in 1995, captained by Gustavo Poyet, they won the Spanish Cup again (on penalties against

Celta de Vigo) and in the following season enjoyed a fine campaign in the European Cup Winners Cup, beating Feyenoord in the quarters and Chelsea in the semis, before facing Arsenal in the final in the Parc des Princes in Paris. With the scores level at the end of full-time, with the match about to go into extra time, former Tottenham player Nayim collected a pass on the half-way line, and, knowing the whistle was about to blow, hit it as hard as he could towards the Arsenal goal, more than 50 yards away. The rest is still the stuff of Arsenal nightmares. The ball looped goalwards. Keeper David Seaman saw the danger late, back-pedalled in an increasingly desperate manner towards his goal, made an attempt at a backward jump to catch it, but could only push the ball into the inside of the roof of the net. It was a gutting experience for Arsenal fans – I watched it in the Highbury Barn pub (I was living nearby) and saw the TV set being smashed with a chair on the final whistle.

Fernando was in the stadium.

"Nayim, Nayim, Nayim," he smiles. "He provoked the biggest emotion I have felt in the whole of my time as a football fan. I had goose pimples (in Spain 'chicken pimples') all over my body. I couldn't believe it. I hugged a complete stranger. I think he was French."

Fernando does not seem the type of man who is inclined to hug foreign strangers.

Zaragoza won the cup again in 2001, again against poor Celta, this time 3–1 in extra time. But they finished 17th in the league, and were relegated the next season.

"Since then, we have had problems. To understand Zaragoza, you have to understand the city. We come from one of the most important cities in Spain with a rich history. And we have always had a football team to match. We might not have ever been the best team in the country, but we have always played with spirit. The people are passionate football supporters. Supporting Zaragoza, being Zaragozista, means we love our team to play attacking football. We would rather lose 5–4 than win 1–0. Last year we played in the Segunda for the first time since the '70s. We are a Primera side, one of the top ten sides in the history of Spanish football. And last season we were promoted without passion, without joy, playing boring football under a manager who only wants results, and doesn't mind how to get them."

He is talking about Paco Flores, who joined the club from Espanyol after rising through the ranks of the Catalan club. Not the greatest player, Flores made his name getting results with limited resources (Espanyol traditionally sell all their best players at the end of the year) and actually won the cup in 2000. In season 2002/03 he guided Zaragoza to second place in Segunda, and his president Alfonso

Soláns bought wisely in the summer (Milito being joined by Brazilian international and former Real Madrid player Savio from Bordeaux and high-scoring striker David Villa from Sporting de Gijón). Yet, after a poor start to the season in which Zaragoza have struggled to score goals or win matches, Flores, a round-shaped bald man, is very much in the firing line of the fans and press. Being a football manager in Spain means having one of the most precarious positions in the country; they are sacked with alarming regularity. Sometimes clubs go through three or four in a season. In Primera there are only three managers who have been at their clubs more than two seasons, none more than four. Flores' days already look numbered.

"Flores is all very well as a manager in Segunda" continues Fernando. "But he doesn't know how to manage a team in Primera."

On the way back I see there is a showing of Mozart's opera *The Magic Flute* in the local theatre. I go to the box office and get the last ticket. It costs 12 euros for a neck-stretching view, but I enjoy the show. There's something familiar about the plot. It's about a prince who comes to a foreign land and struggles to succeed there. But he works hard and, in the end, becomes the king of the country.

## TUESDAY OCTOBER 28TH

In the morning, dying to see if Beckham's playing, I buy a copy of *Marca* and the local sports paper *El Equipo*. I ask the vendor who will win the game tonight.

"Madrid," he replies, in one of those black-tobacco voices Spanish men get shortly before they die of lung cancer.

"How come?"

"Because of our trainer. Flores. He's not a first division trainer. The players score one goal, then they start defending. You need to score at least two, if you want to make sure of winning a game. We are too fearful. We must change the manager."

I take the papers to a classy-looking cafe, aptly enough called 'El Real', and read them with a coffee. Beckham will not play. He hasn't even travelled. Queiroz does not want to risk him not being available for the game in the Bernabéu against Athletic de Bilbao. Guti will again play in his place. This is disappointing, but at least it will give me the first-hand chance to see how El Real click without the Englishman. What if they win at a canter, with Guti brilliant? Could Beckham then lose his place in the side?

This is a very interesting possibility. Guti, who has been at Real Madrid for nine years, and in the first team for eight, is very much the man who has ended up losing out to Beckham's arrival. And in a way he is the most similar player to Beckham at the club, a skilful midfielder with a precise pass, and a great sense of positioning and running off the ball. What's more, he has interestingly cut, dyed-blond hair, and is fancied by all the teenage girls. You wonder, if Madrid had bought a defender instead of Beckham, and trusted in Guti in the central midfield role, wouldn't they be a better side?

I also learn that Carlos Queiroz finally decided not to take the AVE train, but to fly instead. He didn't mention the chasm in the hill, just said that flying was quicker. Hundreds of fans were left waiting at the station in vain. No Beckham, no Real Madrid, only a trainload of travellers.

A few hours later, I get a bus to the game, and sit opposite three old fellows. I can't hear what they're saying, but it's clear they are going to the match. One of them is wearing a beret, two have cloth caps. They carry sticks. They are dressed as old men; perhaps they will be the last generation to dress like this. It suits them. They are good friends, lively, fun. They get off at the stadium, head for a bar, laughing at one another's stories. I follow them to see where they are going (such is the life of a lonely traveller) when I see a huge crowd of people, cordoned off around one of the entrances to the stadium. Waiting for the Real Madrid team bus. I decide to go and join them instead.

I'm sure that when Albacete come to town there won't be a mass of people waiting for them. But Real Madrid are Real Madrid, and so I wait, and wait. Like drug dealers and attractive girls, Real Madrid have a licence to arrive late. There is the usual mixture of anticipation and boredom. Over the far side, near where the coach will enter, I can see an old woman remonstrating with a security guard. She is waving a stick and shouting.

I've picked up the match-night edition of *El Equipo*, given out free before the game like a programme (Spanish teams don't generally produce official pre-match publications), and I take a look. The headline is 'Real Madrid – without Beckham – return to play in the Romareda.' He's that big now. It's almost like 'The Doors – without Jim Morrison – arrive in town.' The coach turns up, to a mixture of jeers and cheers. The players' names are shouted as they get off the bus.

"Rubén! Solari! Zidane! Zidane! Guti!"

But the star of the show isn't there. There is no Beckham, there are no screams, no fainting girls. This is just a football team.

Shortly afterwards I walk past the old lady I've seen earlier. She's got one thing to say, and she's repeating it at the top of her voice, over and over.

"We must get rid of Paco Flores. We must get rid of Paco Flores. We must . . ." I realise that this was what she was remonstrating with the security guard about. I contemplate going to ask her why, then I look her in the eye, and realise this might not be the best idea.

With about 15 minutes to kick-off I decide I really want a half-time sandwich, so I queue to get one. Then I hurry to the stadium. Just about all the seats are full. I find my row, high behind the goal, and can see it's all full. I have to shuffle along past scores of legs, incurring scores of Spanish curses. There's a small boy in my seat, sitting next to another small boy. They are about seven.

"That's my seat." I say, to the general area.

"What number are you?" asks a dodgy-looking, unshaven, gum-chewing guy.

"36."

"These seats are all odd numbers. You must be over there some-where." He points me the way I came. Kick off is looming. Why didn't I arrive earlier? I shuffle away, past the same legs, the same curses. Then I realise that he's lied to me. That the numbers are even. I make the same trip back. The curses get louder.

"That's my seat. Your kid's in my seat."

"Well, someone is sitting in our seat. We had to move."

"But that's my seat. Anyway, you lied to me."

Another fan points to three empty seats in front.

"Just go there, will you?"

I give up, sit in the right hand seat. After a couple of minutes I see a curly-haired young man and a dignified-looking old man shuffling towards me.

"You're in my grandfather's seat," snarls the young guy. Suddenly I'm in the wrong. I move to the seat on the left. I keep looking round at the unshaven guy who's put his kid in my seat. He's smirking.

In front of me the fans have put up a huge banner, so I can't see the players run out, as the tannoy plays the sort of anthem you normally associate with Latin dictatorships. Then a commentator reads the players' names and numbers out, but he leaves the surname to the fans. Thus.

Commentator: Con el número uno! César . . .

Fans: Lainez!

Commentator: Con el número seis! Gabriel . . .

Fans: Milito!

The first half starts with a terrible foul by Zinedine Zidane, who isn't booked, presumably because he's Zinedine Zidane. There's a lot of noise coming from a 500-strong group to my right and down, who have a banner reading 'El Colectivo'. They have a bandleader with a megaphone, who has his back to the pitch. They are making a lot of noise, and Zaragoza respond to it, with Savio particularly lively, attacking down Real's right flank. Zidane is robbed of the ball and does a second bad foul. Again he isn't carded. Shortly afterwards you Pavón does a rather innocuous foul, and gets a yellow card, paying for the sins of his French compañero.

The teams swap chances. Savio hits a free-kick just wide of the post. Real shoot across the box, but nobody touches it in. Milito, having made a run into the Real box, delicately taps the ball past Casillas. There's a tremendous noise from the fans as the ball trickles towards the unguarded goal . . . "waaaaaaaaaaaaaaaaaay . . ."

only to hit the post . . . "ooooooooooooooooh . . ." then get cleared by a desperate Real Madrid defender . . . "aaaaargh!"

The match settles into shape with Zaragoza getting everyone save striker David Villa behind the ball when Real Madrid get possession. Real are playing the same formation – four at the back, a 'doble pivote' and a diamond attack. But the difference between the teams is Guti, who is masterful in the Beckham role, the start of all Madrid's movement, a blur of accurate passing and intelligent off-the-ball running. Real start getting the upper hand. Raúl is desperate to score – a lot has been made of the fact that he made his debut here nine years ago, nearly to the day. A nervous 17-year-old, replacing the great Emilio Butragueño, he missed three sitters. Today he is having no more luck, as chances are being made . . . and wasted.

At half time I have my own silver sandwich to enjoy, as Spanish punk music blasts out of the tannoy. I notice the kid next to me, who turfed me out of the seat, is wearing an 'Espana' t-shirt, something that would be unthinkable in Barcelona. There is no separatist movement in Aragón: it would be rather like 'the Essex Revolutionary Army'. The subs are playing piggy-in-the-middle on the pitch. Most of them are kids – Portillo, César, Rubén, Borja. But amongst them are two Argentinians, Cambiasso, who started the season in the team, and Solari, an international for his country. I wonder how soon it will be before Beckham has to suffer the same ignominy of being piggy in the middle at half time.

Real attack into our goal in the second half, which gives me a good chance to see Milito first hand. He is brilliant, blocking shots, making tackles, coming out of defence with the ball. His partner in central defence, Alvaro, is equally dynamic. Raúl and Ronaldo hardly get a look in. After 20 minutes Real do manage to hit the bar, and the ball falls to Ronaldo's feet. He hits it over the bar. I realise I'm quite pleased.

"Lárgate gordo," (go away, fatty) shouts the grandad.

As the match continues, and continues to be scoreless, the fans get more raucous. Real Madrid continue pressurising, but they are leaving gaps at the back and Zaragoza are able to counter. It's incredible that it's still 0–0. Then Pavón commits a second foul.

"A la calle," shouts the grandad (to the street). A red card is produced, and the young player trudges disconsolately off. The two kids behind me, the seat-nicking little seven-year-old brats, stand up and sing "Jódete, jódete, jódete" (a triple fuck off). Everyone laughs. They are a different generation from the grandad, they won't grow up so dignified. The unshaven guy, the seat-nicking bastard, smirks proudly. He's obviously taught them all they know.

For a while it's like Madrid have the extra man, and they press for a winner, which would put them top of the league. I realise something interesting is happening: I quite definitely don't want them to score. If Beckham were playing, that would be one thing. But without him . . . no way. And, what's more, I would be pleased if Zaragoza score. It has taken Beckham's absence to make me understand something that was latent all along. I am not a natural Real Madrid fan. However marvellous their skills, I find it difficult to support the team with all the money, who always win. The establishment team. I have a similar attitude to Manchester United. I clench my fist.

"Come on Zaragoza," I murmur.

El Gordo is substituted, as is Zinedine Zidane. The game comes to a near standstill, as Real Madrid seem to tire. The referee keeps giving them free kicks, when there seems to be no foul. Is he being blatantly biased against Zaragoza or am I biased against the referee? The El Colectivo lads are having a fine old time down below. A draw will keep Real Madrid off the top of the table – Depor will remain a point ahead with a game in hand. The final whistle goes. I'm pleased.

## RESULTS: JORNADA 8

| | | | |
|---|---|---|---|
| MÁLAGA | 2 | ZARAGOZA | 1 |
| **REAL MADRID** | **3** | **RACING** | **1** |
| DEPORTIVO | 2 | VALENCIA | 1 |
| VALLADOLID | 2 | ATHLETIC | 0 |
| ESPANYOL | 0 | CELTA | 4 |
| REAL SOCIEDAD | 1 | OSASUNA | 0 |
| BETIS | 3 | ALBACETE | 2 |
| VILLARREAL | 3 | SEVILLA | 3 |
| MALLORCA | 1 | BARCELONA | 3 |
| MURCIA | 1 | ATLÉTICO | 3 |

| ZARAGOZA | 0 | REAL MADRID | 0 |
|----------|---|-------------|---|
| RACING | 0 | ESPANYOL | 1 |
| BARCELONA | 3 | MURCIA | 0 |
| VALENCIA | 2 | CELTA | 2 |
| DEPORTIVO | 0 | MALLORCA | 2 |
| ATHLETIC | 2 | MÁLAGA | 1 |
| OSASUNA | 2 | BETIS | 0 |
| ALBACETE | 2 | VILLARREAL | 0 |
| SEVILLA | 1 | VALLADOLID | 1 |
| ATLÉTICO | 4 | REAL SOCIEDAD | 0 |

## WEDNESDAY OCTOBER 29TH

I buy a copy of *Marca* in the morning, which alerts me to the fact that the magazine *Capital*, roughly the Spanish equivalent of *The Economist*, has an article about the parlous state of Real Madrid's finances, run by their president Florentino Pérez.

Pérez' wiliness with money became evident from the smart way he got into power at Real Madrid in the first place, back in 2000. Pérez, a Madrileño, first became locally famous as a city councillor for the now defunct UCD party, a right-wing group which came to power in Spain in the period following Franco's death. When Felipe Gonzalez' PSOE (socialist party) won the general election he moved into business, where he became hugely successful, building the second-biggest construction business – called ACB – in the country. In 2000, a complete unknown in the football world, he stood in Real Madrid's presidential election against Lorenzo Sanz, as a rank outsider. Sanz's position looked safe – he had been in power five years and won two European Cups – but the club was in huge debt and the president had made himself unpopular by insisting his son, the defender Fernando Sanz (now playing for Málaga), was in the team.

During the run-up to the election, in July 2000, Pérez announced that he would bring Barcelona's star player Luis Figo – who had just played brilliantly in the Euro 2000 competition and was considered the world's best player – to the club if he won. This was an amazing offer to Real fans. Not only would they be getting one of the world's best players at the Bernabéu; they would also be stealing him off their bitter rivals, Barcelona. Pérez announced that Figo had already signed a pre-contract under which he would have to pay him the equivalent of £20 million if he (Pérez) won the election and Figo didn't consequently come to Real Madrid. Figo immediately denied this in an interview with the newspaper *Sport*, and in the same interview he promised Barça fans that he would be playing in Barcelona the next season. But his agent, Jose Veiga, did admit that he had had a meeting with Pérez.

Whatever the case, Pérez felt so confident of getting his man, he offered to pay all the Real Madrid socios (members) free season-tickets if Figo didn't play – a cost which would have been covered by Figo's penalty payment if he didn't move to Madrid. If such a 'pre-contract' actually existed, that is. It was a smart move by Pérez. His popularity went through the roof. The idea of Real stealing their arch-rivals' star player was too much for many to resist. And free football for a season if he didn't! Perez won 60 per cent of the votes to become Real's 14th president. Figo was a Real Madrid player by the end of the month.

I pick up a copy of the magazine for the three-hour train journey back to Barcelona. It makes interesting reading. The article wonders whether the 543 Real Madrid shareholders who recently re-elected Florentino Pérez as president of the club (there were six abstentions, no-one voted against him) were fully aware of the financial implications of his regime.

According to the magazine, in 2001/02 Real Madrid took in a total of 192 million euros, but spent a total of 290 million. So how did they announce a profit? By, it seems, taking into account a large chunk of the money they have received by selling their old training ground, Las Rojas.

The training ground was originally sold to the club, back in 1955, on the condition that it would be used as a sporting facility if Real Madrid sold it on. For this reason Sanz, who wanted to sell the place, too, couldn't. Pérez' application to have the property reclassified by the local government, to allow the land to be used to build skyscrapers on, went through the requisite government department remarkably quickly. The government itself promised to buy at least one of the skyscrapers. But what, suggests the magazine, if somebody challenged the government's role in the affair, and Pérez had to give back the money? Economist Gerardo Ortega is quoted as saying 'the dotcom crash would seem like a joke compared with Real Madrid's demise.'

And there are further discrepancies. The magazine states that in Pérez' first year in charge, a 102 million euro debt was registered as being a 31.5 million euro profit. And how? By counting a 117 bank loan from the Caja Madrid y Sogecable – to be paid back over 11 years – as being part of that year's income. As the loan was made on the back of the sale of the land, again Pérez would have to give it all back in the case of a ruling against him in a court.

Before the sale of the training ground, Real Madrid's debts – up to 180 million euros – were legendary. The club is expected to be paid a total of 374 million euros for the sale of their property. But, with deficits of over a hundred million a year thanks to their huge wage bill – 60 per cent of their income goes into their players' pockets – they are living on a knife-edge even if the skyscrapers do go up in the place where the team trained for nearly 50 years. The money from the sale won't last more than a few seasons. What will happen, wonders the magazine, when the goose stops laying the golden egg?

Pérez, it surmises, believes that merchandising, and particularly shirt sales, will be the answer. He is hoping that Beckham will sell 140 million euros worth of shirts over the next three years. This explains his policy of buying 'galácticos', and paying them huge wages, whilst filling the team up with 'Pavones' who get a fraction of the amount. But, concludes the magazine, how can he be sure this will happen when you can buy fake Real Madrid shirts for a third of the price in the centre of the city? And, as the sale of Claude Makelele to Chelsea shows, how long will the 'lesser' players put up with being paid a fraction of their team-mates' wages?

The article raises a number of questions I want to work out over the course of the season. Real Madrid are a fantastic team to watch, a collection of the world's best players with a penchant for attack at all times. As they inevitably leave space at the back, they are also relatively easy to score against. Games tend to be very open, and are likely to be high-scoring over the season. It's going to be great fun watching Real's attempt to win the league, whether I support them or not. But is Pérez's experiment the glorious dream of a libertarian connoisseur, trying to create the perfect team, whatever the risk? Or is it simply another example of a businessman trying to make the most money possible out of his business, treating the players and fans as commodities? Has Beckham been bought by Pérez as the latest brushstroke on a masterpiece canvas? Or is he simply the latest mercenary to sign up for the president's extravagent money-making machine?

**SATURDAY NOVEMBER 1ST**

Real Madrid v Athletic de Bilbao is the Saturday evening match chosen to be farmed out to all the local TV channels, which means that I get to see it in the comfort of my own flat, albeit with Catalan commentary. I rent the flat for 750 euros a month. Uncommonly for Barcelona, it's a 'dúplex' which means that Brenda doesn't have to sit through the whole game: she can read upstairs as I shout and fume and deliver imperfectly phrased Spanish insults at the referee.

Beckham has been spending considerably more than me on his accommodation in Madrid. This week the Spanish newspapers have been full of a story originally printed in *The Mirror* about his extravagant hotel expenses. Beckham has allegedly racked up a stunning 620,000 euro bill in his eleven-week stay in the five-star Santa Maura hotel, in which he has been renting two first-floor suites. The bill was broken down and included 18,000 euros for the parking of his fleet of five cars, exactly the same number of pairs of shoes that I own, and presumably representing a similar choice dilemma in the morning. Beckham has brought to Spain an Aston Martin, a Porsche, an Audi A8, a Lexus and a Range Rover, all of which are located in restricted valet parking bays. His bar bill is said to have totalled 10,000 euros, with room service coming to an impressive 27,000 euros. He has allegedly spent 12,000 euros on TV and videos (presumably not many being of Pedro Almodóvar or Carlos Saura films). His 76,000-euro restaurant bill was for specially produced English-style food. So much for acclimatisation.

Following persistent rumours about his marriage being in trouble, Beckham has also been busy going out with Victoria in Madrid, publicly signalling that they are very much an item. Earlier in the week, the Beckhams had been filmed kissing and cuddling in the Plaza de Oriente, in front of the Palacio Real in the centre of Madrid. They have also been reported to have dined in the Ritz (bill 1,800 euros) and the Hard Rock Café (bill 40 euros).

It's a mark of Beckham's increasing popularity in the country that the story about the hotel bills has invariably been accompanied by a quote from a member of staff about Beckham being the hotel workers' favourite customer, 'always pleasant and polite'. But while Beckham has been given almost entirely positive press since he arrived in Madrid, especially since he proved himself so comprehensively on the football field, his wife has been treated with little but disdain by the Spanish media. Back in July, on her arrival by Beckham's side when he signed for Real, it was reported that she disdained to sign autographs for her fans, and that she wore heels 'that never ended'. There has been very little of positive note since, a matter not helped by the fact that she is said to have stated that Madrid 'smelt of garlic', a comment which is always brought up when her name is mentioned (and one she denies having made). Spain is the country where *Hello* magazine was devised, and the country's appetite for celebrity-related tittle-tattle is enormous. The Beckhams have become the target for a number of rumours about their marriage, with Beckham only needing to be in the same room as a single woman to set off reams of speculation. Notable examples include his SFX agency assistant Rebecca Loos, Spanish supermodel Esther

Cañadas, with whom Beckham was seen chatting during Ronaldo's birthday party in October. There was also the famous-for-being-famous Nuria Bermúdez, who turned up uninvited at Beckham's hotel and publicly stated her intention to bed the Englishman with the words: "Be scared, Victoria Beckham. You ought to be trembling. David is gorgeous. He will be targeted by women wherever he goes, but I will be in the front of the queue."

Beckham has been able to get away with his eccentric dress sense, because he has shown that he is good footballer, and he has been taken into Spanish people's hearts for his honest endeavours on the pitch. His wife, however, is not greatly admired for her talents, and is merely seen as being an oddity – and a threat. Despite the fact that the couple have just rented a new home with an eye to buying it (a six-million euro mansion in the upmarket suburban district of La Moraleja), it is greatly feared that Victoria Adams will take her husband back to England.

His presence, at least, is assured this evening. Beckham pulled out of a training session as late as Thursday morning with a recurrence of the muscle strain that kept him out of the Racing and Zaragoza games. But he is considered to be fit enough to play in a match which it is vitally important for Real Madrid to win – both for sporting and political reasons.

Athletic de Bilbao are a curious club in that they are entirely composed of Basque players. They were formed back in 1898 by northern Englishmen, wear the colours of Sunderland and have an English name, but they have been following this strict regionalist policy for 40 years. No foreigner or Spanish player brought up outside the Basque country and Navarra is allowed in the squad. Despite this severe limitation (imagine Newcastle only playing Geordies) the team has never dropped out of the top level of the league. Or perhaps because of it. The idea is that the players should play with a passion potentially lacking in their more mercenary, multicultural rivals. The game against El Real, then, is a fascinating clash of ideologies.

The Basque country has a population of 2.5 million people, and enjoys some degree of political autonomy from Madrid. 30 per cent of the people speak fluent Euskera, the Basque language which is uncon-nected to any other European tongue. This figure is actually increasing – schools in the Basque country teach all their subjects in Euskera. The odd nature of the language makes the team a commentator's nightmare. Today Aranzubia, Gurpegi, Iraola, Etxeberria and Urzaiz are in the starting line-up.

As the game is about to kick off, the cameras pan in on José María

Aznar, the Spanish prime minister, who will be hugely satisfied if Madrid win today's match. Aznar has been a 'socio' (member) of Real Madrid since he was seven years old and his centralist policies have long aimed at trying to limit the autonomy of the Basque region. His heart, then, is presumably in his moustache-dominated mouth as Athletic start the match on the attack, at great pace, worrying the Real Madrid defence into making basic mistakes. Within ten minutes Iker Casillas is forced into making two fine saves, first from a header by Ezquerro, then after a one-on-one with Jonan. The game continues in the same pattern for the first half hour, with Athletic attacking in waves and creating chance after chance. Casillas is manificent, saving from Etxeberria with an outstretched foot, and Tiko with his hands. Then, out of nothing, a goal for El Real. Ronaldo, loitering on the edge of Bilbao's box like a man waiting for a night bus, gets the ball from Helguera, and scores with the minimum of fuss. The goal doesn't change the pattern of the game. Beckham gets a yellow card for a foul on the edge of the box. The resulting free kick by Tiko looks destined for the top corner of the goal until it is magnificently tipped over by the diving Casillas. I make a cup of tea.

The second half sees Athletic attacking in droves again. Of the outfield players, only Beckham seems capable of putting up any resistance. Within a minute he shows the multi-faceted nature of his game, shooting just wide, then seconds later turning up in his own box to rob an opponent and end yet another Athletic attack. On 52 minutes Ronaldo receives the ball again in a dangerous position, runs past several defenders and hits a cross-shot into the goal. 2–0. The injustice of it! I throw a handful of peanuts at the screen, then have to stoop down to pick them up again before Brenda comes downstairs.

Bilbao don't seem too put out. Again they attack, again Casillas keeps them out. An amazing statistic is flashed up onto the screen. Casillas has made 10 saves. Aranzubia, his opposite number, has hardly made one, and is completely fooled when on 72 minutes Ronaldo draws him and passes the ball across the box for Figo to score into an empty net. 3–0! It is the most undeserved score-line I have seen for a long time, perhaps in my life. I am crestfallen. On 88 minutes Beckham is substituted, and receives a standing ovation from the crowd. Casillas has time for one more save, and on the final whistle the ovation is for him. "Iker, Iker" chant the crowd, as the camera pans in on the young goalkeeper. And then at Aznar, standing on his feet clapping, a broad grin on his face. His most pressing problem with the Basque country has been solved by the best striker in the world . . . and a young man making a strong claim to being considered the best keeper.

| CELTA | 0 | RACING | 1 |
|---|---|---|---|
| MURCIA | 0 | DEPORTIVO | 0 |
| **REAL MADRID** | **3** | **ATHLETIC** | **0** |
| VALLADOLID | 2 | ALBACETE | 0 |
| MÁLAGA | 2 | SEVILLA | 0 |
| ESPANYOL | 0 | ZARAGOZA | 2 |
| BETIS | 1 | ATLÉTICO | 2 |
| VILLARREAL | 1 | OSASUNA | 0 |
| REAL SOCIEDAD | 3 | BARCELONA | 3 |
| MALLORCA | 0 | VALENCIA | 5 |

**LA CLASIFICACIÓN**

| | P | W | D | L | F | A | Pts |
|---|---|---|---|---|---|---|---|
| VALENCIA | 10 | 7 | 2 | 1 | 21 | 5 | 23 |
| **REAL MADRID** | **10** | **7** | **2** | **1** | **23** | **9** | **23** |
| DEPORTIVO | 10 | 7 | 1 | 2 | 19 | 8 | 22 |
| OSASUNA | 10 | 5 | 2 | 3 | 12 | 8 | 17 |
| BARCELONA | 10 | 4 | 4 | 2 | 14 | 10 | 16 |
| ATLÉTICO | 10 | 5 | 1 | 4 | 13 | 13 | 16 |
| RACING | 10 | 4 | 2 | 4 | 13 | 11 | 14 |
| ATHLETIC | 10 | 4 | 2 | 4 | 12 | 12 | 14 |
| VILLARREAL | 10 | 3 | 5 | 2 | 11 | 11 | 14 |
| VALLADOLID | 10 | 4 | 2 | 4 | 14 | 18 | 14 |
| BETIS | 10 | 3 | 4 | 3 | 13 | 13 | 13 |
| MÁLAGA | 10 | 4 | 1 | 5 | 12 | 14 | 13 |
| REAL SOCIEDAD | 10 | 3 | 4 | 3 | 12 | 14 | 13 |
| SEVILLA | 10 | 2 | 6 | 2 | 12 | 13 | 12 |
| ZARAGOZA | 10 | 3 | 2 | 5 | 8 | 10 | 11 |
| CELTA | 10 | 2 | 4 | 4 | 13 | 14 | 10 |
| ALBACETE | 10 | 3 | 0 | 7 | 10 | 15 | 9 |
| MALLORCA | 10 | 2 | 2 | 6 | 9 | 20 | 8 |
| MURCIA | 10 | 1 | 4 | 5 | 7 | 16 | 7 |
| ESPANYOL | 10 | 1 | 2 | 7 | 8 | 22 | 5 |

# SEVEN
# SEVILLE

# SEVEN
# SEVILLE

## WEDNESDAY NOVEMBER 5TH

Jesús is not going to change his mind. I am in the press office of the Ramón Sánchez Pizjuan stadium, in the bowels of Sevilla FC's hulking white bullring of a ground, to see if the press accreditation for myself and my girlfriend Brenda, who has come along to take photographs, has come through. Sevilla's press officer is showing me the fax that I wrote a few days ago and my publisher sent through. There are two letters written large in the margin. The letters, forming the same word in Spanish as English, are 'N' and 'O'. They are underlined three times.

He's as sweet as can be about it, in his sing-song Andalucian accent. "I'm afraid the whole world wants to come to the game," he says. "We have reporters from all over. TV companies, radio stations. There are journalists coming from Japan. I'm afraid we simply haven't allowed accreditation to editorial houses. You can't come. I'm really sorry."

I have also asked to interview Sevilla's goalkeeper, Antonio Notario, reputed to be one of the best in the league.

"How about the interview?"

"Oh, that's fine. I'll ask him tomorrow morning. Should be no problem. Look, I'm really sorry you can't get into the match."

I know that I can get a ticket from the taquilla, so it's no big deal. "Don't worry, Jesús," I say, and offer my hand. It is a common name in Spain, and particularly in Seville, one of the most pious cities in the world, famous for its Easter celebrations where locals carry statues of the Madonna round the crowded streets. When my hand comes out of the handshake there is something left in it. Two small objects. They are two little pin badges, with the crest of the club.

"A little detail," says Jesús, with a smile. He's a big man with a big smile, a likeable man. It's the most pleasant rejection I've had in my life.

There is no queue for the ticket office: I exchange 60 euros for one of the cheap seats, at the top of the stadium, behind one of the goals, in the 'fondo norte'. I'll go on my own; Brenda's decided not to come to the match. She'll watch it in the bar with two friends we have met up with in Seville: Roger (who I went to Real v Mallorca with) and his Uruguayan girlfriend Patricia. In the club shop I make a very boy-not-accompanied-by-girl purchase. An orange Sevilla training top with a blue v-neck.

Later on the four of us go on a tapas crawl in La Triana, a district of the city the other side of the Río Guadalquivir from the city centre, away from the huge cathedral, the Moorish Alcazar castle, the orange trees lining the narrow streets and, most importantly the large number of American tourists who inhabit the Santa Cruz tourist trap. We head into a large bar with blue-and-yellow tiled walls, and pictures of bullfighters dating back 75 years. La Triana is the barrio where one of the greatest bullfighters of all time, Juan Belmonte, was brought up in the 1920s; the bar looks like it hasn't changed much since then. We order four glasses of fino and a bowl of prawns in oil and garlic. Fino is a dry white sherry which is made in nearby Jerez and is much more drinkable than the local red and white wines.

I've left my orange shirt in the pension, but I'm wearing the Sevilla pin badge on my jacket. The barman, an old guy with brushed-back dyed-black hair, sees it as he brings in a ceramic dish full of sizzling prawns.

"What's that?" he says.

"A badge."

"It's not a badge, it's a stain. Ugh! A horrible dirty stain! I've a good mind not to serve you."

I know what's going on. The taxi driver who drove us here has been talking about how Seville's population is split between fans of Sevilla and those of Real Betis. There is no sectarian reason for the split as in, say, Glasgow, or a geographical one, as in the London teams. Sevilla are considered to be the 'posh' side, and Betis the working class club, but largely it is a family thing. Which makes the rivalry intense. And our waiter is a Betis fan.

We've hardly had time to make inroads into our prawns when the guy is back.

"I've found something to get rid of that horrible ugly stain," he says. He produces a sticker, which he sticks over my Sevilla badge. It reads 'Real Betis' with the badge of the rival club.

"There you go, that's better," he says, and walks off.

On our way out, half an hour later, I am accosted by another waiter. He was watching my earlier encounter with his colleague.

"What's that you are wearing?"

"It's to cover a stain."

"I insist you take it off. You cannot cover a stain with a stain. Take it off."

My waiter comes back.

"You'd better not take that off."

"Take it off."

They are both deadpan. I assume this is a joke, but it's performed in a deadly serious manner. These two have probably argued about football every day for years, and this is a regular showdown.

"Take it off."

"Don't take it off."

"I'm going," I say, and walk out of the bar, trying to maintain a smile. Safely down the street I take off both the sticker and the badge, and put them in my pocket.

I've walked into a small example of the biggest footballing rivalry in Spain outside Barcelona-Real Madrid. The rivalry got out of hand in 2002/2003, when a security guard got beaten up by six Sevilla fans before the derby, in full view of TV cameras, which broadcast the images around the world. Antonio Orrego, who was trying to stop the fans from interfering with Betis' pre-match preparations, got so smashed up by one fan with a crutch that he had to spend the night in hospital. Later on in the game Betis goalkeeper Toni Prats was attacked on the pitch by another Sevilla fan. In the corresponding fixture this season, played the same day as Real Madrid played in Vigo, the government asked the fans to be calm in what the police classed as a 'high risk' game. There were no unseemly incidents – a rarity.

## THURSDAY NOVEMBER 6TH

The next day I'm in a Seville fan club near the Sevilla stadium, in the commercial district known as Nervión (the former name of the stadium). I've arranged to meet the just-retired president of the club, Seville's member number 59, an old man by the name of Raúl. His first Seville match was back in 1936 (a 2–1 win over Athletic de Bilbao) he tells me, before I can get a drink. He became a member in 1946. "I couldn't afford membership before that, so I just paid game by game. Things have changed in Spain."

In 1946, Seville were champions, having won an exciting run-in against Barcelona and Athletic de Bilbao, thanks to their double strike-force of Arza and Campos. "Arza was brilliant, a winger, the Gento of Sevilla, and the only Pichichi (league top scorer) Seville have had." They have never won the league since.

Raúl is keener to talk about the times before he was alive than the modern era. "You're British," he says. "The club was formed by the British. In 1905. They worked for the Río Tinto coal mine nearby. The first manager was called Mr O'Connor. He was an engineer in the mines. The club were then nicknamed 'Los Primitivos'. And you know Beckham? Well, he wasn't the first British player to play in Spain. We had the first. He was called Mackenzie, and he played in our first league side in the '20s." He shows me a picture of the team on the wall; sure enough, there he is, a blond amongst brunets, one of eleven smiling figures in white shirts and shorts.

Raúl tells me about Seville's history – how they have been one of Spain's top teams since the war (in Spain the term 'the war' refers to the Spanish Civil War) but have never had enough money to translate that into a sustained period of success. How they have not won anything since a cup in 1948. How the fans are hungry for success. Is he excited by Real Madrid coming to town?

"I am excited by any game. But our real rivalry is with Betis, not Madrid."

"Did you ever consider supporting Betis?"

"Of course not. I am a born and bred Sevillista."

"How did you choose which team to support?"

"My family has always been Sevillista. And always will. I tell you . . . there's only one way I would become a Bético."

"How's that?"

"If Lopera became President of Sevilla, I would become a Bético." You might remember Manuel Ruiz de Lopera, Betis' gaunt president, trying to scupper the broadcast of Madrid's first game earlier in the season. The thought of Betis' eccentric leader tickles Raúl's humour. "Lopera. Sevillista. Ha ha ha. I would become a Bético. Ha ha ha."

I have an awful lunch (I have found it difficult to find good food in Seville) and then I head for Sevilla's Ciudad Deportiva, about five kilometres out of town, to watch the team train, and to do my interview with Notario, the goalkeeper.

It's an impressive place, with a couple of training pitches, quite a big stand, and a cluster of white-painted buildings. The players are playing piggy-in-the-middle in small groups. I recognise the shaven head of Darío Silva, Seville's fiery Uruguayan attacker, who made himself famous in the 2002 World Cup by falling over virtually every time he got the ball. He's having a heated argument with another player, claiming the ball went out of bounds, and therefore he shouldn't be piggy any more. In the end the other player gives up and goes into the middle.

The players are called together for a talk, and, whilst walking off the training pitch, one of them performs the most amazing feat I have ever seen done with a football. Standing about ten yards behind the goal, and 15 yards to its left, a young, slight, dark-haired player kicks the ball with intent. It floats towards its destination, curls round the post, bounces on the line, and ends up in the goal. It's Beckham times ten! If he can score from behind the goal, what will he be able to do from a corner? I wander over to a young spectator, who has given the player a cheer and a wave of the hand, after his goal.

"Who was that? Who scored the goal?"

"José Antonio Reyes. Local boy."

"Did he mean it?"

"Of course he did. He's brilliant. Everyone wants him. Arsenal want him. But we want him, too. He's our best player." Again that sing-song accent. I've seen Reyes play, I should have recognised him. He's a winger with speed and flair. Seville have slapped a 100 million euro buy-out clause on his contract.

Jesús turns up on a moped. A gaggle of journalists surround him, and he tells them the news.

"Alfaro is renewing," he says. Pablo Alfaro is Sevilla's bearded 34-year-old central defender well-known for kicking opposing attackers hard in the shins. "And Darío has said yes." This means that Silva will do a press conference after training.

I wander up to him, ask him if the interview's been set up. He smiles broadly. "I'll ask Antonio," he says. "I can't see a problem." I tell him about the trouble his pin badge has got me into. He laughs.

Twenty minutes later I'm talking to Antonio Notario, the goalkeeper. I've never met a more friendly footballer – he comes out to chat to me on the terraces of the training ground, doesn't even bother changing. I'm interested in how he feels a couple of days before the Real Madrid game. And particularly before facing David Beckham's free-kicks and corners. Has he spent time studying them?

"Spent time! Ha! I've spent so much time with Beckham's video that I could be his wife!"

A huddle of kids is collecting around us, listening into the conversation, and this is the cue for a couple of lewd comments by the older ones. The laughter attracts more people. Pretty soon my little interview has an audience of about 20.

"What makes Beckham such a good corner kicker?"

"He manages to make them go up, then come down again. It's a rare skill – I've only seen Betis's Assunçao do it, too. It's very difficult to defend as a goalkeeper. You just have to keep your concentration, and only catch or punch it if you are sure you can make it."

His words are nearly drowned out by boos from the kids at the mention of the rival player from Betis.

"Do you get nervous before playing against a player like Beckham?" More jeers from the lads.

"Nervous? No, not nervous. There is no room for fear in football. On the contrary, I'm looking forward to playing."

"How about his free kicks?"

"He's good. Very good. The thing about free kicks is that you position the wall to cover one side of the goal, and you cover the other. But Beckham is capable of curling the ball over the wall and in the top corner of the part of the goal you are not covering. If a player does that there is nothing you can do apart from . . ."

He moves his head from side to side, eyes looking upwards, as if watching the ball into the back of the net.

"How does that feel?"

"How do you think it feels? You are helpless. It feels terrible. But it is important to remember that it is not your fault."

I've seen from Notario's statistics in my *Marca Guide* that he was born in Barcelona, and I say he doesn't seem Catalan, that he seems to have the local accent.

"I'm Catalan by birth, but that's all," he says. "My parents were working there for a short time. I'm from round here, really," he says.

"You can see that, you've been most generous with your time," I joke (Catalans are reputed to be mean). He smiles.

Afterwards I meet the others in a Real Betis peña in Santa Cruz, near the cathedral. It's a curious place, a cheap working class bar shunned by the tourists despite being fronted by a beautiful terrace lined with orange trees. I eat a bowl of delicious fresh gazpacho, followed by a number of glasses of fino. It's as warm as an English summer evening. Some local kids are standing on the top of a bench and leaping in the air to try to reach the oranges on one of the trees. After a while I walk over and pick one off, then drop kick it towards them. They kick it around like a football, and pretty soon it is mush. They want another one. I pick another, and another. Then I stand in front of a doorway, and make out that I am a goalkeeper. I think of Notario earlier in the day, and wonder how he is feeling, before his showdown with Beckham and co. It inspires me. Oranges come in thick and fast, sometimes two at a time, but I manage to save them all, mostly with my feet. The kids start going wild. Eventually one gets in a shot that goes past me. I feign dejection and sit down again at our table. The door/goal in front of us opens, and a woman comes out, stepping in the squelch that has formed at her threshold. She doesn't seem to mind.

## SUNDAY NOVEMBER 10TH

On Sunday afternoon Brenda and I climb up the Giralda tower, which dominates Seville's huge cathedral. There are no steps – you walk up a slope, reach a little plateau, turn 90 degrees, walk up another slope, etc. I ask the guy in front, who has a white beard and a beret, why there are no steps. He has a strange look in his eye.

"It was the Arabs. The Arabs! They built the tower so horses could go up. Horses! They were crazy! They used to throw them off the top. The horses! They were crazy." I whisper to Brenda that they were not the only ones.

The top offers a splendid view of Seville's winding organic streets, designed by the Moors who inhabited the town for 800 years. There are so many tourists that we have to queue up to have a look from the 20 or so viewpoints round the top of the tower. I look out for the football stadium where the match will be on tonight, and catch a glimpse of one of its white walls, a mile away out of the crowded rooftops of the old quarter, in the more modern Nervión district. Then I look back around the red rooftops of the old city, realising that I've fallen slightly in love with it.

We head back to the Betis peña. The city has a double bill of football tonight. At 7.30 Betis are playing Barcelona in the Nou Camp in Barcelona, then at 9.30 Seville are hosting Real Madrid in the Nervión. We pull up a table and order a menu del día which arrives as the match kicks off. There are about a hundred fans in the room, of all ages, some sitting on chairs, some on the floor, tense, virtually silent, focussed on the football, hardly a drink between them. We are an incongruous group tucking into our food. I have a plateful of spinach with chickpeas. Betis launch an attack. A header just wide. There are oohs, and the place relaxes.

"Are you showing the Sevilla-Real match afterwards?" asks Roger to the barman.

"No, of course not," he says.

"Of course not?"

"We would not dirty our screen with images of Sevilla! Our clients would go mad! The only time we show Sevilla is when they are playing Betis . . ."

I hurry down my dessert (flan, a sweet Spanish version of crème caramel) and leave. I don't tell the barman I'm going to watch Sevilla. Crossing the main road, just to the north of the old town, there's a roar of motorbikes, followed by several police cars, followed by . . . the Real Madrid bus. It's become a familiar sight, a sleek dark monster full of millions of pounds worth of footballer, heading into the stadium to try to turn the party (Real Madrid are coming to town!) into a wake (they stuffed us).

Twenty minutes later I'm in the Sevilla peña near the stadium. It's walkable from the old part of town. It's packed with pre-match drinkers. They are not showing the Betis match on their television.

"We never show Betis in here," says the peña president, who has recognised me from my previous visit and beckoned me over. Then, lowering the volume of his voice conspiratorially, "but we all know that they are losing 1–0."

He shows me into his office, the inner sanctum of the club. There is a big red and white flag with the Sevilla crest. Propped up next to it is a large framed picture of the Madonna, with tears running down her porcelain cheeks.

It starts raining as I head towards the stadium. A season in the sun, indeed. Outside the stadium the usual bustle and excitement. People are hurrying into the ground past chestnut-sellers, not doing great business, smoke billowing from the makeshift chimneys of their white prams. Everybody else has an umbrella.

It requires a good deal of trial, error and enlightened guesswork to find my place, high up behind the goal, and to its left. The Sevilla ultras, thousands of them, are massed below me, slightly to my right. Between them and the goal there is a vast net. I wonder if it is to stop the ball going into the crowd or from objects being thrown onto the pitch. An enormous flag with the Sevilla crest is unfurled over a large section of the crowd. The Real Madrid players run out, all dressed in black. The requisite boos turn to cheers as the all whites of Sevilla follow. Then the anthem.

The Real Madrid side line up for kick-off in front of me, and it is an odd sight. The defence looks very makeshift. Roberto Carlos is injured, so Raúl Bravo, who has been playing in the centre, takes his place on the left. In the middle are Helguera, who has been playing in midfield, and Rubén, who hasn't been playing at all. On the right is Pavón, who has moved from the centre, replacing Míchel Salgado, suspended. Three out-of-position youngsters and a midfielder. In front the 'doble pivote' is made up of Guti and Beckham, two attack-minded players playing in defensive midfield positions. Then things look a little stronger, with Raúl, Zidane and Figo lined up behind Ronaldo. It's a lop-sided affair, with the Zidanes in attack and the Pavones in defence. A risky business, and a reminder that Real Madrid might be one of the richest clubs in the world, but they have very little experienced strength in depth.

The teams swap a couple of tame shots, then Sevilla break down the right. Young Rubén skews a header across the goal, Helguera gets his head on it and it somehow ends up in the Madrid net. Five minutes, 1–0 to Sevilla, and mayhem all around me. Everyone's on their feet;

they can't believe Sevilla have scored so quickly. There is mass hugging. Three guys in front of me light up celebratory cigarettes: it looks like a ritual they follow every time there's a goal.

Beckham loses the ball soon after the kick-off. Martí puts a ball across from the right; Darío Silva dummies it, it continues through to Reyes, who puts it straight into the path of Darío who has continued his run, shaking off his marker. The Uruguayan slots it into the net. The guys in front are on their feet again. They haven't even finished their cigarettes! Everyone is standing, myself included. People are laughing. Embracing one another. Looking each other in the eye, with disbelief.

"Coño!"

"Magnífico!"

"2–0!"

The guys in front extinguish their cigarettes, and Real Madrid get a free kick outside the box. Beckham steps up . . . and hoofs the ball into the wall. 'He's due a bad'un,' I write in my notebook. Then Sevilla get a free kick as Guti fouls Reyes.

"Guti maricón!" chant the fans in front. Most everyone in the stadium stands on their feet and starts clapping their hands in unison as Darío Silva runs up . . . and puts the free kick wide. Beckham loses the ball again and again. Darío Silva shoots just wide, then misses a volley that would have made the score 3–0. Then Reyes scoops the ball into the air and into the path of the little Brazilian full back Alves, who heads the ball over the advancing Casillas, following it to make sure it goes into the net. It is 3–0, with less than 15 minutes gone! We're up on our feet again. This is incredible! The guy behind me grabs my shoulders, and gives them a shake. I'm yelling "gooool, gol, gol!"

Soon after the re-start you can see that poor Rubén has lost it. He boots one ball straight into touch under no pressure, like a Sunday-leaguer. He skews another clearance terribly, then gets booked for a mistimed tackle on Reyes. On 24 minutes his number is held up on the touch-line. There is an excited chatter. Queiroz is taking him off! He isn't even injured! I feel enormous pity for the kid. This could be his last game for Real Madrid. Solari, the Argentine international midfielder, comes on. Queiroz puts him on the left, moving Raúl Bravo into the centre with Helguera.

It doesn't make much difference. Reyes, who is playing brilliantly, robs the ball from Pavón, who isn't. The central defender is having a nightmare in a position he's unused to. Reyes kicks the ball into the middle where Casquero is waiting to thump it past Casillas. Goooooooooooooool! Gol gol gol! More mayhem, only even more exaggerated. One of the guys in front gets out a goatskin of wine and starts squirting it in and around his mouth, then in and around his neighbours'. I don't know if they know each other. Eventually I sit down again on a bocadillo sandwich in silver paper that has ended on my seat. The Real Madrid players are standing around the pitch, looking at each other, hands on hips. There is no communication. Beckham looks particularly pissed off. And you know what? I'm delighted.

Almost everyone in the stadium starts jumping up and down chanting something I can't make out. I'm jumping up and down too, there's nothing else to do. I'm not sure if the joy I feel is vicarious or real. I ask the girl next to me to write down what the fans were chanting. She laughs, and writes 'Qué bote Nervión'. (The Nervion Stadium should jump).

Queiroz reshuffles his defence again. Pavón is pulled in from his right-back purgatory, and into the centre. Raúl Bravo, a left-footer, goes to right back, his third position of the night, and the third player to be tormented by Reyes, who almost immediately puts the ball through his legs and collects it on the other side. Sevilla, scenting blood, search for a fifth before half-time. They get a free-kick outside the box – it hits a hand in the wall. The whole crowd apart from one shout a word in unison.

"Mano!"

One person shouts something completely different at exactly the same time.

"Handball!" It's me.

The referee doesn't give the penalty. I reflect that the day that I auto-matically say 'mano' will be the day I've really learnt to speak Spanish.

"It was only because it was Beckham's hand," moans the guy behind me. Another foul on the edge of the box, this time against Antoñito, isn't given by the referee. It's been drizzling but now it starts pissing down. You can't hear the half-time whistle for the rain.

"It's as if Real Madrid are playing in white, and Seville in black," says a guy down his mobile phone. There is a lot of laughter. "I don't care now if we win 4–0 or 4–3. I'll never be this happy again," says one of the cigarette guys. A pop singer, announced on the big screen as Rosa, starts singing on a makeshift stage on the halfway line, accompanied by three gyrating dancers. Thousands in the crowd start gyrating in the same manner. I wonder how poor Rubén is spending his half-time.

Sevilla nearly score after the break, but inevitably step down a gear, and Real Madrid start stringing a few attacks together. Raúl belts the ball over the bar from ten yards, like I might have done. Then Ronaldo scores a brilliant goal out of nothing, a shot from the edge of the box, and doesn't even crack a smile. Suddenly I get nervous. There's half an hour to go. Real Madrid only need three goals to equalise. One every ten minutes. If any team can . . .

I needn't have worried. The rain continues to pour down, and it puts out any spark of Madrid recovery. If anything it is Sevilla who look more like scoring, though the referee seems to have decided that the capital's team shouldn't be humiliated any further, giving a string of decisions against the home team. The whole stadium, which is steeply banked, is a sea of umbrellas. I haven't got one – I'm crouched into as small a ball as possible, trying to minimise my surface area, waiting for the final whistle. Guti gets sent off for a vicious kick, Darío Silva for walking off too slowly after being substituted. There is a Mexican wave of umbrellas – a remarkable sight. Then the whistle goes.

I join my friends in the Betis bar afterwards. Roger tells me that Betis lost 2–1 to Barcelona. The barman had refused to show the Sevilla game afterwards. By the time they had found another bar that did have it on, Real Madrid were already 3–0 down. He doesn't look too happy about it.

## MONDAY NOVEMBER 11TH

Brenda and I have to catch a night train to Barcelona, and before doing it we have a fino and tapas crawl around the centre of Seville, to say goodbye to the place. In the bar we have decided is our last stop, before getting a taxi to the train station, we debate whether or not we have time for a last glass of fino and a final tapa. We risk it. I'm wearing my orange Sevilla top, with a green anorak over it. The waiter points to the shirt.

"Look, he's got a Sevilla shirt on!" he says to a group who've just arrived in the corner, two middle-aged guys and two women. I close my jacket over it.

"This is green," I say, foolishly, meaning that Betis play in green, that I'm not favouring one team or the other.

"No, it's the mister," says the barman, pointing at the group. Slowly I understand. The mister, the manager, it can't be . . . it is! It's the Sevilla manager, Joaquín Caparrós, along with the technical director, Monchi Rodríguez, and their wives. The whole group now is looking at me. I wander over, heady with wine, still heady on the 4–1 victory, heady with the whole experience of Seville.

"That . . . was . . . a dream!" I say to Caparros. "4–1!" My Spanish is coming out all tangled up, I am an obvious tourist. 'Thank you, thank you. You have . . . made me . . . happy." Brenda looks a little alarmed.

"Have to go . . ." I say. "To Barcelona." The four of them are grinning. I pick up my rucksack, and we're out into the street, looking for a taxi.

## RESULTA: JORNADA 11

| ZARAGOZA | 1 | CELTA | 1 |
|---|---|---|---|
| ATHLETIC | 1 | ESPANYOL | 0 |
| DEPORTIVO | 2 | REAL SOCIEDAD | 1 |
| ALBACETE | 0 | MÁLAGA | 1 |
| ATLÉTICO | 1 | VILLARREAL | 0 |
| MALLORCA | 4 | MURCIA | 1 |
| VALENCIA | 1 | RACING | 2 |
| OSASUNA | 1 | VALLADOLID | 1 |
| BARCELONA | 2 | BETIS | 1 |
| **SEVILLA** | **4** | **REAL MADRID** | **1** |

## LA CLASIFICACIÓN

| | P | W | D | L | F | A | Pts |
|---|---|---|---|---|---|---|---|
| DEPORTIVO | 11 | 8 | 1 | 2 | 21 | 9 | 25 |
| VALENCIA | 11 | 7 | 2 | 2 | 22 | 7 | 23 |
| **REAL MADRID** | **11** | **7** | **2** | **2** | **24** | **13** | **23** |
| BARCELONA | 11 | 5 | 4 | 2 | 16 | 11 | 19 |
| ATLÉTICO | 11 | 6 | 1 | 4 | 14 | 13 | 19 |
| OSASUNA | 11 | 5 | 3 | 3 | 13 | 9 | 18 |
| RACING | 11 | 5 | 2 | 4 | 15 | 12 | 17 |
| ATHLETIC | 11 | 5 | 2 | 4 | 13 | 12 | 17 |
| MALAGA | 11 | 5 | 1 | 5 | 13 | 14 | 16 |
| SEVILLA | 11 | 3 | 6 | 2 | 16 | 14 | 15 |
| VALLADOLID | 11 | 4 | 3 | 4 | 15 | 19 | 15 |
| VILLARREAL | 11 | 3 | 5 | 3 | 11 | 12 | 14 |
| BETIS | 11 | 3 | 4 | 4 | 14 | 15 | 13 |
| REAL SOCIEDAD | 11 | 3 | 4 | 4 | 13 | 16 | 13 |
| ZARAGOZA | 11 | 3 | 3 | 5 | 9 | 11 | 12 |
| CELTA DE VIGO | 11 | 2 | 5 | 4 | 14 | 15 | 11 |
| MALLORCA | 11 | 3 | 2 | 6 | 13 | 21 | 11 |
| ALBACETE | 11 | 3 | 0 | 8 | 10 | 16 | 9 |
| MURCIA | 11 | 1 | 4 | 6 | 8 | 20 | 7 |
| ESPANYOL | 11 | 1 | 2 | 8 | 8 | 23 | 5 |

# EIGHT
# PAMPLONA

GOLFO DE VIZCAYA

Osasuna

Real Madrid

OCÉANO ATLÁNTICO

MAR MEDITERRÁNEO

N
W E
S

# EIGHT
# PAMPLONA

**FRIDAY OCTOBER 29TH**

Crang! The shutters of the tobacconist pull down when I'm still 20 yards away. There's bound to be another one a bit further up in the old part of Pamplona. But as I walk up the street shutters are pulling down all around me.

Crang!

Crang!

Crang!

What the hell is going on? It's only 1.30 in the afternoon. I've only just arrived. I need to buy a top-up card for my mobile phone to sort out the interview I'm trying to arrange with Osasuna FC's captain, Cruchaga. I need to ring before two.

Crang!

I ask a guy standing outside a toy shop, before he pulls down his shutters.

"Everything shuts at 1.30 here, amigo. You won't find a top-up card."

But, after 15 minutes of frantic searching, I do. There's a guy with greasy hair and an anorak in a little locutorio, a place where immigrants can ring home on the cheap. It's ten to two.

"I just have to get this bit of paper in. It's a bit fiddly," he says.

He's trying to feed a blank receipt with a shaky hand into a small black machine. He keeps getting it into the hole, then turning on the machine, but it won't take. I want to have a go myself. I really want to have a go myself. Five to two.

"It's no good, amigo. It won't go in."

I run out of the place, desperately looking for a phone box. I wait a minute outside one, but the old woman inside looks well entrenched in her conversation. I run a block, through the red pedestrian lights, across an oncoming car. I've seen a free phone box. I put in 30 cents, dial the number. I get a funny tone. The number hasn't registered. I don't get my money back, despite concerted bashing at the button and swearing. I have no more change. All the shops are shut. I won't get through now, it's well gone two. Welcome to the provincial city of Pamplona.

Welcome back, actually. Pamplona is the home of the biggest professional disaster of my life. I got a job here in the autumn of 1990. I was an English language teacher, and I wanted to try out living in Spain, having spent three years in Italy. So I applied for a job I saw in an English newspaper and received a letter back with the terms and conditions.

The jobs I'd had in Italy were good ones, with a fair contract and small classes (maximum 12), mostly made up of adults. When I arrived in Pamplona I immediately realised that I'd made a mistake. This school did very few lessons on its own premises – it got most of its money from sending its teachers out to state schools in the area. My first lesson was with 36 eight-year-old children. My Spanish was a week old. They couldn't speak a word of English.

They were well-behaved kids, who put their hands up before they spoke. For about five minutes. Then they realised that I was not like their usual teachers and all hell broke loose. I spent half the time picking them up and putting them back behind their desks. I had learnt the Spanish for shut up ('cállate') but only in the singular. I did not know how to apply it to more than one person. I had to repeat it over and over again, looking at each offending individual, with less and less authority in my voice, as the whole class realised – for the first time in their young lives – the joys of a teacher losing control.

"Cállate. Cállate. Cállate, cállate, cállate. Cállate. Cállate. Cállate. CÁLLAAAAATE!"

It was mayhem, and it got worse, like a military occupation slipping out of control. One day, about three weeks in, one of them got a scalpel out of his bag, and started waving it about. I decided it was time to resign. I told the head that I was not qualified to teach armies of primary school children, let alone ones with whom I didn't share a common language. Within a month I was out of there. I moved to Barcelona.

As I look out of the phone box I realise that, amazingly, I am in the very square – a busy central roundabout with a fountain in the middle – where the school was based. I look up to where it used to be, and see, to my relief, it is no longer there. Out of business.

I eat a menu del día lunch. I ask for typical stuff from the Navarra region. Risotto with nuts followed by trout with bacon. I've given up drinking for a month before Christmas: I wash it down with water. Pamplona has given me the blues. It's famous for being the party town of Spain, the setting for Hemingway's *Fiesta* where every July herds of

Americans and other tourists run with the bulls in the San Fermín celebrations. But it's the end of November, there is no fiesta, and the
weather is terrible. This region is well known for having constant drizzle
(known as 'txirimiri') in the winter months. The streets are dark, the sky
is grey. God I hate this place.

I read about Beckham with my coffee. He has just received the OBE
from the Queen. There are pictures of him wearing a morning suit and
carrying a top hat. Posh has dressed up as if to go to a funeral and is
wearing a hat which looks like a small but perfectly poised flock of birds
passing over her head.

"I love Spain, I love Real Madrid, and I love my life," he is quoted as
saying. "This is the best honour I have ever had . . . better than my
football medals."

It's been a positive week for the England captain. At the weekend he
scored a 'golazo' (great goal, in Real Madrid's 2–1 home win over newly
promoted Albacete. Beckham broke the deadlock in the 37th minute,
picking the ball up in midfield, seeing space for a shot about 25 yards
out, and hitting it over the keeper and into the top corner of the net.
I watched the game in the city of Figueres, Salvador Dalí's birth and
death-place, having just looked at a possible wedding venue with
Brenda. The barman was a Madridista and made no secret of it when
the goal went in.

"Venga Beckham!"

He reacted with less exuberance to Albacete's equaliser just a minute
later, a spectacular edge-of-the-box volley by Parri, and shifted around
nervously for the rest of the game, his tension relieved in the 87th
minute when Zidane scored a late winner with his head. It was a victory
Real Madrid scarcely deserved. Beckham, however, came out of the
game with credit: *Marca* gave him another '2' with the comment 'golazo'.

He can't, it seems, put a foot wrong in Spain. I open another article
about him in the *Diario de Navarra*, the local paper. It's about how well
he has done since he arrived. It says that some players (naming Guti
as an example) look pretty but don't sweat. But Beckham is different.
He is a hard worker, he doesn't mind getting his hands dirty. It goes
into his past, saying that he grew up in 'the agitated neighbourhood' of
Leytonstone, the 'birthplace of punk rock in England' (forget Camden
Town). I enjoy the way it describes his free kicks. "His strike from outside
the penalty area is unique. He arches his body 100 degrees so his
instep contacts the ball with a cross between violence and geometry.
The ball does an exaggerated parabola, picking up height in its aerial
trajectory to suddenly drop, like lead. He does the same at both posts."
It strikes me that I have hardly heard a bad word said about Beckham

for weeks. His conquest of Spain seems complete. But has he, I wonder, reached the summit of his parabola?

I go to El Baluarte, the big, new, clean, grey-slate slab of an art gallery, which is trying to do for Pamplona what the Guggenheim has done for Bilbao. There's an exhibition about Navarra, comparing it to a similar-sized region in Japan. Navarra is a relatively small mountainous area south of the Pyrenees; it borders on France to the north, the Basque country to the west, La Rioja to the south and Aragón to the east, and is influenced by all four. Pamplona is the capital – half of the region's 250,000 inhabitants live there. The north of the city is very influenced by the Basque Country, the southern half is more Spanish. The kingdom of Navarra enjoyed its zenith 1000 years ago, during the Moorish occupation of the peninsula, when Pamplona was the capital of Christian Spain. It has since spent most of its time defending its dwindling territories; it fell into French jurisdiction in the Middle Ages, and was eventually divided between France and Spain. Spanish Navarra maintained an independent set of rights (the fueros) which entitled it to its own system of taxation, courts and customs, even under Franco's dictatorship (Navarra was a Fascist stronghold in the Spanish Civil War). This history has resulted in a race of people who are hugely defensive of these rights. Even the name of the gallery ('baluarte' means bastion) is reflective of the defensive mentality of the place.

When I leave the gallery it has stopped raining. Pamplona's 18th-century citadel, built to protect it from the French army of Napoleon, is still intact. The area has been turned into a park. I walk around it, admiring a work by the sculptor Eduardo Chillida, who used to be the goalkeeper for neighbouring Real Sociedad. His sculpture is a hulk of rusty metal, clashing nicely with the green of the grass. The huge ramparts of the citadel, black with damp, are overrun with moss and weeds. From the bottom you can see how impenetrable they were, how impossible to overcome. I muse that football teams often take on the character of their city. Osasuna, Pamplona's team, have the best defence in the league, equal to Valencia and Deportivo de la Coruña, having conceded just nine goals all season.

What do you do all on your own in a grey city when the November drizzle doesn't let up? (It's started again.) I wander into a café, order another milky coffee, and read more of the local papers. They are full of the match – Real Madrid coming to town is the second most exciting thing to happen to this town all year. They talk of the morbo of the match: how Real have lost here for two years running; how the boys from Osasuna will pressurise Real from the kick-off; how the Navarros will not give the galácticos the sort of welcome they relish; how the pitch is small and rough and the fans are hostile.

An assessment of the hostility of the locals is recorded in the first-ever travel book, written by the French priest Amery de Picaud in 1120. Pamplona lies on the traditional route from France to Santiago de Compostela, and it owes much of its importance to the fact that it was a major stop-off point on what was the most holy pilgrimage in Europe. Of the Navarros, de Picaud (writing an account of the pilgrimage route) states: "These people dress badly. They eat poorly and drink worse. Using no spoons they plunge their hands into a communal pot and drink from the same goblet. When you see them eat, you think of pigs in their gluttony; and when you hear them speak, you think of dogs barking. They are perverse, perfidious, disloyal, corrupt, voluptuous, expert in every violence, cruel and quarrelsome, and every one of them would murder a Frenchman for a single sou. Shamefully they have sex with animals." When you're playing away on a cold November evening, you don't want 20,000 of this lot breathing down your neck, willing you to make a mistake. This is what Beckham and co. can expect tomorrow night. The thought cheers me up a bit.

I walk along busy four-lane streets to the large chain-run hotel where Real's bus is due to arrive at 8.05. I get there at about ten to. Here the fans aren't perfidious cut-throats, out for blood. There are about 500 teenagers waiting, predominantly girls. They are out for autographs, and to catch a glimpse of their heroes. At first I wait with them, then self-consciousness (what's that middle-aged bloke doing there?) drives me round the other side of the crash barriers. My press card helps me through.

It looks like the girls have been there some time. Some are getting hysterical. One is holding a life-size poster of a shirtless Beckham. Another has a poster of Iker Casillas. Occasionally they burst into high-pitched versions of the stadium songs.

"Campeones, campeones, oé, oé, oé!"

There are several false alarms as cars arrive through the cordon, their occupants scrutinised, then ignored when they prove not to be young, talented, good-looking football players. Occasionally TV reporters wander over with their cameras, shining a spotlight on a section of girls, who behave exactly as required, screaming and waving their Real Madrid scarves and posters.

This is Florentino Pérez' evangelisation process in full working order. Five hundred more Real Madrid fans to buy shirts and scarves, alarm clocks and pillow cases. One of the girls, about 15, has tears running down her cheeks and is baring her teeth with the emotion of it all. A car arrives and there are screams as its driver gets out. A short, 50-something nondescript man wearing glasses, and a grumpy-looking woman. It's Pérez! He walks three yards in front of me, and I shoot him with my digital camera; it could just as easily have been a gun. Anyway, if it had been I'd only have winged him – the picture which reveals itself is of his elbow.

When the coach arrives the screams reach fever pitch. The coach I know so well, as it rolls from stadium to stadium, a slick dark blue machine full of Zidanes and Pavones. And the screaming starts in earnest. You know who the highest pitch is reserved for. Beckham-mania is catching on.

Half an hour later I'm upstairs in a conference room, waiting for Carlos Queiroz to give us his pre-match press conference. I move one of the net curtains to peek out at the entrance to the hotel outside. There are still a hundred or so die-hards outside. There is great excitement at the appearance of a face. I could be a player! I close the curtain, then open it again. They're pointing up at me! I realise how sad I'm being, and go back to my seat.

Queiroz comes in and earnestly answers the earnest questions that are put to him. Spanish football could do with a big injection of Jimmy Greaves-style humour. The Portuguese 'Mister' is a bright man, miles from the bluff English and Scottish managers, a man who likes to speak in metaphor.

"What do you think of the hostile atmosphere your players are bound to receive? The ground is small and the pitch is bad," asks a haughty-looking woman.

"The pitch cannot score goals," says Queiroz. He doesn't smile, he rarely does. There's definitely something of the Bela Lugosi about him. Or is it Boris Karloff? Maybe he has his wife in stitches back home.

I've got a question. I am determined to ask one in a press conference before the season is out. I've written it down on my pad. "What does it feel like to have an official of the British Empire in your team?" It's exciting when you have a question ready in a press conference. Every time the manager stops talking you're ready to say it, your heart's pumping, you raise your shoulders and . . . someone else asks another serious question about the state of Roberto Carlos' foot, Figo's ankle or Zinedine Zidane's calf muscle. Then, when it's your turn, the fat guy next to the manager asks 'is that all?' and unless your question is brilliant, pertinent and thought-provoking, you're going to look like a right idiot. Every time I look down at it, my question looks less brilliant, less pertinent and less thought-provoking. It's not even funny. Next time.

## SUNDAY NOVEMBER 23RD

On the morning of the match I get out of my grubby pension as soon as I can and shelter from the drizzle in the nearest presentable bar, with a coffee and the local papers. There is reams of stuff about the match – much of it talking about the morbo between the teams.

I learn that referee Socorro González once claimed that an Osasuna-Real Madrid game he had just refereed was 'worse than Vietnam'. Osasuna's former striker Jan Urban remembers so many objects being thrown at Madrid midfielder Míchel when he was trying to take a corner one time that the referee asked him to switch sides. And, worst of all, in the game which succeeded the shocking death of Real Madrid legend Juanito in a traffic accident in 1992, the Osasuna fans sneaked a pig into the ground and released it onto the pitch at half time. The pig was wearing a Real Madrid number '7' shirt, Juanito's old number.

Part of today's morbo lies with Osasuna's young right midfielder, Valdo. Valdo has said that if he scores, he 'will celebrate, out of consideration to the Osasuna fans'. The young player is another Real Madrid reject, a canterano who grew up with the Pavones and opted to move to get to play first-team football. He is one of the reasons that Osasuna, who have never won a trophy in their history, a team which has spent more time in the Segunda than the Primera, is currently in fourth position in the table, and this year's 'equipo revelacion' (surprise package). Osasuna, managed by a former Mexican national coach, the smiley Javier Aguirre, base their game on pressurising the opposition into making mistakes and then breaking fast. Some are branding it antifútbol. It is a destructive game-plan, the antithesis of Real Madrid's careful possession game.

Osasuna (whose strange name means 'health' in Basque, and is what you say when you raise your glass) usually give Real Madrid a good game in El Sadar. Of the 25 games Real have played here, they have lost nine and won eight. This is seen as being a poor record. *Gara,* the Basque country's pro-separatist newspaper, remembers Osasuna's past successes. They have beaten all the great Real Madrid sides – that of Di Stéfano and Gento, that of Camacho, Juanito and Santillana, that of 'La Quinta del Buitre' (Buitragueño, Míchel, etc.) and that of Ronaldo and Raúl. They have beaten the country's premier team in the last two seasons. The drum-beating is intense. They only problem is that people seem to be expecting a shock result. And if you expect an upset, you are likely to get upset yourself if it doesn't happen.

Walking towards town I come across a procession of giants. A ten-foot Moorish warrior is dancing around, swinging from side to side, to the shrill sound of a number of one-handed 'txistu' flutes. The Moor has human legs, a framed body covered by an elaborate costume, and a papier-maché head, with turban. I walk close to take a picture; he looms over me. Scary. Ahead of him are five other giants – I overtake them one by one. At the front is a king, and in front of him human-sized figures with big papier-maché heads and three-cornered hats, who are running around hitting little children with sponges in nets attached to sticks with a bit of string. They are hitting kids as young as three or four, quite hard. It must be quite a scary and intimidating experience. I ask an old man what the occasion is.

"San Saturnino."

"Sorry?"

"San Saturnino. The patron saint of Pamplona. It is San Saturnino's day today."

San Saturnino and Real Madrid all in the same day. Another reason for fireworks.

Osasuna's El Sadar stadium is a half-hour walk out of town. Whenever I arrive at a new stadium I take a walk around it to size up the territory. This one is so far into the outskirts of the city that one side of it looks onto a ploughed field. There are scores of people waiting on the road between the field and the stadium – the players' entrance, where the team bus comes in. I've had enough of buses. I wander around to the front of the stadium. There is a bar built into the wall of the stadium – it's already full of standing customers. They have the music on very loud – the aim is for people to sing and dance rather than to talk. It's working.

The music is a cross between Basque folk music and football terrace chants. There's a group of ten or so friends dominating the bar, mostly wearing the red Osasuna shirt, holding up their scarves and singing along. They're in their twenties. One of them is doing a local dance with intricate footsteps, holding his arms up above his head. They are all having a great time. The barmen are busy pouring pints of whisky and coke. Everyone seems to be slightly drunk. Occasionally they burst into song.

"Sí, sí, sí, sí. Hijo de puta, Madrid!" (with the 'd' of Madrid silent, as is the custom in these parts).

A drunk guy with a beard comes up to me.

"Cinco cero," he says to me (five nil). He repeats it several times in case I haven't got it.

"Cuatro cero solo," I reply (only four nil).

"CINCO zero," he insists. Someone hands him a beer he really doesn't need.

There is a rumpus outside. I rush to the door. A group of about 150 young fans are carrying square banners, some red, some black, and singing. It's the same song.

"Sí, sí, sí, sí. Hijo de puta, Madrid!"

I leave the bar and follow them. One of them has an Irish flag around his shoulders, another has wrapped the Basque separatist flag around his hips. They must have marched in together from town.

"Pacharán, pacharán, pacharán," sings the leader (to the tune of 'Here we go') and they all stop at a stall by the stadium wall, lowering their flags and jostling for the attention of the one guy serving. A sign says '1.80 Euros, Pacharán'. It's the local speciality drink, a sweet red aniseed liqueur which packs a punch and leaves you with an almighty hangover. I know this from bitter-sweet experience.

I walk into the stadium, past a bouncer in a red beret with an infra-red gun who lets me through the turnstile when I show him my pass. And up some stairs to the press section of the ground. There are a number of little boxes with glass fronts . . . mine is near the end of the stand, with a good view of the singing end of the stadium to my right, where the red and black flags flutter.

"Shall we open the window, get a bit of atmosphere?" says the man to my left, about 55, mid-length black hair, posh English accent. Then he offers his hand.

"James from the *Financial Times*."

"I'm Alex," I say. I hate all that identifying with your company stuff. We get chatting.

"I'm the guy who wrote the *Barça* book."

"Jimmy Burns?"

"Jimmy Burns."

"I read your book. Enjoyed it."

I offer my hand again. I'm not lying; it's a great book. I open the window. The noise level goes up. The atmosphere infects this little corner of England (the Spanish correspondent of *The Times* is in the same cubicle). And it's quite an English atmosphere in the stadium, too – there's only room for 19,000 in El Sadar and, apart from a few 120 euro seats, it's full-to-brimming, with the steep-sided terraces coming right down to the touch-line. As we are perched high in the main stand which dwarfs the other three, we enjoy a view of the whole pitch, the whole stadium, and the bright lights of the city behind it.

When Real Madrid run on and when, a few minutes later, they first get possession of the ball, the shrill whistling from just about everyone in the ground is deafening. But they rarely keep it for long in the opening stages of the game. Osasuna's 'pressing' tactics are extremely effective, and when they win the ball they get it to their attack quickly and directly. Real's slow passing game doesn't seem suited to the conditions. Much has been made of the terrible state of the pitch, and there are some patches where the turf is a different colour, and others where the green grass is turning to brown mud.

On ten minutes the ball comes to Bakayoko on the edge of the box. The former Everton striker traps the ball with his right boot, and dips his shoulder, fooling Helguera who goes flying past him. Then with his left he thumps the ball into the net. It's a fantastic goal. I make rather too much noise for a neutral in the press box. The whole place goes mental. I get thumped in the face with a scarf someone is waving about in front of me. And then (one of the benefits of being in the press box) I get to watch the goal again and again in slow-motion action replay on the little TV above my head.

Osasuna aren't finished. They continue to rob Real Madrid and pour their attackers forward. They should have a penalty, but Aloisi goes down too late. A brilliant pass to the Australian striker from Bakayoko is hit straight at the keeper. Both men, who found it hard to make an impact in the English Premiership, are tearing Real's defence apart. Real can hardly get the ball: Beckham is running around a lot, though not to much effect. Osasuna just can't get the second goal you feel they will need to win this game. Bakayoko finds space down the wing but passes the ball behind Aloisi, who is free on the right. Then the African striker does a spectacular back-heel to the Australian, who fires the ball straight at the keeper.

"Whoever isn't jumping up and down is a Madridista!" shout the crowd. Nearly everybody in the stands is bouncing. I feel like getting up myself.

Real Madrid get a corner early in the second half. Beckham slowly walks down to take it. The fans in the area are up on their feet, gesturing, whistling and throwing screwed up balls made from the silver foil that their half-time sandwiches were in. Beckham, as if to show that he's not being put off by them, stands for ages in his bullfighter pose, looking at where he's going to put the ball. It's a show of bravado. It's provoca-tive. A silver ball hits him on the shoulder. He releases his pose, turns round and starts remonstrating with one of the recogepelotas (ball boys), pointing to the bit of his shoulder that was hit. Then, with an accusing finger, at the boy.

"Puto Beykan oé, oé, oé!" sing the fans in front of me. The guy in front who hit me with his scarf earlier is jumping up and down, waving the thing dangerously near my nose. I understand now why they have the windows in the press box. Another one is doing a cuckold sign, making two horns out of his index fingers, suggesting that David is not the only Beckham playing away tonight.

Real Madrid are playing terribly, but Osasuna are running out of gas. They bring on a couple of subs to try to keep up the tempo, seeing that Real are not up for this game, that they've got no fight in them, that they are there for the taking. Only Beckham is showing guts in the middle of the field, doubling his efforts, spurred on by the crowd that whistles his every touch of the ball. Guti, his partner in midfield, might as well not be there.

Half an hour into the second half, Beckham gets the ball inside the Osasuna half, takes his time, and passes a long ball straight into the path of the sprinting Ronaldo. The Brazilian lets it run, bides his time, and kicks the ball on the run past the keeper. 1–1. My heart sinks.

The fans to my right start waving their red and black flags again.

"OS-A-SU-NA" they shout. But the team has run itself into the ground. The game peters out. So does Beckham, who holds his hand up to the bench, and limps off, to a huge 'pitada' (abusive whistles). The corner incident has infuriated the crowd. He sits on the bench, puts an ice pack to his leg. Does this put him in danger of missing Real's next two games, against Atlético de Madrid and Barcelona?

Osasuna get a free-kick outside the box in injury time. The mop-haired midfielder Pablo Garcia curls it round the wall, but well past the post. Casillas doesn't bother diving. The referee blows the final whistle. It's all over. I head for the mixed zone.

I decide to tail Beckham, to see if I can get a feel of what it's like to be in his shoes. So when he comes out of the changing room, instead of standing in front of him with the rest of the pressmen, I stand right behind him. It's an odd feeling. There are scores of journalists vying for his attention, pushing microphones and dictaphones in his direction; a couple of TV cameras, too. "David, David . . ."

"Becks, just a word . . ."

"David, that pass you . . ."

It's chaos. He bides his time, stops for the English journalists, says his piece, a calm figure in the mayhem. I take a photo of the back of his head with the pressmen in front. Then, when he's satisfied their requests, he turns to leave. I follow him, one pace behind. He walks out into the cold night where hundreds of fans, standing behind crash barriers, are waiting for a glimpse of their heroes. As soon as his recognisable figure comes into sight there is a scream from both sides. "Beykan, Beykan," they shout. We've exited the door almost simultaneously, I'm lapping up the vicarious kicks. Beckham walks quickly into the waiting coach. A security guard stops me from following him right up to the vehicle, ushers me back inside the mixed zone. It's time to go home; I've got my own bus to catch, a night bus to Barcelona.

## RESULTS: JORNADA 12

| | | | |
|---|---|---|---|
| BETIS | 0 | DEPORTIVO | 0 |
| REAL SOCIEDAD | 0 | MALLORCA | 1 |
| VILLARREAL | 2 | BARCELONA | 1 |
| VALLADOLID | 3 | ATLÉTICO | 1 |
| MÁLAGA | 0 | OSASUNA | 0 |
| CELTA | 0 | ATHLETIC | 2 |
| ESPANYOL | 1 | SEVILLA | 0 |
| RACING | 1 | ZARAGOZA | 2 |
| **REAL MADRID** | **2** | **ALBACETE** | **1** |
| MURCIA | 2 | VALENCIA | 2 |

## RESULTS: JORNADA 13

| | | | |
|---|---|---|---|
| ALBACETE | 2 | ESPANYOL | 1 |
| **OSASUNA** | **1** | **REAL MADRID** | **1** |
| ATLÉTICO | 2 | MÁLAGA | 0 |
| BARCELONA | 0 | VALLADOLID | 0 |
| DEPORTIVO | 0 | VILLARREAL | 1 |
| MALLORCA | 2 | BETIS | 1 |
| MURCIA | 2 | REAL SOCIEDAD | 2 |
| ATHLETIC | 1 | RACING | 2 |
| SEVILLA | 0 | CELTA | 1 |
| VALENCIA | 3 | ZARAGOZA | 2 |

## LA CLASIFICACIÓN

| | P | W | D | L | F | A | Pts |
|---|---|---|---|---|---|---|---|
| VALENCIA | 13 | 8 | 3 | 2 | 27 | 11 | 27 |
| **REAL MADRID** | **13** | **8** | **3** | **2** | **27** | **15** | **27** |
| DEPORTIVO | 13 | 8 | 2 | 3 | 20 | 10 | 26 |
| ATLÉTICO | 13 | 7 | 1 | 5 | 16 | 10 | 22 |
| BARCELONA | 13 | 5 | 5 | 3 | 17 | 13 | 20 |
| OSASUNA | 13 | 5 | 5 | 3 | 14 | 9 | 20 |
| RACING | 13 | 6 | 2 | 5 | 18 | 15 | 20 |
| ATHLETIC | 13 | 6 | 2 | 5 | 16 | 14 | 20 |
| VILLARREAL | 13 | 5 | 5 | 3 | 14 | 13 | 20 |
| VALLADOLID | 13 | 5 | 4 | 4 | 18 | 20 | 19 |
| MÁLAGA | 13 | 5 | 2 | 6 | 13 | 16 | 17 |
| MALLORCA | 13 | 5 | 2 | 6 | 16 | 22 | 17 |
| SEVILLA | 13 | 3 | 6 | 4 | 16 | 16 | 15 |
| ZARAGOZA | 13 | 4 | 3 | 6 | 13 | 15 | 15 |
| CELTA | 13 | 3 | 5 | 5 | 15 | 17 | 14 |
| BETIS | 13 | 3 | 5 | 5 | 15 | 17 | 14 |
| REAL SOCIEDAD | 13 | 3 | 5 | 5 | 15 | 19 | 14 |
| ALBACETE | 13 | 4 | 0 | 9 | 13 | 19 | 12 |
| MURCIA | 13 | 1 | 6 | 6 | 12 | 24 | 9 |
| ESPANYOL | 13 | 2 | 2 | 9 | 10 | 25 | 8 |

# NINE
# BARCELONA

GOLFO DE VIZCAYA

OCÉANO ATLÁNTICO

Barcelona

Real Madrid

MAR MEDITERRÁNEO

# NINE
# BARCELONA

## SUNDAY NOVEMBER 30TH

I'm woken by the bus driver at 6.30 am telling us that we have arrived in Barcelona. We are approaching Sants station. "There has been a spate of bag robberies, so be careful," he says. The bus virtually empties, but I stay on. Everything's still blurry. I've managed to sleep most of the six hours from Pamplona to Barcelona by wearing my puffa jacket back to front so the hood comes over my face, obliterating three of my senses in a stroke.

I'm getting off at the next stop, Estació del Norte, but my bag is in the hold, so I stand by the window to check that no-one steals it. There is a mob of people outside. I see a squat dark-haired woman with what could be my bag. She sets off towards the train station, round the back of the bus, and I look out of the opposite window, and study her shrinking figure. It does look like . . . It IS my bag! I run to the door of the bus; it's locked. I see the driver outside, and bang on the window. BANG BANG BANG! "Déjeme salir!" Let me out!

He comes round and unlocks the door. It seems to take an age. A fat guy who looks like he's just woken up himself. I shout to him that my bag's been stolen and I run to where I last saw the woman. No sign. I run into the train station: one of the biggest in Europe. Already buzzing with people. But no sign of her. She could have gone any of ten different directions. I haven't got a hope. I walk back to the bus, trying to remember what was in the bag, a miserable inverse version of *The Generation Game*. My favourite top. My glasses. My *Marca Guide*. The bottle of pacharán. Those posters I bought of the San Fermín celebrations. The cuddly fucking toy.

"Somebody loses their bag nearly every day. I don't know what to do. I warned you. Didn't I warn you?"

"You didn't warn me," I mutter, "that you were going to lock me in the fucking bus."

Be warned. Barcelona is a full of bag thieves. When walking in public places keep your hand on your wallet. And never leave your bag in the hold of a bus if you can possibly get it inside. The number of visitors to the city I've met who've been robbed is unbelievable. But I live here. I feel such a mug. I'm home.

I'm not the only Englishman in town this week. Real Madrid and David Beckham are coming this Saturday. It's derby week, which means that nobody is talking about anything else. They call the Barcelona-Real Madrid derby 'El Clásico' and it's reputed to be the hardest show in the world to get a ticket for. I haven't got one.

El Clásico is much more than just a football game. The whole of the country talks about the match all week: even football-haters take sides. It would be easy to say that conservatives who believe in a unified Spain governed from Madrid support Real Madrid, whereas liberals who want more power in the provincial capitals side with Barcelona. But that would be an over-generalisation. Many Spanish kids choose between Real Madrid and Barcelona well before they are old enough to be politically aware. Many Spaniards support their local club and either Real or Barça. They might choose because they like a particular player, because they like the kit or because of family connections.

For Catalans, with few exceptions, there is no such choice. Barcelona's slogan is 'Més que un club' (Catalan for 'more than just a club'). For more than a hundred years, since its foundation, Barcelona FC has been inter-twined with the cause of Catalan national identity, a card which the current club president Joan Laporta has been playing as trump throughout his first season in charge.

It's a strong identity. Catalans have as much in common historically and culturally with France as with Spain. The Catalan language is a first cousin of Provençal, which used to be the main language in France south of the Loire. 'Please' in Catalan is 'Si's plau' – it's 'por favor' in Spanish. 'Thank you' is 'merci'. Despite Franco's attempt to kill the Catalan language in the '40s, '50s and '60s it is now more widely spoken in the region than Castilian Spanish, even amongst the children and grandchildren of Spanish migrants he introduced into the region.

The Catalans are very different in personality from the stereotype we have developed of the brash, outgoing Spaniards. They are generally a serious, hard-working lot, renowned for their carefulness with money. They tend to be hard to please and hard to get to know. When you live in the region it is often exasperating how rude people are to you in shops and in the streets (though Catalans maintain that if you do make friends with them, they will stay your friend for life). The national dance, the sardana, sees people stand in circles, holding hands, performing intricate foot movements to music from the tenora, a shrill, oboe-like instrument. Concentration is the key – it's a far cry from the exuberance of flamenco. Catalans don't like bullfighting, either. The Barcelona city council has declared itself 'antitaurina' (anti-bull-culture). One bullring in Barcelona has closed down, the other is largely for the tourist market.

Catalans prefer to celebrate their feast-days by making human towers, up to ten storeys high. These 'castells' require the admired qualities of reliability and team-work rather than the flair and individualism so appreciated by many other Spaniards (in bullfighting, for example, and flamenco). I was briefly a member of a castellers society last year. As I weighed nearly 16 stone, they put me at the bottom, rather than the top (a place reserved for the star of the show, a 6–7 year-old child). It was always a sweaty, uncomfortable and back-straining experience. A frightening experience, too, because if your legs are the ones that buckle, you might be responsible for the collapse of the tower, and injury to the people who fall off. But, as you might imagine, it's good for camaraderie.

The Museum of National History of Catalonia on the old harbour quay in La Barceloneta explains in some detail why the Catalans are so proud to be Catalan. I've been there several times, to try and understand this inscrutable race. The Moors invaded as far as what is now Catalonia, but were pushed back south of the Río Ebro, and the loosely-linked group of counties in the area (administered from Barcelona) became a buffer zone on the border between the Moorish and Christian world, establishing a feudal system which gave the peasants certain rights. There is hence much less Moorish influence in the architecture or language of Catalonia than in the rest of Spain, much of which was divided into caliphates (small kingdoms) for around 500 years, and called Al-Andalus. In the tenth century, the Latin term 'Catalonia' started being used for the area.

The most powerful Count of Barcelona, Ramon Bereguer, married the Aragonese princess Petronella in 1137, allying Catalonia to the existing kingdom of Aragón. Although the new kingdom was generally known as 'Aragón' its capital was in Barcelona. Their great-grandson Jaume was an expansionist, taking control of Mallorca, Ibiza and Valencia from the Moors. These places all still speak a form of Catalan as a result of this. With Moorish influence on the wane, Barcelona became the centre of a Mediterranean empire that stretched as far as Athens and included much of southern Italy in its domain; in the 13th and 14th centuries Catalonia/Aragón was the most dominant power in the whole of the western Mediterranean.

In 1469 Ferdinand of Aragón and Isabela of Castilia married, uniting the two kingdoms, bringing most of the Iberian peninsula together in a single alliance. Barcelona retained its own parliament and laws, but lost political clout as Ferdinand assigned a more prominent role in the government of the new country to Castile.

Twenty-three years later Colombus 'discovered' America. He caught up with Ferdinand and Isabela to tell them the news in Barcelona, but ironically he was ringing the death knell for the port city. The Mediterranean became something of a backwater as the Atlantic became the most lucrative trade route. Spain started colonising what is now Latin America, plundering its riches.

By the time Ferdinand and Isabela's great grandson, Felipe, moved the Spanish court to Madrid, what is now called 'Spain' (a collective word for the two kingdoms and the lands they conquered, derived from the Latin 'Hispania') was the most powerful and richest nation in the world. Madrid's power grew as Barcelona's waned, the latter becoming little more than a provincial port, increasingly governed from the capital.

There were two significant attempts by the Catalans to force independence, the Reapers War in 1640, and the War of the Spanish Succession, ending with the siege of the city in 1714. Neither of them were successful. The region regained some prestige and wealth in the second half of the 19th century, when Barcelona became the industrial capital of the country, largely producing textiles, and was dubbed 'the Manchester of Spain'. The Catalan language had largely fallen out of use in the city by then, but the fast-growing bourgeoisie which developed subsequent to industrialisation started a movement, called Catalanismo, which saw the return to (and sometimes the invention of) traditional Catalan values and cultural movements. Barcelona burst out of its city walls in this period – this is when most of its 'modernist' architecture designed by the likes of Antoni Gaudi was built. It was in the heyday of this period that Barcelona FC was formed. The city also had became the centre of the new labour movement, as workers struggled for rights. These workers formed the bulk of the city's new football club's increasing support base.

In 1931, when the short dictatorship of Primo de Rivera fell, and alongside it the monarchy, Catalonia was finally declared to be an independent republic. Barcelona became the capital of the new state, governed by left-wing idealists. This wasn't to last for long. In 1936 Francisco Franco, a Fascist general who believed strongly in a united Spain ruled from Madrid, started an uprising against the new government and Spain was ideologically split, taking sides in what became the Spanish Civil War (just referred to as 'La Guerra' – the war – in Spain). It was a bloody, vicious war. Mass graves are still being dug up. Many Spaniards still go strangely silent if you bring up the subject.

By 1939 Franco had won the war – and Barcelona was made to pay for its opposition to him. Retribution was vicious with anybody connected with the republic either executed, imprisoned or forced to flee. Through the Guardia Civil, a military police force, Franco enforced political orthodoxy and subjugated the Catalan people with brutal efficiency, encouraging neighbours to 'denounce' one another for anti-establishment sentiments and executing and imprisoning thousands.

Understanding that his authority was weakest in Catalonia and the Basque country, Franco attempted to destroy regional culture and language in these regions. It was forbidden to speak Catalan in public – espousing Catalan nationalism was an imprisonable offence. This brutal reign of terror lasted until his death in 1975.

There was one place, however, where people could sing and shout in Catalan. Barcelona FC's stadium in Les Corts became the only place where locals could express their nationalism and opposition to the regime. The stadium was the only place large numbers could gather, and offered individuals anonymity. The police couldn't arrest 60,000 people at a time.

Once a year this nationalism was even more keenly felt than normal. Real Madrid have, since before the times of Franco, been considered to be the team of the establishment. Franco, based in Madrid, used the club as a form of Spanish ambassador at a time when his Fascist regime found it hard to win friends abroad. The capital's team, in the time that it was winning European Cup after European Cup, was one of the few Spanish exports that was allowed through the borders. Many maintain that referees used to openly favour the team from the capital in their decisions. It was important for them to win La Liga so they could qualify for the European Cup (if they ever failed to win the tournament and get automatic qualification). So, the argument goes, referees used to routinely rule against Barcelona, even when they were playing other teams than El Real. Many maintain that they still do . . .

**TUESDAY DECEMBER 2ND**

I'm in Les Corts, the name of the district in which the Nou Camp is situated. The stadium is part of a massive complex which dominates the area – little of the old part of what used to be a small village outside the city limits of Barcelona remains.

But I'm half a mile away from the Nou Camp. I'm looking, as a matter of fact, for the Old Camp.

"Could you direct me to where the old stadium used to be?" I ask a man in his sixties. His age is relevant, the stadium was pulled down in 1957.

He smiles. I've scored a bullseye first throw.

"Why, there," he says, pointing over a main road to an eleven-story block of flats. "All those flats there, and the ones behind. That whole area: that's where Barça used to play."

He looks ruefully at the block of flats, perhaps seeing it in a different light again. Perhaps remembering the roar of the crowd, the thrill of the theatre.

"Yes, that's where Barça used to play."

Barça played in the Les Corts stadium from 1922 to 1957 in the period when football really caught the imagination of the Spanish people, an urban sport in a country whose cities were quickly growing in size. This was also in the period before and after the Civil War (the championship was suspended during the hostilities). Barcelona played Real Madrid in the stadium during the period of Franco's most brutal oppression (After the '60s his 'dictadura' (dictatorship) became less oppressive, being toned down to a 'dictablanda'. This is a Spanish play on words: 'dura' means hard, 'blanda' means soft.)

I walk around what used to be the pitch area. Behind the flats there is a little park which people are using for their dogs to shit in. It's sad. St Mirren were the first team to play Barça in the stadium, losing 1–0 to the Blaugrana team, before the inauguration proper in which 26,000 fans watched the Scots beat Notts County 2–1 to lift the Lansome Cup. The paucity of the opposition shows how high up the international football hierarchy Barcelona FC were at the time but the stadium became the setting for some of the most famous matches in the history of Spanish football. Its initial capacity was 26,500; eventually this was increased to 60,000.

There are several 'clásicos' against Real Madrid which stand out. Like the game in 1935, during the second Republic, which Barcelona won 5–0, with a 'poker' (four goals) from Martí Valtolra. Like the 1943 clash, which finished 5–5, the most goals ever scored in a league game between the two teams, and still cited as one of the best games ever seen in Spain. Like the 5–0 two years later, when former Barça hero Josep Samitier was manager and Barça went on to win the league. And, best of all, like the 7–2 thrashing Barcelona dealt to their arch rivals in 1950. 7–2 against Franco's Madrid! Imagine that.

Walking through the park, being careful where I tread, I see a sign with a football on it, with a line through it. Then I see that it is not entirely a sports-free zone. In the area I estimate would originally have been one of the penalty boxes, there is a concrete five-a-side football pitch. And there are a few men kicking a ball about, obviously about to start a game. I wander over, stand by the fence, and wait till someone has to retrieve a ball.

"Can I play?"

I feel silly doing this, six months shy of 40. But this is ground once graced by Josep Samitier, by Ladislao Kubala, by Alfredo Di Stéfano, by Ferenc Puskas. This is hallowed concrete. I haven't even got the right clothes, and my shoes are way unsuitable. But I'm desperate to follow those illustrious bootsteps.

"Go on then, as long as you go in goal."

I call to mind the great Ricardo Zamora, Barcelona's keeper in the '20s, who used to wear a black flat cap and a white polo-neck jumper. He would have made countless saves in this very area. Zamora, the legend goes, used to intimidate the opposition into petrification in front of goal: his name is still used for the award given to the Primera keeper who lets in the fewest goals in the season. A cross comes in, which I go to the edge of my box to try and catch. I don't reach it, though, and the ball is headed over me and into the goal. Damn.

I do all right after that, and am even allowed to go out on pitch for ten minutes. As I play, I try to imagine the roar of the Catalan crowd around me, try to evoke ghosts from the past, try to soak up some of the spirituality, the power and the passion that this patch of land must still possess from the thousands of people who have screamed and shouted and cried here. I try to imagine myself as a Barça midfielder attempting to score a goal to send the crowd into raptures, cocking a collective snook at Franco's regime. I drop a shoulder, and find space for a shot. It drifts harmlessly wide. Never mind.

## WEDNESDAY DECEMBER 3RD

I'm in Las Parras, a tiny bar in La Barceloneta crammed with small old men with leathery faces. La Barceloneta is where the city's fishing port has been for 250 years – this is where the fishermen come to watch the football. Barça are about to play Málaga in La Liga. In Andalucía. It's a long way for the players to go three days before El Clásico against Madrid. I get chatting to a guy at the bar, who, hearing my foreign accent, asks me where I'm from.

"Inglés," I reply.

"Como el puto Beckham" he retorts (Like whorish Beckham). We get talking and the I bring up the subject of the Alfredo Di Stéfano affair, which I've been looking into.

Di Stéfano is another key to the morbo felt between Barcelona and Real Madrid. David Beckham isn't the first blond superstar to make a big impact on Spanish football. Exactly 50 years before the Englishman's arrival at Real Madrid an Argentinian player they called 'La Saeta Rubia' (the blond arrow) arrived in the country, and helped turn Real Madrid from a struggling mid-table outfit which hadn't won the league for 20 years into the best club team the world has ever seen. What rankles in Catalonia is that he should have been playing for Barça.

Alfredo Di Stéfano, who is still on the Real Madrid board 50 years after joining the club, was very, very nearly a Barcelona FC player – he even turned out for them in a friendly against Bologna of Italy. That he didn't sign for the Catalan team, it is often claimed, is down entirely to Franco wanting him to play for Real Madrid. And if Franco hadn't intervened in the player's transfer, the argument continues, Real Madrid would not be the club they are now, and Barcelona would be the world's number one football team.

In 1948 Di Stéfano left his Argentine club River Plate (with whom he'd made his name) to join high-paying Millonarios of Colombia at a time when football in that country was booming. Millonarios became known as 'the Ballet in Blue' for their elegant football, winning four titles in five years; Di Stéfano established his reputation as a phenomenal footballer, a complete player who roamed the whole pitch to defend, to set up attacks, and to score spectacular goals. When Millonarios played a friendly in Madrid in 1952, Barcelona's chief scout Josep Samitier (Barcelona's most famous player until then, a glamorous pin up, possibly the best footballer to have until then played in Spain) was impressed with Di Stéfano's performance. As was Madrid president Santiago Bernabéu. A race to sign him ensued.

Bernabéu, who had fought for Franco on the Catalan front, had just invested a fortune in buying Real Madrid a new stadium (which, of course, currently bears his name). However, the team he had playing in it was second rate (they had just avoided relegation) and needed some new blood – a foreigner to inspire the other players, like the Hungarian Kubala was doing at Barcelona.

Barcelona, however, were quicker off the mark, sending a team of lawyers and money-men out to South America to negotiate a deal. There were complications: negotiations needed to be made with both River Plate (who still had the player on their books) *and* Millonarios, and the Catalans were unwilling to agree to the Colombians' demands. They had every chance, it seems, to close the deal but haggled too much, allowing Real Madrid time to send in their own negotiators to try to gazump the signing.

This is when the Spanish Football Association (like all official bodies at the time, a branch of Franco's government) acted, passing a law banning the acquisition of foreign players. They relented in the case of Di Stéfano . . . as long as he signed for both clubs. A complicated arrangement was made whereby it was agreed that Di Stéfano would play for Real Madrid in 1953/4 and 1955/6, and for Barcelona in 1954/5 and 1956/7.

Barcelona fans, who had been following the affair in the papers all summer, were outraged at such an outcome to what had seemed a foregone conclusion, and the Barcelona president, Martí Carrera, soon resigned over the matter. The regime that replaced him decided to sell Barcelona's share in the Argentinian for a handful of million pesetas, and Di Stéfano became a Real Madrid player. The rest is football history. El Real won the league in his first season, and an amazing five European Cups that decade. Ever since his signing el Madrid (and they *are* often referred to simply as 'el Madrid') have been the dominant side in Spanish and European football, something which rankles in Catalan hearts.

"He should have been ours," says the man in the bar to me. "And what then?"

The whole affair was brought to mind in the summer of 2003 when Beckham was available on the transfer market, having fallen out with Alex Ferguson at Manchester United. At the time little-known 40-year-old lawyer Joan Laporta was lying sixth in the opinion polls in the election race for the presidency of FC Barcelona, up for grabs after the resignation of Joan Gaspart.

Barcelona's directors are voted for by the socios (club members); Barcelona had over 90,000 at the time. For 22 years, between 1978 and 2000, one man was the president of Barcelona, Josep Lluis Núñez. They were successful years – Barça won seven championships in that time, and, importantly, the European Cup in 1992. But Núñez was seen by some as having become too powerful at the club, which he was starting to run, according to his detractors, like a personal fiefdom.

Laporta, a young lawyer of 34 at the time, was one of the mainstays of the Elefant Blau (Blue Elephant) fans' group, which was formed to represent Barcelona fans' interests and which, with the support of Johan Cruyff, proposed a vote of no confidence in Núñez in 1998. The veteran president survived the attack – Barcelona were then the champions, after all, and on their way to another championship.

However Núñez felt politically damaged and decided not to stand for the elections in 2000. Joan Gaspart, his right-hand-man throughout his presidency, ran in his place. Laporta put his group's weight behind Luis Bassat, Gaspart's main rival. Gaspart won fairly easily.

But Gaspart's 934-day reign was a complete disaster. Under his control the club lost direction, it lost important players, it lost money. Most importantly it lost games; lots of games. When Gaspart resigned on February 12th 2003, Barça were in unchartered territory. 150 million euros in debt, they were two points away from relegation. Another disciple of Núñismo, Eric Reyna, took over till the end of the season and managed, with the help of new trainer Raddy Antic, to steer Barça to a UEFA Cup place.

And so to the summer and the 2003 election. Lluis Bassat was the front-runner, a publicist who had lost against Gaspart in 2000, and had won 19,000 votes. Other names in the hat were Jaume Llaurado, Josep Martínez-Rovira, Jordi Majo and Josep María Minguella. In sixth place at the bookies was Joan Laporta, the handsome young lawyer. In 2000 Núñez had called the Elefant Blau 'a bunch of terrorists': Laporta was seen as being a little too much of a loose cannon to be a serious candidate.

Until his masterstroke, that is. "I'll buy Beckham if you vote for me," he announced suddenly and brilliantly, although he had had no contact with the player. Beckham's selling power soon became apparent. Immediately Laporta shot up to second in the opinion polls, and people started listening to what he really had to say. The young lawyer stood for a clean sweep of the Nou Camp, for youth, for energy, and for an emphasis on Catalan nationalism. He made overtures to Manchester United, who agreed to sell Beckham to Barcelona. But Beckham didn't want to play in Catalonia. On voting day Laporta won a landslide victory over Bassat. The very next day Beckham signed for Real Madrid.

"I never said I'd definitely buy him, just that I'd try to," said Laporta, in his victory press conference and, remarkably, no-one seemed to mind that much.

The affair hardly made Beckham popular in Barcelona, and in the run-up to the match the Barcelona popular football press have been attempting to stoke up their readers' sentiments against the Englishman. Barcelona's equivalents of *Marca* and *As* are *El Mundo Deportivo* and *Sport*, both of which let the reader know in intimate detail the goings-on at the club, both of which are sold throughout Spain. As far back as October there was a story in *El Mundo Deportivo* trying to create a bit of 'morbo' around a supposed slight of Barça (and by association Barcelona) by David Beckham. It accused Beckham of trying to antagonise the Barça fans with what it claimed to be an incendiary statement. His words? "I won't mind taking the corners at the Nou Camp."

Beckham was clearly not trying to be antagonistic, but he probably didn't realise just how touchy the subject of Real Madrid players taking corners in the Nou Camp is. Luis Figo used to be the Real corner taker. Figo, remember, who had broken the hearts of the Barcelona fans after committing the ultimate football betrayal a player can make, a direct move from the Nou Camp to the Bernabéu (or vice-versa). It was brave of him to try and fulfil his dead-ball responsibilities: the corner-taker is subject to enormous abuse from away fans, and is within a stone's throw of two separate stands. Not that it was stones that were being thrown. The Barcelona fans came to the stadium prepared. Every time Figo stepped up to take a corner he was pelted with a variety of objects, including a mobile phone, a J&B whisky bottle and, bizarrely enough, a suckling pig's head. The game had to be temporarily abandoned because he couldn't take a corner, for fear of his life. The match finished 0–0 and as a punishment for their fans' misbehaviour, Barcelona were eventually ordered to play two of their home games in a stadium other than the Nou Camp. Since then Figo has relinquished corner-taking duty, handing it over to Beckham. And you do wonder . . . will the Englishman get the same sort of treatment from the Barcelona fans, having snubbed Barcelona in order to play for Madrid?

It's strange thinking about one match (El Clásico) while watching another (Málaga v Barcelona) and you can see that a similar process is going through the minds of the Barcelona team. They are playing very poorly. The old fishermen in the bar are not happy. The men smoke while they eat, they smoke while they drink, they smoke while they shout their comments at the television. Mini soliloquies, disgruntled in tone.

Barça this season have been a terrible disappointment, despite the regime change, and you can hear it in the voices and see it in the eyes of the grumpy old men. Grumpy and getting grumpier. Within eight minutes Málaga have scored . . . Salva shoots the ball straight through young Victor Valdés' ineffective attempt at a save. There's a silence in the bar, followed by more disgusted shouts. One guy, the spit of Harvey Keitel, remarks that he will shit on the milk of the referee's mother, then lights up yet another cigarette. Before he has finished it, an unmarked Salva has scored again, this time with his head. Again Valdés' energetic dive gets him nowhere near the ball.

"Donkey," shouts Harvey, and starts a monologue aimed at nobody in particular about how bad Barça are, how they should sack Rijkaard the manager, how they need 11 new players.

"Ten," says his mate. "Ronaldinho's OK."

"And Puyol. You wouldn't want to get rid of Puyol."

"OK, we need nine new players."

It's started badly, but it gets much worse for Barcelona, as the bar gets smokier and the old men get angrier. After half-time, Salva scores a third, and is substituted with Diego Alonso. Within 30 seconds of coming on, Alonso has got a fourth. I decide to leave, to catch the start of the next part of the double bill in another bar: Real are playing against Atlético de Madrid in the Bernabéu.

I cycle to a Madrid-friendly bar I know just behind the Barcelona town hall in the old part of town. It's run by an Andalucian fellow with short grey hair who unfailingly dresses all in black. Perhaps it's a disguise: he is an unashamed Real Madrid fan. And he's smiling when I make it to the bar. I've just missed kick off.

"Ronaldo," he says. "14 seconds."

"Sorry?"

"Gol! Gol de Ronaldo!"

And the little logo in the top left corner confirms it. The game is little more than two minutes old, and Real Madrid are already 1–0 up against their city rivals.

This bar is less crowded; people are quiet about their allegiance for Real Madrid during derby week in Barcelona. Atlético rally, and you can sense the nerves from the five or so single men sitting at separate tables, quietly watching their team play their second-most-hated rivals, without making too much noise about it. Then, about halfway through the half, Beckham gets the ball in his own half, sees a run from Raúl, launches a forty-yard pass directly onto his head. Raúl spots that Atleti's lumbering rock-star keeper 'El Mono' Burgos has come off his line, and, without breaking stride, heads the ball over him and into the net.

That's it, game over. Much of the pre-match hype has been about Beckham facing up once again with Diego Simeone, the Argentine who recently admitted to getting the England player sent off in the World Cup second round in France '98. But Simeone is playing in defence, and Beckham is playing deep in Madrid's midfield, so they rarely meet up on the pitch. Instead everyone is left talking about Ronaldo's brilliant goal – he ran through the Atleti defence straight from kick-off – and Beckham's brilliant pass.

"How do you like playing 'a lo inglés?' (English-style)" I ask the barman, halfway through the second half.

"A lo ingles?" he asks.

"The long ball game. Beckham's speciality."

"As long as they are accurate, I don't mind how long they are."

He tells me that Barça ended up losing 5–1; that their only goal was scored in his own net by former Real Madrid player Fernando Sanz. He says this with a smile on his face and a happy glint in his eye.

"What'll the score be on Sunday?"

"I have no doubt in my mind that Real will win. Which will make me a very happy man. It will mean that I will have a tranquil time for the next five months. If Barça win, I won't hear the end of it, God help me."

God help *me*. I still haven't got a ticket.

**FRIDAY DECEMBER 5TH**

I pop into a bar in the Eixample district of central Barcelona for a cup of coffee and a croissant having unsuccessfully tried to pay my electricity bill in the office of FECSA, the electricity company. I lock up my bike outside. It's about 11 am. There's a copy of *Sport* on the table. I flick through. Of course, it's full of stuff about the derby.

A paragraph takes my eye. 'Barcelona will put 400 tickets on sale to the general public for the Real Madrid game at 9am this morning. Purchasers must provide ID and can only buy two tickets each.'

Hmm. Four hundred tickets, two hours ago. I wonder if it's worth the bother. Then I decide to go for it. I pay my bill, jump on my bike, cycle through the park and past the marina to my flat, pick up my passport, realise I've left my bag in the bar, cycle back to the bar, pick up my bag, cycle to the metro station at the top of the Ramblas, get a train to María Cristina, and walk the ten minutes or so to the stadium. I ask a few questions, and find the right place, where they sell tickets to Barcelona's museum. There are four ticket windows open, about five people waiting in a line at each window. I join a line.

"Are they . . . um . . . selling tickets for the Real Madrid game?"

"It seems so."

"I can't believe it. Two days before the game!"

Within five minutes I'm at the window. I ask for two tickets, and am told they won't be next to one another. I don't care at all. I leave the tickets in the pages of my passport and ring Brenda, elated.

"I've got tickets for the game!"

"Which game?"

"El Clásico!"

"That's nice."

"I got one for you! For the derby. Barça-Real Madrid!"

"One for me? How much did you spend?"

"75 euros. I know it sounds a lot, but . . ."

"If you're spending that sort of money on me, you can buy me some shoes."

I now have an extra ticket for the Barça-Real Madrid game, and a forthcoming 75 euro shoe bill, to boot.


**SATURDAY DECEMBER 6TH**

It's the morning of the game and all the buses have two little Catalan flags above their windscreens. You can feel the derby buzz in the air. I'm waiting by the main post office for a lift to nearby Sitges to play in a football game of my own. The first match of a new veterans' team of ex-pat Brits. As I wait, I read *El Mundo Deportivo*. The headline reads *'Once Puyoles'* (*eleven Puyols*): it wants all 11 Barcelona players to play with the sort of passion and commitment shown by their centre-back Carles Puyol. Puyol is a muppet-haired man who contests every tackle and dubious refereeing decision with rottweiler enthusiasm. He often reminds me of a Sunday League player – he has an ungainliness about him that belies his undoubted skill in a way that almost makes you surprised every time he does something good. You can imagine him winning the 'effort' prize at school. This big, slightly clumsy central defender has become the darling of the Barça fans, which says a lot about the sorry state of the club. It is a position that has recently been filled by the likes of Cruyff, Maradona, Romario and Rivaldo.

When we have our team talk, we realise that we have one goalkeeper and ten centre backs. We are ten Puyols. We can't all play in the same position: I am put on the right wing. I'm 6'2" and 16 stone: it's not my best position. Moreover I'm up against a player who used to turn out for Espanyol. He's not their only star: Anthony Quinn's son is playing at centre-forward. They are all over us, and all over me, in particular. I do a lot of running round in circles and when the ball does come to me I'm so knackered, my feet don't obey my brain and I embarrass myself by putting the ball into touch, or into the path of opposing players. I'm taken off after 20 minutes. Young Rubén comes to mind. We lose 4–0. Afterwards I sell my extra ticket (cost price) to the manager's brother, down from London for the weekend, who's been playing centre-forward. He's pleased. I spend much of the money on a post-match paella lunch in the sun on the terrace of a restaurant on the marina quay. It beats a pie and a pint in the local boozer. Even for pub-level footballers, there are advantages to a move to Spain. Not that I'll get picked again. Never mind, there are more important games to be thinking about.

The Nou Camp is the stadium I have been to most in Spain. I went there several times when I first lived in Barcelona in 1990/91, when Zubizarreta, Koeman, Bakero, Guardiola, Stoichkov and Laudrup formed the backbone of a brilliant team, managed by Johan Cruyff, which won the title at something of a canter. It was nicknamed 'El Dream Team' and Barça have never reached such heights again. Real Madrid finished a poor third that year, sacking John 'Benjamin' Toshack along the way. It was the first of four consecutive league title wins for Barça. The '90s was a great decade for the club: they won the league a total of six times, and lifted the European Cup (in Wembley in 1992) for the first and only time in their history.

The '90s saw a number of classic clásicos in the Nou Camp. In 1992 Barça played Real on the first day of the season and won 2–1 with a last-minute goal by Hristo Stoichkov. It was the perfect start to what would turn out to be a championship-winning season. In 1996, Barça beat their big rivals 3–0 with two goals from the otherwise ineffective Bosnian, Kodro, and another from Luis Figo, later, of course, to switch allegiance. In 1999, on Valentine's Day, Luis Van Gaal's Barça enjoyed another 3–0 win, with two goals from former Real Madrid player Luis Enrique and a third from Rivaldo. Again they went on to win the title. El Real haven't got many good memories of the Nou Camp in recent years in La Liga. This year, the year of Beckham, Real Madrid arrive having not managed a league win in Barça's stadium since November 1983, more than 20 years ago.

It feels like this might soon change. The new decade (whatever it ends up being called) has not been so kind to Barcelona FC. Barça haven't finished higher than fourth this millennium, and only just managed to qualify for the UEFA Cup in 2002/3, after flirting with relegation. I've been watching them quite regularly, and there is something deeply wrong, not just with the current team, but with the club as a whole. There is a pessimism, a heaviness, a hysteria that pervades the whole institution. Barcelona FC seems sick. Players and staff who join seem to get infected. Laporta, a doctor called bedside when a priest might have been more apt, already looks grim-faced. Even the joyful Brazilian playmaker Ronaldinho, who will not be playing today because of a thigh strain, has lost his goofy smile.

The exit from the María Cristina metro station leads you up to Diagonal, an eight-lane highway leading out of town, flanked by stylish skyscrapers and gushing modern fountains – this is the banking district. There is a flow of people down the sidewalk – men, women and children of all ages, many wearing the maroon and blue colours of Barcelona FC, others the yellow and red stripes of the Catalan national flag. A few locals are struggling with shopping bags among the crowd – Barcelona always play late, they never play during shopping hours, they do not want to disturb the city's vital trade. There is no singing, or shouting or joking. The mood is serious. What looks to be the worst Barcelona side for years is about to be put to the test against the mighty galácticos. National pride is at stake. The form sheet says that Barça will lose – but Barça simply cannot lose. Two decades unbeaten against their 'eternos rivales'. Yet the fear of defeat is almost palpable in the air.

From Diagonal you turn left down Avinguda de Joan XIII and the vast form of Europe's biggest stadium comes into sight. It's a huge red-brick dome, an ugly sight, truth be told, prettied up slightly by the scarf-selling stalls crowding its base. I am stunned to see that several of the ticket windows before the main entrance are open – and doing business. There aren't even queues! Barcelona have more members than there are seats in the stadium, which is why it is normally next to impossible to get tickets for the Real Madrid game. But season ticket holders have the chance to sell their tickets back to the club, which then sells them on. And it seems that thousands must have done this: around me, a good proportion of the languages being spoken aren't Catalan, or even Spanish. I hear German, Italian, English. Lots of English. Catalans are noted for their fickleness – I once saw Newcastle play in the Nou Camp in the Champions League in front of a 3,000 crowd (largely wearing black and white, 10 per cent in Mexican hats), because Barça were out of the competition and it was raining. But this is a different matter. It seems that many have stayed away from El Clásico this year, and sold their tickets on. This is unthinkable. It must be the fear, the wretched fear of losing at home to the big enemy for the first time for a generation.

I find my seat with half an hour till kick-off and finally El Clásico starts to live up to its billing. I am on the second tier of three, halfway between the halfway line and the goal. It's like being inside a vast cauldron lined with people; you look up for the sky, and up again, and there it is, a small circle above the masses. As soon as I sit down Real Madrid run on for their warm up. Only half the seats are full, but I've never heard such a cacophony of shrill whistling. There's a tone of hatred I've never heard in whistling before. Then Barcelona run on and the whistles turn to cheers.

You can tell a lot about the two teams from the way they do their pre-match warm ups. The Barcelona players are spread unevenly across their half of the pitch, to my left, stretching, in little groups of three or four. The Real Madrid players come out together and stretch in a circle, obviously talking to one another. My eyes strain for Beckham, then find him, on the far side of the circle. I wonder what he is thinking, in the centre of this cauldron of hate, which is filling up fast.

An assistant runs on to the Real half and places a number of training cones in a small oblong, and Real start playing a game, bibs v non-bibs, a possession game, with no goals. Beckham, bibbed up, looks in good form. Queiroz, an incongruous figure in his trademark narrow-lapelled brown suit, stands nearby, studying his men. The Barcelona players are passing the ball around and taking the odd shot at goal, like so many Sunday League players. Rijkaard is nowhere to be seen. In my year and a half in the city I have developed a dislike for this slightly hysterical club, its self-importance, the mood a defeat inflicts on the whole city, and I don't know who I want to win the game. Or lose it.

The players stroll back to their changing rooms, and the huge screen at the back of the stand behind the goal shows a cartoon in which caricatures of the Barça players get into spaceships and start firing footballs into little goals to the Star Wars theme tune. It's stupid – out of place, pathetic, a huge miscalculation, a trivialisation of the events about to unfold. Then, even worse, a four-piece rock band come on to perform the Barça hymn, the singer straining to add melody to the words, normally sung with the solemnity of a national anthem.

> One flag unites us,
> Blue and red in the wind.
> A valiant shout: we have a name everyone knows:
> Barça, Barça, Baaaarça!

The singer, looking embarrassed, says 'Visca Barça' ('long live Barça') in Catalan, before slipping up with a 'gracias' (thank you) in Spanish. He might well be embarrassed. These supposedly populist touches are Laporta innovations and they do little to add to the atmosphere of the game. What more atmosphere could you need?

Then there's another Laporta touch, and this time a more serious one. A tannoy announcement is made that the outgoing President of Catalonia, the dwarfish Jordi Pujol, a wily politician who has been chipping away at winning political concessions for the region for 20 years, is present. Will everyone stand for the national anthem, Els Segadors?

The Catalan anthem commemorates the Reapers War, the Catalan peasants' uprising against Spanish troops in 1640, a vain but bloody quest for Catalan independence, in which the put-upon local peasantry savagely attacked Spanish troops with their farm tools. It is a very controversial addition to El Clásico, as the song is little short of a call to arms against Madrid's central rule, banned by Franco, but also legislated against by subsequent more democratic politicians.

> 'Triumphant Catalonia
> Will once again be rich and bountiful.
> Drive them off these people,
> So conceited and arrogant
> A good blow of the sickle,
> Defenders of the land,
> A good blow of the sickle!'

The songs aren't finished. The tannoy blares out another, more traditional, version of the club anthem and this time the fans join in. The Boixos Nois, the violent ultras behind the goal to my left, wave their

Catalan flags and red and white flags of Barcelona's patron San Jordi (St George). The 'Boixos' have not been turning up to matches after a dispute with Laporta (he has stopped giving them free tickets to the game, they have started painting death threats on his garage door). But they have decided to come to El Clásico 'to lend the team support when they really need it.' Virtually everybody in the stadium raises their voice in unison to the last words of the anthem, myself included. I've worked out which team I'm going to support.

> *Blau grana al vent,*
> *un crit valent,*
> *tenim un nom,*
> *el sap tothom,*
> *Barça!, Barça!, Baaaarça!!!!*

The guy on the tannoy reads out the players names as their faces appear on the big screen. Real Madrid first . . . and everyone's waiting for Figo.

"Con el número diez, Luis . . ."

The rest is drowned out in a sea of boos, whistles and cat-calls. A fat bloke in front in a smart red jacket stands up and gives Figo the Spanish equivalent of the v-sign, the 'corte de mangas' a clenched fist with a slap on the bicep from the other hand. He does this about ten times, to the refrain:

"Hijo de puta; hijo de puta; hijo de . . ."

Beckham's name gets an animated response, but only about half the decibel level of Figo's. It's pretty clear who the bad guy is in tonight's pantomime.

The tannoy reads out the Barcelona players, saying the first name, and leaving the crowd to shout the second.

"Giovanni . . ."

" . . .Van Bronkhurst." It doesn't quite work.

There is about ten seconds of silence for a former Barcelona goalkeeper who's just died, and Real Madrid kick off. They get a 'pitada' (a shrill whistling) whenever they are in possession. When Roberto Carlos gets the ball, the fat guy in front starts making monkey noises. When Figo gets the ball, the whole stadium boos and whistles. Beckham is largely ignored, though the first time he gets a free-kick, out near the bye-line on the other side of the pitch, a banner is unfurled right in front of him, in the third row of seats.

'BECKHAM IS A WANKER' it reads, in English. That's all. It is quickly rolled up again.

Real start on top. Barcelona keep losing the ball.

"Hostia puta," says the fat guy, when Motta, Barcelona's number 23, a young Brazilian with curly hair, gives it away. 'Hostia', meaning 'the host' (the bread given to worshippers in Catholic masses), is possibly the second-most common swearword in Spain, here linked with the first.

Beckham, who seems unfazed by the atmosphere around him so far, goes to take a corner. There's plenty of abuse, but no hard electronic objects or animal organs. Lots of camera flashes, too. A pigeon has got into the stadium and is flying around in a panic, unable to work its way out.

It's a pretty boring first half, football-wise. Barcelona are playing the game like an away match, keeping all but one behind the ball when Real have possession, amid that uproar of whistles. When the home team do get the ball, they lose it quickly, often to Beckham, who is a busy, scurrying little figure. Then, with ten minutes or so to play in the first half, the Englishman kicks a precise cross-field ball to Zidane, who plays it immediately into the path of Roberto Carlos, whose shot is deflected into the goal. Silence. Absolute silence? Not quite. I hear some faint echoey yells, look opposite me across the pitch, and notice 100 or so tiny-looking Real Madrid fans opposite, jumping up and down. Then there's an eruption of indignation from the other 97,900 in the stadium. The fat man is up on his feet again, swearing at the referee, the Barça defence, the manager . . .

The referee blows for half-time and the man walks up a couple of rows. He pulls a couple of tinfoil parcels from a rucksack, opens one of them. He offers the open package to another guy I assume he's friends with.

"Do you want a croquette?" he asks. "My aunt made them."

"We are playing with too much fear," says his friend. I can hear the same word ('paura') being muttered all around me, its three syllables carrying, somehow, more power than its English equivalent.

Rijkaard changes tactics in the second half, presumably realising that such fear will get him nowhere. He puts on two wingers, ex-Arsenal player Marc Overmars and Portuguese starlet Quaresma. Immediately Barcelona have more urgency about them. We have a game on. And a streaker, who makes about three strides onto the far corner of the pitch before being rugby-tackled by a security guard and escorted off. The Boixos Nois, behind the goal, are raising the tempo, waving flags and chanting: "Barça, Barça, Baaaarça!"

But it's Real who keep making the better chances. Beckham, who seems to be everywhere, puts in a fine cross with his supposedly weak left foot, which Raúl heads limply over when even I, and I'm not joking, might have scored. Barça push forward, looking for the equaliser, and the game is wide open. Patrick Kluivert beats the full-back, is tripped in the box, but shuns the dive. The chance comes to nothing. Then he performs a brilliant diving header, straight at Casillas.

Real counter-attack. With 15 minutes to go, Roberto Carlos passes from the left to Ronaldo who, without much fuss, puts the ball past Valdés into the net. I look over to the tiny Real fans who perform their scaled-down celebrations. The Real Madrid players huddle together, jumping up and down in glee. They think it's all over.

Ten minutes later, Xavi takes a Barcelona corner from the right. Kluivert heads it into the Real Madrid net. 2–1! Game on! I look at the time on the big screen. 83 minutes. Ten minutes left, including added time. I feel a surge of passion I have not felt in a year and a half in Catalonia's capital city.

"Come on Barça!" I whisper.

Less than a minute later, Casillas makes a brilliant save, which is followed by a fracas in the penalty area. This is the last thing Barça need. Real spend the next period taking their time over free-kicks, throw-ins, substitutions.

In the third and last minute of added time, Barcelona get a corner. Obviously their last chance. Everybody is aware that they scored from the last one, everybody looks at Kluivert. Xavi kicks swings it in. There's a slow-motion slam dance in the box. The ball lands in the middle of it, and is headed . . . clear. The final whistle is blown. Roberto Carlos runs across half the pitch towards Beckham, and they jump up and down together, hugging. Beckham's first clásico, and Real's first league win in Barcelona for a generation. Well they might hug.

Afterwards, I meet the English guy I sold the ticket to, in the Bugui Bar on Diagonal near María Cristina station. He's enthusing about Beckham.

"He's like Glenn Hoddle and Roy Keane rolled into one. I can't believe it," he says. I notice that the edge of his wallet is sticking up above the rim of his side pocket.

"Be careful of that," I say and head home, depressed. But not as depressed as the other people on the metro, who haven't taken defeat with a pinch of salt. With Valencia still to play, Real Madrid go three points clear at the top of the table. Barcelona drop to 12th.

## RESULTS: JORNADA 14

| | | | |
|---|---|---|---|
| VILLARREAL | 0 | MALLORCA | 2 |
| REAL SOCIEDAD | 0 | VALENCIA | 0 |
| **REAL MADRID** | **2** | **ATLÉTICO** | **0** |
| VALLADOLID | 1 | DEPORTIVO | 1 |
| RACING | 0 | SEVILLA | 4 |
| BETIS | 1 | MURCIA | 1 |
| ZARAGOZA | 2 | ATHLETIC | 2 |
| MÁLAGA | 5 | BARCELONA | 1 |
| CELTA | 2 | ALBACETE | 2 |
| ESPANYOL | 0 | OSASUNA | 1 |

## RESULTS: JORNADA 15

| | | | |
|---|---|---|---|
| OSASUNA | 3 | CELTA | 2 |
| DEPORTIVO | 1 | MÁLAGA | 0 |
| REAL SOCIEDAD | 0 | BETIS | 4 |
| VALENCIA | 2 | ATHLETIC | 1 |
| ATLÉTICO | 2 | ESPANYOL | 0 |
| MURCIA | 1 | VILLARREAL | 1 |
| MALLORCA | 1 | VALLADOLID | 0 |
| ALBACETE | 4 | RACING | 0 |
| SEVILLA | 3 | ZARAGOZA | 2 |
| **BARCELONA** | **1** | **REAL MADRID** | **2** |

## LA CLASIFICACIÓN

| | P | W | D | L | F | A | Pts |
|---|---|---|---|---|---|---|---|
| **REAL MADRID** | **15** | **10** | **3** | **2** | **31** | **16** | **33** |
| VALENCIA | 15 | 9 | 4 | 2 | 29 | 12 | 31 |
| DEPORTIVO | 15 | 9 | 3 | 3 | 23 | 11 | 30 |
| OSASUNA | 15 | 7 | 5 | 3 | 18 | 12 | 26 |
| ATLÉTICO | 15 | 8 | 1 | 6 | 19 | 18 | 25 |
| MALLORCA | 15 | 7 | 2 | 6 | 19 | 22 | 23 |
| BETIS | 15 | 5 | 6 | 5 | 24 | 18 | 21 |
| SEVILLA | 15 | 5 | 6 | 4 | 23 | 18 | 21 |
| ATHLETIC | 15 | 6 | 3 | 6 | 19 | 18 | 21 |
| VILLARREAL | 15 | 6 | 5 | 4 | 15 | 16 | 21 |
| MÁLAGA | 15 | 6 | 2 | 7 | 18 | 18 | 20 |
| BARCELONA | 15 | 5 | 5 | 5 | 19 | 20 | 20 |
| VALLADOLID | 15 | 5 | 5 | 5 | 19 | 22 | 20 |
| RACING | 15 | 6 | 2 | 7 | 18 | 23 | 20 |
| ALBACETE | 15 | 5 | 1 | 9 | 19 | 21 | 16 |
| ZARAGOZA | 15 | 4 | 4 | 7 | 17 | 19 | 16 |
| CELTA | 15 | 3 | 6 | 6 | 19 | 22 | 15 |
| REAL SOCIEDAD | 15 | 3 | 6 | 6 | 15 | 23 | 15 |
| MURCIA | 15 | 1 | 8 | 6 | 14 | 26 | 11 |
| ESPANYOL | 15 | 2 | 2 | 10 | 10 | 28 | 8 |

# TEN
# MALLORCA

## FRIDAY DECEMBER 20TH

I'm travelling to Palma de Mallorca on a high-speed catamaran without having watched or even found out the score of Real Madrid's previous night's cup match against local rivals Leganés. Brenda and I are to spend Christmas in our respective countries, her in Dublin, me in London. I didn't think it appropriate to spend our last evening together before the holiday in the company of Beckham and co., so I didn't even mention the match. It was quite hard: it is a fascinating encounter because Leganés' squad is made up almost entirely of Argentinians – not Beckham's favourite nationality.

The boat is an antiseptic affair. You're stuck inside the hull; there is no deck to walk out on, no chance to feel the splash of sea air in your face. You watch your progress across the Mediterranean through double-glazed windows. There is a shop, but it doesn't sell newspapers. On the desk, which is fringed with red tinsel, there is a pile of magazines I recognise. The Spanish translation of an official Manchester United Magazine one-off special celebrating the life of Beckham.

He has been much talked about all week. There was an incident in Real Madrid's vital six-pointer home game against Deportivo de la Coruña in the Bernabéu at the weekend which showed the rougher side of Beckham's game. Before the match there was much talk about the fact that Dépor's number 23, the Argentinian Duscher, was the player who injured Beckham's soon-to-be-famous metatarsal bone in a match between Manchester United and Deportivo shortly before the 2002 World Cup, an injury which threatened his participation in the tournament. But it was to be another Argentinian that Beckham tangled with that evening.

The game was a tense, tight affair, a great match of football. Ronaldo opened the scoring at the stroke of half time, putting into an empty net from a pass by Zidane, after a little exhibition of Zidanery had earned the

Frenchman the space to put in the pass. Just after the hour, Dépor's Uruguayan former bin-man striker Pandiani, who had been on the pitch six seconds, slid in an equaliser under Casillas' dive. Either side could have got the winner: it was Raúl who scored it, knocking in a good cross from Roberto Carlos with five minutes left. In the dying seconds of the game, Deportivo (much aggrieved that a seemingly good goal by Luque had been disallowed in the first half) were launching a counter-attack down the right wing through the Argentinian Lionel Scaloni. Beckham, chasing back, knocked the right-back over with a tackle from behind. Scaloni reacted by squaring up to the Englishman; a small ruck ensued involving Roberto Carlos, who came rushing to the Englishman's rescue like a female hippo separated from its calf. Eventually the men were pulled apart and Beckham and Scaloni were given a yellow card each by the referee. Afterwards Beckham tried to play the affair down, but did claim that the Argentinian had refused to shake his hand after the game. Scaloni, on his part, claimed that he hadn't shaken hands because the Englishman had 'touched his genitals' (Beckham's, not Scaloni's).

Which made the Leganés match all the more fascinating. The club, based in a working-class suburb of Madrid, were bought in the summer by the Argentinian concert promoter Daniel Grinbank, the man responsible for bringing the Rolling Stones, Paul McCartney and Michael Jackson to South America. Grinbank had the dream to make Leganés one of Spain's top teams, promising Primera División football within three years. He went about this by hiring two Argentine managers of some repute – Carlos Aimar (ex Logroñés and Celta de Vigo) and José Pekerman (former Argentina youth team manager) – as trainer and technical director. The close season saw a radical and rather ruthless turnaround of playing staff. The new junta got rid of the 17 Spanish players on the books and replaced them with 15 Argentines and a Chilean, most of whom had dual EU nationality. The experiment was not an unprecedented success – Leganés were mid-table when Real Madrid came to town. But what a prospect – a derby against Real Madrid, and a chance for the players and management to tilt at Argentinian football's public enemy number one, David Beckham.

The boat is virtually empty; only one of the passengers has a newspaper, and he is engrossed in the foreign news section. I sit on a table next to him and wait for him to finish. He puts his paper down and I'm there.

"Can I have a read of your paper?"

"Um, I was... um... Ok, then."

It's *El Mundo*, the right-leaning Madrid-based daily. I scurry back to my table with my spoils and hungrily search for the sports section.

'RAÚL AVOIDS A DISASTER' reads the headline, and I realise I've missed one of the matches of the season. On 89 minutes Real were 3–2 down and facing an embarrassing exit from the competition. Then Solari (an Argentine playing against compatriots) scored, to put the match into extra time. Raúl scored the winner on 110 minutes, with 'a wonderful back-heel'.

Real had been 2–0 up (the first goal from a 'stupendous' free-kick by Beckham, the second by Raúl after the keeper had spilled a Beckham shot) but then conceded three goals in quick succession, to find themselves, as the surprisingly mild Spanish expression puts it, 'up to their necks in water'. Beckham had gone off injured. A thigh injury after a bad tackle. He is doubtful for the Mallorca game I'm going to see, before flying straight back to England for Christmas.

The paper jokes that Beckham's body has started to resemble a tourist brochure of Argentina. 'Greetings from Buenos Aires on his left ankle. A memento from Patagonia on his foot; a souvenir from River Plate on his right knee.'

I turn my attention to a potted history of Mallorca in my travel guide. Hannibal was born on the island, it seems, which was called Balearis Major by the Romans (Balearis Menor became Menorca), who colonised the place. The island group was named after its indigenous inhabitants, who were wicked sling-shot throwers (ballein means 'to throw' in Greek).

The island was invaded by the Vandals, then by the Byzantines, then became a pirate stronghold. The Moors took it over in 1076, then it became part of the Aragonés/Catalan empire in 1228. It was taken over briefly by local peasants in the 1500s before being brought under Spanish rule again by Carlos V. In the 1970s it was invaded by lager-swilling tourists from Germany and the UK, each of whom have developed large colonies, the Germans in S'Arenal and the Brits in Y'Baern, otherwise known as Magaluf. In between these lies Palma, the capital of the island, which boasts a medieval cathedral and a modern Primera División team, Real Mallorca, who are hosting Real Madrid on Sunday, three days before Christmas.

Arriving in a city by boat beats being dragged through the arse-end of town on a train, even in the dark. Ports are designed to be looked at from the sea. It's an exciting way to arrive: there it is, spread out in front of you, getting bigger and bigger as you approach. It's a mixture of neon-framed modern and well-lit ancient, with the illuminated cathedral dominating.

I have an agenda. I walk along the seafront (a long marina of bobbing yachts) to my hostel, in Calle Argentina (hah!), drop my rucksack off, and get a taxi to the Son Moix stadium, where I've found out that representatives of all the Real Mallorca peñas will be meeting tonight. I'm running late, though. The taxi drops me the wrong side of the stadium and I have to walk about half a mile, cursing and stomping, to get to the right entrance. A security guard waves me through to the press room, I open a door, and a hundred curious faces look at me. My arrival has obviously silenced proceedings. There is a table on a stage with five men sat in front of microphones and several banks of people seated facing them. Embarassed, I sidle to the back, and they resume their talk.

Everyone is speaking in Mallorquín, a dialect of Catalan, but a pretty incomprehensible one to me. I realise, with a shock, that the man doing most of the speaking is the young-Harrison-Ford-lookalike club president Mateu Alemany, facing his team's fans for what must be an end-of-year meeting. Alemany is a local lawyer, 40, who has been on the club board since the age of 26.

One of the fans is irate. He keeps standing up and waving his arms around. But there is humour in his anger. People are laughing at what he says. You notice more about body language when you don't understand the words. They seem to be talking about changing the name of the club Real Club Deportivo Mallorca (Spanish for Royal Sporting Club of Mallorca) to Reial Club Esportiu Mallorca (the same in the Mallorquín dialect). This goes on for about 20 minutes. The irate fan keeps shouting, the president keeps shaking his head. Then they talk about getting rid of the race track around the pitch of the Son Moix stadium. When the words are similar to Spanish I can understand. "It's like having a motorway round the pitch," shouts the fan. "Get rid of Eto'o. You should sign Fernando Alonso."

When the meeting ends Alemany rushes off. I look at the sheet of paper in front of where he was sitting. It is full of doodles. I make out an anchor and a boat. A couple of clues as to how he's to spend his Christmas holidays. The angry fan is studying me studying the doodles, so I introduce myself. He's friendly, excited to meet a foreign writer. His name is José. He leads me upstairs, where there are a number of tables set with food. It's the Christmas party for the peñas. Tapas, sandwiches, cake, Coke. It's just what I needed. There are some trophy cabinets and I am led to the Copa del Rey – Mallorca are the holders, having beaten Recreativo de Huelva in the final last season. Unfortunately it's behind a glass cabinet. I'd have loved to have lifted it up. I am introduced from fan to fan, and invited by one to join him later in a bar.

"Of course I'll come," I promise.

Before I know it I am being led outside by a fifty-something man named Paco, dressed in a brown suit and sporting a large moustache. He nips into an office and hands me a DVD of Mallorca's Cup Final win in the summer.

"Thank you," I muster. "Um . . . I'm not quite sure where I'm going."

"To the Peña Barralet. They're doing bingo."

Paco turns out to be Real Mallorca's security manager. He drives fast. I put my seatbelt on. This is all going too fast for me.

Twenty minutes later we are in a small bar whose walls are covered with Real Mallorca mementoes. There a pictures of the barman with the Copa del Rey, and signed photos of some of the players. Every time I turn my attention to a new item, the barman shouts out what it is.

"That's a replica of the Copa del Rey."

"That's El Mono Burgos. He used to be our goalkeeper."

"That's a boot from Chichi Soler, our former captain."

There is a game of bingo going on, so no-one else is paying much attention to me. I am offered a Coke, which I accept. I'm still off the beer.

"7" says the caller.

"34."

"23."

"David Beckham!" I shout. Nobody seems to get it. Or rather nobody seems to think it's funny.

When they've finished the sheet, the caller turns his attention to me.

"When are you going to give us back Gibraltar?" he asks, through his microphone. Everyone looks at me.

"We already gave you back Menorca – is that not enough?" I reply. Pretty soon Paco is driving me back to town.

"They play bingo to raise funds to go to away matches," he says. Then he tells me that the Mallorca fans are 'cold', and not to expect a great atmosphere on Sunday. He drops me in the centre of town. I have been in Mallorca three hours and I have received two lifts, a free meal, two Cokes and a DVD. Nice people.


**SATURDAY DECEMBER 21ST**

I'm sitting in the sun on a rock in front of the hunched cathedral. It must be 25 degrees in the sun. I've been walking round the narrow streets of the old part of town, following the route suggested in my guide book, looking at the Arab baths, the modernist palaces and the medieval churches. It's a great place. I'm waiting for a phone call from Gabri, from the local radio station, Onda Cero. He's heard from the Real Mallorca accreditation guy that I'm in town, that I'm following Beckham around. He thinks it's worth a couple of minutes on his show.

The phone rings.

"Gabri?"

"Hi. Bad news. I've just heard Beckham's not playing. He's not even travelling to the game. He's already back in England on his holidays."

"Shit, shit, shit!" I think. "Fuck, wank, bollocks."

"Never mind, Gabri," I say. "I guess you won't want to do the interview."

"No, I still do. If you just hold the line I'll make an introduction and then I'll ask you some questions. It's not live."

Gabri asks me about the book, about the most interesting parts of my trip, about what I've heard said about Beckham on the terraces.

"Go fuck the Queen, Blondie," comes to mind. "Most of what I've heard can't be broadcast," I say.

He tells me he's a great fan of the player, that Beckham's a great fighter. That he has really been surprised by his performances. He wishes me luck with my trip.

It takes a while to get over the news. I wouldn't have come if I'd known he wasn't playing. I could be at home now, in front of the fire, putting up the Christmas tree. Instead I'm all alone in sunny Mallorca. The unseasonably warm weather merely reminds me of how far from home I am. I go for a long walk on the beach, and have an eight-euro three-course lunch looking over the picturesque fishing port of Petrontxelo, wishing for the sleet of London. I envy Beckham his early break.

I wander round bars all day, catching bits of football matches. I watch Bolton equalise against Arsenal in a Scottish pub, and watch Real Sociedad go down 3–1 at home to Valladolid. I'm most interested in watching Valencia's home game against Sevilla so I wind up in a small bar near my hostel. There are two lads in their twenties sitting at the bar, and a middle-aged barman. They are talking football. I've been alone all day, which always makes me shy of strangers. I'm dying for company, though. It's the last Saturday before Christmas. I should be at a party. I sit and nurse a glass of water, watch the match and eavesdrop the conversation.

"I've always said it. The goalkeeper is the most important element of the team. Look at Real Madrid. Look at Iker Casillas. How many times has he saved them? What's more, a secure goalkeeper means a secure defence. Fewer mistakes, less panic. The goalkeeper and the two central defenders. That is the triangle you must base your team on."

It's a typical conversation between Spanish men. There's a silence.

"I was listening to the radio today," says one of the young guys. "I heard a very interesting interview."

My ears prick up.

"There was this Englishman. He's following Beckham to all the stadiums Real Madrid play in. A kind of tour of the country, talking to people, finding out about Spanish football."

"That's me." I say. They look over in disbelief. "I'm that Englishman. You're talking about me!"

Suddenly I am no longer the unwelcome stranger. They all turn round to me. I'm offered a beer. I explain my project.

"Beckham has been a great surprise to me," says the older guy, whose name is Héctor. "He replaced Makelele, and I thought Makelele was irreplaceable. I know this, I am a Madridista. I am from Madrid. Beckham is like a Latin player. He is a fighter. And how he runs. Eleven or 12 kilometres every match. The game brings the tiger out of him. And you know what? The Madrid fans love him. They love him! And you know why? Because he has dos cojones (balls). He is an honourable player, an honest player. He puts his foot in. He fights. He struggles. Real Madrid fans see brilliant players do brilliant things every week. They have grown up on this. They are used to it. Zidane, Figo, Ronaldo; nutmegs, bicycle kicks, dummies. Of course they appreciate all that. But because that is the norm in the Bernabéu, what they appreciate more is a player with honour who is prepared to lay his life down for the club. And they can see that Beckham can do that for them, that he will die for the cause. And that's why he has become such a big hero so quickly."

They ask me if I've met Beckham. I tell them that I hope to, by the end of the season. They ask me what he's like as a person.

"He's very quiet."

"Yes, a man of few words," supposes Héctor. "A man who doesn't like to give too much away."

"Well, he's not a philosopher, if you know what I mean."

"What do you mean?"

"Well, he has great intelligence in his feet, he is capable of spotting runs off the ball, he's very precise with his movements, he has practised every skill until he can do it off pat, but . . . but . . ."

"What are you saying?"

"He's not a great talker."

I don't tell them that I have heard that his favourite hobby is tracing Disney cartoons, and that he was the butt of all the thick jokes in England. I don't have the heart.

Two hours later I am with Dioni, one of the younger guys, in a crowded nightclub on the seafront. Dioni tells me he was a highly promising player until he had a terrible knee injury at the age of 17. Now 25, he has resigned himself to never playing again, and has become a referee, officiating in Third Division matches on the island.

"My girlfriend is Carolina Domenech," he tells me. "You know, Carolina Domenech, the referee!"

Domenech became famous in Spain when she was chosen to officiate the friendly between Real Madrid and Atlético de Madrid in front of 50,000 spectators (and millions of TV viewers) in January 2002. It looked like she would go from strength to strength, but only a few months later she was passed over when it came to choosing a new batch of referees for the Segunda A, and she resigned in disgust, claiming she had been discriminated against.

"Anyway, she's at the other end of the bar, with her parents. I'll introduce you in a minute."

I am pointed out a blonde girl in a red dress who is dancing energetically to Spanish pop music. There are large cotton wool clouds on the ceiling and Dioni's white shirt has gone shiny neon blue. Everything's gone a bit surreal. The music stops, she comes over, we are introduced, and another song starts up again. This is not ideal interview territory.

"So Dioni tells me you were a referee."

"That's right."

"In the Bernabéu."

"Yes."

'Te quiero y quiero más' blasts the music. She looks stern, referee-like. She is enjoying this less than I am.

I make a poor joke, trying to turn the masculine Spanish word 'árbitro' (referee) into a feminine form, 'árbitra'. She's heard this one before, but forces a smile.

"It must have been difficult to be a referee in such a macho country as Spain."

"It is a difficult job anywhere."

The music is hampering my interview style. I'm straining to hear what she says. And it's awful Spanish disco trash. 'Te quiero y quiero más.' There are three or four people crowding round, all their white neon blue.

"And I hear you resigned recently, because you weren't promoted."

"That's right. Now I am the working for the Referee's Association of the Balearic Islands."

The interview fizzles out and she wanders off for another dance. I've been red carded.

I ask Dioni a little about refereeing in Spain.

"It is certainly harder than in England, where from what I've seen on the TV there is less fouling, diving and abuse. You see, Spain is an anti-establishment country. Everybody older than 35 remembers living in the time of Franco. And everybody reacts against it by railing against authority. In football authority comes in the form of the referee. So people shout, and they throw things, and they wave white handkerchieves. Meanwhile the players try to cheat as much as they can get away with."

"So why did you want to become a referee?"

"Because I wanted to be part of football and I couldn't play anymore. And I don't want it to become my career. I have no ambition to move up the ladder. I referee at amateur matches in the Third Division. Sometimes it is hard to make a decision – sometimes you make mistakes. Add the pressure of 90,000 screaming fans and abusive superstars in front of you – no, it isn't one of my ambitions."

### SUNDAY DECEMBER 22ND

I'm sitting having lunch on the afternoon of the match in the Real Madrid peña just out of town, reading *As*, and I spot a little paragraph about the journalists accredited for today's game. "Among the 300 who will be present there are five Japanese, a Brazilian, a dozen or so English, some French and the news channel ESPN. But the most peculiar case is the English journalist Alex Leieh, who lives in Barcelona, who is going to all the matches Beckham plays in the Liga. Alex is writing a book about the English footballer who he follows around everywhere."

At first I bristle at the misspelling of my name, and the misinformation. Follow him around everywhere? It makes me sound like a paparazzo! I'm writing an anthropologically interesting study of Spain using people's interest in Beckham as a vehicle to get me round the country. Can't they see that?

Then my stance softens.

"I'm in the paper," I think. "The article was about me. I'm famous. I'm famous!" This is the sort of reaction journalists have when they read pieces about them, rather than by them.

I happily take the number 8 bus to the stadium. It drops me the wrong side for the main entrance, but the walk is worth it for the view. We are an hour from sunset and the mountains are crisp in the background of the eye-catching redbrick formation of the Son Moix stadium, built for the 1996 World Student Games. It looks like a giant open clam, with arching semi-circular stands along the touch-line. There are several clouds over the mountains that have taken on a deep yellow hue from the sun behind. One, I swear it, looks rather like a camel.

I arrive so early I've got time to kill, and I kill it in the press lounge watching the live round up of other Spanish games being played before the Mallorca-Real match. It is the most impressive such facility I have ever seen – only a glass wall separates you from the pitch. On a whim, I walk through a door in this wall, across the running track, and onto the grass of the pitch, level with the penalty box. On the halfway line the Real Madrid players are walking around in their black suits, like so many Reservoir Dogs, getting a feel for the pitch.

"Paco, your security is crap," I think. Then I'm proved wrong as a man in a yellow anorak approaches me and gently escorts me back to the press facilities.

Much of the pre-match coverage has been about Cameroon striker Samuel Eto'o, Mallorca's 'galáctico' who is half-owned by Real Madrid (he had an unsuccessful couple of seasons there as a teenager, playing just two matches before being let go). My eyes are on him in the first ten minutes of the match, as Real Mallorca tear into Real Madrid in the manner the champions are used to. He's got that languid labour-free assurance that you only see in players of the highest quality – and shows an explosive burst of pace when needed. He dominates this period of the game. On 10 minutes Mallorca attack down the right. Correa passes in from the right wing; the ball goes through Pavón's legs and falls to Eto'o. The African passes the ball back to his long-haired team-mate who has continued a run into the box. Correa thumps the ball through Iker Casillas.

"Goooooooooool!" shouts the tannoy guy. "Goool de . . ."

"CORREA!" shout the crowd behind the goal to my right.

I'd like to say they went mad, but Paco was right. They're a cold crowd, and the atmosphere is not helped at all by the large space between the stands and the pitch, where there are several speedboats on show. This is the period of the game when the fans, behind the team, in a stadium where they are close to the pitch and are vociferous and anti-Madridista (like at Sevilla for example) can really make a difference to the result, and help their team find the impetus to turn 1–0 into 2–0 and even 3–0.

But, though Real Madrid are having another poor game, completely lacking the midfield vision that Beckham provides, completely lacking in ideas, or guts, or leadership, Mallorca don't rub in their advantage. They create a couple more chances, but on the stroke of half time it is Real Madrid who score, with their second attack of the night, culminating in a Raúl near-post header rippling the net. He's unmarked. All around the stadium pockets of fans jump up and down in triumph. I'm suddenly depressed. Bloody Real Madrid always bloody score.

In the second half Mallorca start with some gusto, and Eto'o has a penalty claim denied, then hits the post. After which Ronaldo decides to start playing. He gets the ball on the edge of the box, accelerates, hops over a lunging thin-air tackle by the lumbering Argentinian defender Lussenhoff, and shoots the ball between the goalkeeper and the post. 2–1. Merry Christmas.

Mallorca, to their credit, react well. It's a great game, just without an atmosphere to match. Casillas stops a screamer of a shot by Eto'o, then another shot is cleared off the Madrid line by Helguera. Then, when you think the islanders might equalise, Lussenhoff is completely beaten for pace by Ronaldo, who is pushed over in the box by Nadal. Penalty. Figo steps up to take it. You never feel Figo is going to miss. The Portuguese player places the ball safely inside the post to goalkeeper Leo Franco's left. 3–1, and Madrid go into the winter break top of the table. And a happy bloody New Year.

Afterwards I'm in the mixed zone, waiting with my notepad and a pen, among another horde of journalists. There are no other English, apart from Sid Lowe, of the *Daily Telegraph* and the *Guardian* website, who I've arranged to go for dinner with later. Sid's after an interview with Eto'o; I'm after an autograph from Zidane, as part of a New Year's card for Brenda. I've written on my notepad 'Pour Brenda, Bonne année.' Then I've left a space for the Frenchman's name, and written '(World Footballer of the Year)' underneath. Zidane appears out of the changing room, and I push my book and pen in front of him, as he does a short interview, surrounded by a huddle of 15 or so journalists. He's incredibly shy-looking, as if this sort of attention is a new thing to him, something he's not used to. He speaks so quietly you can hardly hear him, even close up. But shy does not mean obliging. He ignores my book, moves on, does another interview further down the line. I catch up and again I proffer my notebook; again he ignores it. Just before reaching the coach he is stopped by a group of kids insistent on autographs. Third time lucky? Again I push my book in front of him. He picks it up, marks his squiggle, and hands it back. I'm thrilled. No-one would know that the two elongated circles he marked mean 'Zinedine Zidane' but I know . . . I know. Happy New Year, indeed: I'm done for the year. I can go home.

## JORNADA: 16 RESULTS

| | | | |
|---|---|---|---|
| ESPANYOL | 1 | BARCELONA | 3 |
| CELTA | 2 | ATLÉTICO | 2 |
| VILLARREAL | 2 | REAL SOCIEDAD | 0 |
| VALLADOLID | 0 | MURCIA | 0 |
| MÁLAGA | 3 | MALLORCA | 1 |
| RACING | 0 | OSASUNA | 0 |
| ZARAGOZA | 0 | ALBACETE | 1 |
| BETIS | 0 | VALENCIA | 1 |
| **REAL MADRID** | **2** | **DEPORTIVO** | **1** |
| ATHLETIC | 2 | SEVILLA | 1 |

| | | | |
|---|---|---|---|
| REAL SOCIEDAD | 1 | VALLADOLID | 3 |
| ATLÉTICO | 2 | RACING | 2 |
| VALENCIA | 1 | SEVILLA | 0 |
| ALBACETE | 1 | ATHLETIC | 1 |
| OSASUNA | 0 | ZARAGOZA | 1 |
| DEPORTIVO | 2 | ESPANYOL | 1 |
| MURCIA | 1 | MÁLAGA | 2 |
| BETIS | 1 | VILLARREAL | 3 |
| **MALLORCA** | **1** | **REAL MADRID** | **3** |
| BARCELONA | 1 | CELTA | 1 |

**LA CLASIFICACIÓN**

| | P | W | D | L | F | A | Pts |
|---|---|---|---|---|---|---|---|
| **REAL MADRID** | **17** | **12** | **3** | **2** | **36** | **18** | **39** |
| VALENCIA | 17 | 11 | 4 | 2 | 34 | 12 | 37 |
| DEPORTIVO | 17 | 10 | 3 | 4 | 26 | 14 | 33 |
| OSASUNA | 17 | 7 | 6 | 4 | 18 | 13 | 27 |
| VILLARREAL | 17 | 7 | 6 | 4 | 20 | 17 | 27 |
| ATLÉTICO | 17 | 8 | 3 | 6 | 23 | 22 | 27 |
| MÁLAGA | 17 | 8 | 2 | 7 | 22 | 20 | 26 |
| ATHLETIC | 17 | 7 | 4 | 6 | 22 | 20 | 25 |
| BARCELONA | 17 | 6 | 6 | 5 | 23 | 22 | 24 |
| VALLADOLID | 17 | 6 | 6 | 5 | 22 | 23 | 24 |
| MALLORCA | 17 | 7 | 2 | 8 | 21 | 28 | 23 |
| RACING | 17 | 6 | 4 | 7 | 20 | 25 | 22 |
| SEVILLA | 17 | 5 | 6 | 6 | 24 | 21 | 21 |
| ALBACETE | 17 | 6 | 2 | 9 | 21 | 22 | 20 |
| ZARAGOZA | 17 | 5 | 4 | 8 | 18 | 21 | 19 |
| BETIS | 17 | 4 | 6 | 7 | 21 | 22 | 18 |
| CELTA | 17 | 3 | 8 | 6 | 22 | 25 | 17 |
| REAL SOCIEDAD | 17 | 3 | 6 | 8 | 16 | 28 | 15 |
| MURCIA | 17 | 1 | 9 | 7 | 15 | 28 | 12 |
| ESPANYOL | 17 | 2 | 2 | 13 | 12 | 33 | 8 |

# ELEVEN
# SAN SEBASTIÁN

GOLFO DE VIZCAYA

OCÉANO ATLÁNTICO

○ **Real Sociedad**

**Real Madrid**
○

MAR MEDITERRÁNEO

# ELEVEN
# SAN SEBASTIÁN

**THURSDAY JANUARY 8TH**

I've been looking forward to Real Madrid's final away fixture of the first half of the calendar (and their first of the new year) because it takes place in my favourite Spanish city – San Sebastián, home of Real Sociedad. It's the first Spanish city I ever visited (on an Inter Rail holiday in 1984) and I've gone back regularly since.

Donostia, as San Sebastián is called in its native Euskera (the Basque language) is the jewel of the País Vasco (the Basque country), just over the border from the French resort of Biarritz. The city is fronted by a mile-long horseshoe-shaped beach, La Concha (shell), and sheltered by three mountains, one at either tip of the bay, the other emerging from the sea in the middle. A statue of Jesus looks over it, waving a finger in benediction. Or perhaps in admonition: Donostia is a good-looking place which enjoys having a good time. It has a warren of an old town which hosts a crowded street party every Friday and Saturday night. It is the best place I've ever found for tapas (called pintxos in this part of the world); ornate edibles spread across the bar every evening in an orgy of red, white and green.

Coincidentally these are the colours of the Basque national flag, called the 'Ikurriña' by the locals, shaped like the Union Jack, with a white and a green cross on top of a red background. Designed by the founder of Basque nationalism, Sabino Araba, the flag is to be seen all over town. Until the organisation was banned, San Sebastián was also the headquarters of Batasuna, the political wing of ETA, the Basque separatist group. ETA still exists, though it has been considerably weakened in recent years by a concerted campaign to eradicate it by the Spanish and French governments. Periodically, though, you still read about the murder of policemen and judges.

At the weekends there are often ETA-related demonstrations in the centre of San Sebastián. They start with old people carrying pictures of their children on placards, complaining that sentenced ETA members are jailed too far away to visit regularly, in places like the Canary Islands. These gentle folk are often followed by groups of youngsters in balaclavas, who throw stones at the police. The police, a special force called the Ertzaintza, made up of Basques and consequently especially hated by the locals, react with rubber bullets and truncheon charges. They look frightening, like Star Wars storm-troopers, only dressed in black.

A few years ago, sipping coffee at the end of the touristy Boulevard on a warm Sunday afternoon, I was accidentally caught in the middle of one of these riots, and fired upon by the police. I still have a rubber bullet as a souvenir – round, nearly the size of a tennis ball. I had to run into the nearby old town and hide in the shuttered doorway of a bar, petrified by the sight of a muzzle of a gun appearing round the corner before the shutters were quickly upped for me to scurry gratefully inside.

San Sebastián's mixed reputation as party town and ETA stronghold was epitomised in the early hours of January 20th 1994, during the town's all night Tamborrada celebrations, where the townspeople dress as cooks and Napoleonic soldiers and bash drums all night, drinking pacharán and beer and generally going wild. The event celebrates the fact that in 1808 Napoleon's invading army was frightened off by what sounded like heavy gunfire from the town; in fact what little artillery there was, was augmented by the town's cooks bashing their pots and pans. That's what they say in San Sebastián, anyway. That night, almost ten years before this visit, I was in town for the festival.

Well into the night (the party officially starts at midnight of the 19th and goes on until midnight of the 20th), I became aware of ambulances and police. The next day it emerged that José Antonio Santamaría, a former Real Sociedad football player, had been shot in the head by a gunman (a typical ETA execution). It turned out that Santamaría had been dealing in contraband cigarettes, but had been mistaken for a drug runner by ETA, who regularly execute such gangsters. An ambulance took his dead body away; the party continued.

The Basque issue is a complicated one. The Basques have a language which has nothing to do with most other Indo-European languages, which suggests that the race arrived on the peninsula before any other Iberian settlers. Well-publicised research suggesting that Basques were cranially different from other Europeans has recently been dismissed, although pure Basques often have noticeably long ears and noses.

The Basque country largely resisted the Moorish occupation of Spain. Unlike in most other parts of Spain, Basque culture remained relatively undiluted – traditional sports include lifting heavy rocks up hills, and balancing on logs while chopping at them with axes. Traditional music includes the use of instruments unique to the area, such as the txalaparta (a kind of drum) and the txistu (a one-handed flute).

In the major cities the Spanish language is generally used, though anybody educated after Franco's death tends to be completely bilingual, as all state school lessons are conducted in Euskera, the Basque language. The Basque country is a mountainous region full of small towns, and the smaller and more remote the town, the greater the use of Euskera. In some cases young children are losing their fluency in Spanish as they hardly hear it in school or at home. To outsiders Basque is an impenetrable language: it has no Latin roots to help you out.

Here are some useful phrases.

Eskerrik asko – Thank you

Bi garagardo mesedez – Two beers, please

Ile-horia primeran jolasten ari da – The blond lad's playing a blinder.

Basque names stand out from those of their Latinate neighbours; famous footballers such as Etxeberria, Goikoetxea, Zubizarreta and Beguiristain are all from the region.

Franco, in his attempt to impose complete control on the Basque country, didn't get as far as banning Basque surnames, but he did attempt to ban the language and also based a lot of industry in the area, hoping to reduce the Basques' traditional desire for independence by diluting their bloodline.

It didn't work. In the constitutional shake-up that followed Franco's death, the Basque country became one of the 17 autonomous communities loosely ruled by Spanish government in Madrid. But many Basques, while rejecting the violence of ETA, still want more independence from Madrid. The last months of 2003 saw the Basque prime minister Juan José Ibarretxe propose a referendum by the Basque people to decide on the issue of sovereignty, a plan which appalled Aznar and which his sidekick Mariano Rajoy described as 'treason'.

The fact that Real Madrid, for sound enough reasons, are viewed as being 'the team of the establishment' means that their arrival in the region is particularly looked forward to, as a victory for any Basque team over Madrid is seen by separatists as being a kick in the eye for centralists. And fate has thrown Carlos Queiroz's team a double date with Basque opposition: two games in the north in four days.

I'm reading a match report of the first game, played the previous evening, on the coach from Bilbao to San Sebastián, having flown to the former from the UK. (I spent Christmas in London, Sussex and Ireland.) I always seem to be on the move these days. Real Madrid drew Eibar in the Copa del Rey. Eibar is just 50 kilometres from San Sebastián – a rough town of 40,000 inhabitants, where the biggest industry is the manufacture of shotguns. The team are perennial strugglers in the Segunda and the town has gone mad for the arrival of the team from the capital. Many of those who couldn't get a ticket in the 6,000 capacity stadium watched the match from one of the balconies on the two adjacent skyscrapers that dwarf the stadium. Real Madrid didn't deign to play any of their 'galácticos' (Beckham was left at home along with Ronaldo, Raúl, Zidane, Roberto Carlos and Figo), instead fielding a number of their 'filial' (youth team) players alongside first-teamers Guti, Solari and, crucially, Casillas. Eibar countered this by playing *their* second team, as they didn't want to tire out their league players. The match finished 1–1, with Casillas the hero of the night for El Real.

Looking up from the match report, I see a sign for Eibar. Pretty soon we're driving past a town full of red-roofed houses built into the sides of a deep valley. Then the unmistakable sight of floodlights, and a tiny stadium dwarfed by two skyscrapers. I had no idea that the coach was passing by the town.

I arrive in San Sebastián a day before Real Madrid's return to the region, but don't linger in the city long. My friend and host José Mari has arranged for a friend of his to pick me up from the bus station and drive me to nearby Urnieta, about 10 kilometres up into the hills, past Real Sociedad's flashy Anoeta stadium, built (with some panache) in 1993. José Mari runs a language school in Urnieta; I'm dropped there.

I've known José Mari for years. I first met him when he was studying English in London, and working as a waiter. I was introduced to him by an old school friend (a language teacher) who asked me if I wanted to go to the European Cup Final, because a Spanish student of his had got hold of three tickets. I said 'of course' and we sat together as Barcelona beat Sampdoria 1–0 with a wonderful free-kick by Ronald Koeman. Since then I have visited him on numerous occasions and been to his wedding, to Marisa, in 1995. A small guy with enormous charm and energy, José Mari now runs two schools, the bigger one in Urnieta, his home town.

He's teaching when I arrive, but he comes out of the class to greet me. I haven't seen him for years; he looks well. Less hair, though. We hug, and he tells me to get a coffee. He is teaching a class of 12-year-olds till 7.30.

"I've told them you're writing a book about Beckham, and that you're coming in at the end of class. They're very excited," he says. I'm ushered into the teachers' room where I read a couple of chapters of a book by Charles Bukowski I find on the table. I'm nervous: it's been over ten years since I stood in front of a class.

Twenty minutes later I'm standing in front of eight boys and three girls, who are sitting round the room on those chairs that have folding plastic desk-tops attached. The three girls are together, on my left.

"What do you think of Beckham?" I ask.

"He is very beautiful," says one of the girls.

I write the word 'handsome' on the whiteboard, saying that is more commonly used for men. Once a teacher . . .

"No, he is very beautiful," says another of the girls. Everyone laughs.

"He has a very strong right leg," says one of the boys. "But his left leg is not very strong."

"Also, even when Real Madrid lose, he has Victory at home," says another boy (in Spanish 'Victoria' means 'victory').

I do a quick survey. They all want 'La Real' to beat 'El Real' (the Basque team are referred to in the feminine form, the Madrid team in the masculine). Only one is going to the match. They all think Beckham was a good signing for Real Madrid (though for different reasons). They predict the score: 4–0, 3–0, 2–0, 5–1, 4–2 (last year's score), 2–1, 2–0, 4–3, 1–0, 2–1 and 2–3. Everyone boos the girl who makes the negative prediction – but it turns out she's just said it the wrong way round, and meant 3–2.

Much later, after a fine meal made by Marisa (including a salad made with tiny eels and several glasses of pacharán), we check Teletext to see if Beckham has recovered from his ankle injury. He was injured last weekend in Real Madrid's first game of the year, a laboured 1–0 win over Murcia, where a terrible studs-up tackle by Rafael Clavero (a Spaniard, by the way) left him with a gash that required four stitches. I feel a familiar twinge of disappointment as I read the bad news: he's not travelling with the rest of the Real Madrid party. He's definitely not playing. There's even a quote from him about the decision: "The infection has cleared up but I'm still on antibiotics and I thought it better not to play."

## FRIDAY JANUARY 9TH

The next day I wake so late that when we go for breakfast in the local bar José Mari's friends are already drinking beers. One of them is his brother-in-law, Francis; the other is Francis' workmate, Iñaki, the President of Urnieta's Real Sociedad peña, named '5–0' after a famous victory by that score over local rivals Athletic de Bilbao a few years back.

I'm handed a beer, though I'd rather have a coffee. I ask which team generates more passion as opponents when they play in Real Sociedad's Anoeta stadium, Real Madrid or Athletic de Bilbao?

"Athletic de Bilbao create more passion," says Iñaki, "but Real Madrid is usually a better game."

"There is more passion against Athletic, but rarely any violence. We love to beat them, but before the game everyone marches together from the centre of town to the stadium. We are all Basques, after all," says José Mari.

I ask about Beckham, and get the usual response. They are surprised by his work rate, by his fighting spirit, by the amount he runs.

"I think . . ." begins a fat, fifty-something guy, who's been watching the conversation, chewing a toothpick.

He is cut off simultaneously by the three Basque lads.

"Shut up, you're a Madridista," they say, in chorus. He never does reveal what he thinks.

Four beers later we drive into a restaurant in the hills for lunch. José Mari points out Raynald Denoueix's house on the crest of a hill on the outskirts of Urnieta. La Real's Norman-French manager moved to the town – which has 6,000 inhabitants – when he arrived at the beginning of the 2002/3 season.

"Do you see much of him in town?"

"No. He's very French. He keeps himself to himself."

Denoueix did brilliantly in his first season in charge of the team. He took a side that had just avoided relegation and, with just the addition of Valeri Karpin from Celta de Vigo, turned them into a team which just failed to win the Spanish championship, being overtaken by Real Madrid right at the death of the 2002/3 season, after leading the table for most of the year.

So what's gone wrong? This season, with the same manager and almost exactly the same team, La Real are just one place above the relegation zone, struggling to pick up any points at all. They are desperate to beat Real Madrid tomorrow, not for pride or revenge, but mainly because they desperately need the points to avoid being sucked further into trouble. A 2–1 win at Málaga the previous week was their first in ten games, a desperate run of form from a team which, remarkably, are still in the Champions League competition.

"Part of the problem is that we lost some important players, even if they weren't necessarily key ones," says José Mari. His English is very good, especially when he talks about football. "The likes of Tayfun and Khokhlov were good to bring on . . . now we don't have much strength in depth. The Korean, Lee, has done nothing. If anyone was signed to shift shirts, it was him, not Beckham. But it's not just that. There's something funny going on, I'm sure of it."

Lunch, in a big converted farmhouse in the hills, is lentil soup and pork chops, washed down by red wine and orujo de hierbas (a sort of spicy grappa). We return to the bar we were in this morning in Urnieta, and have more orujo, ordered by José Mari's father-in-law, a jovial Catalan with a fondness for conspiracy theories. He reminds me that several years ago, at his daughter Marisa's wedding to José Mari, I sang the Barça hymn with him in Catalan, something I don't remember.

"All the best memories are the ones you can't remember," he says.

There is another guy who joins us, who is introduced as being a Madridista. I ask him why.

"Because my whole family are Madridista. There are nine children. Eleven in the family."

I tell him they should form a football team.

"My mother would go in goal," he says. I ask him if it is difficult being a Real Madrid fan in a small Basque town like Urnieta.

"Only when we lose," he says. "It is very difficult when we lose . . . especially to La Real."

José Mari's father-in-law has been bursting to tell a joke and he's finally found the space.

"In a school in Madrid in the Franco days there's a teacher, who supports Madrid, who says 'put your hand up if you support Madrid.' All but one of the children puts their hand up. The teacher turns angrily to the girl who doesn't. 'Why haven't you got your hand up?' he shouts. 'Because I support Barça,' comes the reply. 'Why do you support Barça?' 'Because my father does, and my mother does.' 'And if your mother was a whore, and your father a thief, would you follow them then?' 'No, miss, in that case I would be a Real Madrid fan.'"

We all laugh.

It's time to leave the bar to get our tickets. A relative of José Mari is good friends with a former director of the club who can get hold of tickets for us. We're going to meet him in a bar near the stadium. We get in the car and drive down the hill to San Sebastián, parking within sight of Anoeta. Ten minutes later we are joined table by the former director, a smartly dressed man in his fifties. He's balding, with a pleasant manner about him. The tone of the conversation is polite. He starts chatting before getting down to the business of the tickets.

"I've just been with John Benjamin Toshack," he says. For some reason I have never fully understood, the Spanish always use Toshack's middle name when they describe him. The Welshman was Real Sociedad manager three times, and has a house in nearby Zarauz. "Funnily enough he has to go to the UK to commentate on the match. He's some expert, as of course he was Real Madrid manager twice, too."

I ask him what Toshack thinks about Beckham.

Pro-file: Beckham shows his best side after the Malaga game

Seeing red: a Valencian Sunday League manager refuses to walk

Deer Vigo: the Rikitriki bar, a shrine to Celta de Vigo

Scarf-ace: Arximelo the Rikitriki owner

Galacticos: Beckham in the presence of genius

Here Vigo: Celta fan singing in the rain

Taking the mic: Manolo el del Bombo gives another interview

The big match: the boys are back in town

Beckhamania: teenage fans wait for the Real Madrid bus in Pamplona

The king and I: giants in Pamplona's San Saturnino procession

El Spice Boy: Beckham's image adorns thousands of bedroom walls in Spain

Question time: Beckham faces the Brit Pack press guys

More than a game: the Barça-Real 'clasico', table football style

Into the cauldron of hate: Beckham runs onto the Camp Nou for his first ever 'clasico' against Barça

Little drummer boy: Lander in San Sebastian

Getting his goat: the author enjoys a slug of 'good Navarra wine' in San Sebastian

Like father... José Mari and Lander in San Sebastian

You looking at me? Racing de Santander fans urge their team on

Collared: the author arranges a trip to the Picos de Europa after the Santander game

'The lads done good': Beckham talks to the press after the Santander game

Holy growl: Figo the dog in the Picos de Europa

True confessions: Don Manuel discusses his Ronaldo problem with the author

Soft landing; Beckham straddles Ronaldo (and not, luckily, vice versa)

Three wise men: inmates of the San Mames old peoples' home next to the Athletic stadium

And then there were four: prescient graffiti in Bilbao

Hostile reception: the Real Madrid bus arrives in Bilbao

Bridge to victory: the old Basque radical *

Redskin: Iñigo the anti-Beckhamista shows off his tattoos

Pride of all Europe: two lions and an Athletic fan

Red, white and blue: Brenda in Bilbao

Basquing in glory: the author and Jose Mari, outside the San Mames

Mane man: Athletic's lion mascot celebrates their 4-2 victory over El Real

Beauty and the beast: from right to left, Beckham and the author

'Not at all': the author interviews Beckham after the Bilbao game

Lest we forget: March 11th mourning notice in Bilbao

Cathedral in the sky: San Mames, 'La Catedral', Athletic's famous stadium

Antimadridistas: Athletico fans' passion for their team is only matched by their hatred of El Real

The joy of the goalscorer: but Beckham's goal wasn't enough to prevent a demoralising defeat for El Real against Zaragoza in the Copa del Rey final

Death in the afternoon: a bull awaits its fate in the Valencian bull-ring

Campeones, campeones oé, oé, oé: Valencia fans celebrate winning La Liga

Flag day: thousands of Valencia fans watched the championship-deciding game against Sevilla on big screens outside Mestalla stadium

Showing his true colours: the author and Manolo el del Bombo celebrate Valencia's championship win

"Whoever doesn't jump up and down is a Madridista".

Hero worship: this isn't why Valencia are nicknamed 'Los Ches'

Nearly there: Valencia score their first goal against Sevilla

'They're not singing any more': there wasn't much celebration in the Madrid supporters club in Barcelona

"I didn't ask him," he says. Then, incongruously, "you know he has a brilliant memory, Toshack. He can remember all the Madrid team's birthdays."

We walk to the stadium, and our companion tells us to wait for a moment, then walks over to the taquilla and comes back with an envelope containing two tickets each worth 65 euros. Jose Mari hands him 140 euros and says 'keep the change' but our companion is insistent on giving it back. The offering and refusal seem like a ritual. We all walk back towards the car together.

"Why did you stop being a director?" I ask him. We are standing outside José Mari's car.

"Because it was all about money. You all sit around a table and all you do is talk about money."

On the way back home we meet José Mari's sister-in-law playing with her four-year old daughter, Patricia, on a swing.

"Which team do you support?" I ask the little girl, knowing her whole family are Real Sociedad mad.

"Madrid," she shouts, with a smile on her face, knowing it is naughty of her to say so. "Madrid, Madrid, Madrid!"

Later that evening we go to a tapas bar in Urnieta. The separatist sympathies of the owners are made obvious by the decor. There is the Ikurriña, the Basque flag, over the bar and several pictures of Real Sociedad round the walls. One depicts the moment before the kick-off between Athletic de Bilbao and Real Sociedad in San Sebastián in December 1975, the first match between the two after Franco's death. The two captains, José Angel Iribar and Inaxio Kortabarria, are holding the still-illegal Ikurriña up to the fans. The latter, Jose Mari tells me, is the only Basque player ever to refuse to play for Spain. There's also a picture of a guy with a moustache hitting a volley. José Mari explains the picture's significance.

He tells me it was taken in the heady early days of democracy after Franco's death. The Basque country was breathing a collective sigh of relief after years of repression. To make things even better in San Sebastián, this coincided with the best Real Sociedad side anyone could remember, captained by Periko Alonso, who demonstrated his passion for the team by insisting on wearing the club badge on the left of his shirt, over his heart, while the rest of the players wore theirs on the right. All season Real Sociedad were neck and neck with Real Madrid in the table. And the title race went to the last minute of the last game. La Real knew that if they drew their last game of the season against Sporting de Gijón in Asturias they would win the league for the first time in their history, whatever Real Madrid did in their game in Valladolid. With a minute to go, Madrid were winning 3–1, and already celebrating, as they knew La Real were trailing 2–1. Alonso put in a desperate cross which was fisted out by the Sporting goalkeeper, Castro. It fell to the boot of the aptly-named Jesús Zamora, who thumped it into the net with some aplomb. It is one of those moments that Real Sociedad fans will never forget, but it wasn't the end of the celebrations. Alonso skippered the team in 1982, too, when a last-game victory over Athletic de Bilbao ensured the team a second consecutive title.

This wasn't the end of the Basque domination. In 1983 and 1984, Athletic de Bilbao's all-Basque XI, fired up by the success of their neighbours, kept the title in the region, with a young Javier Clemente as manager. The policy of only fielding local players is still maintained by Bilbao, though Real Sociedad have started fielding foreign players (the first was Anglo-Irishman John Aldridge in 1989) and last year signed the first non-Basque Spaniard to play for the team for 35 years, since they last won promotion to the Primera in 1967. Sergio Boris, a centre-back signed from Oviedo, was born in Avilés, Asturias. He failed to make much of an impression and is rarely played in the team, but he was representative of a shift in politics by Real Sociedad.

## SATURDAY JANUARY 10TH

The most famous former Real Sociedad player ever is the late Eduardo Chillida, a sculptor whose massive iron works can be seen in cities all over the world. Chillida was the team's goalkeeper in the early '40s – though a serious knee injury forced him out of the game and he went to Madrid to study architecture, and on to Paris to paint. Chillida, who dedicated his life to trying to work out the elusive relationship between time and space, has left his mark on the town with a fantastic sculpture built into the rocks on the east side of town. It is called 'El Peine de los Vientos' (the Comb of the Winds) and is especially worth visiting on a day, like today, when the sea is rough. The sculpture comprises two curved iron claw-like masses protruding from the black natural rock which are pounded by the ocean waves. Holes built into the promenade occasionally produce spectacular spouts of water. It is a reminder of the power of nature, and the ability of man to temper and withstand it.

It's a great place to go to collect your thoughts before a match. José Mari has given me a blue and white scarf to wear, and I have put it round my neck. It is the first time all season I have actually worn any colours to a Spanish game. I have a soft spot for Real Sociedad, from my long association with the town. And my Anti-Madridismo hasn't abated over the Christmas holidays.

We take a short cut over a hill to get to the stadium. At the top is the Costa Vasca Hotel, where we see hundreds of people collected around the entrance. I realise immediately what's going on. Real Madrid must be leaving for the match. We rush across just in time to catch the players getting into the bus. José Mari is thrilled, and takes photos of Roberto Carlos and Ronaldo to show his three-year-old son, Lander, whose favourite word game over the weekend has been the following.

"Which is fatter, a hippo or Ronaldo?"

"Ronaldo!"

Which is fatter, Santa or Ronaldo?"

"Ronaldo!"

Which is fatter, Obelix . . .

Whenever Ronaldo appears on the TV, which he does rather a lot, the kid shrieks 'Gordito' (little fatty). Beckham for some reason evokes the response 'Beckham chulo es' (Beckham is cocky).

There is no Beckham, of course, coming out of the hotel, and the numbers are fewer than usual, but there is plenty of teenage girl presence. The bus edges its way out of the car park, closely followed by a moped with two young girls on it. The passenger wears a Real Sociedad shirt with 'Nihat' (the club's Turkish striker) written on the back, the driver wears a Real Madrid 'Figo' shirt.

We walk down the hill and stop for a drink in the courtyard of a hotel within sight of the stadium. I do as the locals do and get myself a kalimotxo, a wine and cola with ice, which is as refreshing as a beer. A lot of the fans are carrying round plastic bottles full of Coke which, from the sway of their gait, is mixed with something stronger. I ask José what he thinks about the stadium, which replaced an older model next to the train station nearer the town centre.

"Anoeta is a beautiful stadium," he says, "but we all hate the fact that there is a running track around it. The old one was like an English stadium. Here we are too far away to intimidate the opposition. In a few years they have agreed that they will build the seats to the edge of the pitch, which will increase the capacity, too. At the moment it is only 32,000."

It looks bigger. We join the hubbub of blue-and-white clad fans around the building, constructed next to a tree-covered mountain, a mixture of functional concrete sides and an arty, swirling glass roof, then we make our way to our seats.

Inside the roar of the fans is intensified by its echo against the swirling roof.

"The atmosphere is great in the stands, but apparently it doesn't reach the pitch," says José Mari.

Everyone starts whistling as Real Madrid run out, dressed in black, then they hold up their scarves – or the paper versions of scarves that have been laid on all the seats – as Real Sociedad run onto the pitch. The anthem, in Basque, sounds old-fashioned.

*Txuri-urdin*
*Txuri-urdin maitea*
*Txuri-urdin*
*Txuri-urdin Aurrera*
*Beti, Beti maite*
*maite, maitea*
*Donostia, donostiarra'*

I don't understand a word.

A brass band a few rows behind me starts up a tune. There are about five trumpets, a trombone and a drum. It lends a bull-ring tone to the atmosphere as the match kicks off.

The game is tense but essentially dull. Real Sociedad play on the counter-attack. The trouble is that Real Madrid don't seem too keen to attack. Chances are few and far between. Nihat shoots a Beckham-style free-kick (a right-foot outswinger towards the keeper's right-hand post) just wide; Raúl puts the ball over after a punch out by the keeper. Most of the action goes on in the centre of the pitch – both teams seem happy to try and keep possession for long periods without feeling the urgency to score. Suddenly I feel a hand on my shoulder. There's a guy looming over me, with a goatskin wine bottle in one hand.

"What are you writing? Are you the police?"

José Mari explains my task.

"Don't write anything about me. My wife doesn't know I'm here," says the guy. Then he gives us a slug of the goatskin. The jet of wine is thin; you have to squeeze it for a long time to get a satisfying hit.

"Good strong wine from Navarra," he says, taking it back. Then, seeing someone he knows some rows back, he slings the goatskin a good ten yards; his friend catches it and enjoys a slug.

"Falta la rubia," says someone behind, meaning that Madrid are missing Beckham 'the blondie'. At that point Nihat is put through on goal, but Iker Casillas is quick out of his goal and smothers the chance.

"Too bad they're not missing Casillas, too," replies his mate. The Madrid goalkeeper has been good all season. There looks to be no way past him today.

At half-time, as I chew a goat-cheese bocadillo I've bought earlier, another goatskin of wine comes my way. José Mari has made friends with the two guys to his left, as well as the group in front and the goatskin-slinger from before. A sort of community has developed, swapping comments and slugging back the wine. Goatskins, as they don't touch the lips, are a very hygienic way of sharing your drink. Everyone agrees that La Real have had the better of the first half, but they're still not right.

"Nihat isn't as confident as last year."

"Kovacevic is too slow. Shaving his head hasn't changed his luck – he still doesn't look like scoring."

"Denoueix should bring on Xabi Alonso but, as ever, he'll wait until it's too late." The ball boys have run onto the pitch and are having a free-for-all game, all trying to score in Anoeta.

The second half is a little more open, and Real Madrid start with more endeavour. But this means that they leave more gaps, too. The home team's influential Russian midfielder Valeri Karpin is denied a foul by the referee and he bashes the turf like Dick Dastardly. Real Sociedad win a corner, and the clapping bit from Gary Glitter's 'Rock 'n' Roll' is played on the tannoy, to get the fans clapping too. The trumpet band starts up again. Unless I tell you otherwise, every five minutes, the trumpet band starts up again.

The match drifts back into its earlier torpor, but there is great applause when Xabi Alonso, the son of La Real's championship-winning captain of the team of '81, and the club's play-maker, comes onto the pitch. Almost immediately the Basques look sharper, and the ball starts getting moved coherently about the pitch. Nihat receives it outside the box and puts in a cross-cum-shot which drifts over Kovacevic's head. Casillas is put off by the Serb's jump and feebly punches the ball downwards. Karpin, falling to the ground, gets a boot to it and 0–0 has become 1–0. A world of difference. Everybody is on their feet. The goatskin drunkard comes across.

"Write that down. Write that down!"

"I'm writing!"

"Valeri, Valeri, Valeri Kaaaaaaaaaarpiiiiiin!" shouts the tannoy guy. Another goatskin is thrust into my hands. I take a slug.

Remarkably El Real hardly react. La Real start playing possession football. With ten minutes to go, a 75-year-old lady shuffles apologetically in front of us.

"I can't stand any more of this. Either I leave now, or I'm taken out in an ambulance," she says. But it's a toothless Real Madrid, and the ground is filled with 'olés' as the Real Sociedad midfield, strengthened by the arrival of another Alonso brother, Mikel, play keep-ball. The band start playing a jaunty march.

"That's what they play when Real Sociedad are winning the game," explains José Mari. "It's San Sebastián's March." Madrid can't do anything to change the tune. The referee whistles an end to the game.

We walk with the crowd from the stadium to the town centre, and watch the old part filling up for another night of debauchery. Then we catch a taxi back to Urnieta, popping into the bar. I learn that Valencia have beaten Albacete 1–0 away, meaning that they have leap-frogged Real Madrid to go top of the table. This being the end of the first half of the fixture list (all the teams have played one another at least once), Valencia are 'winter champions', an honorary title meaningless in all but the boost it can give to the second half of the season. On the way out I see the Real Madrid fan with the family XI playing darts. He looks miserable, unlike everyone else in the bar. I contemplate on what a difficult time he must have in this Real Madrid-hating, Real Sociedad-loving area.

"Faltaba la Rubia!" he shouts, when he sees me. Blondie was missing.

## RESULTS JORNADA 18

| | | | |
|---|---|---|---|
| ATHLETIC | 1 | OSASUNA | 1 |
| **REAL MADRID** | **1** | **MURCIA** | **0** |
| SEVILLA | 2 | ALBACETE | 0 |
| VALLADOLID | 0 | BETIS | 0 |
| RACING | 3 | BARCELONA | 0 |
| CELTA | 0 | DEPORTIVO | 5 |
| ESPANYOL | 2 | MALLORCA | 0 |
| MÁLAGA | 1 | REAL SOCIEDAD | 2 |
| ZARAGOZA | 0 | ATLÉTICO | 0 |
| VALENCIA | 4 | VILLARREAL | 2 |

## RESULTS JORNADA 19

| | | | |
|---|---|---|---|
| MALLORCA | 2 | CELTA | 4 |
| MURCIA | 0 | ESPANYOL | 1 |
| OSASUNA | 1 | SEVILLA | 1 |
| VILLARREAL | 3 | VALLADOLID | 1 |
| DEPORTIVO | 1 | RACING | 1 |
| **REAL SOCIEDAD** | **1** | **REAL MADRID** | **0** |
| ALBACETE | 0 | VALENCIA | 1 |
| ATLÉTICO | 3 | ATHLETIC | 0 |
| BARCELONA | 3 | ZARAGOZA | 0 |
| BETIS | 3 | MÁLAGA | 0 |

## LA CLASIFICACIÓN

| | P | W | D | L | F | A | Pts |
|---|---|---|---|---|---|---|---|
| VALENCIA | 19 | 13 | 4 | 2 | 36 | 14 | 43 |
| **REAL MADRID** | **19** | **13** | **3** | **3** | **37** | **19** | **42** |
| DEPORTIVO | 19 | 11 | 4 | 4 | 32 | 15 | 37 |
| ATLÉTICO | 19 | 9 | 4 | 6 | 26 | 22 | 31 |
| VILLARREAL | 19 | 8 | 6 | 5 | 25 | 22 | 30 |
| OSASUNA | 19 | 7 | 8 | 4 | 20 | 15 | 29 |
| BARCELONA | 19 | 7 | 6 | 6 | 26 | 25 | 27 |
| MÁLAGA | 19 | 8 | 2 | 9 | 24 | 25 | 26 |
| ATHLETIC | 19 | 7 | 5 | 7 | 23 | 24 | 26 |
| RACING | 19 | 7 | 5 | 7 | 24 | 26 | 26 |
| SEVILLA | 19 | 6 | 7 | 6 | 27 | 22 | 25 |
| VALLADOLID | 19 | 6 | 7 | 6 | 23 | 26 | 25 |
| MALLORCA | 19 | 7 | 2 | 10 | 23 | 34 | 23 |
| BETIS | 19 | 5 | 7 | 7 | 24 | 22 | 22 |
| REAL SOCIEDAD | 19 | 5 | 6 | 8 | 19 | 29 | 21 |
| ALBACETE | 19 | 6 | 2 | 11 | 21 | 25 | 20 |
| CELTA | 19 | 4 | 8 | 7 | 26 | 32 | 20 |
| ZARAGOZA | 19 | 5 | 5 | 9 | 18 | 24 | 20 |
| ESPANYOL | 19 | 4 | 2 | 13 | 15 | 33 | 14 |
| MURCIA | 19 | 1 | 9 | 9 | 15 | 30 | 12 |

**TWELVE**
# MADRID

GOLFO DE VIZCAYA

OCÉANO ATLÁNTICO

**Real Madrid**
○

**Villarreal**
○

MAR MEDITERRÁNEO

# TWELVE
# MADRID

## SUNDAY JANUARY 18TH (BARCELONA)

The newspapers suggest all week that Beckham will not be fit for Real Madrid's match against Betis in Seville, so I decide not to go. I've already been to Seville. There's no point in going again if he's not playing, I figure. I've hardly seen Brenda for weeks. I decide to book a plane to Madrid for next weekend's league match instead, at home to Villarreal, and watch the Betis game in the Real Madrid peña in L'Hospitalet, with all the old guys, the immigrants from the Franco years who've never made the switch to Barça.

When I get *Marca* on the morning of the match, there's a shock. There's a picture of Beckham at Seville railway station, being tripped up by a dumb-looking girl in a red track-suit top. It's a brilliant picture, but it's bad news for me. 'VUELVE BECKHAM' screams the headline. 'Beckham returns.'

It's still not sure he'll make the team, though. He's hardly trained all week. I arrive at the peña ten minutes before kick-off, with Brenda, in time to watch a little of the pre-match coverage. We find room at a table right in front of a large screen in the bar section of the peña. (We haven't announced our arrival beforehand, and there is a very large 'STRICTLY MEMBERS ONLY' sign hanging on the curtain of the main room.) The bar is packed. They show the Real Madrid team and formation. I look to see if Beckham's playing . . . and there's his name, in central midfield, next to Helguera. Damn!

I'm watching the match with Brenda, who starts noticing the sort of things that I would have otherwise missed.

"Beckham's hair is not quite long enough to keep in the new, lower sort of pony-tail he's wearing," she says, during the warm-up. "Look, there's a little strand that keeps getting in his eye, which he keeps having to tuck back in. I bet that'll annoy him all game." She's the only woman in the place.

"Anyway," she continues "wasn't I reading in Hemingway the other day that pony-tails are just allowed to be worn by bullfighters? I think he fancies himself as a bit of a matador."

Whatever the case, it looks like Beckham shouldn't have been risked. He's playing deep and, forced into an ultra-defensive mode by the Betis players who attack Real Madrid from the off, he's hardly getting a touch. The Betis right winger, Joaquín, rumoured to be moving to Real Madrid next season, is a constant menace, torturing Roberto Carlos down the flank. The number 11 is a frustrating player, who often disappears for entire matches. Tonight he is turning it on, giving a wonderful display of how a mixture of pace and skill can destroy a defence. Real often bring the best out in opposing players. On five minutes Roberto Carlos, beaten for pace, knocks the local hero over in the box. You can hear 50,000 voices appealing for a penalty. It looks a sure thing. The old men around me sit, nervous, waiting for the referee.

"No era penalti," says the guy on my left, with white hair and a tweed jacket. You can tell there has been no debate in his mind.

"No, no era penalti," agrees his mate.

The referee doesn't give it. On the replay you can see that it was a clear penalty. Así gana el Madrid.

Then on 18 minutes, Joaquín goes down again in the box, this time after a sandwich challenge by Raúl Bravo and Michel Salgado. Again the roared appeals from the TV crowd, again the derisive comments of the peña crowd, again the referee waves play on. On 33 minutes Beckham gives the ball away in midfield. Fernando shoots, Casillas feebly palms the ball to the edge of the six yard box, and Joaquín gleefully volleys it into the net, before running to the sideline and doing a mad, contorted goal celebration which brings to mind Ian Curtis from Joy Division. El Heliópolis, Betis' stadium (officially named Manuel Ruiz de Lopera after their current chairman) goes wild. Can they repeat the drubbing dealt out to Real Madrid by their rivals Seville?

At half time everyone in the bar is in a bad mood, especially one short man with a clipped beard who shouts at a teenage kid who has walked into the members-only section without being a member. Nobody likes to see their team losing, but when you are used to success, it seems even harder to bear.

"Madrid's defence is terrible tonight," I say to the barman, as I get a beer.

"It's not just the defence. It's the whole team. We are playing as if we have only just met one another. We are shit."

"And Beckham?"

"Beckham was the cause of the goal. He wants too much time on the ball for the position he is playing in. The goal was his fault."

When I get back Brenda has a go at the referee.

"He's terrible. Is he a professional?"

"Yes, though he probably has another job, too."

"That's ridiculous. They pay so much to the likes of Beckham and Zidane. How much do they pay the refs?"

"Um . . . more than they used to. But not much."

"It's clear that the referee is not as good as the players. It's ridiculous. Of course you're not going to get good referees if you don't pay enough. He should have given two penalties there. It should be 3–0!"

These are not views that would go down well with the old men of the bar, muttering into their coffees, smoking their fags. Just as well she's speaking in English.

The second half isn't as electric as the first. Betis have tired themselves out running at Real Madrid. And on the hour Ronaldo does what he's best at doing. Scoring a goal from nothing. He gets the ball from Zidane, commits the goalkeeper with a drop of the shoulder and a step-over, and passes the ball into the goal from an acute angle. 1–1 and a perfect example of what a difference he makes to the team. The old man to my left jumps out of his seat, clenching his fist at the screen in the same movement. It's a sign of relief rather than joy. Sometimes I don't think it would be that pleasant being a Real Madrid fan.

There is more to come. Tote, the former Real Madrid striker sold to Betis at the beginning of the season, does an outrageous 'rabona' – a pass with his right foot after crossing it behind his left one, surprising everyone, including his team-mates. Then a Beckham corner is headed goalwards by Helguera, only to be cleared off the line by a Betis defender. In the dying seconds Figo dwells too long on a shot from outside the box, which is blocked.

"Hijo de puta!" shouts the man in the tweed jacket. It's the last action of the match. There is little conversation. A draw in Betis is not seen as being a good result. The bar clears pretty quickly. Brenda's still upset.

"It just doesn't seem fair," she says. "The referee gave Real Madrid the draw. Do they always give the decisions Real Madrid's way like that?"

## RESULTS JORNADA 20

| | | | |
|---|---|---|---|
| MURCIA | 2 | CELTA | 2 |
| VALLADOLID | 0 | VALENCIA | 0 |
| BARCELONA | 1 | ATHLETIC | 1 |
| DEPORTIVO | 4 | ZARAGOZA | 1 |
| MALLORCA | 1 | RACING | 1 |
| OSASUNA | 1 | ALBACETE | 1 |
| REAL SOCIEDAD | 3 | ESPANYOL | 1 |
| VILLARREAL | 2 | MÁLAGA | 0 |
| ATLÉTICO | 2 | SEVILLA | 1 |
| **BETIS** | **1** | **REAL MADRID** | **1** |

### WEDNESDAY JANUARY 21ST

As if to prove her wrong, Beckham is sent off in Real's next game, a Copa del Rey quarter-final against Valencia at the Bernabéu. This has been billed as 'the battle of the giants' with Valencia sitting at the top of the table, a point above Real Madrid. Real win 3–0, with two late goals rendering the second leg in Valencia a week later virtually meaningless. Beckham is booked on 68 minutes for something he has said to the referee, meaning, as the commentator points out, that the ref 'is obviously fluent in the language of Shakespeare'. Then, on 88, he catches up with Valencia's little Argentinian playmaker, Aimar, in possession on the half-way line and tackles him from behind, clipping his heels and knocking him over. With the score-line as it is, it is a naive foul to commit with a booking to your name. The referee pulls out a red card. Beckham looks aggrieved. The crowd give him a standing ovation as he leaves the field and he makes his usual gesture of clapping each stand as he leaves the field.

Beckham will miss the next leg of the semi, but is not criticised for his sending-off by the Madrid-supporting football press the next day. Far from it. Hugo Gatti, *As'* outspoken Argentinian commentator, writes 'the applause that Beckham got on leaving the field should not go unnoticed. He earned it with his great passing game and his ballsy performance in the middle of the field. He's Madrid's most solid player, and this makes him the player most honoured by the Madrid fans.' The sending off is big news in the English papers, but is hardly worth a side-note in Spain. Beckham's post-match comments are quoted. "I definitely didn't think it was deserved because I just clipped the back of his ankle. I don't even know what the first card was for. Even if I did say something to the referee he wouldn't have understood it. It's different for English players in Spain. The mentality here is different. You can get away with things in the Premiership that you can't get away with here. But I've got no problem with the ref. It's his decision and that's that."

## FRIDAY JANUARY 23RD

After all those trains, getting the aeroplane from Barcelona to Madrid is a joy. I'm going to see Madrid play Villarreal in the Bernabéu, to see how Beckham is going down in the capital, his home city in Spain. I take a Spanair flight on the Barcelona-Madrid shuttle; flights leave hourly, and, if there's room, you can buy tickets in the airport as if you were getting a bus. I leave my flat at 7am and am in the new Real Madrid training ground by 12 o'clock, courtesy of a lift from my host this weekend, Sid Lowe, who picks me up from the metro station, gives me a cup of tea in his flat, and takes me for a terrifying 20-minute motorway ride to Las Rozas, the satellite estate to where Madrid temporarily moved their training ground earlier this season.

Sid is the Spanish football correspondent for *The Guardian Online* service and for the *Daily Telegraph*: unlike the other 'Beckham correspondents' in Madrid he has lived in the country for several years and speaks fluent Spanish. He hasn't got rid of his UK car, though, and every lane change seems to be a calculated high-speed risk; moreover he has taken on the Spanish habit of giving a running commentary of how bad the other drivers on the road are.

This is slotted in between other nuggets of information about the set-up of the Beckham correspondents in Madrid, and gossip about the player.

"I pray to God that Beckham doesn't go at the end of the season: he represents a significant proportion of my livelihood . . ."

"Go?"

"Yeah. Listen, it's quite likely. Posh simply doesn't seem to have moved here. She's always in England. When she does come, she comes at the weekend; that's when he's working hardest. He's only human. He's rented a house; it isn't easy to go back to an empty house, whoever you are . . ."

This is the first I've heard of it. "But he's doing so well . . ."

"I reckon that's possibly counterproductive. What the hell is that fucking idiot doing? Which lane are you in? Make up your mind! About time, too! I reckon if Real win the European Cup, he'll go at the end of the season. He'll want to prove himself here, to have something at the end of the season to show that he made a success of his year. The European Cup fits the bill. If they don't win that, he might well stay until they do."

"But where would he go?"

"Where can he go? Chelsea, I suppose."

Sid tells me about the life of a Beckham correspondent. There are a varying number, at any given time, but four regulars: Eric Beauchamp, of the *Sun*, Simon Cass, of the *Daily Mail*, Anthony Kasternakis, of the *News of the World*, and himself. They go out to training most days, to watch Beckham and to try and grab a word with him afterwards. They go to matches for exactly the same reason. They are always looking for a new angle to sell the Beckham story back home.

"It's actually quite annoying as they are mostly on a different agenda from me," says Sid. "I am interested in Beckham's Spanish experience; how he is fitting in here, how he is adapting to the different style of football and the different style of life; what he thinks of the football culture here. They are looking for a story that will sell in England. They are more interested in what he thinks of Louis Saha moving to Man United. Or how he is supposedly having a feud with the Argentinians. That's the current story: his bloody feud with the Argentinians."

I wonder if any of the journalists follow him from place to place, hound him, shadow him, make his life hell?

"No, the boys are just there to talk to him in the mixed zone after the training session or the game. I think he actually likes us. After all, we are among the few people he meets in his working week who speak the same language as him. But there is one person who follows him from place to place: a photographer who sells his photos to the tabloids. He waits in his car in a lay-by outside his house, and tags behind Beckham wherever he drives. Beckham can't stand him; the other day he saw him at a press conference, recognised his face. 'You can't come in here, you've been following me about,' he said. The guy had to leave. Funnily enough he's the most quiet-spoken, nice-seeming person you could meet."

Las Rozas is a recent development, a soulless new town 20 kilometres north-west of Madrid; a series of identical redbrick blocks of flats, pale yellow chalets and could-be-anywhere shops. A real global village in an increasingly mono-cultural world, and a fitting place for Real Madrid, a collection of superstars from over the world with a large following in three continents. The training ground dominates the area with its six huge sets of floodlights, concrete ladder-like structures, leaning forward as if propped against an invisible wall. There are security men everywhere; this is a closed-door training session, due to the fact that there is a match tomorrow. There is a helicopter circling overhead, making a hell of a racket.

"That's the Villarreal spies," says Sid. Mostly his jokes are good.

Sid shows his accreditation and breezes past the security guard. I haven't had time to pick mine up. I have to ring Paco, Real's hard-working factotum press officer, a man who has been rapidly promoted but doesn't seem, according to Sid, to have left any of his previous responsibilities behind. He sounds hassled. He sounds like he always sounds hassled. He says he will tell someone who will tell someone who will walkie-talkie the relevant security guard. I stand in front of the guard, waiting for this to happen. He has a large truncheon on his belt.

Fifteen minutes later, after being stopped by another security guard, after ringing Paco again and after having to wait for more walkie-talkie confirmation amid the din of the bloody helicopter which is still hovering overhead, I find myself in the mixed zone of the training area. It is situated on a concrete pathway outside a building where the changing rooms are located. There is a line of bright blue crash-barriers on the path, behind which ten or so journalists are standing. Everything is new – no grime, no weeds. The players need to walk past to get to the car park. The journalists are French, Spanish and English. Everyone waiting for their man. Becks has arranged to do an interview with the English guys. The French guy speaks all three languages fluently, talking to everybody in the group. He has cropped peroxide hair and a cheeky grin. He can't stand still, moving from person to person.

"Are you from *L'Equipe*?" I ask him.

"Yes I am."

*L'Equipe* is the French national sports paper, an upmarket *Marca*.

"A Zinedine Zidane correspondent?"

"Mais oui."

"Is he as shy as they say?"

"He is very, very shy. A timid man. But it doesn't matter. Today I have to ask him about his damaged muscle. That is all."

He gives me a piece of cinnamon-flavoured chewing gum. Then he sings a little song and does a little jig.

"Ce soir j'attends Zinedine. Comme chaque soir, comme chaque soir" (Tonight I wait for Zinedine, like every night, like every night).

I want to talk to the Madrid midfielders about what it's like to play with Beckham. Guti's out too quickly for me to catch his attention. He looks expert in avoiding people like me. Cambiasso comes out next, the young Argentine midfield enforcer, who started the season as a titular (first-teamer) but whose opportunities are getting less and less frequent.

"Cambiasso!" I half-shout, as he walks past. I've heard Spanish journalists do this; they use the players' playing names, the ones that they put on their shirt. He's balding, and you can see it more now that his shaven hair of the early season has grown out. He's wearing a polo neck jumper and jeans. He avoids my eye, but holds his mobile phone in my general direction, as if to say that he's busy.

"I just want to ask you about playing with Beckham. What's it like to play with him?"

He's walking away fast, but turns round.

"It's very good," he says. He's got a sarcastic tone to his voice, as if he's letting me know that he's just voicing the party line, and he knows that I know that, but what the hell.

"Es un gran jugador" (he's a great player). That's all. Never even slowed his pace. He's off.

Next up comes Borja. He's a youngster, who's just got into the first team squad. A central midfielder like Beckham, he's played a couple of games this season. I watched him play against Mallorca. He played rather well. I saw him speak to journalists afterwards, too. He seems cultured and intelligent, both on and off the pitch. I'm hoping that the players-give-you-their-attention-inversely-proportionate-to-their-fame rule will come into play here.

"Borja!" I shout. Borja is his Christian name, but the one he has chosen for his shirt. He looks at me, sizes me up and approaches. He's wearing an adidas tracksuit.

"I just want a quote or two about what it's like to play with Beckham."

"It's good."

"Has he changed the way Madrid play? Has he left an English stamp on the team?"

"I think that Real Madrid has changed the way he plays, and has left a Spanish stamp on his game."

"How do you communicate when you play with him?" The helicopter has chosen this moment to hover overhead, as if to emphasis the theme of communication difficulty. He leans his head down towards me, so he can hear me. He has a pronounced Roman nose. He looks a little like Gareth Southgate.

"It's difficult, because we don't share a language. But we understand one another. Football is a language."

"His Spanish isn't so good?"

"My English isn't so good."

"Have you learnt anything from him?"

"A lot. How to pass. How to make space for yourself. How to work hard. How to win possession from the opposition. He's learning a lot, and I'm learning watching him learn. He's a very good player."

He gives me a look as if to say 'is that all?' and I thank him. It is.

Because, without warning, Beckham has come out. He is wearing his blond-streaked hair down to his shoulders, and has on a khaki t-shirt and beige combat trousers. You can see a large jagged blue tattoo coming out from under the sleeve of his t-shirt. He has a very quick word with Simon and Eric, shaking his head and shrugging his shoulders, then he's off. I walk beside him, ask for an autograph. He signs it, without slowing his pace. Without looking at me. I wonder if he is aware of my existence, if he has noticed my presence in so many of the places he has been to in Spain. Somehow I doubt it. I drop back. I drop back. Another journalist, a girl who is writing a book about Steve McManaman, attaches herself to him, walks alongside, asking him questions. He gives her short shrift and she, too, is left in his wake. Beckham is in a hurry and he is not doing any talking. Pretty soon, he's out of sight and in the car park.

Sid comes up. "He had said he'd do an interview today, but he's changed his mind. He must have something on. I wonder what?" Sam and Eric say their goodbyes. They are off down the pub. No story today. Sid is to pick them up later, to give them a lift back to Madrid.

### SATURDAY JANUARY 24TH

I'm back in the working-class La Latina district, retracing my late-August steps. I find the market again, six months more seedy. It's the afternoon, so not all the stalls are open. I find the guy from the 'alimentos' stall: 60ish, with a big Spanish moustache, standing in front of a bank of tins of tuna, anchovies and plum-peeled tomatoes, with a selection of hams and cheeses in a glass cabinet in front of him. Two people are being served, two more are waiting. I let an old lady go in front of me. She buys some ham.

"This one's the sweetest," he says and cuts her off some slices on a big machine. Then it is my turn, and I remind him who I am.

"Six months ago you said you thought Beckham was just signed to sell shirts. What do you think now?"

He smiles. His answer is a PR man's dream.

"Todo lo contrario" ('absolutely the opposite'). "He sacrifices himself every game. I didn't think he would do that. I didn't know he was a worker. He has been good, both effectively and sportingly."

"I think . . ." he continues, "he has changed the way Madrid play. They play more from the back now. More like the English, with one, two passes then, poom, a long ball from Beckham and . . . Gol!"

"A good signing, then?"

"A great signing. One of the best for years."

I walk up towards Lavapiés and pretty soon I find myself in the smoky bar with the nicotine-stained Hieronymous Bosch picture that I went into on my last visit. I think I recognise the barman who spoke to me last time, the man of few words.

"Were you working here six months ago?" I ask him.

"I was working here 20 years ago," he replies. He wears a white jacket, as if he was working in a market.

"I asked you about Beckham six months ago. Do you remember?"

"I remember."

"Have you changed your opinion? You said that Madrid should have signed a different sort of player."

He looks at me slowly and walks away. I don't think he wants to talk. Then he comes back. He's been thinking out his reply.

"I didn't know him as a player, then. I thought he was here to sell shirts. And I wasn't wrong. He *was* brought here to sell shirts. But to play as well. He is a very good player. I see him on the TV (he points up to an old set up high in the corner, that looks like it might be black and white). The fact is, nowadays, you can't afford to buy a good player and pay him all those millions, unless he sells a lot of shirts as well."


## SUNDAY JANUARY 25TH

I walk with Sid to the Bernabéu. His flat is 20 minutes away from the ground. The stadium is in the commercial district of town, surrounded by plush-looking skyscrapers with the name of the company they house in neon at the top. We arrive about an hour early – there are already thousands collected around the base of the stadium, around the scores of stalls selling hats, scarves, photos, flags and those incredibly irritating air-pressure horns that continentals like deafening their neighbours with during important football games.

I decide to ask a cross-section of the community what they think of Beckham. I start with a boy and a girl, both in their early twenties, draped in his-and-hers identikit Real Madrid scarves and hats.

"Qué opinas de Beckham?" I ask.

"I'm sorry, mate, don't speak Spanish."

A London accent.

"You're just here for the match?"

"Yes." The bloke does the talking. "I bought the plane tickets for Sue's birthday. It's a little treat for her. We're staying in a hotel over there."

"Are you Beckham fans?"

"I am," says the girl. "I'm a massive Beckham fan. That's why Andy brought me here."

I've noticed more British accents around than the last time. And there are a large number of Japanese, too. The Beckham tourist market is obviously picking up steam.

"How did you get your tickets?"

"I bought them off the concierge in the hotel."

A tout catches my eye. Addresses me in English.

"You want a ticket. Football?" (As if I might say no, but I would like one for the opera.)

"How much?"

"100 euros."

I ask another guy, who looks a little more desperate.

"35 euros. You want? How many you want?"

"I was just interested in the price."

"Price very good. How many you want?"

"I already have a ticket."

"You want more?"

I shake him off and spot another guy to ask about Beckham. He's wearing enormous plastic glasses, a big Mexican hat and a sign round his neck, saying 'Antonio, rey de los bocadillos' (king of the sandwiches). In a scabbard-type affair around his waist he has a huge hero sandwich, about three times as big as a normal one. A real eccentric. A Freudian psychoanalyst might have some assumptions to make about the sandwich in the scabbard.

"Antonio, Antonio, what do you think of Beckham?" I ask.

"I don't know him."

"I mean as a player. Do you like him as a player?"

"Yes, I love him. He enchants me."

"What do you like about his play?"

"I like his long accurate passes from deep in the midfield. They are like a can opener."

I stop an old fellow of about 80, dressed in a drab brown suit, no hat, carrying a rather smaller sandwich (I assume that's what it is) in a brown paper bag.

"What do you think of Beckham?"

"When he signed I wasn't sure. I was suspicious that he was a media-friendly signing who wouldn't fit into the team. But I have been surprised by his work-rate and his disregard for his shins. I now think that he was a good buy. And I think that he is Real's best player."

"Better than Ronaldo? Better than Zidane?"

"You heard me. Real's best player."

Real Madrid's best player is warming up when I find my seat in the press box. Strangely, he's wearing black boots. He doesn't look nervous, as he did six months ago. But he does look apart from the other players. They're doing short runs across the pitch. I wonder what is going through his mind. I imagine he must feel slightly alienated in a stadium and a team full of people speaking a language he has failed to master. They start playing a five-aside keep possession game. He's very good. He's trying hard. I hope he doesn't get injured.

Half an hour later, after *Hala Madrid* has boomed out the tannoy, the match kicks off. I decide to Beckham-watch. He is playing deep, alongside Guti, more often closer to the line of four defenders than the four attackers he is trying to feed. When Madrid are in possession he strolls around the centre of the field, occasionally making a little darting run to shake off his marker and find the space to receive the ball. When he gets it he scurries around, making sure that he's always in enough space to consider his passing options. Today he is keeping it short, passing to the nearest player, usually Guti, occasionally spreading the ball across the pitch to the full-back or one of today's wide men, Solari on the left or Figo on the right. Used to seeing El Real play away, I am surprised at their fluency and calmness on the ball. Away they are nervous and tentative, allowing the opposition to attack them from the off. Here they are loath to give up possession of the ball, playing it round with calm assuredness. When they do lose the ball, Beckham is a different player, running everywhere, trying to close down whoever's in possession, or cut off who they might pass the ball to. He's very energetic, perhaps overly so, as if to make sure that everyone knows that he is trying hard. Whenever he wins the ball in a tackle – which he does on several occasions – he also wins an ovation from the crowd. They love it and they encourage him to do more of the same. He's playing to the gallery, as ever, and the gallery is encouraging him to be a tough tackler. So the Beckham we know, the precise passer of the ball, is changing into Beckham the enforcer, Beckham the hard-man. But this is a hard-man with finesse, a slugger with a deft k.o. blow in his repertoire.

I'm wondering why I'm feeling a strange warm flush on my face when Real Madrid score, after about 15 minutes. The Argentinian Solari steals the ball in the box and, using the momentum of his run to find space, kicks a hard left foot shot under the Villarreal keeper, Reina. The warmth? There's a vast gas fire, one of hundreds, on the underside of the roof. Real Madrid heat their fans in the winter.

Beckham has nothing to do with the goal, but he sprints to Solari to join in the celebrations. He wants to be part of everything. He takes the free-kicks, he takes the corners. If the ball goes off, he runs to get it, handing it reluctantly to the full back whose job it is to take the throw-ins. He's always having a word with the referee – when Roberto Carlos gets a yellow card, he's up there complaining. I'd love to hear what he's saying. Perhaps Spanish referees all speak English . . .

At half time there's a funny conversation amongst the English journalists about how to write the adjective used to describe the inhabitants of Argentina.

"What's all this Argentine shit everyone's writing?" says Sid. "They're Argentinian!"

"Argentinian comes up as a spelling mistake on Word," says Jimmy Burns.

"I just write 'Argies'," *says the News of the World* guy, Anthony. "There's no point in writing anything longer. They'd just change it back again."

At the start of the second half, Beckham finds himself in the centre-forward position, racing the keeper for a slightly-too-long ball. The keeper just gets there first; Beckham goes down. A defender piles in and there is a bit of a fracas. The referee breaks it up. Beckham jogs off, to huge applause. Another example of the fighting Englishman's gutsy approach. The defender is Arruabarrena. His nationality? Argentinian, Argentine, Argy, have it how you will.

Pretty soon the game as a contest is all over. Guti passes the ball to Ronaldo outside the edge of the box. The Brazilian swerves the ball left-footed round the out-of-position Reina and into the net. It is a stunning goal, a goal out of nothing, his twenty-second of the season.

Villarreal start coming back into the match, and Beckham is even more in the thick of things. He blocks a shot in the box (applause). He has another little flare-up with Arruabarrena (more applause). Figo, Raúl and Roberto Carlos are substituted. With Zidane injured, Beckham is now the senior player in the team. With five minutes left, the substitutions look premature: Villarreal score, a header directly from a corner. Real shift into time-wasting mode. Beckham gets involved in yet another flare-up, this time with the former Atlético striker José Mari, much hated by the crowd. The Villarreal player ends up pushing Beckham away with the flat of his hand on his neck. For this he gets a yellow card. The crowd love it.

"Beykan, Beykan, Beykan," they chant. The ref blows his whistle for full time. Beckham is last off. He has applauded all four sides of the crowd. They applaud back. He knows how to milk it . . .

For the Beckham correspondents the match is not as important as the quotes from Beckham that follow it. It is judged by the editors back home that the English public are more interested in what Beckham says than what he does. So there is an air of tension in the mixed zone behind the players' tunnel in the Bernabéu 15 minutes after the game has finished.

The place isn't just like a building site. It *is* a building site. This is a part of the Bernabéu that hasn't yet been finished. At the moment it is only classed as a 'four-star' stadium, meaning that it isn't good enough to host European Cup finals, unlike the five-star Calderón and Nou Camp grounds. But the club are working on it. And they're not waiting until the close season. There are cables dangling from the ceiling; you have to walk on planks of wood, holding on to scaffolding tubes to get there. In one corner there are hundreds of piled-up blue seats. Health and Safety would have a field day. The equivalent body in bulls-in-the-street Spain is obviously not so powerful. Scaffolding divides the players from the journalists between the dressing room and the exit for the coach.

The English ones have split into two sections. On the right, nearer the changing rooms, are the Sundays (*The Mirror* and the *News of the World*). On their left, out of earshot, are the dailies. They need different quotes. Today the Sundays get first whack because they are going out tomorrow.

"I'll start by asking him if he's injured," says Simon, *The Mirror* man, to Anthony of the *News of the World*. I'm standing right behind them.

"OK, that's good," says Anthony.

"There he is!" Beckham is walking towards us. He's wearing a green forage cap, with his hair poking out the sides. You can see his diamond ear ring. He's got a beige military-looking top on. Military is this week's look.

"Hi mate," says Anthony. Beckham stops.

"How are you?" he says.

MIRROR: Have you got any injuries?

BECKHAM: A cut ankle. No stitches, or anything like that.

NEWS OF THE WORLD: Was it the number three. The Argie guy?

BECKHAM: It was.

NEWS OF THE WORLD: You seemed angry.

BECKHAM: It was just a challenge. It was a football thing. You get them in the game.

NEWS OF THE WORLD: Were you worried about getting a yellow card? (Beckham is one booking away from an automatic suspension).

BECKHAM: Yeah, I didn't want one, but in football you get that sort of thing.

NEWS OF THE WORLD: You passed the ball to Figo 35 times today.

BECKHAM: Did I?

NEWS OF THE WORLD: Were you passing to him because he was unhappy with you?

BECKHAM: Some people were saying some things, but I don't think Luis has got a problem with me. We had dinner together the other night, and he didn't say anything.

NEWS OF THE WORLD: You were passing to him constantly.

MIRROR: Did it make a difference to Real Madrid's pattern of play that Zinedine Zidane wasn't playing?

BECKHAM: He's an amazing player, and when he's not there you notice that. Solari is an amazing player, too, and he scored. Every player is good here at Real Madrid, that's why they're here.

MIRROR: How do you rate your personal performance?

BECKHAM: I'm happy. I worked very hard today.

NEWS OF THE WORLD: José Mari put his hand in your face. What was going on there?

BECKHAM: It was just round my neck a little bit. It was nothing. These things happen in football.

He walks down the line and I shadow him, so I can eavesdrop on his next interview, with the *Telegraph*, the *Mail* and the *Sun*. The guy from the Mail is leading the questioning. You can see that he's already decided what his article is going to be about.

"You've become the enforcer in midfield."

"I think I've been working very hard, if we lose the ball, to get it back as soon as possible."

"Are you finding it to be a different job?"

"Playing in central midfield is a different job from what I'm used to, because instead of looking just one way, you have to get used to looking both ways."

"Roy is a great example of a player in the position you're playing. [He's talking about Beckham's former team-mate at Manchester United, Roy Keane]. Have you had a word?"

"No, I didn't ring him to discuss where I'm playing. We haven't spoken for a while. But he's a good example of a central midfield player; a great player."

The *Mail* guy, Simon, has got his story. He allows Eric, from the *Sun*, to have a go.

"Have you lost anything in your game after changing your position?"

"No. I can play them long balls. That's what I like playing."

"You got another cut on your ankle today."

"Just a little one. On the other foot. There were no stitches."

"You seem to relish the battles and challenges in central midfield."

"To get in this team there are those who have a lot of skill and those who work hard. I like to think I have a little bit of skill and I work very hard."

"Sven's here tonight. Did you know that?" (Sven-Goran Eriksson, the England manager).

"Yeah, we spoke earlier."

"Any plans to meet him later?"

"No. I thought I done alright. I'm happy with my performance."

"Did Sven mention the red card?"

"No, he didn't."

"Did you talk to Mark Palios?"

"No."

This is a question too far. Beckham does not want to talk about the FA executive responsible for the eight-month ban on his friend Rio Ferdinand. The interview is over, he signals with a blink, and walks off.

I'm impressed with the way that the journalists help each other, and give one another space for their questions. I say this to Sid in the pub afterwards. We are with Paul, who has been doing match commentary for the Press Association.

"Well, we have to work together all the time."

I point out that the dailies didn't go heavy on the scraps that Beckham had got into.

"Only because we knew that the Sundays would do that. We assume that they will cover that territory, and we know that they will not fail to mention it. We know that they know how to do their job. So we have to go for different, slightly less obvious angles, as we have second bite of the cherry. It's all different, of course, when the game is on the Sunday. Then we get to file immediately, and get to talk about the more immediate stuff."

Anthony from the *News of the World* turns up. He has short, almost cropped hair, and is wearing a white polo-neck jumper and a beige raincoat. He asks Sid what the weekly papers talked to Beckham about.

"Just his deeper positional play. And a bit about Sven being there."

"Sven was there?"

"You didn't know?"

"I didn't know." Sid looks worried. "Shit! If you file that, I'm a dead man. Eric and Simon will kill me."

Anthony looks sly. "Trust me. I am a man of honour. I will not file. Where is the toilet?"

"I'm not kidding. If you file, I'm a dead man. And that means you're a dead man."

Anthony wanders outside, and Sid starts looking even more worried. Is he filing? Ten minutes later, he's back again. He immediately gets a text message. It is from Eric of the Sun. He shows it to Sid.

ANT YOU R A GENT FOR NOT FILING ABOUT SVEN

"You texted Eric that you knew about Sven?"

"Why shouldn't I?"

"Because he will know that I told you!"

"Don't worry, I won't file."

It is an absurd power game and Anthony is milking it for all it is worth. Soon it is forgotten, and I am deep into a wine-fuelled discussion with him about politics and art, in which he demonstrates how perfectly suited he is to the newspaper he writes for.

"Modern art? I call it modern fart," he says.

| ESPANYOL | 1 | BETIS | 2 |
|---|---|---|---|
| **REAL MADRID** | **2** | **VILLARREAL** | **1** |
| MÁLAGA | 2 | VALLADOLID | 3 |
| VALENCIA | 0 | OSASUNA | 1 |
| ALBACETE | 1 | ATLÉTICO | 1 |
| SEVILLA | 0 | BARCELONA | 1 |
| ATHLETIC | 1 | DEPORTIVO | 0 |
| ZARAGOZA | 1 | MALLORCA | 3 |
| RACING | 3 | MURCIA | 2 |
| CELTA | 2 | REAL SOCIEDAD | 5 |

## LA CLASIFICACIÓN

| | P | W | D | L | F | A | Pts |
|---|---|---|---|---|---|---|---|
| **REAL MADRID** | **21** | **14** | **4** | **3** | **40** | **21** | **46** |
| VALENCIA | 21 | 13 | 5 | 3 | 36 | 15 | 44 |
| DEPORTIVO | 21 | 12 | 4 | 5 | 35 | 17 | 40 |
| ATLÉTICO | 21 | 10 | 5 | 6 | 29 | 24 | 35 |
| OSASUNA | 21 | 8 | 9 | 4 | 22 | 15 | 33 |
| VILLARREAL | 21 | 9 | 6 | 6 | 28 | 24 | 33 |
| BARCELONA | 21 | 8 | 7 | 6 | 28 | 26 | 31 |
| ATHLETIC | 21 | 8 | 6 | 7 | 25 | 25 | 30 |
| RACING | 21 | 8 | 6 | 7 | 28 | 29 | 29 |
| VALLADOLID | 21 | 7 | 8 | 6 | 26 | 28 | 29 |
| REAL SOCIEDAD | 21 | 7 | 6 | 8 | 27 | 32 | 27 |
| MALLORCA | 21 | 8 | 3 | 10 | 27 | 36 | 27 |
| BETIS | 21 | 6 | 8 | 7 | 27 | 24 | 26 |
| MÁLAGA | 21 | 8 | 2 | 11 | 26 | 30 | 26 |
| SEVILLA | 21 | 6 | 7 | 8 | 28 | 25 | 25 |
| ALBACETE | 21 | 6 | 4 | 11 | 23 | 27 | 22 |
| CELTA | 21 | 4 | 9 | 8 | 30 | 39 | 2 |
| ZARAGOZA | 21 | 5 | 5 | 11 | 20 | 31 | 20 |
| ESPANYOL | 21 | 4 | 2 | 15 | 17 | 38 | 14 |
| MURCIA | 21 | 1 | 10 | 10 | 19 | 35 | 13 |

# THIRTEEN
# VALLADOLID

GOLFO DE VIZCAYA

OCEANO ATLÁNTICO

Valladolid
○

Real Madrid
○

MAR MEDITERRÁNEO

# THIRTEEN
# VALLADOLID

**FRIDAY JANUARY 30TH**

Within a couple of hours of my arrival in Valladolid (after a ten-hour train journey west from Barcelona) I am standing in a Latin American dance bar in the city centre. I'm waiting to meet Xavi, who runs an unofficial website about Real Valladolid football club, and his friend Iñigo. We've communicated via e-mail but I don't know what they look like. In front of me a group of eight people are being taught the basics of salsa step-movement by an impatient young woman with a Captain-Scarlet-style microphone and a girth that suggests that she doesn't go in for a particularly energetic style of dancing herself.

Valladolid is in Old Castile, a land of many medieval castles in the flat highlands of the meseta plain north of Madrid, an area which suffers from extremes of weather popularly described as 'nueve meses de invierno, tres de infierno' (nine months of winter, then three of hell). I've always been curious about the city because of its hard-to-pronounce name, and because of Laurie Lee's depiction of it in *As I Walked Out One Midsummer Morning* as 'a foreboding place full of beggars showing their stumps and bored soldiers with cardboard boots'. Felipe III made it the capital of Spain in 1601, moving his court from Madrid, making it the most important city in the world for a very short period in which much of its grandest architecture was built. Then he moved back to Madrid in 1606. There's something about my pension room near the main square that epitomises my first impressions of the city. The room is slightly bigger than the single bed in it, yet a vast and ancient wooden beam runs across the ceiling, disappearing into the wall, suggesting that this scruffy little hole was once part of a space which was altogether more luxurious.

A guy approaches, introduces himself, shakes my hand. He's very smiley, a bit shy. It's Iñigo. He hands me a CD and a blue folder. It's a history of the football club, and a list of the most famous monuments to visit in the city. A gift. How sweet. Touched, I ask Iñigo what he will drink. A pineapple juice. Iñigo answers my questions about modern-day Valladolid. It's the capital of Castilla y León, and the resulting bureaucracy is the source of a lot of jobs for the townspeople. Otherwise there is a Renault and a Citroen factory nearby. The city now has 320,000 inhabitants. "And Valladolid is the rugby capital of Spain," he says, proudly. "We have two teams in the top division."

From capital of the world to capital of Spanish rugby in four hundred years. That's quite a downsize.

Xavi turns up, introduces me to a bunch more people, and we move to a tapas bar. I am presented with a plate of cold potatoes in mayonnaise and a glass of local wine.

"Valladolid is famous for its fine wines," says Iñigo.

"And its potatoes?" I joke.

"It is not particularly famous for its potatoes," he replies, deadpan. "They are just . . . well . . . normal potatoes."

A guy called Julio, sitting opposite, introduces himself. He is part of Valladolid's ultra fan group, Ultras Violetas (the club play in violet and white striped shirts).

"We are extremely right wing," he boasts. Valladolid has the reputation of being a right-wing city. It was a Francoist stronghold during the war, and is nicknamed Fachadolid for its fascist leanings.

Julio turns out to be quite an expert on the ultras fan scene in Spain.

"We are a typically Spanish group. We carry a lot of banners," he says. Other groups model themselves on the Italians, apparently, and a few on the English.

"Like the Boixos Nois from Barcelona. They do not wear colours or carry banners so much. They identify with the English casuals. The Chelsea fans – the Headhunters" (pronounced with a hawk and a couple of vowel transformations). "Or the fans of Meelbal. They are the best, they are the strongest, they fight the most."

It takes me a second or two, then I get it. Meelbal . . . Millwall.

"I saw a documentary in the '80s," I offer, "in which a Millwall fan called Harry the Dog charged the Blackburn end all on his own."

His face lights up. "Arridedog, I know," he says. "Arridedog is very mad."

I wonder whether he admires Arridedog's compatriot, David Beckham.

"Beckham is a good player," he says. "But there are a lot of Spanish players who are just as good. It's just that we don't talk about them so much. We think that foreigners are better than us. This is a problem here. So if a Spanish player scores a good goal it will be shown on the TV a couple of times. If a foreigner, like Beckham, scores a good goal, it is all you will see for a week. We have a player, Óscar, a young player, and one of our best. He scored a volley after a brilliant back-heel from El Chino Losada the other day. It was a lovely touch, but it was hardly shown on the TV at all, because he was not a foreigner. Now if Beckham had done that . . ."

I ask him a bit more about Real Valladolid. He tells me that the club are the 'Real Madrid of Castilla y León', the club the fans of the other local clubs – Burgos, Salamanca, León – love to hate. That they have been in the First Division for the last eight years. That their object at the beginning of every season is to avoid the drop, but that sometimes there is a good year.

"Five years ago we got to the quarter finals of the Recopa (Cup Winners Cup)," he says. "But we have a very big debt. We have a debt of 3,000 million pesetas." The Spanish talk in euros until it comes to talking about large sums, like house prices or the debts of football clubs, in which case they can only converse in pesetas. It makes every sum sound infeasibly big, with all those zeroes.

"How much is that in euros?"

We work it out together. About 20 million euros. 12 million quid.

"That doesn't sound too bad to me," I say, thinking of Leeds or Barcelona.

"Which team do you support in England?" he asks me, to get off the subject. I give him the spiel I give about being born in Newcastle but brought up on the south coast and hence having two teams, Newcastle and Brighton, who I support with the same passion. I always feel a little embarrassed explaining this to football fans, as many see it as a kind of sporting bigamy, something slightly immoral.

"We have a term for that here," he says. "Chaqueteros (jackets). Because these people change their colours when they want. In fact you will see a lot of chaqueteros on Sunday. Whichever team scores first will get a huge cheer. People will decide who they are supporting during the match. Because, you know what? Most of the Valladolid fans are Real Madrid fans, too. Although I wouldn't call them real fans."


**SATURDAY JANUARY 31ST**

I drag myself out of my fourteen-euro-a-night hole (the beams are beautiful but I'd rather have some sort of central heating: it's freezing) in time for a quick aperitif before lunch. I end up in a busy bar in the town centre, with a glass of fine red wine in a large flute, watching a little baby crawl around near the door. He is at the babbling stage. Three drunk men seem to be in charge of him. One is leaning over him, trying to get him to speak his first words.

"Hala Madrid," he says.

"Glblblblblblglmmmmll," responds the baby.

"HA-la MAD-rid."

"Gblmblgblmbl."

It'll take some time, but I'd lay a bet on what his first words will be, and what team he'll end up supporting.

I move to a restaurant round the corner. It is called La Criolla, and is recommended in all the guide books. I get through a succulent bean stew, a plate of goose in raisins, a bottle of red wine and a pudding, which I order because of its name 'gypsy's arm.' I have *Marca* for company. It talks of a Guti-Beckham partnership in midfield, and shows pictures of the Real Madrid squad all wearing Colombia scarves and posing in front of a 'victim of terrorism' on a wheelchair. He turns out to be a soldier from the Colombian army, who has been injured by the FARC guerrillas in the civil war in the country. I wonder how much Beckham knows about the Colombian situation, and how much he has looked into it before lending his support to the government's side of affairs.

The gypsy's arm arrives. It is not, as I have fantasised, a real gypsy's arm, hacked off at the shoulder, hairy and with large rings on several fingers. It is a delicate creamy thing akin to a chocolate log. My bill comes to 33 euros. Beckham's clausula (the price any team will have to pay before they can buy him from Real Madrid while he's under contract at the Bernabéu) – according to *Marca* – is 180 million euros. When you indulge yourself, it is always good to put things in perspective. I'm brought a coffee-with-liqueur compliments of the house.

I plan to walk around town to clear my head. I have even drawn out a route for myself on my city map from church to museum to church again in a big circle taking in all the most significant monuments which characterise the city's glorious past. Half an hour later, exploring the 'beach' on the banks of the Pisuerga river, I see a 50-foot steamboat moored up to a walkway. I walk down the gangway onto the boat.

"Can I get a coffee here?" I ask a chunky middle-aged man in glasses.

"It's not a bar, it's a boat. We have a voyage down the river in half an hour."

"Is it a real steamboat?"

"No, it runs on diesel. Did you say you wanted a coffee?"

"I thought you said . . ."

"Compliments of the house."

"Great."

I get chatting to the three-strong crew. Manolo, wearing a pair of grey overalls, is the mechanic and takes the money on the door. He has a white crewcut. He gives me a large glass of orujo (Spanish grappa) with herbs. A local delight from nearby Zamora. And very strong.

"He knows everything there is to know about Valladolid," says his colleague, Juan, the guy who gave me the coffee, a Chilean, who turns out to be the skipper of the boat.

Manolo tells me that the first ever experiments in underwater diving were performed in the River Pisuerga in 1602, as Felipe III wanted to find a way of recovering treasure lost from sunken galleons. Two men, using bamboo sticks to breathe, stayed on the river-bed for an hour and a half.

"See that old wall there?" he says. I nod. "That's all that is left of Felipe's Palacio de La Ribera, once one of the most sumptuous palaces in Europe. Felipe was Felipe II's son, but he was more fond of hunting and having a good time than administering his empire. They used to have a ramp down which they would throw bulls into the river. The bulls would swim across and then attack the picadors who were waiting on the river bank. Felipe III would walk around the city in an underground system of passageways, so as not to be seen in public. It greatly increased his mystique."

"What do you think of Beckham?" I ask. He looks at me strangely, wondering about this non-sequitur.

"I heard recently that he has already paid back his transfer fee in the money the club have got from shirt sales and other advertising rights using his name," he says. "I am pleased about this. I am a Madridista."

"You, who know everything about Valladolid, a Madridista!" I exclaim. "You are a chaquetero! A turncoat!"

"We were hoping that the Real Madrid team might have turned up for today's voyage. But it doesn't look as if they are going to."

It's a joke. He's been taking in some money, but not much. There's an old couple, a young couple with three children and a guy who appears to be Manolo's brother. But no Beckham, Raúl or Ronaldo. A galáctico-free voyage. I am handed a second glass of orujo with herbs. A very large glass. I fear for my well-being. The captain, who has left us, reappears wearing a smart blue jumper with epaulettes. I salute him. He salutes back. He puts Ennio Morricone's *The Good, the Bad and the Ugly* on the stereo, and walks up to his bridge. The afternoon voyage of the 'Leyenda del Pisuerga' has begun, and it would appear that I'm staying on board.

## SUNDAY FEBRUARY 1ST

I wake up in need of a drink of water and some fruit, but have a café con leche and a couple of tapas instead. It's an early kick-off today – 5pm – so I decide to go straight to the stadium, getting a number 8 bus from the Plaza Mayor in the town centre. At the bus-stop there's a guy who has covered his face with a Real Madrid scarf. He's wearing a Real Madrid cap, and is waving a Real Madrid flag. There's little evidence to doubt his allegiance.

There's a bunch of Irish lads in their twenties on the back seats of the bus and I eavesdrop on their conversation. They are students studying in Valladolid. It is said to be the place where the purest Spanish is spoken (the language is referred to as 'Castellano' in Spain as it originated in Castilla) so there are many foreign students at the university. They talk incessantly about girls: Norwegian girls, Finnish girls, Australian girls, Spanish girls. They seem to be highly sexed – though most men in their twenties are more highly sexed in their conversation than in reality. They are obviously going to the game.

The bus takes about half an hour – the stadium was built on the outskirts of town for the 1982 World Cup. It was used for three matches in England's first round group, Czechoslovakia v Kuwait, France v Kuwait and France v Czechoslovakia; England played their matches in the San Mamés in Bilbao. The bus drops us a ten-minute walk away, through a shopping centre with a Carrefour, a McDonalds, a Toys'R'Us and a C&A. I'm walking just behind the Irish lads. We walk past a group of nasty-looking skinheads, dressed in black. Los Ultra Sur.

"Hello," says one, hearing English. He says it in a menacing way, the hawked 'h' having a cut-throat ring to it. Or maybe that's just my imagination.

"Hello, hello, hello?' he insists.

He is ignored but luckily doesn't make a point of it. I think the Irish guys are oblivious to the danger. We carry on towards the stadium.

A couple of hours later I meet Julio outside the main gate, having picked up my accreditation. Julio has promised to introduce me to the Valladolid ultras, as they prepare their paraphernalia before the match. They are allowed to keep their things in a room in the stadium – they have an understanding with the club. The meeting was originally scheduled for 11am, but moved to the afternoon, because the ultras got drunk last night and were too hungover to make it this morning.

"Look at that guy with the beard. He's the chief of police. The guys around him are plain clothes policemen." He is full of little bits of information, which he divulges in a whisper. He points out the bloke I've seen at the bus-stop, his face still covered by the Real Madrid scarf, who walks past waving his flag.

"Look at the badge on his rucksack," he says. I look. It is a Real Valladolid logo. "He is a chaquetero," says Julio. "That is why he is wearing that scarf. Next week he will be supporting Valladolid."

We watch the Valladolid coach come in. The players are greeted with warm applause. Julio talks me through their names as they come out.

"That's El Chino Losada, who did the back-heel I was talking about the other night. That's Óscar, who scored from the volley . . ." Soon the familiar Real Madrid coach turns up. It gets a much more heated reaction.

"Pucela!" shouts a fifty-something woman next to me. "Pucela, Pucela!" I ask what she means, and Julio explains. "Pucela is the nickname for the city of Valladolid," he says. "It comes from 'Pucelle' which was the name given to Joan of Arc. Some soldiers from Valladolid fought with her, and brought the name back with them. We use it when we talk about the football club. We never chant 'Valladolid', just 'Pucela'." (I can understand why. Even though the natives have developed a way of saying 'Valladolid' incredibly quickly, it's a bit of a mouthful in a football chant. Just try . . .'Clap clap, clap clap clap, clap clap clap clap Valladolid!' Doesn't work.)

The lady is in the minority. Most of the people around are cheering the Real Madrid players as they run the gauntlet from bus to stadium. Security is poor. Beckham comes out looking stressed, and runs into the stadium entrance amid gasps, screams and autograph books.

"Beykan, Beykan," says Julio, in a sarcastic high-pitched voice. He's disgusted with the chaqueteros.

A young man in a bomber jacket with creative facial hair turns up, and is introduced as Edu.

"This is Alex," Julio says to Edu. "He is a Newcastle hooligan." And then, to me, "Edu is the Ultras Violeta's songmaster. He has a megaphone, and everything."

"Do you watch the game at all?" I ask Edu.

"No, I turn my back to the game. I don't care."

"Do you make up the songs?"

"No, I don't." He laughs at the idea. "They are Argentinian songs. Italian. I translate them to make them fit."

"And do you sing all the way through the match?"

"I take a break every now and again, to drink a Coca Cola."

Edu slips off to talk to the chief of police, and then he hurries into the stadium entrance Beckham has just gone into. I assume we're to follow him, but Julio stays put. He shows no sign of going into the stadium, even though there is now only half an hour to kick off. Suddenly something dawns on me.

"Do you have a ticket to get in?"

"No, I don't. I can't afford one today."

"So you can't take me to the ultras?"

"When you go in with your press accreditation they will give you a little orange bib. Then you can go where you want in the stadium."

"They only give those to photographers."

"No, you'll get one, too."

I don't get a bib, but when I get into the stadium I realise that I can wander round it quite freely, so instead of heading for the cabinas de prensa (press boxes) in the main stand, I climb down to where the ultras are behind one of the goals. I have to squeeze under a barrier between the two stands, but it's an easy enough manoeuvre. The entire length of the front row of the stand is covered by a furled up violet and white flag. I take a seat just behind. There are 250 or so ultras collected to my left, already bashing drums, waving flags. One has the confederate flag, another waves a picture of Alex from *A Clockwork Orange*. In front of me there is a concrete moat. I am looking for Edu, so I can get an introduction, maybe sit with them: he is nowhere to be seen. The group burst into song . . .

'Pucela, Pucela!'

The Real Madrid players run onto the pitch for their warm-up, past the Pucela mascot, a yellow castle with legs and an acid house smiley face.

"Hijos de puta!" chant the ultras, about ten times. A few finish the chorus off with a flurry of Nazi salutes. One of them has seen me looking over, scanning them all for Edu's face. He tugs at a friend's sleeve, and they both stare at me. I must look odd with my notebook. They look like they're debating whether to confront me. I head off, back to the safety of the press cabin. The players go back to the dressing room.

The cabin is exactly that, a little wooden box. I find a seat behind a glass window next to Sid Lowe; the atmosphere is terrible because of the window. So I stand on the corridor between the press box and the fans, along with a number of others who have arrived late to find that the number on their ticket doesn't carry as much authority as someone who refuses to budge from the appropriate seat.

The players run out again, and there are cheers and boos in equal measure. The big flag is pulled up until it covers the whole of the stand behind the goal I've just been sitting in. There are some tiny-looking rips in it, through which several fans at a time are poking their heads, waving their scarves. The sun is shining brightly on this stand and the one oppo-site me, which contains about 2000 Real Madrid fans, an astonishingly large number for a Spanish game, where there is little culture of travel-ling to away games. I realise that, despite the name of this book (which was always meant to be taken with a pinch of salt) this is the first daytime match Real Madrid have appeared in since the first game of the season, against Betis. *A Season in the Floodlights*? The hymn is tannoyed out. It sounds like a political anthem from the Civil War.

*Up Real Valladolid!*
*The badge you wear on your chest,*
*Wear it with pride and honour*
*And defend it with passion and respect,*
*Struggling in a fair fight*
*To attain glory, fighting without stopping,*
*for Real Valladolid.*
*The white and violet flag is the symbol of our noble fans*
*And that's why we have to reach our goal,*
*We will rise up together, with strength and tenacity*
*And all together in one voice, we will sing this song*
*Pucela, Pucela, up Real Valladolid!*

There is an oboe-dominated band to my right, which starts up a jaunty tune. Valladolid start the stronger, attacking mostly down the right, where Solari is playing in Roberto Carlos' position, and young Mejía is starting his third game as central (centre back). A header goes over the bar, then the home team win a corner. A player goes up to head the ball . . . and is clearly pulled over by Zidane. I could see it from 50 yards away! The whole crowd could see it! The referee, on the edge of the box, ignores it, and Real clear. 'Asi fucking gana El Madrid' I think, to the accompaniment of many whistles.

Beckham, again, is playing very deep. His short passing game is good, but his long balls keep being over-hit. On a bad day, he looks like the sort of player Graham Taylor kept putting in the England midfield in the early '90s. On 24 minutes another Valladolid attack comes down the right wing. A cross is fired in . . . and Óscar heads the ball into the net. Goooooooooool! I do a little jump, clenching my fists. I look around me, and see the whole crowd, apart from the Ultra Sur, up on its feet, waving scarves and cheering. 'So much for the chaqueteros theory,' I think.

A "Pucela, Pucela!" chant gets going round the ground. The band strikes up another tune. Beckham, making a rare foray into the attack, hits a shot just off target from the edge of the box. Solari gets booked, then holds off too long, allowing El Chino Losada to get another cross in from the right. Óscar is waiting at the far post, and thumps a second header past Casillas. On the stroke of half time. The crowd react in the way you'd expect them to react in the circumstances, 2–0 up against Madrid at half time. Everyone bar the Ultra Sur is on their feet, raising their arms, shouting 'gol!'. Myself included. I'm glad not to be in the press box.

In the interval I walk down the aisle in among the crowd. I see an old fellow pointing at a young kid a few seats in, who is wearing a Real Madrid scarf. He's asking the kid the score. The kid, a little overweight and around 12, pulls both ends of the scarf in frustration. He is close to tears. This will be the one time in the year he can see his heroes, and they're playing terribly, Beckham included. They look very weak down the left. On the bench, Queiroz doesn't seem to have any solutions. César, Borja, Núñez, Portillo, Pavón, Jordi and Juanfran: hardly an all-star cast. And last night Valencia, by winning 6–1 in Málaga, went top of the table. Real Madrid need to win to overtake them again. I'm scanning the fans' faces to see if I can see any secret merengues who've been keeping quiet. There are a handful of glum faces among the smiles.

It's a different Real Madrid that starts the second half. Solari and Figo start probing down Valladolid's right flank, creating two clear chances in the first two minutes of the half. Then, in the third minute, a third attack down the same flank: the ball comes across the edge of the box, and Zinedine Zidane kicks it through a crowded defence and past an unsighted keeper. Game on. Hundreds of fans in front of me rise up to cheer the goal. Where did they come from? I can see plenty of celebrations all across the stand in front of me. The Ultra Sur are happy, too.

Fifteen minutes into the half another Real Madrid attack comes down the right. Figo whips a cross in, it hits a Valladolid player and drops to the ground, a split-millimetre-per-second slower than normal. Handball? Surely involuntary? The linesman holds his flag out eye-height between his hands. The referee points to the spot, then, amid a flurry of complaining violet and white players, shows a red card to Peña, the unfortunate offender. Figo places the ball on the spot, takes a calm run up and sidefoots it past the keeper. 2–2. Now it's the Valladolid ultras who are an island in a sea of celebration. I can't believe it. Most of the fans seem to have changed allegiance according to the score. Momentum is with Madrid now; half an hour to go, against ten men, and virtually the whole crowd on their side. The Valladolid ultras behind the goal try to rally support, but the 'Pucela!' chant doesn't get taken up around them as it was before. Madrid pile forward, creating a number of chances. It only seems a matter of time.

Then Solari commits a foul on the far side, and the referee sends him off, too. This evens things up, and Valladolid start swapping attacks with Real Madrid. It's anybody's game. Zinedine Zidane does a pirouette on the edge of the box (in Spanish a 'ruleta'), fooling the whole defence and winning himself plenty of space for a shot, which he hits over the top. Still, it was an amazing piece of skill and the whole crowd, even the Valladolid Ultras, stand to applaud. It is a wonderful moment. Then El Chino Losada hits the bar with Casillas beaten.

Beckham has become a virtual bystander, losing the ball when he has been in possession, and it is no surprise when he is replaced with ten minutes to go by Juanfran, a youngster making his third appearance. The band starts up to my right. Real's fans opposite initiate a chant, joined by supposed Valladolid fans in the same stand.

"MAD-rid . . . MAD-rid!"

"Pucela, Pucela" retort the fans behind the goal. There are only a couple of minutes to go, and the match seems destined to finish in an honourable draw that would be a fair result, and suit almost everyone in the stadium. Then Ronaldo gets the ball on the edge of the box, wins a yard of space against his compatriot Julio César and hits the ball into the narrow space between the goalkeeper and the post. 3–2. Virtually everyone in my stand is up on their feet, applauding, just as vehemently as they were applauding Valladolid's second goal. Fucking turncoats.

The last few minutes see some frantic attacking by Valladolid, but they can't get a shot in on Casillas. About a third of the seats empty before the final whistle; I'm not sure whether this is Valladolid fans who are resigned to defeat, Madrid fans who are too nervous to watch the end, or chaqueteros who can't decide what they want to happen. The final whistle is greeted by generous applause by everyone who's remained in the stadium. It has been a tremendous game of football.

I have a quick chat with a father and son standing next to me. The son is wearing a Valladolid scarf. They are both beaming.

"Who do you support?" I ask.

"Both teams," says the dad.

"A little bit more Real Madrid," says the son, despite his scarf.

"Whichever team needs the points most," says the dad. "And today that was Real Madrid. We are top of the table again." I hurry out of the stadium. I have a night train to catch to Barcelona.

## RESULTS JORNADA 22

| ATLÉTICO | 1 | OSASUNA | 1 |
|----------|---|---------|---|
| MÁLAGA | 1 | VALENCIA | 6 |
| BETIS | 1 | CELTA | 0 |
| REAL SOCIEDAD | 1 | RACING | 0 |
| **VALLADOLID** | **2** | **REAL MADRID** | **3** |
| VILLARREAL | 0 | ESPANYOL | 1 |
| MURCIA | 1 | ZARAGOZA | 0 |
| MALLORCA | 1 | ATHLETIC | 3 |
| BARCELONA | 5 | ALBACETE | 0 |
| DEPORTIVO | 1 | SEVILLA | 0 |

## LA CLASIFICACIÓN

|  | P | W | D | L | F | A | Pts |
|--|---|---|---|---|---|---|-----|
| **REAL MADRID** | **22** | **15** | **4** | **3** | **43** | **23** | **49** |
| VALENCIA | 22 | 14 | 5 | 3 | 42 | 16 | 47 |
| DEPORTIVO | 22 | 13 | 4 | 5 | 37 | 17 | 43 |
| ATLÉTICO | 22 | 10 | 6 | 6 | 30 | 25 | 36 |
| BARCELONA | 22 | 9 | 7 | 6 | 33 | 26 | 34 |
| OSASUNA | 22 | 8 | 10 | 4 | 23 | 17 | 34 |
| VILLARREAL | 22 | 9 | 6 | 7 | 28 | 25 | 33 |
| ATHLETIC | 22 | 9 | 6 | 7 | 28 | 26 | 33 |
| REAL SOCIEDAD | 22 | 8 | 6 | 8 | 28 | 32 | 30 |
| BETIS | 22 | 7 | 8 | 7 | 28 | 24 | 29 |
| RACING | 22 | 8 | 6 | 8 | 28 | 30 | 29 |
| VALLADOLID | 22 | 7 | 8 | 7 | 28 | 31 | 29 |
| MALLORCA | 22 | 8 | 3 | 11 | 28 | 39 | 27 |
| MÁLAGA | 22 | 8 | 2 | 12 | 27 | 36 | 26 |
| SEVILLA | 22 | 6 | 7 | 9 | 28 | 26 | 25 |
| ALBACETE | 22 | 6 | 4 | 12 | 23 | 32 | 22 |
| CELTA | 22 | 4 | 9 | 9 | 30 | 40 | 21 |
| ZARAGOZA | 22 | 5 | 5 | 12 | 20 | 32 | 20 |
| ESPANYOL | 22 | 5 | 2 | 15 | 18 | 38 | 17 |
| MURCIA | 22 | 2 | 10 | 10 | 20 | 35 | 16 |

# FOURTEEN
# VALENCIA

GOLFO DE VIZCAYA

OCÉANO ATLÁNTICO

**Real Madrid**
○

Valencia ○

MAR MEDITERRÁNEO

# FOURTEEN
# VALENCIA

## SUNDAY FEBRUARY 13TH

I arrive in Valencia at about one o'clock in the afternoon, eight hours before the kick-off of Real Madrid v Valencia, which has the look of a championship decider about it, even as early as February. If Valencia win the game they go top, a point above Real Madrid. If Madrid win, they go five points clear, and surely out of sight. A crucial game, then, one the whole country has been talking about all week. It's a fascinating clash between top and second; between the best attack and the best defence in the league; the best home team at home against the best away team, positive possession football versus negative catenaccio; Ronaldo v Ayala, Raúl v Marchena, Beckham v Albelda. Fascinating knife-edge stuff. I've decided to travel down to Valencia to watch with their fans, rather than to go to the Bernabéu again. This turns out to be an inspired decision.

The previous Saturday both Madrid and Valencia won home games (against Málaga and Atlético respectively) to keep it tight at the top. Ronaldo scored the first goal against the Andalucian side. The second was a powerful free-kick from Roberto Carlos which must have given Beckham mixed feelings. In the words of Roberto Palomar, of *Marca*, the next day: "As Beckham had already hit the same old lady with glasses three times with previous free-kicks, Roberto ran up and said, 'I'm taking this one.' He hit a whiplash shot into the net." Beckham looked tired, running a lot, but to little effect, partnered by young Borja in the centre of midfield. He hasn't scored a free kick in the league since the game against Málaga at the beginning of the season: and, since the ball was passed to him and he didn't hit the dead ball directly into the goal, that is classed in Spain as a goal from open play.

I want to eat paella at Paco's Riua restaurant to see if there is any Ranieri news – he's been back in town, I saw it on the TV. But I'm disappointed to find the shutters down and a sign saying that it's closed on Sundays 'to give the workers a rest'. So I end up in a greasy little place just behind the market. It's seven euros for a three-course meal and half a bottle of wine. You get what you pay for in these places. You could count the chips on two hands and the rings of squid-in-batter on one. I'm not in good company, either. I've bought *Super Deportes*, the Valencian equivalent of *Marca*. On the front cover it has a picture of Valencia players celebrating a goal, with a root vegetable superimposed on top. The headline reads "ENOUGH BLA BLA BLA. ENOUGH 'POOR ZIZOU'. IT'S TIME TO TAKE THE RADISH BY ITS LEAVES. YUM YUM." Inside there is page after page of drum-beating nonsense about the game, with interviews in which key players from both sides say little of any substance. The main concern voiced is that the referee, Tristante Oliva, will be biased in Real Madrid's favour because of what happened to 'poor' Zinedine Zidane in midweek.

In the Copa del Rey semi-final against Sevilla, which Real Madrid were losing 1–0 on the night in Seville but winning 2–1 on aggregate, Zidane was sent off for a supposed foul on Seville's Pablo Alfaro. Alfaro's a gentleman off the field but quite the opposite on it. A couple of weeks before my arrival in Valencia he was pictured putting his finger up an opponent's anus (through the shorts, of course, and on the run), for which he had acquired the nickname 'Dr Alfaro'. In the semi-final in midweek he went up for an aerial challenge with Zidane, and elbowed the Frenchman in the neck. As the World Footballer of the Year was falling to the ground his palm connected gently with Alfaro's pirate-bearded face. Was it a petulant flick? Or just the force of momentum? Only Zidane knows. Alfaro showed acting skills to match his medical abilities and went down mimicking a man who's just been smashed in the face with a baseball bat. Hard. The notorious linesman Rafa Guerrero, known for attracting attention to himself by making outrageous decisions, signalled to the referee that he had seen the incident clearly and that Zidane should be given a straight red card. Nothing for Alfaro. The referee complied. It was a ridiculous decision that added to the conviction that refereeing in Spain is appallingly far behind the standard which should be demanded in the 'best league in the world'. Matters were made worse by Real Madrid's Director of Football Jorge Valdano, who stormed into the referee's dressing room at half time to complain about the decision. An unprecedented move from a supposedly distinguished representative of the club. Soon after the interval, with Sevilla pressing for a second goal, matters were evened up when the referee dismissed Sevilla's Navarro for an innocuous-looking tackle. The Valencian newspaper sees this as being another example of how much Real Madrid bully referees into giving decisions their way.

As a bit of light relief, there's a page dedicated to Valencia's other team, Levante, currently second in the Segunda A table, with a real chance of promotion to the Primera in 2004/5. I realise that they are playing at home, and that it's on in just over an hour. I have time to watch it. What's more, the game echoes this evening's main fare in a couple of ways. The opponents, Leganés, are from Madrid. And the game pits the team with the best home record (Levante) against the team with the best away record.

As you may remember, just before Christmas Leganés, fielding ten Argentinian players, were a couple of minutes away from knocking their neighbours Real Madrid out of the cup (which would have been a bit like Orient beating Arsenal). This feat would have been a great boost to the club. Defeat, on the other hand, seems to have set off a disastrous chain of events. Their president, the Argentinian rock promoter Daniel Grinbank, walked out on the club shortly after Christmas, closely followed by the better paid of their stars (including the former AC Milan player José Chamot) and their managerial team, José Pekerman and Carlos Aimar. The club is now in something of a free-fall, about to drop into the relegation zone. A result is vital in Valencia, to stop the rot.

To get to the Ciutat de Valencia stadium I have to walk over the section of the dried-up river bed which contains dozens of full-sized dirt football pitches, all of which (this being Sunday afternoon) are in use. It's a fantastic sight – a carnival of football with hundreds of fans watching, listening to loud salsa music and generally having a good time. They've obviously turned up for the occasion rather than the standard of football: it's more hoof-and-hope than give-and-go. I approach a man who has stopped on the bridge to look.

"Where are all these people from?"

"They're not Spanish. They're from Ecuador, Colombia, Peru. Immigrants." It stands to reason. It's four o'clock on a Sunday afternoon in Spain, traditionally a time when the Spanish streets are empty as everyone is at home eating lunch with their family.

Levante's stadium is a redbrick affair on the outskirts of town, surrounded, as such stadia are, by high-rise dwellings and busy main roads. I find my seat behind the goal (at 20 euros the cheapest going) and ask the three men behind which players to look out for. They tell me that the centre-forward Aganzo and the midfielder Rivera are Levante's best players. I write this in my notebook.

"Are you here to take them away from us?" asks the oldest amongst them. He thinks I'm a scout.

"Cuéllar is our best player," says another.

"Yes, you can have Cuéllar. Take Cuéllar."

Levante show in the first five minutes why they are near the top of the table, feeding their wingers who put dangerous crosses in for Aganzo, the big number nine. If I *were* a scout, I'd have a good look at the right-winger Limones. Then Leganés start to pack the midfield to stop the ball from getting to the wide men, and start dictating the pace of the game. The crowd – the 25,000 capacity stadium is about half full – start getting impatient. The team is whistled off at half-time.

"Who do you think will win the Valencia-Madrid game?" I ask the guy behind.

"What do I care?"

"Do you not support Valencia?"

"I support Levante. This is the important game today for us."

"What do you think about Beckham?"

"I will worry about Beckham when we go up to the Primera. Not now."

The crowd are shouting "Congo, Congo!" and the man taps my shoulder and points to a striker warming up on the touchline. "That's Edwin Congo. Put him in your notebook." Congo, a Real Madrid reject, is Colombian, and puts in mind an 'international' team of dual nationality players (Alan Brazil, Mike England, Joe Jordan etc). I put that thought in my notebook. The guy looks pleased that his tip-off has led to such a flurry of notes. I think he still suspects I'm a scout.

It's more of the same in the second half, and I realise that Levante will have to buy a whole new team if they are to thrive in the Primera next season. Then, with five minutes left, their midfielder Rivera gets the ball in midfield, plays a one-two with Congo, and kicks the ball accurately into the available space between keeper and post. 12,642 Levante fans (the crowd has just been announced) get to their feet and cheer. The five Leganés fans, in the far corner of the ground, continue bashing their big drum. It looks like a return to the depths of the Segunda B for them. In injury time the ball goes into the crowd, and the bloke who catches it kicks it as far as he can away from the place the throw should be taken from, then bows to accept the generous applause that follows.

It takes about 40 minutes to walk from La Ciutat de Valencia stadium to the Mestalla stadium. It's all big main roads. Valencia seems to have a lot of big main roads. Where are they all going to? Maybe they are just driving around, to kill time before the big game.

I'm going to watch Real Madrid v Valencia in Manolo el del Bombo's bar, and when I get there I know it's a good choice. It is one of three adjacent bars in a square right next to the stadium. All three have set up a number of televisions facing away from the bars (so you can see it from the street) and there are scores of tables and chairs set up in the square. On the screens, Barcelona are beating Atlético de Madrid 2–1. It's still the first half, and Madrid v Valencia doesn't kick off until it's over. The place is already quite full. I wander into the bar. Manolo is serving drinks. I ask him how his hernia is. He tells me it's better and he's ready with his drum for international duty in the forthcoming Spain v Peru friendly.

"A tough game in prospect today . . ." I say. He whistles, and his eyes take on a nervous look.

"Importantísimo. We have to win. If we do not win . . ."

"Do you think that Beckham might have a bearing on the outcome?"

"He is not in the best of form. I fear Ronaldo, and Figo."

"Do you really think Beckham is off form at the moment?"

"I think that Figo is in form. He is the most dangerous."

"And the referee?"

"We will see."

"Do you think that the refereeing in Spain favours Madrid?"

"Let's wait and see."

My interview technique has been diseased by exposure to the tabloid guys in Madrid the other week. Manolo, with his international reputation to think about, is refusing to be led. Or I'm not very good at it.

The bar is the same as I left it, with drums on the ceiling and pictures all over the walls. The old guy with the worn-out lungs who ate the tissue is in the same seat, still chain-smoking. He has two different brands of cigarette in front of him, for a bit of variety, I guess. Manolo puts his big Basque beret on for a photo op, and Luis García scores a third goal for Barcelona.

"Who will win the league?" I ask him. He's busy; punters are flooding in. I am an annoyance.

"We will see," he says.

I get a ringside seat outside the bar next door 'El Pequeño Mestalla'. The square has filled up – all the seats and tables are full, then there is a bank of people standing five or six deep behind. There must be at least 1000 people there. Some kids have climbed about 15 feet onto the plinth of the large statue which dominates the square. It's tense. Very tense. We watch pre-match scenes from the Bernabéu – a large flag reading 'The Radical Ultras Company' (in English); Steve McManaman in the press box; the players warming up. Beckham comes on screen. He looks tense, too. There are a few jeers.

"Maricona!" shouts a guy behind, with a mop of curly hair and a well-filled-out t-shirt with the slogan 'Ni Lo Pienses' (don't even think about it). He is calling Beckham a lesbian.

Valencia start better, and after five minutes, Mista is clean through on goal, only to be pulled up by an offside flag. The crowd are outraged, on their feet, complaining, waving their hands. It is interesting behaviour. Because they are a crowd, and are outside, they are behaving more like a football crowd than a crowd-in-a-bar would normally do. There are cat-calls and whistles and abuse, as if the participants (who are 200 miles away) could hear. Mista is shown by the action-replay to have been onside. The cat-calls, whistles and abuse are repeated. Pretty soon Figo, with a dive, wins a foul.

"Go to the swimming pool!" shouts Ni Lo Pienses, who has taken on the role of bigmouth in the vicinity of the screen we are watching.

Real Madrid try to play their possession game, but Valencia are easily able to disrupt it and look to be the superior side in the first half. Beckham is having a poor game, starved of the ball and inaccurate with his passes when he does get it. His free kicks invariably go over the bar – when he is allowed to take them. Roberto Carlos is taking on more and more responsibility in that respect, though his tend to go into the wall. Just before half time, the Englishman is shown a yellow card after stepping on an opponent's foot. It means that he has accumulated five and will miss the next game, against Espanyol in Barcelona. "Damn," I think, "Damn damn damn damn damn." I have a ticket for the match in my pocket.

I've been drinking a stream of beers throughout the game – there are a couple of waitresses who come running whenever you need one. Everything starts moving fast in the way it does when you've had a few beers. Beckham starts playing better: a couple of times he sets up Raúl, who spurns the chances. And he used to be so deadly. Then Raúl is penalised for a shocking double-footed tackle on the edge of his own area. The crowd are outraged when he is only given a yellow card, and a penalty is not awarded.

"Burro!" (donkey) shouts Ni Lo Pienses. "Arbitro de mierda!"

Baraja's shot goes just wide. A statistic comes up about the distribution of fouls in the game. Madrid 12, Valencia 24. Is this a reflection of biased refereeing?

"Arbitro de mierda!" repeats Ni Lo Pienses, who obviously thinks it is.

Valencia get a corner, the ball comes in and Ayala hits a power header into the goal.

"Goooooooooooool!" Everybody is up on their feet, out of their seats, stepping towards the TV screen. An old guy, to my right, is standing with his head tilted back, his mouth wide open, his arms pushed behind him. He is wearing spectacles, with a string attached to stop them falling off.

"Goooooooooooool!" he yells.

There is just time for people to sit down again, then the replay is shown, and they are up out of their seats again. The second replay gets a huge cheer; the third another. That's it. Back to the match. Fifteen to go.

Valencia are good at defending and attacking on the break, and the game is in their hands. Real Madrid have had a poor night, and they don't look like worrying goalkeeper Canizares. Every time an attack breaks down, the crowd cheer it like a goal. The atmosphere is marvellous. A bus drives past, peeping its horn. Just a minute to play out. An innocuous cross comes over, Raúl falls in the box. The referee . . .

"Noooo."

"Hijo de puta! Nooo!"

. . . points to the spot! He gives a penalty! The replay shows the incident again. Raúl, backing slightly into Marchena, falls over. There is no sort of challenge. There was no sort of danger. And yet the referee . . .

"Noooo! Hijo de cabrón!" (son of a cuckold). Everyone on their feet. Ni Lo Pienses is dumbstruck. The old guy puts his head in his hands again. Disbelief. The fans crowd around the screen as if they are players remonstrating at the referee. On the screen the players are crowding round the referee, remonstrating. He's not going to change his mind now. There is a palpable sense of justifiable outrage. Absolute, genuine outrage! How could the referee have . . .

Figo steps up. He always scores.

"Miss," I think. But he always scores.

He scores.

"Cabrón!" That was me.

Beckham catches up with Figo on the far side of the pitch. The Portuguese knows that the goal is lucky, his celebrations are muted. Beckham has a huge smile on his face. He doesn't care. A Coke can narrowly misses the screen. There's the sound of breaking glass. The final whistle goes. The square virtually empties in seconds.

I get back to my hotel room and say to the night porter, an old guy who I haven't seen before, "The referee invented a penalty. Did you see it?"

"I saw it. Well, you know, you win some you lose some."

Where is his absolute outrage? Why is his blood not boiling, like mine is, that Valencia should have been a point clear but because of the fucking referee INVENTING a fucking penalty they are two points behind?

"You are a Madridista," I say.

"I am," he admits. "And there have been at least three games this season in which a referee has given Valencia the game." It takes me a while to get to sleep.

## RESULTS JORNADA 23

| | | | |
|---|---|---|---|
| VALENCIA | 3 | ATLÉTICO | 0 |
| **REAL MADRID** | **2** | **MÁLAGA** | **1** |
| OSASUNA | 1 | BARCELONA | 2 |
| ALBACETE | 0 | DEPORTIVO | 2 |
| ATHLETIC BILBAO | 2 | MURCIA | 1 |
| CELTA | 2 | VILLARREAL | 1 |
| ESPANYOL | 2 | VALLADOLID | 0 |
| SEVILLA | 3 | MALLORCA | 0 |
| SANTANDER | 1 | BETIS | 2 |
| ZARAGOZA | 2 | REAL SOCIEDAD | 1 |

## RESULTS JORNADA 24

| | | | |
|---|---|---|---|
| MURCIA | 1 | SEVILLA | 3 |
| REAL SOCIEDAD | 1 | ATHLETIC | 1 |
| VALLADOLID | 0 | CELTA | 2 |
| BETIS | 2 | ZARAGOZA | 1 |
| DEPORTIVO | 2 | OSASUNA | 0 |
| VILLARREAL | 6 | RACING | 3 |
| MALLORCA | 0 | ALBACETE | 0 |
| MÁLAGA | 5 | ESPANYOL | 2 |
| BARCELONA | 3 | ATLÉTICO | 1 |
| **REAL MADRID** | **1** | **VALENCIA** | **1** |

## LA CLASIFICACIÓN

| | P | W | D | L | F | A | Pts |
|---|---|---|---|---|---|---|---|
| **1 REAL MADRID** | **24** | **16** | **5** | **3** | **46** | **25** | **53** |
| 2 VALENCIA | 24 | 16 | 6 | 3 | 46 | 17 | 51 |
| 3 DEPORTIVO | 24 | 15 | 4 | 5 | 41 | 17 | 49 |
| 4 BARCELONA | 24 | 11 | 7 | 6 | 38 | 28 | 40 |
| 5 ATHLETIC | 24 | 10 | 7 | 7 | 31 | 28 | 37 |
| 6 VILLARREAL | 24 | 10 | 6 | 8 | 35 | 30 | 36 |
| 7 ATLÉTICO | 24 | 10 | 6 | 8 | 31 | 31 | 36 |
| 8 BETIS | 24 | 9 | 8 | 7 | 32 | 26 | 35 |
| 9 OSASUNA | 24 | 8 | 10 | 6 | 24 | 21 | 34 |
| 10 SEVILLA | 24 | 8 | 7 | 9 | 34 | 27 | 31 |
| 11 REAL SOCIEDAD | 24 | 8 | 7 | 9 | 30 | 35 | 31 |
| 12 RACING | 24 | 8 | 6 | 10 | 32 | 38 | 29 |
| 13 MÁLAGA | 24 | 9 | 2 | 13 | 33 | 40 | 29 |
| 14 VALLADOLID | 24 | 7 | 8 | 9 | 28 | 35 | 29 |
| 15 MALLORCA | 24 | 8 | 4 | 12 | 28 | 42 | 28 |
| 16 CELTA | 24 | 6 | 9 | 9 | 34 | 41 | 27 |
| 17 ALBACETE | 24 | 6 | 5 | 13 | 23 | 34 | 23 |
| 18 ZARAGOZA | 24 | 6 | 5 | 13 | 23 | 35 | 23 |
| 19 ESPANYOL | 24 | 6 | 2 | 16 | 22 | 43 | 20 |
| 20 MURCIA | 24 | 2 | 10 | 12 | 22 | 40 | 16 |

# FIFTEEN
# BARCELONA

GOLFO DE VIZCAYA

OCÉANO ATLÁNTICO

**Espanyol** ○

**Real Madrid**
○

MAR MEDITERRÁNEO

# FIFTEEN
# BARCELONA

## SATURDAY FEBRUARY 21ST

I'm standing outside the Olympic Stadium on the Montjuic mountain in Barcelona, the most beautiful setting for a football stadium I've seen in Spain. It's an hour before the kick-off of Real Madrid's game with Espanyol, Barcelona's second team. The game is vital for both teams, with Real hoping to consolidate their lead over Valencia, and Espanyol desperate for points to climb out of the relegation zone. They call relegation 'El Pozo' (the well) in Spain, and Espanyol have spent the whole season so far up to their necks in the water at the bottom. However, having sacked Javier Clemente and hired capable French coach Luis Fernández, and having spent wisely in the transfer window, they have achieved a string of good results and can now see light above their heads. It would be a rare drop out of the top flight for the Catalan club; Espanyol have always played second fiddle to their more illustrious neighbours but have quite a history themselves. They celebrated their centenary in 2000 and have only spent four seasons out of the Primera in the history of the league.

I've always been interested in why Barcelona residents should choose Espanyol (who have won the Copa del Rey three times, but never the league) over Barcelona (16 Leagues, 24 Cups, 1 European Cup, 4 Cup Winners Cups, 3 UEFA Cups . . .). But I'm a bit nervous to ask the people around me. Espanyol's ultras are notoriously right-wing and violent. I've seen them on the TV lighting fires in the stands to signal their disgust, and waving the old (and illegal) Franquista Spanish flag (the same as the current national flag with a black eagle in the middle, banned after Franco's death in 1977). They have a terrible reputation. Will they mind my prying?

The received wisdom is that most of those who support the club are anti-Catalanista sons and daughters of immigrants who are making a political statement about their allegiance to the Madrid establishment by not supporting Barça. That the team's very name (which means 'Spanish') is a two-finger salute to the Catalan nationalists. But this isn't entirely true.

The club, referred to as 'los periquitos' (the parakeets) in the Spanish press, was formed in 1900 by a student, Ángel Rodríguez, who had watched a few games in England. This was just two years after Barça was set up by the Swiss businessman Hans 'Joan' Gamper. Their original name 'Español' derives from the 'Sociedad Gimnástica Española', whose facilities the club first used. Rodríguez, no doubt aware that the city's existing team was largely made up of British and Swiss ex-pats, insisted on a policy of only playing local players (of Spanish nationality but including many local Catalans). The club soon went bust, but was reformed in 1909. In 1910 they adopted the colours they now wear – blue and white stripes – to recall the flag of Roger de Lluria, a Catalan national hero, medieval admiral of the fearsome fleet of the Almogaver mercenaries.

Español moved into the Sarriá Stadium (a stone's throw away from the present site of the Nou Camp, formerly a haven for escaped parakeets, hence the name) in 1928. They used to attract a loyal following at their compact stadium, known as Can Rabia or 'La Bombonera' (the sweetbox), which was well known for its great atmosphere. This stadium was, incidentally, the venue for the France-Brazil World Cup quarter final in 1982, one of the best World Cup matches of all time. Español were traditionally considered the working class team of Barcelona, the underdogs of the city. They attracted a largely local following from around the barrio, and from Spanish-speaking Barcelona residents who didn't buy into the nationalist image of the city's dominant club (though it's true to say that many of the large wave of Spanish immigrants who moved to Barcelona in the Franco era quickly started supporting Barça in order to integrate into their new surroundings).

In 1995 the club, in an attempt to Catalanise their image, changed their name from Real Club Deportivo Español to Reial Club Deportiu Espanyol. It wasn't so much a change as a translation: they were still called 'Royal Spanish Sporting Club', only they were now called it in Catalan. The shortened form 'Español' became 'Espanyol' pronounced exactly the same, just spelt differently. It was a curious change. They were still 'Spanish' only in a more Catalan way. But a gesture, all the same.

In 1997, broke, the club sold their atmospheric 'sweetbox' ground and rented the Olympic Stadium, built for the 1992 Games and the scene of Linford Christie's gold medal. The track that he ran on is still there between the fans and the pitch, which means that the atmosphere is terrible. I went to see Espanyol-Valladolid a week before the Real game and though a section of the fans was singing throughout the game, the sound barely carried beyond them. It's an ugly open bowl designed for simultaneous track and field events – and an awful place for a football match, especially as its 55,000 capacity is rarely even half-filled for Espanyol games.

It'll be pretty full tonight though, and there are thousands of fans filling up the wide-open spaces around the stadium. I'm checking people's colours, aware that many Espanyol fans are reputed to share their allegiance with Real Madrid. There are a number of Real shirts and scarves on show, though the majority are wearing the blue and white of the home team. I get myself a beer in a kiosk over the road from the stadium (Dutch courage), and approach an old man wearing an owlish pair of glasses and a blue-and-white bar scarf.

"Can I ask you why you support Espanyol, and not Barcelona?"

He smiles.

"I support Espanyol and Barcelona. I used to go and see both teams play when I was younger. But the prices are too dear at Barcelona now, so I only come to Espanyol. I used to live in the next street up from the old stadium."

"Are you Catalan?"

He points to a little yellow and red striped ribbon sewn onto his scarf, the Catalan flag, (said to symbolise the smeared bloody fingermarks of the dying Catalan hero Wilfred the Hairy on his gold shield).

"Certainly. I am Catalan and proud of it. And Espanyol are a Catalan side." I ask him (in Spanish) if he is a Catalan speaker and he tells me a story about how it used to be illegal to speak Catalan in public back in the Franco era. How he was once on a tram, speaking Catalan to his friend, and a plain-clothes policeman showed him his badge under a lapel and said 'speak in Christian' so they had to switch to Spanish.

"It doesn't give you a problem that your team is considered to be the anti-Catalan team in Barcelona?"

"I don't consider it such. Espanyol is just a name."

I find another old fellow with a neat grey beard, who's eating sunflower seeds and spitting the shells out. A couple are stuck in the beard. Still cautious, I figure old men are an easy target.

"I've lived here for 30 years," he says. "I came from Albacete. At first I went to see Barcelona. But I didn't like the atmosphere. Too tense, too serious. So I started going to watch Espanyol. It was much more enjoyable. I've always had a feeling for the little team. And so I became a fan."

"Do you support Real Madrid as well?"

He spits out another shell.

"I hate Real Madrid."

I approach a couple of younger men who are queuing for beer. I address the one who looks fat and jovial.

"I support Espanyol because Barcelona are a Swiss team," he says. "They were originally all Germans and English. Catalans should support Espanyol, because they are not a foreign side."

"Are you a Catalanista?"

"I am a Catalanista. I am a Catalanista, and I support Espanyol."

I turn to a pair of identical twins, further down the queue. They have very short hair, and are wearing blue and white scarves.

"Don't ask this question," says one, and he means it. "Not to us, not to anyone."

At this point a young skinhead nearby kicks over one of the silver chairs at the bar-kiosk. Then he kicks it again, as if it were a football. His friends pull him off, and they head across the road to the stadium. I decide to wait a bit before approaching the next fan. Another young bloke in a blue and white scarf. I've chosen him because he is wearing glasses.

"Why do you support Espanyol and not Barça?"

"Because we are not stupid." He is speaking as well for a much more aggressive-looking friend I didn't realise he was with. Then, in English, "Because we are not donkeys." He decides to expand on this.

"Barcelona was founded by putos foreigners. Espanyol is a Spanish club." He looks angry.

"So it is a political statement, your support of Espanyol?" A question too far.

"That's enough." Then, again in English, "Fuck off." I follow his advice.

There are a number of empty seats as the match kicks off and whole sections of unsold seating have been covered by polythene adverts for major drinks companies. The Espanyol ultras wave large numbers of blue and white flags and chant against the team they hate: not the one they are playing.

"Puto Barça! Puto Barça!"

Guti is out as well as Beckham so Real are playing yet another pairing in central midfield: Zidane and Borja. Solari, Raúl and Juanfran are playing ahead of them, with Ronaldo up front. Real are wearing a new grey away kit. It's an apt choice. The start of the game is an insipid bore. I start up a conversation with the bloke next to me. He has a pointed beard like a medieval nobleman. He tells me he supports both Espanyol and Real Madrid. So who does he want to win tonight?

"We'll see."

He says he used to go to the old Sarriá stadium with 11 friends; all season ticket holders. Only three of them go to the new stadium. The other two couldn't make it tonight. They sold their tickets on.

The referee's decision to give a last-minute 'fantasma' (ghost, ie non-existent) penalty to Real Madrid against Valencia has led to a national debate during the week. The referee's association, headed by former international referee Diaz Vega, have stood by the referee, Tristante Oliva, saying that the decision was a correct one, and telling referees that any contact by a defender in the penalty area, wherever the ball is, should in future lead to a penalty. I wonder how this will affect tonight's referee. Will he favour the home team? Or will he favour Madrid, to show that he is impartial to all the pressure?

"Hostia puta!" (whorish host) shouts my neighbour, when Raúl Bravo gets a yellow card for delaying a free kick. He's wearing his Espanyol hat.

"Asi gana el Madrid," chant the ultras.

Then, on 26 minutes, Raúl chases a ball, closely followed by Espanyol defender Carlos García. The goalkeeper dives at his feet and collects. Raúl goes down. The referee . . . points to the spot! I can't believe it! Another dodgy penalty. I am outraged!

"Hostia puta!" I shout. "Árbitro de mierda!" (Shitty referee). The guy looks at me askance. He's surprised. Was that the wine at lunchtime followed by the beers outside the stadium? Or am I turning into a Spanish fan? Figo's on the bench; Ronaldo strokes the ball in. 'Asi gana el fucking Madrid,' I think.

"Hijo de puta!" I say. If only I had a white handkerchief. Half the fans in the stadium rise up and cheer. I head for the toilet, disgusted. Another dodgy penalty. I can't believe it.

I'm not long back when, at the far end, Iván de la Peña does down from an innocuous-looking challenge by Casillas. De la Peña, a bald Asturian, a false messiah at Barcelona in the late '90s, came back to the city last year to play for Espanyol after failing to impress in Marseille and Lazio. But his contract wasn't renewed by Javier Clemente, and he was left without a club at the beginning of this season. He was 'repescado' (re-signed, literally, re-fished) by Luis Fernández and, a visionary playmaker, has been approaching his best form. It appears he has the key to Espanyol's relegation escape attempt. The referee awards another penalty. It's only the second against Real Madrid this season. He was almost obliged to give it in the circumstances. Raúl Tamudo, Espanyol's busy little Spanish international striker, sends Casillas the wrong way. 1–1.

My reaction to the goal leads to a conversation with the guy at half time.

"Are you an Espanyol fan?" he asks.

"No. I just hate Madrid."

He asks me why? I've been asking myself the same question. It's been bugging me for a while. Why do I hate Madrid?

The longer the season goes on, the more I'm becoming obsessed with Spanish football. The first thing I do in the morning is to go out and buy *Marca*. The topic of conversation I slip most easily into is what's going on in the Spanish football league. I know the goal difference of the top three teams in the league. It's boring Brenda to tears, but I can't help it. I'm becoming a Spanish football fan. And every Spanish football fan I have met either hates Real Madrid or loves them. It is akin to having political beliefs, or being religious. You don't have to think about it, you just feel it. Are you left or right? A believer or an atheist? Anti-Madridista or Madridista? Real Madrid are the most powerful club in Spanish football: if you follow the game you inevitably have to take sides on the matter. But where's my objectivity gone? And why should I hate the most exciting team ever put together?

"I hate them more when Beckham isn't playing," I say, as an excuse. If I can't answer the question yet to myself, I haven't a hope of explaining to anyone else.

El Real turn it on in the second half, with Figo on for the ineffective Juanfran. Zidane performs the Zinedine Zidane Show: every touch is a surprise. Roberto Carlos hits a stunning volley past the keeper from the edge of the box. Raúl Bravo heads in a corner. Then Ronaldo scores one of the best individual goals I have ever seen. Running on to a ball from Cambiasso he dummies to turn right, fooling the keeper, Lemmens, into diving at his feet. Only his feet aren't there. He hasn't even touched the ball, which continues on through. He shimmies left again, and runs the ball into the unguarded net. It's reminiscent of Pele in the World Cup in 1970, only he actually finishes it off. I realise I am in the presence of genius. 4–1, and game over.

"Gordo, gordo," chant the Espanyol ultras, but you can see they don't mind too much. Half the fans in the stadium are on their feet, cheering, including my neighbour, now wearing his Real Madrid hat.

"Gordo, gordo," I chant. It's Ronaldo's 21st goal of the season.

"Imagine how good he'd be if he were thin," says the guy. A few minutes later Lopo scores a consolation goal for Espanyol, but it's much too little, far too late.

Later on that evening I watch the end of the Valencia v Barcelona game. Barça win with a late goal by Gerard, who doesn't celebrate, because he used to play for the home team. Suddenly El Real are five points clear at the top of the table. This depresses me. But, I reflect, should it? Should I be so ungenerous? Real Madrid represent everything I love in football: unbridled flair, devil-may-care attacking home and away. The best collection of attacking players the world has ever seen. A privilege to watch. So why can't I just sit back and enjoy the show?

## SATURDAY FEBRUARY 28TH

I watch Saturday afternoon TV in my flat in Barcelona. *The Football Focus* equivalent *El Día Antes* (hosted by Englishman and former Osasuna player Michael Robinson) show an advert during the show. Not during the ad break, during the show. They believe it to be so good, they think you should see it. The advert is for Pepsi, and it stars David Beckham. He plays a medieval adventurer trying, with the help of some other 'galácticos', to save a village from the clutches of an evil knight who is hoarding all the Pepsi cans.

*El Día Antes* takes the viewers into the chaotic press launch of the ad which took place earlier in the week in Madrid. The place is packed with journalists, desperate to get an interview with one of the stars there. There is no doubt who has top billing. Beckham has turned up dressed in a leather coat with wide fur lapels, like something out of *Withnail and I*.

"What are you dressed as today, David?" asks a sarcastic-sounding English girl.

"I'm not dressed as anything. I'm dressed as me," says Beckham.

There's a story circulating in the British press about Beckham's huge earnings from advertising endorsements – at £6.7 million last year, more than the £4 million he earned as a footballer. You see him smiling at you everywhere you go: full-page ads in newspapers, starring roles in TV commercials, his head and shoulders on advertising billboards. There is even a puppet of him on Canal plus' *Spitting Image* equivalent *La Semana del Guiñol*. You see him playing football, as well, of course. But not as well as he was doing earlier in the season. He's run into a worrying patch of mediocre form.

On Wednesday Real played Bayern Munich in Germany in the Champions League. The match finished 1–1, a score which flattered Real, who played awfully. Beckham was unable to hold midfield, he was outshone by his blond partner Guti. The Spanish team equalised with a free-kick, which wasn't entrusted to Beckham, but to Roberto Carlos. The next day, *Marca* gave the Englishman a '1' – the sixth consecutive time he got this unflattering score. Is there something going wrong? Is this the start of the Beckham backlash?

I watch the game against Celta de Vigo on Sunday evening in a Galician tapas bar on the Barcelona seafront. Valencia have just lost 2–1 to Espanyol up the road in Montjuic, on a pitch covered in snow. This result means a win against Celta will put Madrid eight points clear, just two weeks after being a minute away from losing the leadership to Valencia.

I'm expecting a bit of a Galician crowd, but there is just the usual collection of old-man Real Madrid fans, sitting on their own, moaning when things go wrong. At half time, Celta are winning 1–0, with a goal from Sasa Ilic. There's plenty of grumbling going on.

"What do you think of Beckham?" I ask the old guy in front.

"Is he playing?" he replies, in a rare show of Spanish sarcasm.

In the second half, the inevitable happens. Ronaldo taps in a rebound from the keeper, Zidane heads in a Figo cross, and Figo scores, set up by a fine pass from Beckham. 3–1. It is the first time that the Englishman has had anything to do with a goal since his free-kick in the cup against lowly Leganés before Christmas. On 88 minutes an extremely tired-looking Beckham is substituted, with Cambiasso coming on in his place.

The game finishes 4–2. The next morning, *Marca* is full of Real's good fortune. They are eight points ahead of Valencia and nine ahead of Depor, who lost at home to Barcelona. Without a contender in sight, then, as they hit the last lap of the course. The newspaper's match report ends with a joke "There was an Englishman, a Frenchman, a Brazilian, a Portuguese and a Spaniard . . . and they always won." But they don't go overboard in their praise for the Englishman. Despite his assist, he gets another '1' with the phrase 'big runner'.

During the lunchtime news I watch the Pepsi advert again. There's no doubt that Beckham gets the biggest billing. But at the end of the ad, there is a simulated free-kick as the medieval baddies line up in a wall to try to protect their wagon full of Pepsi cans. One of the players hits an accurate shot at the padlock of the caged cans, and they spill out over the ground. But the kick is not entrusted to David Beckham. It is taken by Roberto Carlos.

## RESULTS JORNADA 25

| | | | |
|---|---|---|---|
| ATLÉTICO | 0 | DEPORTIVO | 0 |
| **ESPANYOL** | **2** | **REAL MADRID** | **4** |
| CELTA | 0 | MÁLAGA | 2 |
| SEVILLA | 1 | REAL SOCIEDAD | 0 |
| VALENCIA | 0 | BARCELONA | 1 |
| ALBACETE | 1 | MURCIA | 0 |
| RACING | 1 | VALLADOLID | 0 |
| OSASUNA | 1 | MALLORCA | 1 |
| ZARAGOZA | 4 | VILLARREAL | 1 |
| ATHLETIC | 1 | BETIS | 1 |

| | | | |
|---|---|---|---|
| VALLADOLID | 1 | ZARAGOZA | 2 |
| BETIS | 1 | SEVILLA | 1 |
| REAL SOCIEDAD | 0 | ALBACETE | 1 |
| MURCIA | 0 | OSASUNA | 1 |
| MALLORCA | 0 | ATLÉTICO | 1 |
| MÁLAGA | 1 | RACING | 0 |
| VILLARREAL | 0 | ATHLETIC | 1 |
| ESPANYOL | 2 | VALENCIA | 1 |
| **REAL MADRID** | **4** | **CELTA** | **2** |
| DEPORTIVO | 2 | BARCELONA | 3 |

## LA CLASIFICACIÓN

| | P | W | D | L | F | A | Pts |
|---|---|---|---|---|---|---|---|
| **REAL MADRID** | **26** | **18** | **5** | **3** | **54** | **29** | **59** |
| VALENCIA | 26 | 15 | 6 | 5 | 47 | 20 | 51 |
| DEPORTIVO | 26 | 15 | 5 | 6 | 43 | 20 | 50 |
| BARCELONA | 26 | 13 | 7 | 6 | 42 | 30 | 46 |
| ATHLETIC | 26 | 11 | 8 | 7 | 33 | 29 | 41 |
| ATLÉTICO | 26 | 11 | 7 | 8 | 32 | 31 | 40 |
| OSASUNA | 26 | 9 | 11 | 6 | 26 | 22 | 38 |
| BETIS | 26 | 9 | 10 | 7 | 34 | 28 | 37 |
| VILLARREAL | 26 | 10 | 6 | 10 | 36 | 35 | 36 |
| SEVILLA | 26 | 9 | 8 | 9 | 36 | 28 | 35 |
| MÁLAGA | 26 | 11 | 2 | 13 | 36 | 40 | 35 |
| RACING | 26 | 9 | 6 | 11 | 33 | 39 | 32 |
| REAL SOCIEDAD | 26 | 8 | 7 | 11 | 30 | 37 | 31 |
| ZARAGOZA | 26 | 8 | 5 | 13 | 29 | 37 | 29 |
| VALLADOLID | 26 | 7 | 8 | 11 | 29 | 38 | 29 |
| ALBACETE | 26 | 8 | 5 | 13 | 25 | 34 | 29 |
| MALLORCA | 26 | 8 | 5 | 13 | 29 | 44 | 29 |
| CELTA | 26 | 6 | 9 | 11 | 36 | 47 | 27 |
| ESPANYOL | 26 | 7 | 2 | 17 | 26 | 48 | 23 |
| MURCIA | 26 | 2 | 10 | 14 | 22 | 42 | 16 |

# SIXTEEN
# SANTANDER

GOLFO DE VIZCAYA

**Racing de
Santander**

**Real Madrid**

OCÉANO ATLÁNTICO

MAR MEDITERRÁNEO

N
W E
S

# SIXTEEN
# SANTANDER

**THURSDAY MARCH 4TH**

I wake up wondering where the hell I am and work out I'm approaching Palencia in northern Castilla y León, after a night train journey in one of the sleeping carriages from Barcelona. Brenda's in a female compartment down the carriage. She's come along to take some photos. She's landed herself a good job in Ireland, and we're going to spend the next couple of weeks together in northern Spain before our enforced separation. We have to change trains here to get to Santander, which is in Cantabria on the north coast: Real Madrid are playing Racing de Santander in a couple of days. In the two hours between trains I buy the papers and look round the centre of Palencia. Hemingway calls it 'a nice Castilian town, with good beer and excellent quail shooting', though I don't partake in either of these pleasures. It's got a high quotient of medieval churches too, though, so I look round a couple. They kind of depress me, as medieval churches have done since my parents used to drag me round them as a kid on family holidays. All that darkness, all those pictures of skeletons. Anyway, my head is so full of the cut and thrust of Spanish football, I seem to have lost the serenity needed to contemplate medieval façades. I used to have it. Didn't I?

The countryside leading up to the north coast is spectacular, but the sports paper I've bought, *As*, is irritating. The paper announces that Real Madrid has an 82.81 per cent chance of winning the league. They are complacent; much more concerned with Real Madrid's match against Bayern Munich next week than the one against Racing this weekend. Beckham is on the front cover – the story about him is that he has just been to Herzogenaurach in Germany to promote a new range of adidas clothing. The company has designed a logo of Beckham taking a free-kick for the new venture. The irony is that he hasn't scored one for ages. He spent half an hour after training the previous day practising them, and he only scored three. The columnist Juanma Trueba suggests that

there are three reasons for Beckham's continuing failure – 'lack of practice, the walls don't go back far enough in Spain, and yabadabadoo'. I
suspect he's suggesting that Beckham's excuses about his failure at
free kicks this year are hot air.

The first sign of snow is on the terracotta roofs of a village called Alar
del Rey. At Mave, you can see that there was recently a covering. Then
we climb higher into the cordillera of hills – by Mataporquera there's a
thick blanket of the stuff. There's nothing like a covering of snow to
cheer you up. I read that Real Madrid have something of a personnel
crisis. Raúl is injured, Míchel Salgado and Pavón are suspended. They
might have to play the inexperienced Mejía at right back. We hit the
peaks of the hill range, and then suddenly the snow has gone, replaced
by large expanses of green. We've reached Cantabria and it's all rolling
hills, cows with bells attached to their necks and detached houses with
steep roofs. Just the odd palm tree there to remind you that you're not
in Switzerland. I contemplate how football in Spain is an urban sport,
and that my travels have almost entirely been to large or medium-sized
cities. It's something I mean to change. We pass through a village called
Boo, then we pull into Santander. We're to spend three days there,
catch the Racing match, then move onto the Picos de Europa, a famously
beautiful mountain range which stretches out over Cantabria, Asturias
and León to see what part football plays in a small rural community, in
the run up to the Bayern game.

From the station we get a taxi straight to the stadium, called El
Sardinero 'the sardine catcher'. It is right next to a beach of the same
name, and opposite a spectacular silver blob of a building, El Estadio
Polideportivo, where they play handball and basketball. The taxi driver
doubts that there will be any tickets left. He calls the home team
'Racing', pronouncing the first syllable as in 'Rathbone'. He is surprised,
when he drops us off, to see that the ticket-office windows are still
open. Pissed-off-looking touts are hanging around waiting for them to
sell out. There's nothing cheap left; the best price we can get is 55
euros, for tickets behind the goal in the South Stand. Afterwards I nip
round to the press office and arrange to get access to the press
conference after the game. Brenda's egging me on to get through to
Beckham after the game and try and ask him a question. We start
working out the best thing to ask him.

**FRIDAY MARCH 5TH**
It's the day before the Real Madrid match, but you wouldn't know it
from *Marca*, which I read in the Café Royalty opposite the pretty ferry

port (in this case not an oxymoron) which brings boats in from Plymouth twice a week. You wouldn't know it from Santander either, as the city, the shop-and-bar-filled centre squeezed between the sea and the parallel hills, the suburbs spilling over behind, goes about its business. *Marca's* journalists are still obsessed with Beckham's lifetime deal with adidas – quoted as being worth up to an incredible 241 million euros – and his free-kick goal drought. They report that after yesterday's training the reserve team keeper Jordi Codina bet Beckham ten euros that he couldn't score a free kick against him in three attempts. And that Beckham couldn't. They mention that Beckham is suffering from flu and is doubtful for the match, though they put him in the little diagram of the team that they suggest will turn out the next day, alongside Guti in the centre of midfield (though behind Guti might have been more accurate).

The paper is also looking forward to the midweek Champions League match against Bayern Munich, and is full of outrage at UEFA for their ban on Roberto Carlos for hitting French player Martin Demichelis during the first leg. They are building up quite a campaign, suggesting that Bayern Munich have pulled strings in UEFA to keep him out of the game between the two clubs. Hardly anything about the match against Racing. I ask the waiter, a bald impassive man who might otherwise be a butler or a snooker referee, what he would ask Beckham, if he had the chance. "I don't like football," he replies. He pauses. "But I would ask him if he could give me some of his money."

Just before lunch I have a glass of Rioja (I'm told there are no good local red wines) in a dusty old bar in the centre of town, where there is a flange of old men who look like they have nowhere else to go. The most talkative one keeps walking behind people, touching his throat, and scaring them by talking loudly in their ear in a dalek voice that exits through his voicebox. There is a short blind man leaning face-forwards into the bar, white stick in hand, who occasionally bursts into spontaneous fits of raucous laughter, which unfailingly turn into a hacking cough. I get talking to Miguel, who is wearing once-smart clothes: a blue coat and a greasy tie knotted tight under a frayed collar. He is a Real Madrid fan, and a Racing fan too. We're speaking in Spanish but he occasionally utters bursts of polished but formulaic English.

"Beckham is a perfect English gentleman," he says. "A great diplomat. A fine advertisement for your country. Tony Blair must to pay him money. He could do great things for your country. He has the touch of the King Midas. He is the world's number one of marketing."

What he would ask Beckham, if he had the chance? He comes up with a number of options.

"I would ask him about strange English customs. Like why do all prices have '99' at the end? Why don't they serve free tapas with drinks? [we have been given a cup of broth, with soggy bread bits]. And I would ask him what he thinks of Spain. What his opinion is about our cities, and our customs. Does he like us? We like him."

This gets me thinking. How much does Beckham know about Spanish customs and Spanish cities? He goes from the airport to the hotel to the stadium. There's little difference to him, presumably, between one city and another. In Madrid he's followed everywhere by what has now become a fleet of paparazzi. He can't have got to know the city like anyone else would have: he can't exactly wander round the streets. And how interested is he, anyway? He's arriving in Santander tonight: will he know which region he's in? Or even which coast he's on? Spain knows all about him . . . but how much does he know about Spain? This seems like a good question to ask him. I write it in my notebook.

I've read that the Real Madrid players are staying in the Hotel Bahía, on the seafront-side of the town centre and that they will arrive about 8.30 tonight. After lunch Brenda and I wander into the restaurant of the hotel, and ask to reserve a table for dinner. The dining room is split into two sections by a sliding wooden panel. On one side four or five tables have been set up for a party of about 30 people. It must be for Real Madrid! We choose a table right next to the panelling. We will be able to hear them talk!

We take a walk along the quays on the pretty seafront of this lovely city, built on one side of a wide estuary full of little sailing boats. We're heading for El Sardinero to watch Racing train. I've requested an interview with the goalkeeper Ricardo, who spent last season at Manchester United, only managing one game but becoming good friends, by all accounts, with Beckham. An inverse experience: a Spaniard goes to England for a year and virtually nobody notices, so he comes back.

Pretty soon the quayside turns into a sandy beach, which leads to the Magdalena peninsula, which has been turned into a national park. The stadium is just the other side of the peninsula, past the city's extravagant Baroque casino. When we get there, there is no training going on. I find the press guy. "Sorry, change of plan," he says. "They are training behind closed doors tonight." No interview.

We decide to walk back over the hill that leads into the centre of town. We get a bit lost and ask directions of a short, middle-aged woman with blonde hair and bad teeth. She takes us in the right direction, and points us out the five-star Hotel Real, a magnificent white pile set in its own grounds overlooking the sea, where she says Real Madrid usually stay.

"What would you ask Beckham, if you met him?"

She pauses, and smiles. "If I could have his lovely diamond earrings. He could just tell his wife he lost them."

We have a drink in the hotel's plush bar, with its sea views. We get nuts, crisps and olives with the drink. We chat to the waiter, asking why Real Madrid are not staying here this year, why they are down in the Hotel Bahía, which only has four stars.

"Who knows? Perhaps they can no longer afford to stay here. All those wages for Beckham."

We get a taxi down to the Bahía. The driver is a Racing fan. So what would he ask Beckham?

"Ask him to go easy on Racing. Not to play too hard. We need the points."

We arrive at the Bahía at exactly the same time as Real Madrid. There are about 500 fans flanking the entrance to the hotel. I see Beckham's head; his dark roots bobbing through the gauntlet. He's travelled, then. His flu can't be that bad. The kids go mad. We hear the usual chorus of names as the players run through.

"Figo. Figo! Zidane! Solari!"

There is a line of ten-year-old kids, standing on a wall, spitting. Their leader is a fat 14-year-old in a Racing shirt, wearing a scarf, buccaneer-like, over his forehead.

"What would you like to ask Beckham?" asks Brenda, who's bolder than me. The older one snarls contempt at the question, and the others look up at him to provide an answer that reflects this contempt.

"Ask him if he would lend me his woman," shouts the boy, and his mates laugh their approval. The smallest one spits again.

A couple of minutes later we follow through the same doors the players have just rushed through. The crowd outside the hotel has thinned, but the bar is packed with excited fans, happy to be in the same building as their heroes. We order a vermouth, and wander through to the empty restaurant. The five-course special costs 35 euros each. It seems worth it. Just us and Real Madrid in the same dining room. Maybe we'll meet them. Request a little chat with Beckham. That's the sort of thing people do in the restaurants of posh hotels, isn't it?

Not many other guests turn up in the restaurant. We sit smugly, as the waiters take a trolley full of bottles of water through to the big table. They wouldn't drink wine, would they? Ours is a long meal, though they bring one course quickly after another – small portions of delicate food served on large white plates with flourishes of sauce squirted on the side. A bottle of good Rioja.

"The players will probably eat pasta and drink water," I drone. Brenda is getting a little sick of football. Can't I talk about anything else? And where are the players? It's getting late. 10.30! What time are these bloody footballers going to eat?

At 11 there's a hubbub at the door. At last! We look to see who's heading the party. A woman? Aged about 30? And another? And another. Pretty soon there's a crowd of about 25 women, dressed to party, being led to the tables behind the panels, and one bloke, with a stockbroker haircut and a stripy shirt. No footballers. We eat our fancy puddings in silence. After five courses I'm uncomfortably bloated. What a waste of money. Afterwards, in the bar, Iker Casillas is sitting in the corner, talking to a girl. I order a brandy. They say that the bar is closed, that I can't have one. This trip is not going to plan.

## SATURDAY MARCH 7TH

Things continue in the same vein the next day, the day of the game. At 11.30 I turn up to the Hotel Continental, where Florentino Pérez is scheduled to meet the Santander-based Real Madrid peña at noon. I'm told the meeting has been cancelled. I've read in *Marca* that a priest from the village of La Vega in the nearby Picos de Europa mountains has challenged Ronaldo to a game of football in the Hotel Bahía – if the priest wins, Ronaldo has to pay for the upkeep of some of his mountain churches. As I arrive I see a number of media types leaving the place. The guard at the door doesn't let me in, tells me the priest doesn't want any journalists to witness the 'game'. I give up, meet Brenda, and we go for lunch in a dark bar with a suit of armour and hundreds of dusty bottles of wine stacked up on the walls and ceiling. I eat the biggest T-bone steak I have had in my life, so rare that, gnawing the bone, I remind myself of one of the pre-historic man-monkeys in *Quest for Fire*. Brenda looks at me with something approaching panic.

We take the same walk to the stadium as before, walking past the bobbing yachts, the enormous brutalist-style theatre and along the city's wide stretches of sandy beaches, past the casino, and into the usual scarfed-up throng heading for the game. What a way to get to the match. On a viewing platform looking out to sea, some Real Madrid fans pose for a picture with a flag of their club. The sky is a deep blue and there are numerous sailing boats just shy of the horizon. The fans carefully wrap up the flag again and put it in a bag. I ask them what they would ask Beckham, if they had the chance.

"Ask him why he is trying so hard." says a guy in glasses. "We think he's trying harder than he did in Manchester. Is it because he is worried that he won't otherwise get into the team?"

We find our seats, on the first row of the second tier behind one of the goals. The capacity of the place is just 23,000 and it's going, they say, to be full today for only the fifth time in its 26-year history. The teams warm up. A tired-looking Beckham, not yet wearing his shin pads, stands on one touch-line passing looping balls to Roberto Carlos, who stands on the other, passing them back. It looks like he's over his 'flu. A few hundred Madrid fans in the opposite stand start up a chant, which is joined in by the hundred or so Real Madrid fans sitting in a pen directly in front of us.

"Maaaaaaa-drid. Maaaa-drid."

It is echoed by a louder chant from all four sides of the stadium.

"Raaaa-cing, Raaa-cing." The players run out to the usual boos and cheers, and Racing's anthem comes over the tannoy.

> 'Racing, Racing. Ra ra ra!
> A la bin, A la ban, A la bin bon ban
> Racing! Racing! Ra ra ra!

Míchel Salgado's suspension means that young Mejía, a centre-back who has only played three first-team games, is filling in at right back, and from the opening moves of the game you can tell Racing have been told to target this flank. Twice in the opening minutes the Uruguayan winger Regueiro skips past the long-haired youngster and puts in a cross – twice the subsequent header flashes just wide of the post. The referee, Medina Cantalejo, flashes three yellow cards in the first five minutes, for no apparent reason but to impose his strutting authority. Racing get a corner which is only half cleared by Casillas, dropping towards Racing's Benayoun. The ball loops as if in slow motion towards his boot and he winds up for a shot: there's plenty of goal to aim at. I feel my knees starting to make the rise of triumph. They are stayed by a black flash which leaps across the six-yard box and miraculously blocks the shot. Beckham. Fifteen minutes gone and it could already be 3–0 to Racing. But it's still 0–0.

"You have to take your chances against Real Madrid," says the old fellow next to us to his two grown-up sons. And then, as if to prove his wisdom, Solari scores a goal from nothing at the far end of the pitch to put Real in front. The little section in front of us starts jumping up and down and hugging. Shortly afterwards Real get a corner: Beckham goes to take it, showered by abuse, but well lit by a hundred camera-flashes. The ball is headed over the bar. A let-off. "Real have to take their chances against Racing," jokes the son. Then there's a free kick to our right (Mejía has brought down his tormentor Regueiro), the ball falls to Benayoun on the six-yard box, and this time there is no miraculous saving tackle as he places it carefully into the unguarded corner of the net. The father hugs his sons. A firework goes off behind the stand opposite.

"Beckham wears his socks differently from the other players," says Brenda, in the way that people who aren't terribly interested in the game alert your attention to something that you might otherwise have missed. "You know, he's not naturally cool, like Guti is. You can even see it if you compare the way they run. And that's why he's a trend-setter, and Guti isn't. Guti follows fashion, Beckham just wears what he feels like, and because he's got style, it works."

Real Madrid get their first dangerous free-kick about 40 yards out of the box. Beckham and Roberto Carlos both shape up to take it. It's the Brazilian who shoots . . . way over the bar.

"He's so low to the ground," says Brenda. "Like a little tank."

Real Madrid are much better in the second half than the first. Once Figo starts coming back to help young Mejía, they don't look half so vulnerable, and start building attack after attack. Beckham takes a couple of free-kicks into the box, and, with Real Madrid frequently in possession around Racing's penalty box, starts assuming a more attacking role. In the first half he could have been Vinnie Jones. Then on 73 minutes, after jumping for a ball with Beckham, Ronaldo falls over, and crumples into a heap behind the goal. He is helped off the pitch by Real's physio.

"Gordo, gordo," shout the crowd, ungenerously. You can see from the way he is hobbling that he won't be playing for a while. It's a terrible blow for Real Madrid. And I have a niggling suspicion that it was Beckham who knocked him over. Young Antonio Núñez comes on in his place.

"Núñez for El Gordo!" says the old guy. "I'll settle for that."

But it's Núñez who creates the best chance for El Real to score in the second half, going down in the box after a challenge by a Racing defender. The referee doesn't give anything.

"Asi gana el Racing," shouts one of the Real fans in front of us. It's the closest they get to wrapping up the game. Deep into injury time, Mejía, who looks like he has toughed out his nightmare, gets a red card for a hand-ball. The referee, who has so far waved ten cards, shows a couple more, to Beckham and even Queiroz, for complaining about the earlier decision. Shortly afterwards he blows the final whistle.

I rush out of the stadium and, showing my invaluable press card, get myself and Brenda into the mixed zone, which is little more than a small corridor between the changing room and the road outside. She's got her camera round her neck. The place is packed with journalists and TV cameramen. Anthony, the *News of the World's* man and Eric, the *Sun's* man, argue about where the Sunday paper man should stand.

The *Mail* man, Simon, turns up, and announces that he's off to the Queiroz press conference. The *Mail* have been banned from Beckham's post-match talks for an article they have printed about him. "Ask him about the tonsils, and that shit," shouts the *Sun* guy. The two seem to have a little agreement on quote-sharing. I start rehearsing my question for Beckham in my head. I've chosen the one about him not getting to know Spain. It sounds foolish, all of a sudden. After about five minutes some of the Racing players start trying to force their way through. It's a terrible struggle for them to squeeze through the crowd. Then Roberto Carlos comes out.

"Roberto, Roberto Carlos," shout the reporters, but he doesn't want to talk. He looks around him with some dismay, then pushes his way out through the crowd, using that low centre of gravity, those tree-trunk legs, to their full effect. Next up is Ronaldo. Injured Ronaldo, who takes one look at the crowd and heads back into the dressing room. The Racing press guy, Antonio, comes out, and makes an angry speech to the effect that the Real players will go straight to the coach without going through the mixed zone. The scrum relaxes its tension.

I walk outside the door and take a look at the excited crowd, waiting behind a cordon of silver crash barriers and policemen, and the familiar team bus. Why this uproar? Why are people so interested in catching a glimpse of the players they have just seen doing something interesting (playing a game of football) doing something very uninteresting (getting on a bus)? Why are all these pressmen so interested in getting quotes off the players, which are likely to be boring and clichéd? Then I see Beckham scooting towards the bus, a coffee-coloured scarf trailing over his shoulder, with the *News of the World* guy heading him off like a fullback after a striker who has beaten the offside trap. He catches him five yards short of the bus door. By the time I get there a throng of pressmen, jabbing microphones and cameras, has already formed. Boy, these guys are quick. Do they train? The questions rain in, about his performance, his form, his tonsils. I can't get a word in edgeways. Brenda is next to me taking photos.

"David, David," I keep shouting, but he never looks my way.

"David, the Spanish . . ."

"David, how well do you . . ."

"David . . ."

Occasionally he feels a spit of rain and looks up into the sky, his diamond ear-rings glinting, to hint that it's bloody cold out here and he's still got flu. After three minutes the hacks have exhausted their questions. I make one last attempt . . .

"David . . ."

. . . but it's too late. He's into the bus. Damn, damn, damn. I feel a crushing sentiment of self-loathing. I'm not cut out to be a tabloid hack.

Back in the mixed zone, I meet the priest who challenged Ronaldo to the game of football and arrange to meet him in the Picos de Europa the next day, to ask him about the whole affair. Then I go to a nearby bar and watch the second half of Valencia v Deportivo while eating an enormous plate of sea-snails with a pin and drinking several cold beers. Valencia turn 1–0 into 3–0 with two very late goals against a 10-man team that starts leaving gaps at the back to try and equalise. This puts the East-coast team six points behind Real Madrid. The championship race, it seems, is not yet over.

## SUNDAY MARCH 7TH

There *is* a Beckham backlash. I thought he did a fine defensive job in the first half (that saving tackle!) and was fluent in his passing in the second, and I was wondering whether *Marca* would give him a '1' or a much-needed '2'. He gets a '0', with the comment 'he didn't do anything.' As if this clearly untrue statement is not enough, the journalist Roberto Palomar finishes his match report off with a damning criticism of the Englishman.

'David Beckham should be entered into the chapter of disasters,' he writes. 'His regression in the last few weeks has been evident. First he played and ran. Then he ran, and played. Afterwards, he only ran. Yesterday he neither played, nor ran. The best that he did was to hug Ricardo.' I look to *El País* to find something more reflective of my opinion of Beckham's performance. But there is just more damnation, albeit more poetically put. 'Guti's game grew as the match progressed,' writes the serious daily, 'but next to him he found the latest version of Beckham, who has lost his identity. Right now, he's acting as Guti's water-carrier. He runs all the miles in the world, but he doesn't manage to find where he's going, directed by a force akin to chaos. He's lacking a map of the game.'

We're moving westwards, in a bus, through the stunning rock-walled valley that funnels the road from Santander into the Picos de Europa. We're going to try to find the Ronaldo-challenge priest, Don Manuel Muela, even though I'll have missed my appointment with him by at least five hours (there's only one bus a day). I read the relevant tourist literature on the bus, while trying not to miss what it's talking about out the window. By all accounts we're heading to one of the most beautiful and remote regions in Spain, inhabited by wolves, bears, wild boar and simple rustic folk. The bus pulls into its final destination. Potes is a touristy town with a large medieval tower, completely surrounded by mountains which look like the ones children draw: craggy and snow-capped and marvellous to behold. We get a taxi up to La Vega, eight kilometres up, and look for a pension. It is off season and we are spoilt for choice. We decide against the one with the Land Rover outside, scared off by the seven dead foxes hanging on the rear bumper. We go for the Casa Leny, with a noisy torrent – the Río Frío – fast-flowing right past our bedroom window. Twenty-seven euros a night seems a good price for such tranquillity.

Later on I go for a walk up the side of one of the wooded mountains near our house, with views of larger, snow-capped peaks either side. After about half an hour the only sign of human life is the line of cotton on the ground that marks out the path to take. I can feel the freshness of the air in my delighted lungs. I have found a stout stick which is the perfect size to help me up the steeper bits of the slope. The further I get up the mountainside, the more liberated I feel. This territory is devoid of man, which means that it is devoid of man's most addictive pasttime: football. I feel purified, clean, serene. I come to a level piece of land, look into the abyss below and shout, with all my might,

"FUCK YOU BECKHAM!"

I am free.


## WEDNESDAY MARCH 10TH

But not for long. The priest, Don Manuel, a small, wiry, grey-haired man of 42, is obsessed with a football matter. He tells me and Brenda about it at length as he takes us on his weekly walk through mountain paths from one parish to another to deliver Mass. The craggy scenery is stupendous, and Don Manuel is looking good, too. He is dressed in a black cassock and a pair of hiking boots, with a black rucksack on his back, presumably for the host and wine. He has 15 churches in his patch. He spends three days a week walking between them to deliver the midweek Mass, then on Sunday drives round all the ones he can reach in his car. He's a busy man. But at the moment he welcomes all diversion. He has a nagging problem.

It all started in September on a trip with some of his parishioners to Málaga, where Real Madrid were playing the local team. Don Manuel, from Santander, is a Racing fan, but he is also a Real Madrid fan and has loved the Brazilian national team since they awakened his interest in the game in the 1970 World Cup tournament in Mexico. So he decided to make his way to the hotel that Real Madrid were staying in before their game against Málaga FC, to try to arrange an interview with

Roberto Carlos and Ronaldo. He waited in a back room, and to his surprise, Roberto Carlos walked in.

"He looked at me with dismay, wondering what this priest might want with him. I told him about how I was a fan of Brazil, how I admired his play, and how I loved watching Real Madrid. How all my parishioners were Real Madrid fans, and how we all watched the matches together in a little bar in La Vega in the Picos de Europa. He just nodded, shook my hand, and when I was through, left."

Next up was Ronaldo, who was, apparently, far more chatty than his compatriot.

"He asked me about the Picos, and I said that he should come and visit. I said that I would challenge him to a game of football, and if he lost he would have to visit my parishes. That I would hide the ball in the folds of my cassock as I do with the children: like this I would definitely beat him. It was a joke really. He laughed and laughed. I gave him a cross of St Christopher and a rosary for Roberto Carlos, which I had forgotten to give him before."

The matter got complicated when Don Manuel met a journalist of the local *Diario Montañés* newspaper at a dinner just before Christmas, and told him the story, giving him a picture of himself with the Brazilian striker that he had had taken after their interview. The journalist made the story into a back-page feature of the Sunday edition, exaggerating the nature of the challenge made to Ronaldo, saying that the player had agreed to pay for the repair of a number of churches if he lost the little contest with the priest. It also made public Ronaldo's half-joking 'promise' to come and visit the area. Sunday being Sunday, Don Manuel had a hell of a day playing it all down with the parishioners of his 15 churches.

Since Christmas the priest has been busy getting together a proposition to Florentino Pérez, with the help of the local town hall, and the Racing de Santander president, Ángel Coterillo. He had arranged to give this proposition to Ronaldo and Pérez on the morning of the Racing-Real game in the hotel Bahía.

"The trouble is," laments Don Manuel, "by the time I got to the hotel, the news had spread and there were dozens of journalists waiting for me. When I saw Ronaldo he was furious with me. He didn't want to talk to me, let alone play a game of football with me. He thought that I had led him into a trap." There was no game, then, and the journalists were all sent away, at which point I had arrived on the scene. The priest, however, was interviewed on the TV and the radio. The story was spreading. It had Roberto Carlos-strength legs.

"Now I don't know what to do. Wherever I go, whoever I see, people ask me when Ronaldo is coming. I don't even know if he is! I have asked for him and one other player – perhaps it will be Beckham – but it is all in the hands of Florentino Pérez and Ronaldo himself. And he looked so cross with me! I don't know what to do. It is very damaging. I think this whole affair will do me nothing but harm. It is getting to the point where I find it hard to sleep."

Thinking the matter over, I realise that there isn't much in it for Florentino Pérez to get Ronaldo into the Picos. The population is very old (there's little work for youngsters) and all the men seem to support Real Madrid anyway. They're definitely not the football-shirt-buying type – they seem to prefer dirty woollen jumpers with holes in them. I advise Don Manuel to keep the matter on a back-burner and to pass over the responsibility to the Town Hall, so he can't be blamed if it all goes wrong.

"How can I put it on the back-burner?" he says. "It's all anyone wants to talk to me about!"

At the village of Enterrias we are joined by a friendly Alsatian dog which accompanies us for the next couple of hours along the mountain paths. The priest is often a good 20 yards ahead of us, used to running zig-zaggedly down hills and hauling himself up steep footprint-stepped slopes, so the dog keeps a beat between him and us. Each time he finds us, he greets us with the sort of enthusiasm humans reserve for airports and weddings. Eventually we wind up back in Enterrias. Brenda and I sit on a bench looking up at a stone church, where we can see the priest ringing the bells to announce his arrival to the village people. The dog is at our feet, happily panting. A young woman in an apron turns up and says,

"There you are."

She's talking to the dog.

"What's his name?"

"Figo."

"After the footballer?"

"Of course. Out last one was called Míchel (after the Spanish international Real Madrid player of the '80s and '90s)."

"Not Beckham."

"The next one will be called Beckham."

I tell her how the dog has been with us for the past three hours.

"He'll follow anyone. It's getting ridiculous. The other day he turned up in Potes, 15 kilometres away. People are always ringing up to say they have found him. Our number is on his collar." She has a rope with her, and she ties it to his collar and drags him up the hill. It's quite a task. He's planting his feet, whining, looking back at us sorrowfully.

Mass over, we set off down the hill. As we are approaching the next village, after about 20 minutes walk, we hear a familiar yelp. Figo has liberated himself from his rope and tracked us down. He's all over us, delighted to have found us again. We're more ambivalent about the reunion. There's no way we're going to trail back up the hill. The priest gets out his mobile phone.

"I'll ring up the owners," he says.

There's a mumbled conversation.

"He says we have to hit him with our sticks and he'll stop following us and go back home."

We look at Figo. He looks at us. The priest starts prodding him gingerly with his stick. But he's obviously not cut out for corporal punishment, not even with a dog. There's no way either Brenda or I are going to start hitting him. We continue down to the village, dog at our heels. We reach a house, where a man is sitting outside in wellington boots and a woolly hat. The priest explains the problem.

"Just hit him!" says the guy. Several other family members come out of the house.

"That's the thing," says the priest. "We can't bring ourselves to."

The six or seven members of the family start laughing. I do too. They offer to do the hitting but we refuse to allow it. We start chatting. I tell them the dog's history of following people and its Real Madrid-related name. They agree to tie him to a gate-post until we are well gone.

"Hey, Father," says the guy in the wellies. "Now we've got Figo, but when are we going to get Ronaldo?"

"Yeah, when's he coming?" They're all still laughing.

"We'll see," says the priest, more seriously, and we scurry off down the hill.

Later on that evening I'm in the local bar, watching Real Madrid play Bayern Munich in the Champions League. It's an extremely tense game: Real have to win to proceed to the quarter finals. In the bar there are ten or so villagers, watching intently. This constitutes approximately a third of the male population of the village.

"There are usually more, but it's on terrestrial TV, so the others will be watching at home," says Chico, a grey-haired man who earlier in the day picked me up hitch-hiking down to Potes.

"And where's the priest?"

"I haven't got a clue. He never usually misses a minute. Perhaps he's with Ronaldo. El Gordo's not on the pitch."

At the mention of the priest the barman, a jovial, fat, grey-haired man, says, "Did you know that the latest research has found that Jesus Christ was Spanish?"

"What do you mean?"

"He was still unemployed and living with his mum and dad at the age of 33."

On the half hour, Zidane scores a volley from several yards out. I'd like to say the place erupted, but these village folk seem to be reticent with their emotions. There's quite a bit of fist-clenching. Chico lights a cigar. And they continue watching the TV, grim-faced.

As the second half kicks off, Don Manuel walks in, greets everyone. I'm delighted to see him. He's been listening to the first half on his radio in his car, he says. Room is made for him to sit down on a chair in front of the TV. He rests his head against a pillar behind. He is more vocal than his parishioners.

"That's clearly a yellow card!"

"Play with more width!"

"What a foul! They're criminals, these Germans!"

"Help him, help him, help him, good God!"

He turns to me at a certain point.

"I don't know what to call this phenomenon. Talking to the TV as if you were at the match. I always do it."

Beckham hits the side-netting with a free-kick. Then Raúl, too, hits the side netting. Bayern launch attack after attack. The minutes tick by. With a couple to go, the priest stands up, rotates 360 degrees, and sits down again. The others are quiet, grim-faced. There is a fight on the pitch – Guti gets a yellow card. Then the final whistle. Real are through. Everyone pays up and leaves. They look slightly less dour than usual. They slap the priest on the back with obvious warmth on their way out. I say my goodbyes. I've met most of these guys over the last four days. Last to go is the priest. He looks radiant. I've grown to like him enormously.

"Good luck with Ronaldo," I say. His face drops.

| RACING | 1 | REAL MADRID | 1 |
|---|---|---|---|
| OSASUNA | 1 | REAL SOCIEDAD | 1 |
| CELTA | 1 | ESPANYOL | 5 |
| VALENCIA | 3 | DEPORTIVO | 0 |
| ATHLETIC | 1 | VALLADOLID | 4 |
| ZARAGOZA | 1 | MÁLAGA | 0 |
| BARCELONA | 3 | MALLORCA | 2 |
| ALBACETE | 1 | BETIS | 0 |
| SEVILLA | 2 | VILLARREAL | 0 |
| ATLÉTICO | 1 | MURCIA | 1 |

## LA CLASIFICACIÓN

| | P | W | D | L | F | A | Pts |
|---|---|---|---|---|---|---|---|
| REAL MADRID | 27 | 18 | 6 | 3 | 55 | 30 | 60 |
| VALENCIA | 27 | 16 | 6 | 5 | 50 | 20 | 54 |
| DEPORTIVO | 27 | 15 | 5 | 7 | 43 | 23 | 50 |
| BARCELONA | 27 | 14 | 7 | 6 | 32 | 23 | 49 |
| ATHLETIC | 27 | 11 | 8 | 8 | 33 | 26 | 41 |
| ATLÉTICO | 27 | 11 | 8 | 8 | 33 | 32 | 41 |
| OSASUNA | 27 | 9 | 12 | 6 | 27 | 23 | 39 |
| SEVILLA | 27 | 10 | 8 | 9 | 38 | 28 | 38 |
| BETIS | 27 | 9 | 10 | 8 | 34 | 29 | 37 |
| VILLARREAL | 27 | 10 | 6 | 11 | 36 | 37 | 36 |
| MÁLAGA | 27 | 11 | 2 | 14 | 36 | 41 | 35 |
| RACING | 27 | 9 | 7 | 11 | 34 | 40 | 33 |
| VALLADOLID | 27 | 8 | 8 | 11 | 33 | 39 | 32 |
| REAL SOCIEDAD | 27 | 8 | 8 | 11 | 31 | 38 | 32 |
| ZARAGOZA | 27 | 9 | 5 | 13 | 30 | 37 | 32 |
| ALBACETE | 27 | 9 | 5 | 13 | 26 | 34 | 32 |
| MALLORCA | 27 | 8 | 5 | 14 | 31 | 47 | 29 |
| CELTA | 27 | 6 | 9 | 12 | 37 | 52 | 27 |
| ESPANYOL | 27 | 8 | 2 | 17 | 31 | 49 | 26 |
| MURCIA | 27 | 1 | 11 | 14 | 23 | 43 | 17 |

# SEVENTEEN
# BILBAO

GOLFO DE VIZCAYA

**Athletic
de Bilbao**

OCÉANO ATLÁNTICO

**Real Madrid**

MAR MEDITERRÁNEO

# SEVENTEEN
# BILBAO

## THURSDAY MARCH 11TH

We get an early-morning bus from Potes to Santander and a quick connection to Bilbao, where Real are to play their next away match against Athletic. The terrible news starts filtering through on the radio as we approach the Basque city. There's been a bomb in Madrid. 20 dead, then 30, then 40. Basque terrorist group ETA is earmarked for responsibility. When the bus arrives in Bilbao, we rush to a bar, where we watch the shocking scenes on the TV. A train just outside Atocha station has had part of its roof blown off. We learn that it is one of three trains that have been attacked simultaneously. At least ten bombs. The pictures are horrific. Bits of bodies, pools of blood, bulked-out body bags. Scenes from hell. I imagine her mouth open in surprise, melted to her seat. For some reason I imagine her rush hour relief in finding a seat the seat when she got on the train. The death toll keeps rising. 140, 150. 180. Over a thousand injured. The bars are full; everyone is looking up at the screen. Nobody is talking much. You can tell what is going through their minds. First the horror, then the doubt. Could it be possible that fellow-Basques were responsible for such an atrocity?

We are on our way for a weekend in the UK, before returning to Bilbao for the match against Real Madrid. On the way to the airport bus we walk past a school. Two hundred or so children are standing in the middle of the playground, silently paying tribute to the dead. We stop and watch, paying our own respects, stunned, sad, exasperated, scared. Security is tight at the airport. There is a general election in three days. We are due back in the country on polling day. The right-wing PP (Partido Popular) have been enjoying a significant lead in the opinion polls. Everything has been pointing to a third consecutive term of office. They are strong on their anti-ETA rhetoric. If it was the Basque terrorist group who planted the bombs, they will gain significant political capital from the fact. But what if it wasn't? If the atrocity was Al Qaeda-related, then the PP, who dragged Spain into an unpopular war in Iraq (over 90 per cent of the Spanish were against the war) could be deemed indirectly responsible for the blasts. On the TV in the airport bar, PP deputy prime minister Mariano Rajoy insists that the atrocity was carried out by ETA. But it doesn't add up. They usually target judges and policemen, and not civilians. They normally give warnings. Why would they suddenly change their modus operandi so much? This looks like a much better-organised group. Aznar is standing down; Rajoy is the new PP candidate for prime minister. What is he doing making the speech anyway? Shouldn't it be Aznar? Is he trying to look statesmanlike in order to gain more political credibility before the election? We board the aeroplane five hours after the blast, looking carefully at fellow passengers and their bags. It is a strange time to be leaving the country.

### SUNDAY MARCH 14TH

I miss Real Madrid's home league match with Zaragoza two days later, a dress-rehearsal for the forthcoming Cup Final and a game nobody wanted to play. I don't even know the result until I pick up the next day's *Marca* on arrival back in Bilbao on the Sunday, the day of the general election. There is a design of a black mourning ribbon (the shape of the AIDS awareness ribbon) superimposed on the newspaper's logo. The sign is everywhere you look. We left a country in shock, we return to a country in mourning. A country wondering where to direct its anger. And, bizarrely, a country going to the polls.

In such circumstances football seems trivial, but the football fixtures have gone ahead. Real Madrid, playing a weak team to save players for the forthcoming Copa del Rey final (Figo, Helguera and Guti on the bench, Ronaldo out injured) were lucky, it seems, to get away with a 1–1 draw. There was a poignant minute of silence, candles on the seats of Real Madrid season ticket holders killed in the blasts. Real played poorly; it's hardly surprising. *Marca* forget the political situation in order to talk about Real's footballing 'crisis' (two consecutive draws): Beckham comes in for the most criticism. He makes the front page (with the headline 'it wasn't the right day') and is awarded one point, with the sort of comment that usually follows a '0': 'he's still lost'. Julián Ruiz 'The Lawnmower Man' writes 'I don't want to add impetus to Beckham's mounting crisis, but something's clearly going on. The rumours that he and his family haven't managed to get to grips with Madrid have been confirmed. This is the crucial point. If he doesn't overcome this crisis, the slippery slope is alarmingly steep.' Ruiz is referring to the fact that Beckham hasn't yet bought a house, and has cancelled his son Brooklyn's future enrolment in the local school. That his family are still living in England, only coming to Spain at the weekend (when he is working). *Marca's* 'Question of the Match' is 'what has happened to make Beckham lose form so much in the last few games?'. A possible answer is discussed in an article a couple of pages further on, leaked by the *News of the World*, in which Beckham states 'I have signed a four-year contract with Real Madrid, and I want to stay here . . . all the speculation surrounding my return to England is rubbish.' He categorically denies a meeting with Roman Abramovich. An 'I don't want to go to Chelsea,' in effect, but the sort of denial that inevitably adds flames to the fuel of rumour. He is playing like a man who is suffering from homesickness.

Beckham's perceived problems seem so trivial at a time like this. The country is going to the polls after the worst day of bloodshed since the Civil War. It has now been ascertained that it was a group 'linked with Al Qaeda' which planted and detonated the bombs. There have been angry demonstrations in front of the ruling PP party headquarters. Millions of marchers all over Spain have been blaming the government. Not only are they deemed to be responsible for incurring the wrath of the Al Qaeda terrorists against a country which overwhelmingly did not want to join the Iraq war, they have clearly been trying to pull the wool over the public's eyes by insisting against all evidence that Basques, not Muslim fundamentalists, were responsible for the atrocity.

We arrive at our host José Mari's flat in Urnieta, in the Gipuzkoa region of the Basque Country, late in the evening. The election results are coming through on the TV. Enough seats have been counted for the result to be in no doubt. The PP's absolute majority has been overturned. The Socialist Party is going to win the election, after eight years in the wilderness. Zapatero is to replace Aznar as President of the government. It is stunning news. A genuine surprise. José Mari is delighted.

"They lied to us. It looked like they were going to get away with the *Prestige* oil-spill disaster and with following Bush into the Iraq war, when the whole country was against it," he enthuses. "But they didn't get away with lying to us. The Spanish are many things, but they are not stupid." Zapatero gives a grateful and graceful victory speech. Just before turning in, I ask José Mari which football team the new prime minister supports.

"Barcelona," he says. Then, with a wry smile, "Real Madrid are no longer the team of the establishment."


**WEDNESDAY MARCH 17TH**

We've been staying for a few days in an 'Agroturismo' a farm-house in the mountains near Urnieta, where we walk up a different green mountain peak every day, over gurgling rivers, through forests of upright tuning-fork-like trees, past cows with alarmingly sharp horns. It is peaceful, restful and a million miles from the terrible goings on in Atocha, the new political winds and the urban hurly-burly of the football season. Brenda has just been offered a good job in Dublin and she is seeing as much of Spain as she can before she goes back home, using my timetable as a framework. We are spending some quality time together, in a quality environment, before our estrangement. For one reason or another football has been taken off the conversation menu. I break the news of Wednesday's game on Tuesday.

"It's, er, the Cup Final tomorrow."

"The Cup Final? Which Cup Final?"

"The Spanish Cup Final. La Copa del Rey. Real Madrid against Real Zaragoza. I'm afraid I have to go to the bar to watch it. It's work. Beckham's playing. Do you want to come?"

She doesn't. I have to walk seven kilometres down a winding country lane to the nearby village of Urnieta to get to a bar that I've been told has it on. José Mari is going to join me later. When I get there, one minute before kick-off, the bar is pretty full. But the screen is showing the news in Euskera, the incomprehensible Basque language. At two minutes past nine, the barmaid flicks channels. The players are standing round the centre circle, heads bowed for the minute of silence. The bar falls silent, too. You are never too far from the memory of those terrible scenes. When it finishes, the crowd in the stadium start singing. The atmosphere sounds terrific. In the bar it's the opposite. The 25-or-so drinkers, mostly young men, don't look up from their conversations at the screen. Are they not interested? At least there's an old guy, with the requisite old guy tache-and-cigar combination, sitting at the bar, as rapt by the game as I am.

The match, ironically enough, is in Barcelona, in the Olympic Stadium in Montjuic where I watched Real Madrid thrash Espanyol just three weeks ago, before their and Beckham's 'crisis' started. And, to rub in the fact that I'm in a bar in the Basque country and not the stadium back home, it turns out to be one of the best matches I've seen all season. Real spend much of the opening stages of the game in Real Zaragoza's half, keeping possession of the ball, but not threatening to do much with it that might endanger the Zaragoza goal. Then, on 25 minutes, they get a free-kick about 30 yards out. Beckham and Roberto Carlos line up to take it, Beckham kicks it. The ball loops in the air, over the wall, past the energetic dive of the keeper, hits the inside of the post . . . and ripples the inside of the side netting. Goal! Or to translate the commentator, 'Goal, goal, goal, goal, goal! Goal from David Beckham! Goal from David Beckham in the Olympic Stadium.'

The crowd in the bar don't share the commentator's enthusiasm. Nobody looks up from their conversation. The old man at the bar shows no emotion either way to hint at who he's supporting. I'm not sure whether to be happy or sad. I'm supporting the underdog, but I'm also up for my man. Beckham is clearly delighted. It's nice to see a grin on his face. He reels away and runs to the bench, arms outstretched. Is this the end of his 'crisis'? He kisses his wedding ring, even though Victoria Beckham is the only Real Madrid wife not at the match. A superb goal, and a great platform for Real Madrid to build on.

Minutes later Real get another free-kick outside the box. Beckham brushes Roberto Carlos aside. Another arcing shot, this time to the near post. Which it hits but this time on the outside. Goal kick. The Englishman allows himself a wry grin. He's found his range at last.

The match swings one way then another. Just five minutes after Beckham's goal, Zaragoza are level. Savio makes his way to the bye-line, loops the ball over Casillas, and Dani, Zaragoza's recent signing from Barcelona, controls the ball on his knee and thumps it into the goal. The boys in the bar give away the fact they have been paying attention, they've just been pretending not to. Their arms are in the air, celebrating a goal against the old enemy from the capital of Spain. Real Madrid have been pegged back! Then, a minute before half-time, the Asturian striker Villa, about to take a shot on the edge of the six-yard box, is up-ended by Guti. He picks himself up to kick the resulting penalty past Casillas, following it with a fine celebration, mimicking the Asturian way of pouring cider, from a bottle over the head into a glass at the hip. Zaragoza 2 Real 1. One of the lads jumps onto a bar stool, raising his arm in the air, aping the goal celebration. The old fellow has still not flinched. He merely takes another puff on his cigar.

Within a minute of the second half kick-off, Real are back on level terms, with a free-kick by . . . Roberto Carlos, who has brushed Beckham away. 2–2. The lads have largely left the bar, to watch the match back home. "May the worst team win," one guy says to me on the way out (meaning, of course, Zaragoza). José Mari, who has been teaching up till now, joins me. I ask him who he's up for.

"I'm Basque."

"But who are you up for?"

"Zaragoza, of course. Anyone but Real Madrid."

The old fellow is still watching. I've still not worked out who he supports. He shows no emotion when Cani gets booked twice within five minutes to leave Zaragoza with 10 men, which should put Real into the driving seat. But doesn't. 'Los galácticos' are clearly exhausted. Beckham is particularly tired in the second half; the commentator is rarely bothered with the awkward pronunciation of his name. It's Zaragoza making all the chances, and Real are pleased to hear the whistle on 93 minutes, pleased to get a couple of minutes' rest before extra time.

The number on the field soon evens up when Guti, who has been one of Real's better players, gets sent off for a second bookable offence. Real must be trying to dig deep to get the winner, but they can't find the gear. Zaragoza, with Movilla the composer in midfield, start looking more likely winners. Five minutes into the second period of extra time, substitute Galletti takes a pass on the edge of the box and kicks it across Casillas and into the goal. 3–2! His shirt comes off and he disappears under a pile of Zaragoza players. Queiroz brought Portillo on for Solari before the end of normal time but, despite his players' tiredness, he makes no further substitutions. Just before the final whistle, Figo gets a kick in the chest and Real a free-kick.

"That should have been a yellow card," mutters the old guy, finally showing his colours. The resulting dead ball comes to nothing. The final whistle is the signal for exuberant celebrations from the Zaragoza players and fans. Before Zaragoza captain Luis Carlos Cuartero is handed the cup, the old fellow leaves. The camera pans in on King Juan Carlos handing over the large silver trophy, then in on the Real Madrid players standing on the pitch, watching, dejected, divided, a team of individuals each standing alone with his thoughts: a neat counterpoint to the minute of silence at the beginning of the match. Beckham looks like the loneliest and most lugubrious man in Spain. I feel sorry for him, but not for long. What a game! José Mari offers me a lift back to the farmhouse. But first we drink a celebratory glass of pacharán. Zaragoza goalscorer David Villa is interviewed on the screen above our heads. "I don't know if this means anything, but I'm dedicating this victory to the people who were killed in the Madrid blasts," he says. His joy is tinged with sorrow. The awful images come back. That woman melted into her seat. The body bags. The sickly sweet pacharán is hard to swallow. I feel guilty for having been taken so far away from the gravity of the tragedy by the excitement of a football match. Then I think 'but what a match!'.

On the way back José Mari tells me something interesting. "You know," he says, "the way that old guy wasn't letting on that he was a Real Madrid fan was very typical of the way that people are in the Basque country about politics, because of the extreme opposition of views. Nobody talks about politics unless they are sure the person they are talking to is of the same political opinion. That's just the way it is. But after March 11th, the atmosphere seemed to change. I noticed it in my lessons. People suddenly wanted to hear other people's opinions about politics. The events were so shocking and sudden that it opened everybody up. I hope that that will be a lasting thing."

"Do you think it will be?"

"We'll see."

## FRIDAY MARCH 19TH

Bilbao is enjoying something of a renaissance. It's traditionally been viewed as a dour, industrial and unappealing city, but the Bilbaínos are working hard to change this image and they're doing well. The city is built in the valley created by the Ría de Bilbao estuary, and the con- urbation snakes along the banks of the river, fattening out in the centre like a snake that's eaten a sheep, overlooked by the looming presence of the ever-present green valleyside. It's in this central area that the town hall is concentrating the new structures that have changed the city's look so drastically in the past decade: a couple of fancy bridges, a flash conference and exhibition centre, and the Guggenheim Museum, quite simply the most stunning piece of modern architecture I have ever seen.

This is my second visit to the museum, but it still packs a major impact. It's like a pile of massive popcorn containers, wrapped in silver foil. It's like a fleet of shiny silver ships' hulls on a turbulent sea, in dispute over which way to sail. It's like . . . extremely difficult to describe. Look at the pictures. Go yourself, if you haven't been. It's something you'll never forget. The Guggenheim is often accused of being more interesting outside than in, and I'm not that impressed with the temporary exhibition on offer (the impudent jigsaw figures of Jean Dubuffet). But there's some great pop-art stuff in the permanent exhibition, including an optical-illusion steel house by Roy Lichtenstein, three giant, bright-red, head-and-armless statues of Venus by Jim Dine, and Andy Warhol's 150 Marilyns, scores of images of the last great blonde icon . . . before now.

"He'd definitely have done Beckham," I say to Brenda.

"Only if he died," she replies.

Afterwards Brenda, who is wearing an Athletic de Bilbao scarf that José Mari has given to us, waits on the far bank of the river to take a picture of the Guggenheim with somebody typically Basque walking in front of it. We are hoping to sell a feature on the game to a football magazine. We wait and wait, but nobody comes along so I arrange for an old guy in sunglasses sitting on a park bench to put on the Athletic de Bilbao scarf and walk in front of her. She snaps him. Then he starts talking. And can he talk.

He tells us how he is Basque and proud of being Basque and that he wants the Basque Country to be separate from Spain. He tells us that he wants this to be achieved by peaceful means. He says that when he was eight years old in 1937 he went to sleep as normal in the same flat as his parents and four brothers and sisters, and when he woke up he only had a brother and a sister left – the others had been killed by a Fascist bomb. That his surviving sister had lost her legs in the attack. He tells us that he abhors violence, that he was disgusted to be living in a country which took part in the war on Iraq, a war which he sees as being waged in order for the United States of America to be able to obtain oil at a good price. He thinks the Madrid bombing was a direct consequence of the war, and he is delighted about the downfall of the PP.

He also tells us that he is a big supporter of Athletic de Bilbao, and that he is very proud of the club's policy of only playing Basque players. Tomorrow's game is the highlight of the season and little would give him as much pleasure as Athletic beating El Real. The Real team represent two things he hates: Madrid's centralism and capitalist globalisation. He's interesting, but he likes an audience, and we're there nearly half an hour, despite many attempts at farewell.

"Great, thanks for your time . . ."

"Great. Couldn't agree more. It's been great to meet you . . ."

"Look, we really have to . . ."

Then I decide to cut my losses, and find out the Basque left's view of David Beckham.

"I admire him for his spirit and his play. He is a fighter and he is a very good passer of the ball. But what has he got to do with Madrid? In a way, everything, because Madrid was the centre of an empire and an empire needs mercenaries. But in a way, nothing. Why should Madrid be allowed to use its unfairly gained riches to buy the best players in the world to try to assert its dominance over the rest of the peninsula? If Real Madrid win the league it means that they have bought the best team. If Athletic win, it means that, that season, the Basques are the best players. It means something real, it means something genuine."

I ask him when Athletic last won the league, though I already know the answer.

"1984. But we have never been out of the Primera. Only Real Madrid and Barcelona can say that as well. Of that we are very proud. Even though I'll tell you one thing: I would rather support an all-Basque Athletic in the Segunda than an Athletic with non-Basques in it in the Primera."

I don't mention this, but Athletic's Basque policy isn't entirely strict. They allow players in the team who have been born and brought up in Navarra, a neighbouring region with just as many Spanish as Basque influences, and there are two players who were born and brought up in La Rioja, which is about as Spanish as you can get. The rules have been stretched for them because of their patronyms: Aranzubia and Ezquerro both have Basque roots.


**SATURDAY MARCH 21ST**

We get a swish new tram to the ugly corrugated-iron tub of a stadium just outside the town centre. It's three hours before kick-off but the

flag-and-scarf stalls are already set up, the silver-foil-wrapped sandwiches are piled high (like an edible Guggenheim) and men and women
in red-and-white shirts and the occasional large beret are already walking
through the barrio, singing. The stadium is called 'San Mamés' (after
the fancy hospice building next door) but nicknamed 'La Catedral' and
duly revered as one of the holy sites of Spanish football. Athletic have
been playing here since 1913; no Spanish club has played longer in
one ground. The San Mamés has a capacity of 40,000. Today it is
unlikely to sell out: the management have made the match a 'día del
club' (club day) meaning that season-ticket holders have to pay to watch
the match. This, and the fact that many people have left the city for
the extended bank holiday (yesterday was San José day) means only
30,000 are expected to show up to see Athletic (pronounced 'Atletic,
with an almost silent 'c') play Los Galácticos.

There's a line of bars just opposite the side of the stadium where they
sell the tickets and I've arranged to meet Iván in one of them. He's the
father of Cesar, the bar owner, and is club member number 15, which
means only 14 people have been going to see Athletic longer than him.
Like many Basques he has piercing blue eyes. They are lit with fond
memories of the first great Athletic side, which won the second and
third league championships in Spain, in 1930 and 1931.

"Blasco, Careaga, Castellanos, Irquizu, Roberto, Muguerza, Garizurieta,
Bata, Chirri, Iraragorri, Gorostiza." He reels off the names with the ease
with which certain baby-boomers can tell you the line-up of the Leeds
side of the early '70s.

"I'll tell you a story that no-one knows." He's enormously enthusiastic.
"When we were kids, eight or ten years old, we used to sit on the wooden
planks they put behind the goals. We didn't have watches, of course:
not many adults did, let alone kids. But there was the clock of the
Misericordia." He takes me out of the bar and shows me a clock on an
ornate belltower of the large hospice next to the stadium.

"We used to look at the clock and when it was three o'clock we would
shout at the referee 'start the game, whistle-blower, it's time to start
the game!' And when it was twenty to five we'd shout 'finish the game,
whistle-blower, it's time to finish!' Put that in your book. That's something nobody knows."

He has little to say about the current Athletic team, or even the team
that won the league twice in the '80s. What he wants to talk about is
the great side of the early '30s.

"The manager was an Englishman called Mr Pentland. He made them
run up the hill where they now have the funicular railway, to make
them fit. He used to make them shoot at the goal in practice. If they

missed the goal, they had to shoot five more times. That meant that when the Bilbao players shot, they never missed the goal. Iraragorri was the best. When Irraragori shaped up to shoot, the goalposts shook in fear." He is entranced with the memory of it all and wants to tell it to me, for me to write it down, to tell the world for him. "One day the goalkeeper Blasco was injured before the game against Barcelona, and his substitute Ispizua was not so good. So the defence said to the goalkeeper, 'don't worry, we will not let them past; they will not even shoot at the goal. We will die before we let them past. They were 11 lions that day, I remember it. They only let Barcelona shoot once, and they scored. But Athletic scored 12 goals at the other end. Twelve! It is still a record in Spanish football." He says the word 'leones' (lions) with the roar of the beast in question: Athletic are nicknamed 'the Lions' for their passionate style of play. I wonder how he sees today's match going. It takes him a while to get back to the present.

"We will win. We will be 11 lions again. We will beat Madrid."

The streets around the ground are full of fans, with a large proportion of them wearing the team shirt and others sporting other accoutrements. Two guys are dressed in lion suits, a number wear outlandishly large berets, there are three guys with identical t-shirts with the legend 'Beckham me la suda' ('suck it, Beckham'). We hear an uproar: the Real Madrid coach is coming in. We rush round, and there's a crowd of red-and-white shirts hurling abuse at the Real players as they run into the stadium. One guy, an enormous skinhead, is holding up a banner, unfavourably comparing the footballer with Bobby Charlton and Bobby Moore.

"He's just there to sell shirts," says the skinhead, whose name is Iñigo, and whose cut-off denim jacket is full of badges bearing the name of English punk bands of the '80s: UK Subs, Cockney Rejects, Peter and the Test Tube Babies. "Real Madrid are not a proper football team, they are the team of the government. They represent Spanish oppression of the Basque country." He shows me his tattoos: one of Obelix, his head shaved, wearing red-and-white striped leggings. One of a lion dressed in Athletic kit. One of a guy lifting a huge stone in front of the Basque flag, with the legend 'Basque country' written above. He shows me his dog, Lona.

"How will you get the dog into the stadium?"

"We're not going in. I can't afford a ticket to see Athletic any more. I'm off to the old town now to watch the game on the TV. I only came here to show Beckham my banner." The prices are, in fact, scandalous. We've paid 90 euros each to get in. José Mari got us the tickets and has now joined us.

The stadium is only three-quarters full when the club anthem comes over the tannoy in Euskera.

*Athletic, Athletic, eup!*
*Athletic gorri ta zuria . . .*

The teams come out together, in two neat lines, as if it were a cup final, and stand around the centre circle for a well-kept minute of silence for the Madrid massacre. Two children, dressed in Athletic kit, let a pair of white doves out of a box, and everyone cheers. Normally such a cheer is just a release of energy as the match starts. I'm sure I can hear more in this one. People have been deeply affected by the bomb, and it is never far from their thoughts. One of the doves takes a while to find its way out of the stadium.

The first half is a bore. Football seems trivial after all that's happened. Real Madrid look tired and lacklustre, but Athletic don't seem to be able to capitalise on it. Beckham's 'crisis' is continuing, despite a change of hairstyle: the ponytail is gone, his hair is loose. So is his play. He loses the ball several times; his long balls don't seem to find their man. There is little action of any note until five minutes before half time, when Helguera gives the ball away to Athletic's graceful play-maker, Yeste, who is sporting a toned-down version of the Mohican haircut he's had since Christmas. The haircut has so far seen him score five goals. He makes it six with a careful shot past Casillas. Gol! The crowd is up on its feet in an unexpected explosion of celebration. Suddenly there is some atmosphere in the ground. I take the opportunity to go to the toilet.

When you're in the toilet of a football ground you know from the noise the crowd is making what sort of thing is happening on the pitch. I've just started pissing when I hear from a roar of expectation that Athletic have started another attack. There's another roar; this time of indignation. Too soft for a penalty. Then the crowd start a slow rhythmic clap. A free-kick! I rush out the door into the open air and see . . . the ball go into the net! A header from the free-kick! 2–0! There's definitely an atmosphere about the place now; the crowd can't believe it. Neither can the Real players, who slowly take the ball back to the half-way line, looking at one another in recrimination.

"Athletic, Athletic, Athletic," chant the crowd, drowning out the sound of the half-time whistle. We have a football game.

At half time there's a brilliant video on the big screen, made by the club to try to recruit season-ticket holders. There is a game going on in the San Mamés in which all the players and the referee are naked. The commentator is commentating as normal. Then a fan runs onto the pitch, fully clothed, in an Athletic shirt. The players stop playing. "A streaker on the pitch! It's disgraceful!" shouts the commentator as a couple of naked policemen lead him off to the accompaniment of boos from the crowd.

I'm tempted to make some 'Emperor's new clothes' link Beckham. The fact is he's playing as poorly as I've seen him play in a long time. He's so far back in defence he's almost playing in the centre-half role from the days the old fellow was talking about earlier in the bar. Guti is the dominant partner in the midfield pairing; at one point, ten minutes into the second half, he runs to where Beckham is in possession and takes the ball off him, as if he doesn't trust him with it.

By this time, Real have pulled one back, a goal from Raúl in the first attack of the half. Athletic, though, have stepped up their game – Beckham has to foul Yeste to stop an attack and is forced on one occasion to boot the ball out of touch like a Sunday League centre-back. I see '23' being held up on the electronic scoreboard but it's for Athletic's midfielder, Tiko, who is replaced by Orbaiz. Athletic press for the third, and clinching goal . . . then Real break, Roberto Carlos crosses for Raúl, who shoots the ball past the onrushing keeper. 2–2! They scarcely deserve it.

The fans are getting louder and louder – there are no Real Madrid fans in sight: the whole of the crowd is yelling for the home team. Valverde, Athletic's manager, brings on their skilful attacker, Ezquerro, who is booked within five seconds, surely some kind of a record. But it doesn't put him off being the focal point of Athletic's increasingly frenzied attacks. On 75 minutes there's a foul wide outside the Real box. Ezquerro curls in a far post cross. Casillas dithers, Del Horno, the Athletic left back, heads the ball into the net. Everyone's on their feet. 3–2!

"Beste Bat, beste bat," chant the crowd in Basque. I ask José Mari what this means.

"'Another one'," he says. "They want another one."

It isn't long in coming. Del Horno receives the ball, runs into the area, checks to send Helguera flying in front of him and, without breaking stride, rolls the ball past Casillas, who flinches as if expecting a cannon-ball shot. 4–2! A drubbing!

But not enough for the crowd, which started the match subdued, but is now in great form.

"Beste bat, beste bat, beste bat."

They so nearly get two more, but Casillas is brilliant on a couple of one-on-one occasions.

Beckham has disappeared for quite some time, but suddenly appears on the right wing, collects the ball and puts in a fantastic curling low cross for Guti, which the Madrileño fails to put into the net. It's a reminder of what Beckham can do so well and within a couple of minutes he's down there again, chasing a ball down the line, finally brought down by Del Horno. He gets up, angry, there's a bit of pushing and shoving, then by the dugout the electronic board shows his famous number. On his way to the bench, to be replaced by Cambiasso, he kicks a plastic bottle in anger.

"Beste bat, beste bat," shout the crowd, as Casillas saves another one on one. I find myself joining in, my first meaningful words in Euskera.

"Beste bat, beste bat."

Then the crowd change language.

"Qué bote San Mamés!" they shout (San Mamés must jump). Soon everyone is jumping up and down. When the final whistle goes, three quarters of the crowd raise their scarves, Kop-like, above their heads. It's a sight to remember.

We haven't got a moment to lose, though. We rush through the corridors of the stadium, myself, Brenda and José Mari, and a flash of my press card gets all three of us into the mixed zone. Within a couple of minutes Queiroz is delivering a lugubrious press conference. Anthony Kasternakis of the *News of the World* approaches me.

"You speak Spanish. Can you ask him about Beckham's reaction to being taken off?"

I point to José Mari.

"He'll do it." Before the poor guy knows it, he's been handed the microphone and he's asking a question which is being broadcast on national, and international, TV.

"Excuse me," he says, giving away the fact he's not a journalist by being too polite. "I would like to ask what your response is to Beckham's angry reaction to being substituted. Thank you very much."

Queiroz gives a deadpan reply about frustration being a normal reaction after a bad defeat.

I see Quique Guasch, TVE1's perma-tan interviewer, who always goes up to players after the game, pretending to be their friend, asking them questions in a manner that sometimes disarms them into being more truthful than they might otherwise be. I decide to see how his own tactics work on him, biding my time, approaching him and slapping him on the back.

"Quique! What did you think of Beckham's performance?"

He doesn't flinch. "Appalling! He looked tired. But it's not just that. He's playing out of position." He's serious, miles away from his on-screen persona, but friendly enough.

"Too far back?"

"Far too far back. He's an attacking player. And he's being played in an ultra-defensive role. Of course he's not doing well! Of course he's tired! He wasn't bought to replace Makelele, he was bought to attack down the wing!"

"But Florentino Pérez, on Beckham replacing Makelele, said he's got rid of a carthorse and bought a racehorse."

"If you buy a racehorse, you don't use it to plough fields."

There's a sudden hubbub, and Beckham comes out to face the press, the only Real Madrid player to do so. His hair is still down. He's wearing a suit and fat-knotted tie, pointy shoes. A Louis Vuitton bag is tucked under his arm. He looks pissed off, humbled, upset. Eric, from the *Sun*, leads the questioning. As usual, he replies with short, honest but highly-sanitised answers. Yes, he's disappointed with the result. No, Real didn't play well. Yes, his own form is suffering. He turns to go. This time I'm determined to ask a question.

"David, David . . ." I shout.

He turns to me. This is my big moment. I have David Beckham's attention. There are still microphones being jabbed in his direction. My girlfriend is pointing the camera at us.

I want to be positive. An image of him running down the wing and delivering a superb cross to Guti comes to mind.

"Do you ever miss playing on the right wing?" I blurt.

He looks disgusted with my question.

"Not at all," he says.

"Not at all?"

"Not at all." He turns away, and walks off towards the coach.

My heart is beating fast. I realise that you have to be far more subtle with your questioning in the cut and thrust of the mixed zone, if you want to keep the conversation going. If I wanted to be a tabloid journalist I'd have a hell of a lot to learn from the likes of Eric and Anthony. But then I realise that I've just had a conversation with David Beckham, however short, and a smile spreads across my face.

## RESULTS JORNADA 28

| REAL MADRID | 1 | ZARAGOZA | 1 |
|---|---|---|---|
| REAL SOCIEDAD | 2 | ATLÉTICO | 1 |
| BETIS | 1 | OSASUNA | 1 |
| ESPANYOL | 0 | RACING | 1 |
| VALLADOLID | 2 | SEVILLA | 0 |
| MALLORCA | 4 | DEPORTIVO | 2 |
| VILLARREAL | 2 | ALBACETE | 1 |
| MÁLAGA | 2 | ATHLETIC | 1 |
| MURCIA | 0 | BARCELONA | 2 |
| CELTA | 0 | VALENCIA | 2 |

## RESULTS JORNADA 29

| ATHLETIC | 4 | REAL MADRID | 2 |
|---|---|---|---|
| DEPORTIVO | 1 | MURCIA | 0 |
| ATLÉTICO | 2 | BETIS | 1 |
| ALBACETE | 2 | VALLADOLID | 0 |
| SEVILLA | 0 | MÁLAGA | 1 |
| ZARAGOZA | 1 | ESPANYOL | 1 |
| RACING | 4 | CELTA | 4 |
| OSASUNA | 2 | VILLARREAL | 1 |
| VALENCIA | 5 | MALLORCA | 1 |
| BARCELONA | 1 | REAL SOCIEDAD | 0 |

## LA CLASIFICACIÓN

|  | P | W | D | L | F | A | Pts |
|---|---|---|---|---|---|---|---|
| REAL MADRID | 29 | 18 | 7 | 4 | 58 | 35 | 61 |
| VALENCIA | 29 | 18 | 6 | 5 | 57 | 21 | 60 |
| BARCELONA | 29 | 16 | 7 | 6 | 48 | 32 | 55 |
| DEPORTIVO | 29 | 16 | 5 | 8 | 46 | 27 | 53 |
| ATHLETIC | 29 | 12 | 8 | 9 | 39 | 37 | 44 |
| ATLÉTICO | 29 | 12 | 8 | 9 | 36 | 35 | 44 |
| OSASUNA | 29 | 10 | 13 | 6 | 30 | 25 | 43 |
| MÁLAGA | 29 | 13 | 2 | 14 | 39 | 42 | 41 |
| VILLARREAL | 29 | 11 | 6 | 12 | 39 | 40 | 39 |
| SEVILLA | 29 | 10 | 8 | 11 | 38 | 31 | 38 |
| BETIS | 29 | 9 | 11 | 9 | 36 | 32 | 38 |
| RACING | 29 | 10 | 8 | 11 | 39 | 44 | 37 |
| VALLADOLID | 29 | 9 | 8 | 12 | 35 | 41 | 35 |
| REAL SOCIEDAD | 29 | 9 | 8 | 12 | 33 | 40 | 35 |
| ALBACETE | 29 | 10 | 5 | 14 | 29 | 36 | 35 |
| ZARAGOZA | 29 | 9 | 7 | 13 | 32 | 39 | 34 |
| MALLORCA | 29 | 9 | 5 | 15 | 36 | 54 | 32 |
| CELTA | 29 | 6 | 10 | 13 | 41 | 58 | 28 |
| ESPANYOL | 29 | 8 | 3 | 18 | 32 | 51 | 27 |
| MURCIA | 29 | 2 | 11 | 16 | 23 | 46 | 17 |

# EIGHTEEN
# ALBACETE

GOLFO DE VIZCAYA

**Real Madrid**
○

Albacete ○

MAR MEDITERRÁNEO

# EIGHTEEN
# ALBACETE

**THURSDAY APRIL 1ST**

I step out of Albacete's functionally designed train station and look around me. It's my first sight of the city with one of the worst of reputations in Spain. There are tower blocks to my left and right. The sky is a looming grey. A refrain is going round in my head with the annoying insistence usually reserved for singles by – say – the Spice Girls. It's a little rhyme the Spanish say about the town. 'Albacete, caga y vete; Albacete, caga y vete; Albacete . . .' It means 'Albacete, have a shit there and leave.' The *Rough Guide* I had until it was stolen in Barcelona made similarly dismissive comments, something along the lines of 'Albacete has plenty of accommodation, but there is absolutely no reason to use it.' The town is famous only for its production of knives. As I walk past the football club's merchandise shop (a square box, locked up for lunchtime) it starts raining. I have come to this inland town of 150,000 inhabitants in the south-east of the country, determined to prove its critics wrong, and have a damn good time. But if first impressions are anything to go by . . .

The city's football team, Albacete Balompié, are due to play Real Madrid in a couple of days time. I love the name of the club: 'balompié' is a Spanish translation of 'football' – only the other way round: 'ball-foot'. Albacete have surprised many people this season. They are without a single well-established star, and are coached by a man, César Ferrando, who was head-hunted from Valencia's B-team without any experience of Primera or Segunda División management. Yet, with eight games to go, they have already virtually assured themselves of safety from relegation in a season which has so far seen them concede just 38 goals, only two more than Real Madrid. And this after losing their first three games on the trot. A plucky team: a team that you have to like. A team who play attractive football in a clean all-white kit, bearing (courtesy of the local tourist board) the name of the area's local hero: 'Quixote'. We are in La Mancha, the setting for Cervantes' novel *Don Quixote*, in which the self-delusive errant knight of that name tilted at windmills with a tin-pot hat and a cardboard shield.

Albacete's forthcoming encounter with Real Madrid, however, brings to mind the older legend of David and Goliath. 'El Alba' has less than half the annual budget of any other club in the Primera. Their compact little ground, 'El Carlos Belmonte' (named after a former mayor of the city, an architect who designed and inaugurated the stadium), has a capacity of just 17,000. Their president, Ángel Contreras, owns a shop which sells lamps: during the week you can find him serving at the counter.

"Half the players in the squad are on loan from other teams," says Jesús Gualda, the president of the Albacete peña collective. I'm sitting in the office of his small insurance company, alongside his mate Parrita, and they're showing me pictures of the team's rise from regional football to their current heights. "Contreras has built up an entire squad for less money than it cost Real Madrid to buy David Beckham," he continues. "And Beckham's salary would pay El Alba's entire wage bill," he exaggerates.

They're an interesting pair, my two new friends. Jesús is the serious one, a neat man with gold-rimmed glasses who is eager with facts and information. He tells me of the club's formation in 1940, of the 1974/5 season when they went up to the Tercera (Third Division) after an incredible campaign in which they scored 111 goals. Of their previous stint of five years in the Primera in the early '90s. Parrita has more swagger about him. He is the club's 'animator' who takes a drum to the ground and directs the singing. There's something of the Frank Worthington about him. "I am great friends with Manolo el del Bombo, "he tells me. "I was the inventor of 'El Grito del Alba' (the Alba chant)."

"How does it go?" I ask.

"Alba," he chants as a reply, and claps three times.

I ask Jesús about the average attendance in the Carlos Belmonte.

"Fourteen or fifteen thousand," he replies. "It was only eight or nine thousand last season. You know, when Real Madrid paid all that money for Beckham, they were benefiting El Alba as well. There are at least 3,000 more season ticket holders than there were the last year we were in the Primera. Different sorts of people, too. More women; more young girls."

Jesús is a busy man who keeps wandering off to speak on his mobile phone, leaving me to talk to Parrita. I ask him if this, in his opinion, is the best-ever Alba team.

"No way," he says. "In 1991–92 we were one minute away from qualifying for the UEFA Cup. Do you remember when Tenerife came back from 2–0 down to beat Real Madrid 3–2 with a last-minute goal which meant that Barça, not Real, won the championship?"

I tell him that of course I do.

"Well, that goal also lifted Tenerife above us in the table, and robbed us of our finest hour." He tells me that 70% of Alba fans also support Real Madrid. "That wasn't a popular goal round these parts," he adds.

Parrita tells me that there was recently an international match played here: Spain against Northern Ireland.

"There were only 200 Northern Ireland fans, but they made more noise than us," he says.

Jesús comes back from another phone call. "They drank all the beer there was in town," he adds. "By the way, I've just been speaking to the local TV station. I said that you were here, and they're coming round to do an interview with you. I hope you don't mind."

I do. I hate television interviews. I get nervous, freeze, feel like I'm back at school. They terrify me. Suddenly I'm fidgety and awkward.

"Not at all," I say. "Doesn't bother me. That's great."

Within five minutes in walk two men: a homely-looking middle-aged fellow in a brown pullover with a TV camera on his shoulder, and a young curly-haired guy in a trendy red track-suit top, holding a large blue microphone.

"Hi, I'm Cristo," says the young guy.

"First Jesús, then Cristo," I say. He doesn't crack a smile. They stand me against a wall with a poster for the forthcoming match as a backdrop. Then Cristo, pointing his blue mic at my face, asks me a series of odd questions about my book, questions designed to satisfy his curiosity as a journalist rather than that of the average viewer.

"How can you afford to do all this travelling?"

"I'm being given an advance by my editorial house. I stay in cheap hotels, travel by train, steer clear of taxis and expensive restaurants."

"Does Beckham know about the book?"

"Um, no, he doesn't."

"What do you think he would think if he did?"

"Um, well, I don't suppose he'd mind. I mean, I'm using him, if you like, to tell the reader about Spain. It's not about him, really."

My translation here suggests I was speaking Spanish more fluently than I really was. Sometimes, under pressure, it all comes out muddled up. I'm not giving a good interview, and I can see it in Cristo's face.

"Was that alright?" I ask afterwards, in the bar.

"Fine," he says, again without smiling.

"I'm in town three hours and I'm already being interviewed on the local TV station," I say.

"That's the Beckham effect," he replies.

The Beckham effect was apparent last weekend in the Bernabéu. Madrid faced Sevilla, the team that thrashed them off the park in Andalucía in the autumn. I watched this game in the Real Madrid bar in the centre of Barcelona. El Real more than got their own back, winning 5–1, with two goals from Ronaldo, and two assists – both brilliant passes – from Beckham. The Englishman broke his recent run of bad form, getting awarded a '3' the next day by *Marca*, with the comment 'pletórico' (literally 'abundant'). He was substituted, limping, in the 84th minute, coming off to a standing ovation from an adoring crowd. Maybe the backlash is over. Maybe now his season will finish on a high. Maybe he will follow the classic graph of a new player at a club: explosion-regression-consolidation.

There's a sci-fi film festival on in the local Filmoteca and I've been meaning to spend the evening there, but I soon realise that I am now officially a guest of Jesús. He takes me for a meal in a local restaurant and tells me of his job as president of the peñas. He has to liaise between the fans and the players; between the fans and the management; between the fans and the police. It's an important role, with no equivalent in the UK. He does it for the love of the club: he isn't paid a peseta. He has contacts with all the other peña owners round the country. At one point he hands me the phone, and there is a familiar voice on the other end. It is Arximelo, the guy with the bar in Vigo.

"Hombre," says Arximelo. "How are you?"

We eat a plate full of fried squid, and a plate full of fried gristle. I wouldn't recommend the latter. Jesús insists on paying. Then we go to his mate Parrita's bar 'Parri's Palace'.

By now it's midnight and the place is packed. People are sitting at tables, drinking heavily. This is immediately apparent: each table has at least one open bottle of spirits on it.

"Parrita sells bottles for 20 euros. It's much cheaper than drinking it by the shot," says Jesús. We sit at a table with three guys who are involved in running a football school. There's a thin old guy, a fat middle-aged guy and a young guy called Luis who keeps pouring me glasses of J&B. I dub them Florentino, Valdano and Quieroz, according to their roles in the school. One bottle finishes, another is bought. I am given a tracksuit from the school. I get into an argument about Real Madrid with Valdano, the fat guy, a Real supporter.

"I am an anti-Madridista," I declare.

"How can you say that? El Real is the best club in the world."

"The richest club in the world."

"So what? Does it matter whether they are rich or not? Being the richest club in the world is just part of being the best."

"But it is unfair. Being the richest club gives them a head start over the others. It's not an even playing field." (Again, I'm being generous here with my Spanish. I say something like 'the pitch is steep' which I need to spend about three minutes explaining.)

"Look, football is a business, just like every other. Real Madrid are the most successful company in the business, and hence the best football club. It's as simple as that."

"But it's sport! It's not business!"

"The two are the same thing. Sport is business, and the richest club is therefore the best."

"It should be more about how good the local players are, not who can buy the best players."

"Go and support Athletic de Bilbao, then."

"I might just go and do that."

We've been waving our hands and raising our voices. The other three at the table have been occasionally joining in. The J&B has been flowing. The whole conversation has lasted over an hour. Afterwards I realise that I've lost my head a little.

"Sorry about that," I say to Valdano later.

"What do you mean, sorry?"

"Our disagreement. No offence meant."

"Offence? What do you mean offence? What's the point of going out and drinking loads of whisky if you can't have a good old argument about football?"


## FRIDAY, APRIL 2ND

My first thoughts are hazy memories of the night before. Another bar, me insisting that I pay for at least one round, a lift home from Jesús, who hadn't been drinking on account of a course of antibiotics. I look at my watch. Quarter to one. I sit up with a start. Jesus! Quarter to one! I jump out of bed, start throwing on clothes. I have an interview at one o'clock at the training ground with Pablo Ibañez, Albacete's young central defender, one of their most influential players. I get the lift downstairs, get reception to call a taxi. Within five minutes it's arrived. Within ten I'm at the training ground. Five past one. There are sometimes advantages to being in a small town.

On the train down to Albacete I read an article about Pablo. He is the player with the most 'minutes' in the Primera this season. In Spain this is a big deal. One of the statistics regularly given out about players is how many minutes they have played in the league. When a young or formerly injured player is thrown on at the end of the game it is said that the manager is 'giving him minutes'. Pablo, I read (in *Marca*, of course) has managed 2,637 minutes this season. He has been 'titular' (in the starting XI) in all 30 matches, but was taken off injured against Betis after 27 minutes. The article says that he has only been given three yellow cards all season, a remarkable statistic for a central defender in Spain. Not surprisingly his performances have made him much coveted by other teams. The article intimates that he will be off to Atlético de Madrid next season.

Albacete Balompié's out-of-town Ciudad Deportiva (training ground) is a one-storey concrete building which hardly disturbs the flatness of the dusty local terrain around it (we're in the south east of the huge Meseta plain: there isn't a hill in sight). I walk through the entrance, down a corridor, past a huddle of autograph-hunters and wait outside the dressing-room door. The Nigerian player Nawal comes out, and tells me Pablo is still inside. Pretty soon the defender himself walks out.

"Let's go to the Bar Málaga to do the interview," he says. He's tall, with short spiky hair. Zipped up woollen cardigan. Friendly guy.

"How far is it from here to Málaga?" I ask.

"About 200 kilometres. Why?"

"A joke. You said that we were going . . . never mind."

We walk into the bar.

"What do you want to drink?" he asks. "A beer?"

I'm still a little drunk from the night before, hence the rubbish joke. A beer's the last thing I need. "A coffee with milk. I was out with Jesús from the peñas last night. Too many beers."

"Oh, Jesús," he says, and gives me a knowing smile.

He tells me a little about his career. He made his debut for the club at the age of 20 a couple of years ago and hasn't missed a game since. He's heard the talk of Atlético's interest but doesn't want to think about next season until this season is over. Albacete still have to make sure they avoid relegation. He has to take each game at a time. And next up is Real Madrid.

"What did you feel like when you woke up this morning?" I ask. "How long did it take you before you realised that you were playing against Real Madrid tomorrow?" I often try dumb questions like this, in order to try and humanise players.

"Not long. But I'm not a maniac about football. I don't think about it all the time. I like to separate my life and my job. I like to think about other things, too. Like in the morning, what to have for breakfast." He has three tapas in front of him, and the thought of breakfast makes him pick one up and eat it. It's a little tart with tuna in it. I look at it enviously, starving. I haven't had anything to eat today.

We get to talking about Beckham, who Pablo rates very highly as a player. I ask him where he was when Beckham scored in the game against Albacete in the Bernebeu. I draw a picture of a football pitch, and an 'x' for Beckham. He takes the pen, draws another couple of 'x's alongside.

"I was here, marking Raúl," he says. Then he draws a line towards Beckham's 'x'. "Then, when I saw Beckham had found the space for a shot, I tried to block it. He was too quick, though. I didn't get near it. What a goal."

I ask him how he feels that Beckham is reputedly getting paid more than the whole Albacete team put together.

"You don't think about that sort of thing. In fact when you get on the pitch you have to forget entirely that you are playing against Real Madrid. You have to forget Beckham is Beckham, Raúl is Raúl and Ronaldo is Ronaldo, and just treat them as opponents."

"What about giving away free kicks outside the box? Hasn't the manager told you to be careful about that with the likes of Beckham and Roberto Carlos around?"

"He may talk about that tomorrow, I don't know. We're always encouraged not to give away fouls outside the box, anyway."

"You don't give away many fouls yourself, judging by your yellow card record."

"When I jump, I try to jump clean, without using my elbows. When I tackle, I try to get the ball."

After our conversation finishes, I shake hands with Pablo and he wanders off to the bar to have a read of the paper. After taking a couple of final notes, I go up to the bar to pay.

"No, no, no, no," he says. "We'll settle that." I'm finding it difficult to spend any cash in Albacete.

Talking about money, over lunch I read the sports section of *El Mundo* which gives details of Real Madrid's new contract with adidas, worth a total of 130 million euros. And it's adidas who are supplying the kit! It talks about Florentino Pérez's attempt to make Real Madrid into a global brand of the size of the likes of Warner Bros or Disney. Of how they now receive between three and six million euros for every friendly they play. That they have plans to launch a TV station around the world, and have 300,000 'card-holders' (who've bought the right simply to be associated with the club), that the club has licensed a total of 800 products. That the European and Asian markets are assured, and that the next big push will be for the United States and Africa. It's interesting material in the light of my shouting match with 'Valdano'. And it makes you wonder what chance little Albacete have of derailing the Real Madrid express tomorrow.

I go and watch Ed Wood's '50s B-movie *Plan 9 from Outer Space* in the Filmoteca, planning to go straight from here to the nearby Gran Hotel (in the same square) to watch Real Madrid's arrival in town. The film, which has gained cult status due to its amateurish awfulness and the Johnny Depp movie *Ed Wood* about its making, stars Bela Lugosi. It is a happy coincidence. I have long thought that Carlos Queiroz has more than a passing resemblance to the Hungarian horror movie star. Now is my chance to make a direct comparison. And sure enough I am right, although Lugosi's character spends most of the film raising his cape in front of his face (Lugosi actually died four days into the making of the film).

I am surprised when I scuttle out of the cinema (happily I have to miss the finale) to see the size of the crowd waiting outside the Grand Hotel for Real Madrid. I show my press card to a policeman and walk to the hotel entrance, which is situated in a narrow street just off the square. I'm with the rest of the local press. Cristo is there, his blue microphone in his hand, dressed in what appears to be a safari suit. Thousands of fans have turned up and are squashed onto the pavements behind yellow crash barriers the length of the road. I am standing right next to the most crowded section where a single crash barrier cordons off the pavement, to allow players off the coach and into the front door of the hotel. Sardined into this funnel are the most dedicated of the crowd, mainly teenage girls who have been waiting for a couple of hours (I saw them before the film started). There is little doubt who they have come to see.

"Beykan, Beykan, Beykan," they chant. One of them holds up a poster of the Englishman, topless. The crowd gets more and more hysterical as the estimated time of arrival of the Real Madrid coach (8.30 pm) approaches. There are several false alarms, triggering a cacophony of high-pitched screams.

I grow alarmed at the poor security as the crowd gets bigger, packing into the small available space. The single crash barrier blocking off the pavement by the door is starting to be pushed forward. A five-year-old boy, crushed against the barrier, starts crying – a policewoman forces people back to free the child. I start visualising the barrier falling over, and the horrendous crushing of people that would ensue. I am in a moral dilemma. Do the police know what they are doing? Should I say something? What if I say nothing and there is a disaster? They seem more concerned about checking that everyone in the press area has accreditation (a number of chancers have infiltrated our ranks) than about crowd safety measures. It'll be fine. I'm over-reacting.

"I am afraid that the barrier will fall over when the coach arrives," I say to a policeman standing next to the pressure point. "I'm afraid there might be a disaster."

"Nooooooo," he says, in a reassuring voice. It doesn't reassure me. Should I go to a higher authority? There's a plainclothes policeman obviously organising things down the way.

The level of the screams reaches an unprecedented pitch and I see the coach slowly making its way towards us. Fans have jumped over the barriers and are banging on its side. As it approaches us, what I feared would happen, happens. Once the vehicle has passed them, those further down the pavement, enclosed in the pen formed by the barriers, push forward to try to get a better look at the stars as they leave the coach. The door opens, and they appear right in front of me: Míchel Salgado, Borja, Mejía. Everyone's going mad. The single barrier to the left of the entrance, bearing the weight of hundreds of fans, leans further forwards. Several policemen rush to the scene and try to hold it up. Figo comes out, the fans surge forward. I can see a look of desperation on one cop's face as he signals for reinforcements with his arm. What's going to happen when Beckham leaves the coach? I wonder if I can stop him in some way. I contemplate jumping in to help push the barrier back, but by the time I have weighed up the possible consequences (crushed legs come to mind) the whole space is filled up with police pushing for all they're worth against the force of the crowd. The screaming intensifies. Are they cries of panic, or adulation? The barrier bends further forward, the police look to be losing their battle. More screaming, a level I have never heard before. I gesture at the crowd to step back, pushing my palms forwards in the air, frantically. A policewoman is doing the same by my side. The level of noise is incredible. Suddenly, the pressure subsides. The screaming dies down. The police relax, stand straight, start looking at each other. Crisis over. I look round. All the players have left the coach and gone into the hotel.

I walk through the lobby towards the area designated for Queiroz's press conference. I spot Beckham, leaning coolly against the wall by the lift, with his trademark Louis Vuitton bag tucked under his arm, oblivious to the near disaster that he has just generated. I'm still shocked by it. And it comes to me that maybe the hysteria has been stage-managed. Real Madrid normally stay in the Parador (state-run castle-cum-hotel), a few miles out of town. There were more likely to be scenes like that if they stayed right in the town centre. Then I remember Santander, where they changed from their normal hotel in the suburbs to another one right in the centre that seemed less suited to their needs. And I start suspecting a policy whereby the team is being placed as centrally as possible IN ORDER to attract huge attention. That the whole hysteria-on-arrival-in-town thing is part of Florentino Pérez's evangelisation process, in order to widen Real's appeal, in order to hook the teenage girls to a life of Real Madrid support.

Queiroz arrives in the room and sits at the table for his interview. He does not pull his cape over his eyes.

"Are you surprised at the level of interest the team's arrival here generated?" asks one woman.

"It happens wherever Real Madrid go, so I am not so surprised," says the Portuguese manager, in that deadpan manner he has. "Everybody wants to be close to the Real Madrid team. I can only thank the people for dedicating some of their free time to achieving this objective."

He is asked about the game. He says that Albacete are a very good team, and that Real will have to run a great deal to beat them. And that Beckham, who has passed a fitness test, will definitely play. The whole thing lasts five minutes.

I meet an Englishman (wavy mousy hair, glasses, smart suit) who I earlier saw being interviewed before the arrival of the coach. He had been handing out leaflets advertising his English language school, Monkey Business. The leaflets are a stroke of marketing genius.

'Shout at Beckham in his own language!' they read in Spanish. Then they give three things that the crowd might shout, first in Spanish, then with an English translation.

"Pa victoria la del Alba!"

('There's no victory' – a play on his wife's name.)

"Beckham pederás, pero qué bueno estás!"

('Beckham, you're going to lose, but there's no-one as gorgeous as you.')

"El Alba es el queso mecánico."

('Alba is the clockwork cheese' – La Mancha is famous for its cheeses, and this is a play on the term *Clockwork Orange* – Kubrick's film and Burgess' novel – which is often used as a symbol amongst the ultras in Spain due to the violent nature of its protagonists.)

He's called Chris, and he's very pleased with himself.

"Apparently the leaflets were mentioned in the *Daily Telegraph* yesterday," he says. "My mum rang me and told me."

I ask him about the Beckham effect on the town.

"Incredible," he says. "This is the biggest thing that's happened here for years."

He goes off and has a word with the owner of the hotel, then comes back. "That's the last president of the club. I used to teach his son English. So I'm in there." He's off again, but he turns round before he's out the door. "Small-town stuff," he says, winking.

## SATURDAY APRIL 3RD

I've been invited to watch a local under-16 match by Luis, who poured me all the whisky that is still causing me a throbbing headache 30-odd hours later. He's the manager of the team, called Molinos (windmills). Even though we are 100 kilometres off 'the Quixote trail' there are frequent references to La Mancha's favourite son. He picks me up at my hotel, drives me to a sports complex on the outskirts of town, and pretty soon I'm standing by the side of a sand pitch watching an earnest game of teenage football alongside the substitutes, the managers and a couple of dads. Rather incongruously, I'm taking notes. On 20 minutes there is a flare up between Luis and Molinos' central defender, Pedro.

"You're pushing up too much. That's the third time you've let them though," shouts Luis.

"Oh shut up. Leave me in peace," replies Pedro.

"Right, that's it!" shouts Luis. "Referee. Referee!" He rolls one hand round the other over his head, signalling he wants to make a change. Then he turns to one of the substitutes, still sitting on the bench.

"What are you waiting for? Get your track suit off! GET YOUR TRACK SUIT OFF!" He starts pulling at the boys track suit bottoms, yanking them off his legs. "Now get on the pitch." Pablo has sat down on the bench, tight-lipped with indignation, tears in his eyes.

The match is a tight affair between the top and second in the table ('the Real Madrid and Valencia of this league' as Luis puts it.) The teams are well-trained and the match is still 0–0 in the second half. One player has caught my eye – Molinos' number 25, 'Depe' who has dyed blond hair and is wearing two fake diamond ear-rings. He is even playing in Beckham's position in the centre of midfield. On 70 minutes he hits in a long shot that bounces well in front of the goal. Molinos' big striker Pablo nips in front of the keeper and heads it over him into the goal. "GOOOOOOOL!" shouts Luis. The players all run to the corner, jumping into each others' arms like professionals.

It looks like the goal is worth three points until the last minute of the game, when Molinos' right-back Alberto needlessly gives away a corner. The ball isn't cleared properly and one of the opposition players shins a rebound it in the net. More professional-style celebrations. Luis looks crestfallen, but soon picks himself up. "We're still top of the table," he says. "On goal difference."

I'm driven to Jesus' office and taken by him to the stadium, which resembles a corrugated-iron submarine from the outside. We are allowed to wander freely round and meet the fans of the 'Curva Rommel', Albacete's singing end, who are preparing a 'mosaico'. They are putting long strips of cellophane behind all the seats, which the fans are to hold up when the players run onto the pitch. The cellophane is in two different colours, maroon and white. It displays the logo of the sponsor of the event, a national beer-maker.

"It looks like Indian colours," says Jesús to one of the cellophane-cutters. He means that it's red and white, like the colours of Atlético de Madrid.

"It's maroon, not red. It's the colours of the Castilla La Mancha flag."

"Why are you called the Curva Rommel?" I ask him. This has been bothering me. It sounds suspiciously Nazi.

"Because of Rommel Fernández. An Albacete player from Panama, who was killed in a car crash while he was playing for the club. He was very popular here."

"Not because of Rommel, the German general?"

"Not because of the German."

Cristo walks past with his blue microphone. He's wearing a grey pinstripe suit.

"Hey, Cristo, you getting married?" says Jesús.

It's a lovely day, and the stadium, a compact one-tiered place renovated as recently as 1999, has a wonderful look to it, all shiny seats gleaming in the hot sun. Jesús takes me into the dressing room area where there is a row of photos from throughout Alba's history: former Real Madrid player and Spain and Real Madrid manager José Antonio Camacho (remembered in World Cup 2002 for his sweaty armpits) playing for the club during the famous 111-goal season; a young Parrita bashing his drum; Luis holding a pig dressed in Alba colours; Rommel Fernández' car wrecked against a tree.

"Soon there will be a picture of today's match up here," says Jesús. "Our famous victory against the Real Madrid of the galácticos." I feel a surge of excitement in my breast: a vicarious hit of David's butterflies before attempting to slay Goliath.

I've got a few hours to kill before the game, so I go to the city's most famous restaurant, Nuestra Casa, to try some of the local food and see what the papers have to say about the game. I try the Manchegan gazpacho – nothing to do with the refreshing Andalucian soup, but a partridge and rabbit stew on a bed of unleavened bread – then a plate of meat and sausages so big I can't get halfway through it (this is rare behaviour on my part). The paper shows pictures of the team coach arriving at the hotel and talks about the great sense of expectation there is in the city for the game. It's a sell-out and tickets are going for up to 300 euros. The paper talks of a new species of tout: not a professional but a fan who covers the cost of his season ticket (around 200 euros) by buying an extra ticket for the Real Madrid match at the reduced rate offered to club members and selling it on outside the game at an hugely inflated price.

My ticket has been arranged through the press office, but when I pick it up I am surprised to see that it offers me 'standing room' in the 'Marcador' Stand, not a place in the press box. I'm also given a laminated card allowing me free access all over the ground. I'm happy to have anything: outside, with two hours still to go, it's very much a seller's market with fierce negotiations at every corner. I start nosing round, taking photos: a match like this brings out the eccentric in people. There's one group walking around with a three-foot sandwich they've made, singing Albacete songs.

"What's that for?" I ask.

"It's to eat at half time. And we're going to see if Ronaldo wants some."

One guy is dressed as a bat, another as a clown. Chris, the English teacher, has employed two girls to hand out his Beckham leaflets. Oddly, they refuse to have their photo taken. Everyone is wearing their colours – Real Madrid and Albacete fans are happily mingling in the sunshine without a hint of unease. Spring has arrived, finally. An electronic thermometer reads 22 degrees. I take a picture of a fan wearing a number 23 Albacete shirt with the name 'Delporte' on the back. Delporte is Albacete's version of Beckham, a Frenchman who dyes his hair blond and wears it in a pony-tail.

"El Becks de la Mancha," he says, as I take the photo with the blue wall of the stadium as a backdrop. I like the phrase: it has a ring to it.

"Hey, you looking to buy a ticket?" says the number 23's mate. "200 euros." I tell him I've already got one.

I find my 'place' inside the stadium half an hour before kick-off. It's on the concrete walkway between two tiers of one of the main stands, leaning against an advertising billboard. It's not a great place. But I've got my 'access all areas' card, so I decide to see if I can upgrade, and stroll round the stadium, taking pictures, looking for an interesting spot. I walk to La Curva Rommel, and they're already singing a song. It's the grandly named 'Grito del Alba' (Alba shout), which Parritta claims to have invented.

"Alba, clap clap clap. Alba, clap clap clap."

Chris the English teacher has paid for an advert for his school to be repeated over and over on the big screen, which is otherwise advertising local restaurants and car salesrooms. His voice keeps coming across the tannoy singing, in English, 'Come on Alba, come on Alba." I notice a little gate at the bottom corner of the stand which opens onto the pitch. I pin my 'Access all areas' pass onto my jacket and walk though it and onto the grass. Can I possibly be allowed here? A security guard glances at my pass, but doesn't say anything. I walk down the touch-line, towards the dug-outs. The atmosphere is more intense here. Photographers are sitting on their silver boxes, or on white plastic chairs. None are free. On the other side of the dug-out I spot a pile of unused chairs. There's a roar from the crowd and the players run onto the pitch, from the players' tunnel behind one of the goals. The 'mosaic' goes up around me. It looks marvellous. I walk behind the dug-out, still undecided as to whether I'm allowed pitchside, as the substitutes and management sit down on their benches. There's Quieroz, Solari, Núñez! Right next to me! I stop, a rabbit caught in headlights, then blink and move on. The best thing, I figure, is to act like I know what I'm doing. I pick a chair off the pile, and set it down next to a guy with a badge saying 'Camara'. I've got my own camera round my neck, a little zoom thing, which looks silly next to all the huge zooms on sticks the other guys have got. A security guard picks up a chair, sits next to me, lights a fag, smiles. He holds it cupped in his hand so nobody can see it from afar.

"This should be good," he says and I realise I'll be allowed to stay. It should be good, he's right. Albacete v Real Madrid! The highlight of the year in the little La Mancha city! And I have an amazing view, almost exactly the same view as I had of the kids' match this morning. I indulge in a brief daydream in which the ball gets cleared my way, I stand up, trap it with my chest, control it on my knee and volley it back onto the pitch.

There is a minute of silence for the March 11th victims broken by two or three idiots shouting obscenities, then the match kicks off. I have a great view of the Real back four, defending the goal to my right. My eyes are on Beckham, and on Pablo, the Albacete player I interviewed, who starts the game well, making a box-to-box dribble the way only the best centre-backs can do, and then performs a perfectly executed goal-saving flying tackle on Ronaldo on the edge of the box. I remember saying him how careful he had to be not to give away free kicks, and, sod's law at work here, soon afterwards he slices through Ronaldo about 25 yards out from goal. Free kick. Pablo looks disgusted with himself. But who's going to take it?

Real Madrid have obviously been working on this. Beckham walks up to the ball, picks out a tuft of grass from underneath it, and throws it away. He and Roberto Carlos both shape up to kick the ball. The goalkeeper has positioned his wall somewhere in the middle, to cover both options. Beckham takes a slow run-up from an acute angle from the left; Roberto Carlos trundles in from directly behind it. The Englishman slows to a halt, the Brazilian carries on and hits a powerful shot which flashes into the net. It looks like it's hit someone on the way, wrong-footing the keeper, but at 80 mph it's difficult to see clearly. People all over the ground rise to their feet, although one stand is Madrileño-free. The Curva Rommel, to my right, raise a defiant chant.

"Al-ba-ce-te, Al-ba-ce-te!"

Albacete, who don't deserve to be down, start playing with more urgency, which creates gaps in their defence which Real Madrid try to exploit on the break. Alba have more possession, Real create more chances. Beckham has a shot which curls over the bar, Guti another which is tipped away by the keeper. Beckham, having put a couple of long passes wide early on, is playing in the scurrying fashion in which he often approaches away matches – tackling a lot, passing short more than long. He gives the ball away a couple more times, but also shows his class with an unexpected back-heel which frees space for Zidane.

The half-time whistle sends the players out of the dug-out again. Cristo walks past: he's wearing a leather jacket and a pair of flared jeans, bleached down the front. Right in front of me Cambiasso, Nuñez and Solari play a game of keepie-uppie 'donkey' which they enjoy enormously from the way they are joking and laughing. Then the rest of the substitutes join in and it turns into a game of piggy in the middle. Chris' advert comes on the big screen.

"Come on Alba. Come on Alba."

My view of the start of the second half is obstructed by the Real Madrid midfielders who are warming up right in front of me. You can't exactly say, "Hey, Solari, mate, get out the way, would you?" Borja, Solari and Núñez look the most likely to come on. I try to watch proceedings through the gaps between them as they go through their intricate and at times rather balletic warm-ups. Beckham is all over the pitch but Albacete, who have begun to dominate the game after bringing on two substitutes, are by-passing the midfield by pumping balls forward to their big striker Mikel and trying to make something from his knock-downs. Mikel, a Basque, is one of those players who uses his Christian name as his playing name. Small wonder – his surname is Agirregomezkorta. Queiroz calls over to Borja and the board-man holds up his board. Number 16! It's Guti who comes off. I can clearly see the disappointment on his face. It's a defensive substitution – Borja is a strong, muscular midfielder.

Then, on 70 minutes, Albacete concede another foul outside the box, this time about 30 yards from goal, right in line with where I'm sitting. This time Beckham doesn't make to take it, instead insinuating himself into the wall. The Brazilian hits the ball, it seems to hit Figo on the way, and Real have another goal. The Curva Rommel is stunned into silence. This is completely undeserved by Real Madrid.

Alba bring on their most skilful player, Líbero Parri, and he curls a free-kick over the wall. A trumpet in the Curvas Rommel blows a lament, and the whole crowd shout 'olé'. This happens two or three times in a row – from down here you can really feel how the crowd affects the players, and Albacete start moving the ball round with more confidence. Parri receives it outside the box and hits a great cross-shot which bounces in front of Casillas and into the net. 2–1! Ten minutes to go! Game on. The whole of the Curva Rommel is bouncing up and down waving their scarves in circles above their head.

Real Madrid, with Zidane just substituted (Solari finally gets out of my way) start doing all they can to waste time. It is very unbecoming for a team of 'galácticos'. Ronaldo is replaced by Núñez and the inevitable chant is incredibly clear from my close-to-the-dug-out position.

"Gor-do, gor-do"

Albacete attack frantically when they get the ball, and Parri puts another long-shot into the side netting. Beckham falls as if pole-axed by a tackle, the referee waves play on. The boardman holds up his precious information. Three minutes. The trumpet starts up another refrain, the crowd keep on shouting and Albacete continue on the attack. The ball bobbles in the box, Mikel has a shot . . . blocked. The final whistle. The dug-outs clear of their occupants. The stands clear of fans. I'm left sitting ringside, contemplating what I've just seen. Real win and go four points clear, with Valencia still to play tomorrow.

Afterwards I go back to Parri's Palace and meet various members of the Curva Rommel who are handed their personalised bottles of J&B (their names are scrawled in marker pen on the label) as they walk in the door. On the screen in front of us Barcelona's unlikely title charge effectively ends with a 0–0 draw at home to Villarreal. I am introduced to Jesús' 14-year-old daughter, Lidia, who goes to all the Alba matches with him.

"Who do you support?"

"Alba."

"Even when Beckham is playing?"

"Yeah, I love Alba."

"What do you think about Beckham?"

"He's gorgeous. I have three posters of him on my wall in my bedroom."

"What's gorgeous about him?"

"He's so guapo" (good-looking).

"Did you ever have any pictures of footballers up on your wall before he came to Spain?"

"No way."

Later on Chris the English teacher turns up. He's very drunk and deep in the throes of his 15 minutes of fame.

"I've been interviewed by nine TV stations and eight radio stations," he says. "I was in the *Sun* and the *Telegraph*. It's really opened my eyes to how the media works. It's been a snowball, a fucking snowball. I haven't had one extra enrolment yet, mind."

"Come on Alba," shout the Curva Rommel guys at him.

"Come on Alba," he shouts back. Something tells me it's going to be another big night.

### SUNDAY APRIL 4TH

I walk through Alba's unlovely city centre, across the ring-road and down the tower-block-lined road to the station. The sun is shining. I have *Marca* in my hand. The headline is 'THE LUCK OF THE CHAMPIONS'. It turns out that the second goal was turned in by Figo's hand. Beckham is given a '1' with the comment 'untirable'. I feel sorry for Albacete, though Espanyol's defeat in Seville means they are relatively safe from relegation. I've grown fond of the team in a short time, and fond of the place, too. A place where I tried and tried to put my hand in my pocket but was never allowed to pay. A town where I was shown great kindness by complete strangers; a town where I made friends; a town where I had to get a new bag to carry all the presents I'd been given. And something Luis said late in the night at Parri's Palace is going round my head. "They say something about Albacete that's more accurate than 'Caga y vete' (shit and leave)," he muttered. "They say 'when you arrive in Albacete you cry. But when you leave you cry too.'"

### RESULTS JORNADA 30

| | | | |
|---|---|---|---|
| **REAL MADRID** | **5** | **SEVILLA** | **1** |
| RACING | 0 | VALENCIA | 3 |
| BETIS V BARCELONA: MATCH POSTPONED, EVENTUALLY 1–1 | | | |
| CELTA | 0 | ZARAGOZA | 2 |
| VILLARREAL | 0 | ATLÉTICO | 0 |
| MURCIA | 2 | MALLORCA | 0 |
| REAL SOCIEDAD | 1 | DEPORTIVO | 2 |
| ESPANYOL | 2 | ATHLETIC | 1 |
| MALAGA | 1 | ALBACETE | 1 |
| VALLADOLID | 1 | OSASUNA | 1 |

## RESULTS JORNADA 31

| | | | |
|---|---|---|---|
| SEVILLA | 1 | ESPANYOL | 0 |
| **ALBACETE** | **1** | **REAL MADRID** | **2** |
| BARCELONA | 0 | VILLARREAL | 0 |
| OSASUNA | 1 | MÁLAGA | 1 |
| ATHLETIC | 0 | CELTA | 0 |
| ZARAGOZA | 2 | RACING | 2 |
| MALLORCA | 1 | REAL SOCIEDAD | 1 |
| DEPORTIVO | 2 | BETIS | 2 |
| ATLÉTICO | 2 | VALLADOLID | 1 |
| VALENCIA | 2 | MURCIA | 0 |

## LA CLASIFICACIÓN

| | P | W | D | L | F | A | Pts |
|---|---|---|---|---|---|---|---|
| **REAL MADRID** | **31** | **20** | **7** | **4** | **65** | **37** | **67** |
| VALENCIA | 31 | 20 | 6 | 5 | 62 | 21 | 66 |
| DEPORTIVO | 31 | 17 | 6 | 8 | 50 | 30 | 57 |
| BARCELONA | 31 | 16 | 8 | 6 | 48 | 32 | 56 |
| ATLÉTICO | 31 | 13 | 9 | 9 | 38 | 36 | 48 |
| OSASUNA | 31 | 10 | 15 | 6 | 32 | 27 | 45 |
| ATHLETIC | 31 | 12 | 9 | 10 | 40 | 39 | 45 |
| MÁLAGA | 31 | 13 | 4 | 14 | 41 | 44 | 43 |
| SEVILLA | 31 | 11 | 8 | 12 | 40 | 36 | 41 |
| VILLARREAL | 31 | 11 | 8 | 12 | 39 | 40 | 41 |
| BETIS | 31 | 9 | 12 | 9 | 38 | 34 | 39 |
| ZARAGOZA | 31 | 10 | 8 | 13 | 36 | 41 | 38 |
| RACING | 31 | 10 | 9 | 12 | 41 | 49 | 38 |
| VALLADOLID | 31 | 9 | 9 | 13 | 37 | 44 | 36 |
| REAL SOCIEDAD | 31 | 9 | 9 | 13 | 35 | 43 | 36 |
| ALBACETE | 31 | 10 | 6 | 15 | 31 | 39 | 36 |
| MALLORCA | 31 | 9 | 6 | 16 | 37 | 57 | 33 |
| ESPANYOL | 31 | 9 | 3 | 19 | 34 | 53 | 30 |
| CELTA | 31 | 6 | 11 | 14 | 41 | 60 | 29 |
| MURCIA | 31 | 3 | 11 | 17 | 25 | 48 | 20 |

# NINETEEN
# MADRID

GOLFO DE VIZCAYA

OCÉANO ATLÁNTICO

**Real Madrid**
○
**Atlético de Madrid**

MAR MEDITERRÁNEO

# NINETEEN
# MADRID

## MONDAY APRIL 5TH

The first I hear of the Beckham crisis is a phone call from my mum on Monday morning.

"They say he's had an affair."

"Who says?"

"The tabloids. It's all over the news."

I rush out and get *Marca* in my local newsagent. There is no mention of the affair, so I go down to one of the kiosks by La Barceloneta marina and buy the *Sun*. It's a sunny day, and I wander down to the shoreline of Barcelona's tatty city-beach near my flat to have a read. The waves are high and there's a shoal of surfers 20 yards out to sea, like seals in their black wetsuits. The wind flaps the pages of the paper so I shelter behind a palm tree. The first eight pages are dedicated to the Beckham news. It is alleged that Beckham's former PR girl, Rebecca Loos, slept with him on several occasions in the autumn. There are transcripts of the text messages that he is alleged to have sent her, with stars replacing the naughty bits. There are a lot of stars. It's like doing a crossword puzzle.

The Spanish have no equivalent newspapers to the red-top British tabloids. There's little need: they have hours of tittle-tattle on the TV, in programmes such as *Cronicas Marcianas* (Martian chronicles) on the Berlusconi-owned Canal 5, in which several presenters spend several hours every night shouting at one another on the subject of celebrities and their private affairs. There are also a number of glossy magazines which interest themselves in the same material. Spain is where *Hello* magazine originated (the Spanish version is called *Hola*); its imitators include *Sorpresa* (surprise) and *Interviu*. *Sorpresa* is the magazine that printed the pictures of Beckham out in the nightclub with Rebecca Loos back in October.

These magazines are collectively known as 'la prensa rosa' (the pink press). Normally footballers aren't considered to be targets for la prensa rosa or the TV gossip programmes, which tend to concern themselves with movie actors, flamenco singers, bullfighters and the Marbella jet-set, as well as anyone with any royal connections. But Beckham has bucked the trend, because people who are not normally interested in football are interested in him. I've heard that some of his team-mates are worried that because of Beckham, they too will be considered fair game for Spain's technicolour rumour mill. So far his family-man image has worked in his favour: now the gossip hounds really have something to get their teeth into.

## TUESDAY APRIL 6TH

Or as the *Sun* puts it: 'Beckham Crisis, Day 2'. Most of the Spanish newspapers have ignored the Beckham allegations, but the serious national daily *El Mundo* gives it a page, with the headline 'Is Beckham unfaithful?' The article, as much as anything, is interested in the British tabloid press' predilection for scurrilous stories. The Spanish call our tabloid papers 'la prensa amarilla' (the yellow press), a translation of the American term, coined in the 1890s, for the sensationalist New York papers owned by William Randolph Hearst and Joseph Pulitzer, after the cartoon strip *The Yellow Kid* in Pulitzer's *New York World* newspaper. Spaniards believe these papers brought America into a war against Spain in Cuba by exaggerating the nature of Spanish atrocities in the island. *El Mundo* is slightly scornful of the *Sun's* reporting of the text messages, and how the affair has created a debate in England. It publishes an old picture of Loos standing next to a pissed-off-looking Victoria Beckham. Beckham's wife is holding their second son, the infant Romeo, who looks like he is celebrating a goal. It also discusses the potential damage the allegations could have on Beckham's media image and the millions he amasses from it.

Today the Real Madrid players have something else to worry about: the second leg of the Champions League quarter-final against Monaco in Monte Carlo. Beckham was booked for a needless foul late in the first leg, meaning an automatic suspension from the second, in which Real have to protect a 4–2 lead. It looked at the time suspiciously like Beckham had got himself booked so he could sit out the match in France and have a clean slate for the semi-final. As it happens, the fact that he isn't playing gives him the opportunity to join his wife on a family skiing holiday in the Swiss Alps.

*Marca* again ignores Beckham's personal problems. It leads today's edition with a picture of Ronaldo looking into a crystal ball, foreseeing 'la décima': Real's tenth European Cup win. They don't seem worried about the Monaco game. I watch it in a bar with a big screen in La Barceloneta. There are about 30 people there and everybody seems to be up for Real Madrid. I am the only person under 60; the others are presumably migrants from the Franco era who never switched allegiance to their new city's team.

"Do you think they'll miss Beckham?" I ask the man on my right, who's wearing a baseball cap and smoking a cigar. He grunts a reply through Walter-Matthau jowls that I don't quite understand.

"He's not a happy man at the moment," I continue. "Problems of the heart."

"I don't care what he does in his free time," growls the man. "I just care what he does on the football field."

After 36 minutes he's up and cheering as Raúl scores an opportunistic goal to put Madrid 5–2 up on aggregate. I consider going elsewhere to watch the Arsenal-Chelsea game: this one seems all over.

A goal late in the first half by the Monaco captain Giuly changes my plans. And a couple of minutes after the break, a cross comes in from the left and Morientes outjumps Mejía to head the ball into the top corner of the net. Instinctively I shout 'gol!' and clench my fist, which gets me 30 nasty looks. It's a bitter pill for the old guys to swallow. Morientes is a Real Madrid player on loan to the French team, a popular striker exiled by Pérez as part of his 'Zidanes and Pavones' policy. The camera pans in on the Real Madrid president, who is trying not to look at Prince Albert of Monaco, two seats away, dressed in a long Monaco scarf and acting just as the fans around him are, jumping up and down and raising his arms in the air.

It is time for Real Madrid to react, but they don't seem to have enough energy to launch the attacks needed for a goal that would clinch the tie. Remarkably, on 66 minutes Giuly scores a third goal for Monaco, a cool back-heel from around the penalty spot that drives the French crowd wild and makes everyone in the bar put their head in their hands. These guys with their brandies and their filterless black tobacco cigarettes are really grumpy now. Another shot of Prince Albert's antics doesn't help matters. The score is now 5–5 on aggregate, but Morientes' away goal in the Bernabéu means that Monaco go through if the score doesn't change.

It doesn't. In fact Real have absolutely nothing in reserve, and it is the Monagasque side that comes closer, hitting the bar and the post in the closing minutes. On the final whistle the Real players' body language says it all. Many of them collapse on the pitch, then eventually walk off, heads down, funeral faces to match their black kit. A couple of weeks back a unique treble looked on the cards. Now there's just La Liga to go for. If Beckham, with all his fighting spirit, had been playing, would they have surrendered so meekly? I wonder, in the midst of his reunion in Switzerland, whether he managed to even watch the game.

## SATURDAY APRIL 10TH

Real Madrid's disastrous exit from Europe has placed the club firmly in a semi-official state of crisis which has been dominating the pages of the football press in Spain. *Marca*, keeping a dignified silence on Beckham's personal problems, followed the defeat with a brilliant front cover showing Raúl face-down on the Monte Carlo turf after the game, with the headline 'THE END'. But Real are still a point ahead of Valencia in the league and, with Beckham back, are looking to the game against Osasuna to try to erase the memory of their defeat.

For Beckham, the best place to escape his personal demons is presumably the football field. Rebecca Loos has this morning revealed more details of her alleged affair with the England captain in the English press, and there are rumours that a second girl claiming to have slept with Beckham are to be revealed tomorrow. His wife has travelled to Madrid to watch the game, with Brooklyn in tow, in a brave show of support. It's Saturday night and I watch the game in a crowded bar, with the sound turned down. But the pictures alone are revealing enough. As the game kicks off the cameras pan in on Victoria: she's wearing a skimpy black chiffon top, despite the fact that everyone else is in scarf, coat and hat. Spring takes its time to warm up Spain's land-locked capital. Then the cameras pick up on the bigger crisis. The Ultra Sur reveal a huge banner reading 'What would the result have mattered if you'd lost with honour? Monaco was shameful.'

I've barely found my seat when Osasuna score. A long throw flies in from the left, Salgado and Mejía both jump at the ball, knocking each other over, and it bounces into the path of former Real youth-teamer Valdo, unmarked on the far post, who shoots it past Casillas. Three Real Madrid players are lying on the ground as Beckham angrily kicks the ball into the net again. The Keystone Cops come to mind. Barely two minutes have been played and in the next 15 minutes the Osasuna right-winger could, maybe should, have three more goals, volleying one cross over, heading another into the side-netting and a third straight at a relieved Casillas.

Beckham is playing well, running like a madman, but the rest of the team seems devoid of ideas and energy. This is summed up on the 20th minute when, carrying the ball over the half-way line, the Englishman spots the Osasuna keeper off his line and tries a speculative lob which ends up in the roof of the net. Every time Beckham does anything the camera finds Victoria up in the stands. We see Brooklyn run off crying, obviously upset by all the hullaballoo. His mother chases him up the aisle. The next time Beckham gets the ball, the camera focuses in on their empty seats. Things aren't much better on the pitch. Osasuna continue pressing from the front, forcing Madrid into errors and winning a number of throw-ins, which, with the Real Madrid defence so shaky, seem more dangerous than corners. And it's from a throw-in that the second goal comes, just before the break. Casillas comes out too far, fails to get the ball and the Uruguayan Pablo García calmly and gently lobs the ball into an empty net. 2–0 to Osasuna.

The second half continues in much the same manner as the first. Beckham, obviously enjoying the catharsis of playing, is the only Real Madrid player running. He receives little support, at one point having to perform a 30 metre u-turn with the ball, chased all the way by an Osasuna midfielder. He sprays passes long and short but they come to nothing. He is denied two penalties as he tumbles in the box. His free-kick leads to a Helguera goal, which is disallowed for offside.

Osasuna 'sentence' (as the Spanish put it) the game on the hour. Again Valdo finds himself in space on the right, with time to measure a perfect cross to Moha who heads the ball past Casillas. By this time half the crowd have left. Many of those who have stayed wave white handkerchiefs: a sign of disgust at their team's performance. The cameraman assigned to focus in on people in the crowd has decided that the collective crisis is bigger than Beckham's personal one and we keep seeing an ashen-faced Florentino Pérez. The final whistle is a relief to all concerned. Beckham is shown walking towards the tunnel. He is usually magnanimous with his applause to the Bernabéu crowd; this time, his face contorted in disgust, he only gives them three short claps.

**SUNDAY APRIL 11TH**

Beckham comes under fire from all sides in the Spanish press. *Marca*, remarkably, give him another '0', with the comment 'Forrest Gump'. Presumably this is a reference to the fact that he runs and runs without any evident goal, rather than a pointer to his intelligence quotient. There is again no reference to his personal affairs. *El Mundo*, however, dedicates a double page spread to the Beckham crisis. There's a four-box cartoon showing Beckham, wearing his Real Madrid shirt, which has somehow lost the '3' from its '23'. He looks around and, aghast, spots the number lying on its side on the top of Victoria's head, like a pair of horns. In Spanish the expression 'poner los cuernos' (putting on the horns) means to cuckold someone. There are a series of articles revealing everything Rebecca Loos has said about the alleged affair in the English tabloids, as well as Beckham's insistence that the stories are 'ludicrous'. There is also an article taken from the *Observer,* lamenting the fact that the British public has blamed Victoria's reluctance to move to Spain for Beckham's alleged conduct, saying that this sort of attitude shows that, despite the feminist movement's successes over the last century, prevalent attitudes are still in the Victorian age. The whole business is given as much space as Real's disastrous defeat to Osasuna, and for all *El Mundo's* angling to show how the situation has highlighted the oddness of the British press, the detail and space devoted to it makes you wonder how much the newspaper is simply attempting to sell more copies by titillating its own readership with the lurid details.

## RESULTS JORNADA 32

| | | | |
|---|---|---|---|
| ESPANYOL | 1 | ALBACETE | 1 |
| RACING | 1 | ATHLETIC | 2 |
| MÁLAGA | 3 | ATLÉTICO | 1 |
| VALLADOLID | 1 | BARCELONA | 3 |
| VILLARREAL | 0 | DEPORTIVO | 2 |
| BETIS | 0 | MALLORCA | 2 |
| REAL SOCIEDAD | 2 | MURCIA | 0 |
| REAL MADRID | 0 | OSASUNA | 3 |
| CELTA | 0 | SEVILLA | 0 |
| ZARAGOZA | 0 | VALENCIA | 1 |

**TUESDAY APRIL 13TH**

*El Mundo* carries details of an interview with an alleged 'lover number two', Sarah Marbeck. It comments on the oddity of the fact that she kept the text messages she allegedly swapped with Beckham for two years. In the messages Beckham – who is still insisting that the stories are 'ludicrous' – is referred to as 'Peter Pan' and Victoria as 'Wendy'. Marbeck is known as 'Tinkerbell'. There is a funny coincidence here. Real's forthcoming opponents Atlético de Madrid carry the name of a different Hollywood film on their shirts every month. This month the film in question is *Peter Pan*.

**WEDNESDAY APRIL 14TH**

I arrive in Madrid for this weekend's 'derbi', the first of three extremely difficult matches which will be crucial to the success or failure of Real

Madrid's – and Beckham's – 2003/4 season. First up El Atleti – 'los eternos rivales' (the eternal rivals) – in the Vicente Calderón stadium in central Madrid, then 'el clásico' against Barcelona in the Bernabéu, followed by a trip to Riazor, home of Deportivo de la Coruña, the only Spanish team left in the Champions League after their remarkable feat of coming back from 4–1 down in the first leg against champions Milan to win the tie 5–4 on aggregate. A difficult line-up, only tempered by the fact that el Real do not have to fit two Champions League semi-finals between the games (as do Dépor).

I buy the *Sun, El Mundo* and *Marca*, which I read over a couple of mid-afternoon cañas in the bar in Lavapiés. Outside much of the city's male immigrant population – North Africans, Ecuadorians, Dominicans, Sub-Saharan Africans – is going about its business or simply hanging around. Inside is calm and peace: a perfect place to enjoy the news. One story in *Marca* illustrates just how much Real Madrid need a rest. At half time during the Monaco-Real game in Monte Carlo, with the score at 1–1, Giuly apparently went up to his French international team-mate Zidane and asked him if Real could let Monaco win 2–1 so they could save face in front of their home fans (they would still lose the tie 5–4). 'Can't you see we're knackered?' replied Zidane, implying they would be lucky to get away with losing just 2–1. Undoubtedly it was meant as a joke. The problem for Zidane was that Giuly not only reported the conversation to his team-mates in the dressing room (and they came out in the second half all guns blazing) but repeated the conversation and its repercussions to the French newspaper *L'Equipe* after the game. Zidane, a sensitive being, was appalled by the betrayal which, along with the fans' banners railing against the team had, according to *Marca*, put him in a state of depression which had affected his performance against Osasuna.

Beckham can't be feeling much better as his media crisis gets worse, although the second woman, Sarah Marbeck, does not sound entirely convincing, and *El Mundo* has stated that he has put the matter in the hands of his lawyers. Beckham is pictured on a trip to Pizza Hut in central Madrid with his wife and kids, smiling for the camera as if nothing has happened. That morning, however, he can't have been so happy as the players were forced to train in their Las Rojas training ground to a barrage of abuse from 100 or so of their own fans, who had put up a 30-metre banner along the fence reading 'For you, whores and money, for us outrage and repression'. The sign was up for a full 20 minutes before the police arrived to pull it down.

Real Madrid's reaction was immediate. After the training session the players were told that the routine before the game against Atlético was to be radically different from normal. Instead of training in the mornings in Las Rojas and having free time in the afternoons and evenings, they were ordered to report that very evening for a two-day, two-night training camp 200 miles away in La Manga, staying in the Hyatt Regency Hotel, the same place where the incident with the Leicester City players had taken place the previous month. Beckham must have been upset about the decision – he was planning to spend time with his wife and children in the build-up to Victoria's 30th birthday on Saturday – but he kept his silence, as he has done (apart from a couple of press releases calling the allegations 'ludicrous') since his 'crisis' began. Roberto Carlos, on the other hand, gave a press conference in which he was not so diplomatic. "I'm 31 years old and nobody tells me what to do," he said. "If the club wants us to go to a training camp, they should ask us what we think about it first." Team morale does not seem high.

I walk to the food market in La Latina to have a chat with the stall holder who changed his mind so radically about Beckham between August and February. The place seems to be even darker and scruffier than before. It's mid afternoon, there aren't many people around: half the stalls are shut.

"What do you think about him now?" I ask, while buying some goat's cheese marinated in olive oil.

"I'm not sure . . ." he says, rather flustered. Then he composes himself. "Listen, what Beckham does in his private life is his own business. As long as it doesn't affect his performance on the pitch."

"But he hasn't been playing that well. Are you sure that this hasn't had repercussions on his game?"

"That's the thing. It has. But he hasn't stopped trying. And that's the main thing. He runs all game. He covers more miles than any other player. And he is a good player. As long as he keeps trying, everything will come good."

I ask him if he is worried about the game against Atleti.

"Listen," he replies. "This is an Atleti area and most of my customers are Atleti fans. They know I support Real Madrid. If we lose, then I will hear about the game for many days to come. That is not what I want."

I stroll over to the poky little bar with the picture of hell by Hieronymous Bosch on the wall. This time the barman recognises me. I ask him what he thinks about Beckham now.

"I blame it on the money," he says. "They have too much money and too much free time. Of course they're going to get into trouble.

"Money is the whole problem with Real Madrid. There are too many bosses and too few workers. If you have to work for your bread, you will work hard. If you are rich, you won't. Look what happened against Osasuna. They had 11 players who have to work for their bread. Real Madrid didn't. That's why they lost."

His red face seems to have got even redder.

"Who do you want to win on Saturday?" I ask him.

"Atleti. I want Atleti to win. Of course."

The rivalry between the two Madrid clubs goes back more than a hundred years. Atlético de Madrid have a chequered history, which started in 1903, when they were formed as a feeder team for Athletic de Bilbao, wearing the same Blackburn-like colours of blue-and-white-halved shirts (which Bilbao still use as their away strip), and known as 'Athletic' de Madrid. They drew large support from fans in the south of the city where they were based, but their first years were hardly successful. At first they weren't allowed to play in the Copa del Rey, then the only national tournament, because of their ties with the Basque team; their main games were in the regional Madrid league. Their main rivals were, from the start, the team from the north of the city, Real Madrid, then called Madrid Club de Foot-Ball, who became the first side to dominate Spanish football, winning the Copa del Rey in 1905, 6 and 7.

Athletic, desperate to compete with Madrid whom they played several times every year in the regional league, changed their colours to red and white shirts with blue shorts in 1911 and became an independent entity in 1913. This is when they were given their nickname 'los colchoneros' (the mattress-makers) because of the similarity of their shirts to the canvases made to cover mattresses. Still, since only the winners of the regional league (usually Madrid FC) were allowed into the national cup competition, they still failed to make a national impact. It wasn't until 1921 that they managed to qualify, eventually losing in the final to Athletic de Bilbao.

Los Colchoneros owe their first title to a bizarre and rather macabre incident in the Civil War. They were amongst the founder members of the Spanish national league's Primera División but were relegated from it, for the second time, in 1936, alongside Osasuna. (Real) Madrid FC fared much better, winning the league in 1932 and 1933. The league was suspended when the war broke out and not reconvened until 1939. During hostilities Oviedo's Buenavista stadium was completely destroyed (it was used to dig trenches in by the Nationalist Army). It was decided that they could not play in the league and a play-off was called between Athletic de Madrid and Osasuna, three years after they'd been relegated together, to replace the Asturian side. By now Athletic had a new name after having merged with Aviación Nacional, Franco's Air Force. Athletic- Aviación beat Osasuna 3–1 and, under the management of goalkeeping legend Ricardo

Zamora, went on to win the league, finishing ahead of Sevilla. They won again the following season, with a new name, Atlético Aviación (Franco had decreed that foreign names should be banned). Real Madrid, who had now changed their name to its present form, finished a lowly sixth. As the sport gained in popularity, the city of Madrid had a new dominant team.

The confusion over name changes continued. In 1947 Los Colchoneros split with the Air Force and gained their current title 'Club Atlético de Madrid'. This didn't diminish their dominance. In 1947/8 their legendary front line 'La Delantera de Seda' (the silken forwards) started the season with a 5–0 destruction of El Real. In 1949 the team started poorly, finishing the first half of the season in 11th position. They sacked their manager, signing Argentinian Helenio Herrera, and finished the season as champions. Real were nearly relegated. Herrera won a second consecutive title in 1950/51, despite having an injury-prone forward line which became known as 'La Delantera de Cristal' (the crystal forwards).

These were boom years in Spanish football, and Atleti were picking up more and more fans in the city, destined to years of frustration. The balance of power was soon to change. Santiago Bernabéu, fed up of being president of the city's second team, bought Alfredo di Stéfano from Colombian team Millonarios. Real's rise was meteoric. They won 12 of the next 16 titles, and 27 out of the next 50. Atlético have been one of the few other teams to have brought their fans the joy of winning the league (in 1966, 1970, 1977 and as recently as 1996), but their victories were never capitalised on. And, crucially, they have never won a trophy in Europe. Real's rise to domestic dominance coincided with a period in which they conquered Europe, winning the first five European Cups. As a result they became Spain's most popular team, garnering support from all over the country.

But they still aren't Madrid's favourite team. That night I go out for a night on the town with a group of people I meet. It's a wild swinging affair that takes in a number of bars in the area of Chueca and doesn't end until seven in the morning. Nothing compares with Madrid's nightlife. Hemingway put it well when he wrote 'to go to bed at night in Madrid marks you out as a little queer'. I meet scores of people, and virtually all of them support Atlético de Madrid. One of the last coherent conversations I remember is with a journalist called Miguel, an Atleti fan.

"Why do you support Atleti and not Real Madrid?" I ask.

"It's a family thing. My father was an Atleti fan, and his father before him. Most of the people who live in the city support Atleti. You will see that when you go to the Calderón on Saturday. In the Calderón you will see real football fans, not the sort of fair-weather fans that turn up to the Bernabéu. When we went down to the Segunda in 2000, the stadium was still nearly full every match. The atmosphere was tremendous. It still is tremendous. And you know why? Atlético fans support the team. Real Madrid fans just go along to see the team win."

## THURSDAY APRIL 15TH

I go down to Atocha station to meet Sid Lowe, who is coming back from Valencia after doing a television commentary for the Valencia v Bordeaux UEFA Cup semi-final, a game Valencia won 2–1 to qualify for the semis. Atocha was the scene of the bombing just over a month ago that has led to such cataclysmic changes in Spain. Since then, the city has got back to business and Atocha is working as normal. It's a wonderful station, worth going to even if you don't need to catch a train. It has its own palm house, overlooked by the best station café I have ever had a café con leche in. At first, apart from a number of black ribbons (the Spanish sign for mourning), I think that every reference to the atrocity has been erased. Then I find the main entrance (I have come in through the back one) and find a moving sight. The large curved window-front is covered in messages of condolence, wishes for peace, pictures of the dead, flowers, candles. Scores of people are standing there, thoughtfully, contemplating the enormity of the tragedy. One sign reads 'Life must go on . . . but we will never forget.'

Sid takes me to a restaurant in Plaza de la Paja, the original centre of the city when it was just a small town, before Felipe II made it the capital of the world. I gen up on the Real Madrid crisis in general and the Beckham crisis in particular. I wonder if, after everything, Beckham is still talking to the *Sun* and the *News of the World*.

"He's not talking to anyone," he says. "Eric [from the *Sun*] is still doing stuff – for example the signs at the training ground the other day. Anthony [*News of the World*] is lying low."

I wonder if either of them had anything to do with the story. "I don't think either of them knew anything about it before it came out. It's nothing to do with them at all."

"What do you think of the media coverage of the whole business in Spain?" I ask him.

"The football papers have hardly touched it. And I think the prevailing sentiment among the Spanish is 'What the hell? What can you expect? Good-looking guy all on his own out here.' They've come down on his side. Somehow the stories make him more human."

Real's crisis seems more pertinent. The newspapers have shown pictures of the team arriving with long faces at La Manga. *As* is full of a story about Roberto Carlos going to Chelsea; *Marca* is wondering which signings El Real will make in the summer. I ask Sid who the manager is likely to be next season.

"One's thing's for certain, it won't be Carlos Queiroz," he says. "He'll be back to Manchester United. His days were numbered from the start."

"It seems unfair."

"It's bloody unfair. He arrived thinking that he would have Makelele in the midfield and Milito in defence, and he still thought that the squad was short. Milito didn't work out and Makelele buggered off, with no-one to replace them. What's he supposed to do? He's been slated for making no rotations but what can he do? Every match Madrid play is important. Every defeat is seen as being a disaster. He can't just throw kids in. They're used to playing in the Segunda B, the equivalent of the English second division. How can they be expected to make the jump up to the Primera, when every game is a final? Queiroz was shafted from the start, and I, for one, feel sorry for him."

"How important is the derby?"

"Vitally important. El Real need to win it. And, you know what, however tired they are, I think they will."

## FRIDAY APRIL 16TH

I arrange to meet a journalist from *Marca*, Carlos González, in the Bernabéu. He is responsible for deciding how much weight to give to which story relating to Real Madrid in the newspaper. It's strange going to the stadium on a non-match day. There are still people buzzing around. Carlos is covering a meeting between all the presidents of the 'federaciones' of the clubs of the top two divisions. I sit through a boring twenty-minute press conference where men in black suits talk about the common problems they share liaising between fans and the club. Then we go for a caña in a nearby bar.

"Why has *Marca* not even mentioned Beckham's personal crisis?" I ask.

"Because we are a sports paper, and we feel that our readers are interested in sporting matters. Also we need to keep a good relationship going with the players, and we don't want to betray them in this manner. So this is the policy of the newspaper. Anyway, if we talked about all the players' personal lives, we wouldn't have room in our pages."

After he leaves I buy *El Mundo* and a glossy weekly gossip mag, *Sorpresa*, which has a picture of Beckham on the front. *El Mundo* is still going big on the story, talking about Rebecca Loos' latest set of allegations in an interview granted to Sky News. It talks, again, about the curious obsession England has with the story, which it calls 'David Beckham, his alleged infidelities, and two bisexual lovers'. Loos has said, it reports, 'there's something I know about him, an intimate part of his body, that only people who have slept with him know about.' It says that the *Sun* is having a field day, calling Loos the 'sleazy senorita' and joking that the secret could be a tattoo on his buttock reading 'Germany 1 England 5'.

## SATURDAY APRIL 17TH

Matchday. I'm sitting in Michael Robinson's office in the Canal Plus TV studios in Tres Cantos, a satellite town 24 kms from Madrid. You might remember Michael from his playing days as a bustling centre-forward at Preston, Manchester City, Brighton, QPR and Liverpool. I was a regular on the terraces when he played for Brighton and helped them get to the FA Cup Final in 1983. He was one of my heroes when I was a teenager.

I met Robinson ten years ago in the Costa Vasca Hotel in San Sebastián to interview him for the *Guardian* as part of a series about people who live in different European countries from their own. The interview proper, which started at ten at night, lasted 15 minutes. Then Robinson asked me if I wanted a drink. He said that he was having a gin and tonic, and would I like the same? In Spain the size of the drinks you are poured sometimes depends on how much the barman likes the look of you. Happily Robinson was then (and still is) one of the most popular men in the country.

He arrived in Spain to play for Osasuna at the end of his career, and loved the country so much he decided to stay. He got into television and showed a flair for it, so much so that he was soon given his own show by Canal Plus. The channel sells top football matches and Hollywood films to subscribers, but Robinson's show – called *El Día Después* (The Day After) went out to everybody who wanted it, in a decoded format. Broadcast since 1992 on Monday night, it took (and still takes) an irreverent look at the previous weekend's Spanish football.

The show was an immediate success, largely down to Robinson's ideas. Football had previously been treated with long-faced seriousness on Spanish TV and this show bucked the trend. Robinson's presentation style was light and jokey without being facile, and the items on the show were designed to make people laugh and to look at the fans at the games as much as the games themselves. When Míchel, Madrid's sturdy international midfielder, squeezed Colombian international Valderrama's balls in a league match in 1992 (rather like Vinnie Jones famously did to the young Gazza) Robinson ran the moment over and again, backwards and in slow motion, to the music from *the Sting* (*The Entertainer*). This was talked about all over the country, and *El Dia Despues's* ratings soared. Fans started singing 'Michel, Míchel maricon' (pansy) every time the square-jawed midfielder got the ball.

So there I was, all those years ago, sitting with one of Spain's top TV stars. The barman was obviously delighted to be serving Robinson, and the measure he gave him (and me) was enormous. We ended up with large goblets fuller of gin than tonic. Robinson, a great talker, told me things about his career that I couldn't believe, off the record of course. Four gins later I stumbled out of the hotel, stopping briefly to take a picture of him for the paper. The picture, needless to say, couldn't be used.

Ten years later Michael doesn't remember our last meeting. But he seems captivated by the idea for this book. He also wonders if I'm here to dig the dirt up on the Beckham affair.

"Not at all," I say, which is the truth. "I'm interested in what the Spanish think about him."

"There was this whole thing about him being here just to sell shirts when he first arrived," he replies, launching into a monologue that has me furiously scribbling notes. "I was one of the few people who disagreed. David Beckham is the England captain. And I, for one, have never known an England captain who is a tart. It just doesn't happen. Look at Kevin Keegan, Bryian Robson, Terry Butcher, Alan Shearer. Were they tarts? Of course they weren't. They all had fighting spirit. And David Beckham is no different. He is an extremely hard-working, dedicated professional with bags of fighting spirit and the Spanish soon realised that. So that opinion about him being a clothes horse, which was fairly widespread, didn't last long."

He's dressed in a crisp shirt, has his greying hair brushed back, and is wearing rimless glasses that give him an intelligent look which matches the deliberateness of his responses. Every ten minutes or so he lights a Marlboro red.

"What's more," he continues, "he looked so good. He was a sex symbol, with a fighting spirit, not your ordinary guy with a broken nose or a lump over his eyebrows. So he was almost immediately accepted. Not so Zinedine Zidane, who spent half a season trying to find his position when he arrived. They didn't know where to put him."

He takes a pause and lights another Marlboro.

"If anything is likely to go wrong, though, about him being here, it's going to be his marriage. David is a fighter (he uses the Spanish word 'luchador') and they love him for it here. But in Spain most people don't give a monkey's who she is. She wanders round with an entourage of bodyguards and chauffeurs and people think 'who does she think she is?' It must be heartbreaking for her. It was widely reported in the Spanish press that she said that 'everything smells of garlic' in Madrid, and though she denied ever having said it, it had a damaging effect on her image over here. So the only thing that really bothers people about David and Victoria over here is whether the whole business will affect his game or provoke him into leaving Real Madrid. That's the only angle there is."

Another cigarette. This is one of those interviews where you don't need to ask questions.

"Here [on the show] we haven't even mentioned the story. If David was seen a few nights before game pissed as a rat, that would be a different matter. What comes over to them about David is his love of football; he seems to them to be hugely dedicated to the game. And this whole situation hasn't taken anything away from that."

I'm whisked into a plush studio to watch the live broadcast of *El Día Antes* which goes out every Saturday lunchtime. I've seen it before; production standards are high, it's humorous, it's incisive, it's educational. It beats its British equivalents hands down. The biggest talking point of the show is the forthcoming derby. There is an item which shows a grandfather talking to his son about Atlético de Madrid's glorious history. They are going to the match together later in the evening. There are black and white reports of Atlético's triumphs in the '40s and '50s, and colour clips of their more recent successes. The grandfather's voice gets shaky with the emotion of describing all this to his grandson.

"Yeah, but all I want to see is Zinedine Zidane," says the kid.

There is also a piece about Real Madrid's vulnerability in the air. With a music backdrop they show that Real have conceded 16 goals this season from headers, and countless more crosses coming into the box and not being defended properly. The voiceover tells us that this is Real Madrid's Achilles heel, and that all Atlético have to do to score against their rivals is to lob the ball in the box. It shows a picture of Morientes, playing against Real in the Champions League, making this clear to a team-mate with hand gestures.

Afterwards I compliment Robinson on the high standard of the show. He invites me for a coffee in the local bar. I look at my watch. The match doesn't start till ten o'clock at night. There are still five hours to kick off. Plenty of time.

The hours pass quickly. And history repeats itself. A tropical-style downpour outside necessitates our staying in the bar longer than intended. Four huge gin and tonics, countless hilarious anecdotes and a long lesson in the ins and outs of 'Robinsonismo' (the broadcaster's lucid theories on how to make television programmes) later I find myself in a taxi bearing down on the Calderón stadium. The last thing Robinson has said to me is still in my head.

"Real Madrid fans are strange creatures. They hate losing. But if the team is losing 3–0, they think 'fuck you' and want them to lose 6–0. They feel betrayed, and they want the team to feel the same pain."

Things start moving quickly. Atlético de Madrid have asked all their fans to wear their team shirts today, and most of them seem to have complied. There's an hour till kick-off, but from the tumult outside it seems more like ten minutes. I've got press accreditation today (there hasn't been a ticket on sale for weeks) and, trying to find my way to my entrance, I'm blocked by a cordon of policemen. To my left there are 30 or so Ultra Sur corralled against the wall by the away fans' entrance. I start preparing to take a photograph of them but they look so menacing that I think better of it. I bump into the *Daily Telegraph* reporter Paul Hayward, the friend of a friend at home.

"I've just seen some fights down the street. It looks as if it's all about to kick off," he says. The fans are chanting, 'Ultra, Ultra Sur'. It's time to move. We get through the police cordon, flash our tickets into the infra-red machines and are inside the ground. We walk through what seems to be a shopping mall and into our seats. There are a score or so English journalists there, about four times as many as normal. Beckham is back in the news.

The atmosphere is great. The ground has two stands, a grandstand that we are in and a long, curved affair which surrounds the other three sides of the pitch. It's 57,000 capacity is filling up. To my left, behind the goal, there are thousands of Atleti fans already in their seats. They have put up several large banners. At ground level there are caricatures of the 11 Real Madrid players, above them a huge banner reading 'SON ONCE GALLINAS' (they are 11 chickens). Above is another banner, reading 'A POR ELLOS', the Spanish equivalent of 'get into them'. Over the tannoy a voice is commenting wildly on a PlayStation game which is being played out live on the big screen. Atleti get a goal. "El Niño!" shouts the guy. "El Niño scores!" El Niño is Atleti's 19-year-old international striker Fernando Torres. Unfortunately he won't score for real today, as he's suspended. The Atleti fans don't mind. They celebrate the goal as if were a real one, jumping up and down and waving their scarves.

"Atleti, Atleti!" they chant.

There's a great view of the Palacio Real, the royal palace, lit up, to my left. To my right I can see the Manzanares river and cars flashing past, aware, no doubt, that El Derbi is about to kick off. There is a huge whistle as the Real Madrid players run onto the pitch, wearing white. The Atleti fans' collage is completed, as a huge canvas cartoon wolf with gnashing great teeth is dropped down in front of them, presumably to eat the eleven chickens. The Ultra Sur, hemmed into a small section on my left, produce their own banner, a Spanish flag with a sword symbol on it. They set off flares. They carry a placard large enough to read the words 'Honour, Tradition and Valour'. Another banner comes down in the stand in front of me. 'Real Kings of Madrid son los Rojiblancos' it says in a mixture of English and Spanish (Madrid's real kings are the red and whites). The Atleti players run on to huge acclaim and there is an impressive show of red and white scarves. The Atletico hymn comes over the tannoy.

*Atleti, Atleti, Atlético de Madrid . . .*

The first attack is made by the home team as the fans jump up and down, waving their scarves and singing 'Madridista el que no bote' (whoever doesn't jump up and down is Madridista). The attack is broken down on the edge of the box. No matter, the Atleti fans are in fine voice, repeating three times, to the tune of 'here we go', 'Real Madrid, Real Madrid, Real Madrid,' before revealing the song's true sentiment, 'hijo de puta, Real Madrid.'

On five minutes Real Madrid break forward, and the ball is passed by Figo to Solari, who finds himself free on the left of the box. He takes the ball towards the bye-line, sees goalkeeper Aragoneses out of position and expecting a cross, and sidefoots it between the goalkeeper and his right-hand post. Real Madrid are in front! The Ultra Sur cheers are all that can be heard for a few seconds, then the Atleti fans react with their standard song. 'Atleti, Atleti'. Beckham, who has not yet touched the ball, is the first to reach Solari to congratulate him.

The game then dies, with Atlético fouling any Real Madrid player who dwells on the ball, and launching long balls into the box which are easily dealt with by Raúl Bravo and Pavón, the central defenders. Beckham, who has a more attacking role than normal as he is being partnered by Helguera rather than Guti, is having a quiet game. His most dramatic action in the first half is to leap high into the air, in trademark fashion, after a foul by Gaspar, who pulls his ponytail when he finally hits the ground. Beckham calls dramatically for a card. The referee doesn't oblige. It takes Atleti more than half an hour to muster a chance, a header just wide from a corner, closely followed by a shot by Ibagaza blocked on the edge of the box. The Atleti fans don't stop singing, but it's hardly a wolf against chickens out there, more like a pitbull thrown into a ring with an alsatian. I look over to Sid Lowe, sitting next to me, who is writing a piece on the game for the *Observer*, to be sent just after the final whistle. Thus employed, he's unusually quiet. The gist of his piece is that the Real Madrid crisis has been halted in its tracks.

At half time, the euphoric effect of the four monster gin and tonics having turned into a realisation that it is not very professional to drink that much before going into the press box. I chat to the journalists around me, most of whom seem to have developed a similar Anti-Madridismo to me this season. It takes an age for the second half to roll around, but when it does, it's worth the wait. Atleti have a new urgency about them and on two minutes the Greek forward Nikolaidis, on at the break, is sent clear. Pavón lunges from behind him in the box, and knocks him down. Penalty! The young defender gets the red card, Paunovic steps up to take the kick, and blasts it into the net. The Atleti fans go mad. The press box goes mad. I am bashed on the back by the man from the *Times* to my right. 1–1, game on. Sid looks worried, and starts changing the introduction to his piece. The crisis isn't over yet. One point isn't much use to Real Madrid. The game continues at a frenetic pace, with more effort than quality on display. Figo is nearly sliced in half by Nano, then puts Zidane through. The Frenchman's hurried shot is saved by Aragoneses. Then young Jorge gets put through in similar fashion, and has an age to run at Casillas. His inexperience shows; he shoots the ball straight at the goalkeeper, who blocks with his arm. The tension in the stadium is rising. The Atleti fans are sure of a victory: they rise out of their seats as Paunovic heads the ball . . . just wide.

Then on 77 minutes, Real get a corner on the left. Beckham doesn't take it; perhaps he has been relieved of that duty. Figo swings the ball into the box, Raúl goes up with the keeper, who seems to be knocked flying. Beckham heads the ball back into the six-yard box and Helguera, who looks offside, heads the ball into the net from a couple of yards out. 2–1. The Ultra Sur make themselves heard again.

"Surely the ref can't let that stand," says Sid. He does. Sid hacks anew at his introduction.

Atlético have time to react, but, with Real defending deep, can't find the space to create any chances. Casillas easily saves a Paunovic header from a free kick at the far post. The boardman holds up a sign indicating four minutes of extra time; after two of them Beckham is substituted. He claps at the Ultra Sur, as the Atleti fans vent their frustration at him.

'Hijo de puta!'

Then, a real chance. The ball flashes across the box; Jorge sticks out a leg. Connection. The ball whips just past the post. It's virtually the last action of the match. The final whistle is blown. Real's crisis seems to be over. It looks like Beckham, too, has ridden out his. He has got a valuable match-winning 'assist' here tonight, too. He won't be talking to the journalists today, I head into the night, trudging slowly to the metro among a slow-moving crowd of disgruntled Atleti fans, flags pointing down, their colourful attire faded by the night.

## RESULTS JORNADA 33

| **ATLÉTICO** | **1** | **REAL MADRID** | **2** |
|---|---|---|---|
| ALBACETE | 0 | CELTA | 2 |
| ATHLETIC | 4 | ZARAGOZA | 0 |
| MALLORCA | 1 | VILLARREAL | 2 |
| DEPORTIVO | 1 | VALLADOLID | 1 |
| OSASUNA | 1 | ESPANYOL | 3 |
| SEVILLA | 5 | RACING | 2 |
| VALENCIA | 2 | REAL SOCIEDAD | 2 |
| MURCIA | 0 | BETIS | 1 |
| BARCELONA | 3 | MÁLAGA | 0 |

## LA CLASIFICACIÓN

| | P | W | D | L | F | A | Pts |
|---|---|---|---|---|---|---|---|
| VALENCIA | 33 | 21 | 7 | 5 | 65 | 23 | 70 |
| **REAL MADRID** | **33** | **21** | **7** | **5** | **67** | **41** | **70** |
| BARCELONA | 33 | 18 | 9 | 6 | 55 | 34 | 63 |
| DEPORTIVO | 33 | 18 | 7 | 8 | 53 | 31 | 61 |
| ATHLETIC DE BILBAO | 33 | 14 | 9 | 10 | 46 | 40 | 51 |
| OSASUNA | 33 | 11 | 15 | 7 | 36 | 30 | 48 |
| ATLÉTICO DE MADRID | 33 | 13 | 9 | 11 | 40 | 41 | 48 |
| MÁLAGA | 33 | 14 | 4 | 15 | 44 | 48 | 46 |
| SEVILLA | 33 | 12 | 9 | 12 | 45 | 38 | 45 |
| VILLARREAL | 33 | 12 | 8 | 13 | 41 | 43 | 44 |
| REAL BETIS | 33 | 10 | 13 | 10 | 40 | 37 | 43 |
| REAL SOCIEDAD | 33 | 10 | 10 | 13 | 39 | 45 | 40 |
| REAL ZARAGOZA | 33 | 10 | 8 | 15 | 36 | 46 | 38 |
| RACING DE SANTANDER | 33 | 10 | 9 | 14 | 44 | 56 | 39 |
| VALLADOLID | 33 | 9 | 10 | 14 | 39 | 48 | 37 |
| ALBACETE | 33 | 10 | 7 | 16 | 32 | 42 | 37 |
| MALLORCA | 33 | 10 | 6 | 17 | 40 | 59 | 36 |
| ESPANYOL | 33 | 10 | 4 | 19 | 38 | 55 | 34 |
| CELTA DE VIGO | 33 | 7 | 12 | 14 | 43 | 60 | 33 |
| MURCIA | 33 | 3 | 11 | 19 | 25 | 51 | 20 |

# TWENTY
# BARCELONA

GOLFO DE VIZCAYA

OCÉANO ATLÁNTICO

Barcelona

**Real Madrid**

MAR MEDITERRÁNEO

N W E S

# TWENTY
# BARCELONA

## MONDAY APRIL 19TH

I try to take couple of days off the football, but it's hard. I have some travel articles to write about Madrid. I go to a bullfight in the magnificent Las Ventas bull-ring in the east of the city, considered to be the best in the country, with a 25,000 capacity. It's not close to half-full today: it's an early-season novillada, for rookie bullfighters who haven't yet earned the pony-tails which the experienced bullfighters traditionally wear. I'm in the cheap seats in the sun, and this section is full with a mixture of tourists and Spanish aficionados. The young matadors are good at posing and strutting and one gets a series of 'olés' for his capework, bringing the bull close to his body. But they all find it hard to kill the bulls cleanly with their swords. One bull vomits blood before dying and an American girl next to me leaves. La corrida de toros was the major spectator sport before football in Spain, and while there are no banners and singing, the crowd behaves in a similar way to the spectators in a football ground, applauding shows of bravado and hurling abuse at the picadors, the mounted lancers whose job it is to weaken the bull by spearing it in its back. It seems to me that Beckham has been more picador than matador this season: more concerned with damaging the opposition than gracefully going in for the kill.

I also check out the sporting facilities that Madrid is preparing for their bid for the 2012 Olympics, treading a lonely path round the city from swimming pool to swimming pool, ending up in the new half-built Estadio de Madrid on the outskirts of town. One stand is completed, a massive plate-shaped object which has earned the stadium the nickname 'La Peineta' as it looks like a flamenco dancer's comb. The stadium is to be completed, with its capacity increasing from 20,000 to 75,000, if Madrid's bid is successful. The city is certainly on the up. It's a long journey out there, and looking at an empty stadium under a cloudy sky rather depresses me. I feel trapped in this land-locked city. I'm dying to get back to Barcelona, to the sun, the sea. To fresh air, and light. But it won't be the same as it was before I left.

Brenda has gone to Ireland. She's left me here in Spain. I am to join her after the season is ended. I'm rather lonely, and rather sad, in this big city I have never got to understand, or love. I've spent much of the season travelling on my own, but this time there will be nobody to go back to in Barcelona. I can empathise with how Beckham must have been feeling all these months. I wonder if his days in Spain are numbered, with constant rumours linking him to Chelsea. *El Mundo* is trying to draw out the Beckham crisis as much as possible, but the story has no more legs. The sports papers are full of Madrid's winning goal against Atleti. It looks like Raúl pushed the goalkeeper, and Helguera was offside when he headed the ball into the net. It seems unfair; it seems inevitable. Valencia stay top after drawing at home with Real Sociedad, but only on goal difference. They equalised in the last minute: a great goal from Mista. Madrid look to have the easier end-of-season run-in, despite hosting their old rivals Barcelona on Sunday.

The newspapers report a new Beckham haircut. He's shaved it all off. Or maybe Victoria did it, Delilah-style. I think of the young matadors, hoping to earn their pony-tails, and wonder whether Beckham has got rid of his because he doesn't feel he is playing good enough football to merit it. Is it the hairdressing equivalent of rolling your sleeves up? Perhaps it signals a new start in his life, in his Madrid career. Is his crisis over? Is Madrid's? I take a night train to Barcelona. Early on Tuesday morning, I arrive home to an empty flat. Brenda's wardrobe has no clothes in it.

**THURSDAY APRIL 20TH**

El Clásico II is approaching and the war of words has started in the sports papers. Barcelona president Joan Laporta said on Tuesday in *El Mundo Deportivo* that he had a dream in which Barcelona won the game in Madrid, and he celebrated by dancing on the roof of his car in La Castellana, the swanky Madrid thoroughfare where Real's old training ground is located. Helguera replied the next day that if he saw him doing that, he'd push him off. With Ronaldo still injured, Ronaldinho, Barcelona's 24-year-old Brazilian midfielder, is being seen as the man most likely to decide the match. Since losing to Real Madrid in the Nou Camp, Barcelona have been the form team in La Liga. They won their first nine league matches of the year and remain unbeaten in 2004. They signed Edgar Davids, 'El Pitbull', on loan from Juventus in the winter transfer window, and his fighting qualities in midfield have given both Ronaldinho and the Spanish international midfielder Xavi new purpose and freedom. As a knock-on effect, the whole club seems rejuvenated and Barcelona are really up for the game against Madrid. A win will put them four points behind their great rivals, with four games to play. Only three months back they were 18 points behind. And they have the momentum, while Real are tiring.

## FRIDAY APRIL 22ND

The whole city seems rejuvenated, too, as the first summery days of the year bathe the buildings in sunlight. I'm so pleased to be here. It's starting to feel more and more like home, as I keep returning from other parts of Spain, from the unfamiliar to the familiar. When it's hot, La Barceloneta, my seaside barrio, fills up. The swimming pool I've been going to all winter, a wonderful outdoor heated affair which I've virtually had to myself sometimes, suddenly gets packed. You can't get a sun-lounger on the terrace overlooking the beach, and have to make do with a plastic seat. Everyone is excited about the upturn in the weather and the upturn in Barcelona's fortunes. Everyone is excited about El Clásico. I overhear an old man talking about Beckham. He's in the middle of a circle of five or six people but he's the only one talking. He's making them laugh. Judging by the dark colour of his skin, he's one of the perennial bathers who take their clothes off on the beach all year round. He has a white beard, a small pot belly.

"You know what, I'd rather have Ronaldinho than Beckham," he says, doing an impression of the Brazilian player, his thumbs and little fingers sticking in the air. "Beckham wasn't the same after Christmas. I read an article which said that his body wasn't used to getting a winter break, and he never recovered his fitness. But who knows the truth?"

He goes on to make some comments which make his entourage roar with laughter about the differences between the Englishman and the Brazilian. At the beginning of the season the two men were considered to be the two major signings of the season by Spanish clubs, and there is a lot of 'who was the better buy' going on. At Christmas, the on-form Beckham would probably have got most votes, as Ronaldinho was playing in such a struggling team. But Barcelona's renaissance has been punctuated by some amazing goals and moves by the Brazilian (including my favourite where he looks one way and passes the other) whilst Beckham's form has suffered, and there's little doubt who looks the better buy at the moment. There's little doubt who looks more likely to play a key role in Saturday's derby either.

## SATURDAY APRIL 24TH

I decide to watch El Clásico in a bar in my barrio, Jai-Ca, which specialises in seafood tapas and is the home of a Barcelona peña, 'Penya Culés Barceloneta'. 'Culés' means 'arses' and is the nickname of the Barcelona fans, dating back to the days when those without tickets used to sit on a wall to watch the matches and all you could see of them from below was their bottoms. I arrive there three-quarters of an hour before kick-off, but the seven tables and all the seats are already occupied. I park myself in the best standing spot against the bar, in front of the television set. I'm just in time. Soon the place is full.

There are vast wine barrels behind the bar, with bets of what the score will be chalked up on them. It's a sweepstake; you pay three euros and if you win, share the prize money with anyone else who has gone for the same score. I put three euros on 0–0. That wouldn't be my prediction for the game, but only one other person has gone for it and I estimate I'll win 100 euros if no-one scores. At least I'll be right at the start of the game. I also buy a litre of wine which comes in a square, corked bottle. I don't want to keep having to order drinks.

The atmosphere in the bar is already heavy with expectation, and the management push it up a notch by playing the Barça hymn on the loud-speakers. My anti-Madridismo and my return to the city I have  started finally to feel at home in, makes me join in, though I find it hard to phrase the Catalan words. A woman at the table in front of me, her back to the television, stands up towards the end, her arms waving in the air, she conducts the crowd in their singing. She's about 45, with curly black hair, well-dressed in a white cotton jumper. It's a brilliant hymn, one which ends in a crescendo as the popular name for the club is repeated three times.

"Barça, Barça, Baaaaarça!"

They play several versions of the song. A heavy metal version is on when the Barcelona players run onto the pitch. Ronaldinho comes on like a 100-metres sprinter off his blocks; there's a fond cheer. Then a salsa version comes on, and the game kicks off. Figo fills the screen amid whistles and boos. Barcelona fans will never forgive him, but their fortunes seem finally to be on the up after a four-year depression following his treacherous move to Madrid. El Real mount their first attack and Figo is involved. The music is turned off, and the commentary comes on. It's time for serious business now. The noise in the place is incredible. A young guy is trying to make a call from the payphone on the wall in front of me, but can't get heard so he steps into the toilet, and closes the door behind him, the coiled cable of the phone following him in. Beckham, who is difficult to distinguish from Cambiasso with his new haircut, takes a corner. Raúl Bravo heads wide. The tension mounts.

And mounts, and mounts. Real Madrid have started the first half brilliantly and Barcelona are on the back foot. Ronaldinho is hardly in the game: Beckham, Zidane, Cambiasso and Figo are running the midfield. The bar is so crowded there are people on the pavement outside, and others almost directly under the TV screen, looking up. There's no more room and the waiters are finding it hard to squeeze through with their trays. The woman in white still has her back to the screen. She's looking at the crowd.

"More atmosphere, we're too quiet!" she shouts. Then she gets out a kazoo and plays the Barça hymn on it. Many in the crowd sing the chorus.

"Barça, Barça, Baaaaarça!"

But, of course, the players are playing in a different atmosphere, and there are shots of the Madrid crowd at the stadium cheering on their team. And virtually all the play comes from the El Real. Beckham hits a shot over the bar. Zidane shoots low, Barça's young goalkeeper Víctor Valdés can't hold onto it and Raúl is quick to the rebound. Valdés saves again, the ball falling to Roberto Carlos, who hits a thunderous shot which Puyol saves with his face on the line. All in the space of ten seconds. The triple-let off is greeted with joy in the bar. The barman rings an old-fasioned brass bell hanging up behind the bar, and everyone cheers. A song starts up, which most everyone joins in,

'Madrid is burning, it's burning Madrid."

The woman in white looks at my notebook, asks me what I'm doing. She says she is a journalist, too. Politics.

"Why have you got your back to the screen?" I ask her.

"I couldn't watch it." She pats her chest several times to indicate the possibility of a heart attack. "But I watch the crowd. I can tell what's going on from the crowd."

Madrid mount another attack. Valdés makes another save, Raúl heads the rebound onto the crossbar. Puyol makes a weak clearance, Figo hits in a shot, Valdés makes another wonderful save. Another let-off. The bell rings madly. More chanting. Figo gets a yellow card for protesting.

"Ese portugués, hijo de puta es!" chant the crowd. The bell rings for a full 30 seconds. Soon after the referee blows his whistle. Half time. Relief. There's not much wine left in my bottle.

The second half starts in much the same vein. People have relaxed and started chatting, ordering tapas and drinks, and it takes a little time for everyone's attention to turn back to the TV screen. It's a little annoying. A Roberto Carlos near-miss three minutes in gets everyone to shut up.

The tension returns. Cambiasso runs at Valdés, who has received a short back-pass. Valdés neatly sidesteps the Argentinian, who goes flying off the pitch.

"Olé," shout the crowd. The barman rings the bell.

On 53 minutes a Beckham cross floats into the box, Roberto Carlos chests it down and Solari volleys the ball left-footed past Valdés into the goal. 1–0. There goes my bet. There are a few shouts of 'hijo de puta'. I look round to see the majority of the 150 or so people behind me demonstrating identical body language, their heads cradled in their hands, elbows up. I realise that I am in the same position. The TV shows the league table as it would be if this were the final result, with Real Madrid at the top. Valencia are to play later, a difficult away game in Bilbao. "Hijos de puta," I whisper.

Barça's manager Frank Rijkaard reacts to the goal by bringing on Luis Enrique and Kluivert for the ineffectual Overmars and Saviola. In the Bernabéu the fans hurl their abuse at Luis Enrique, a man who made the opposite move to Figo several years ago, swapping the white of Madrid for the red and blue of Barcelona. In the Jai-Ca the Barcelona fans give him an ovation. The bell rings. Barcelona gain more urgency. Van Bronckhorst runs down the left, puts in a looping cross which strands Casillas, and Kluivert heads the ball in from five yards. There's a moment of silence, then the place explodes. Gooool! The Barça hymn comes over the loudspeakers, and everyone sings along, conducted by the woman in white, who is now standing on her chair.

'We have a name everyone knows . . .

Barça, Barça, Baaaarça!'

The goal is shown again, and I watch the crowd watching it. Everyone is grinning, laughing, shouting, waving their arms in the air. 1–1!

Real Madrid now look tired and Barcelona pour forward. Ronaldinho, who has been inconspicuous so far, wins a free kick outside the box and steps up to take it. He looks at the ball, twitches his thumbs, looks at the seven-man wall and shoots over. Then on the halfway line, Puyol and Figo go for a 50-50 challenge. Figo dives in, studs first, and clips the Catalan, who flies into the air as if hit by an explosion. The referee shows Figo a yellow card, then a red. The bell rings wildly, the crowd celebrating as if another goal has been scored. Figo eventually walks off the pitch, muttering dark Portuguese insults. The Barça anthem comes on the speakers again. There is a sense now that Barcelona could win the game. The tension shifts a gear, now laden with expec-tation. Beckham does a jumping-bean dive, even though he doesn't seem to have been touched by Davids, then handles the ball on his return to earth and gives away a free-kick. The whole crowd jeers. It must be the low-point of his career in Spain, caught in slow-motion on camera for all to see.

The clock ticks down. Real Madrid close ranks. Ten minutes to go. Five minutes to go. If Barcelona don't score, they will be seven points behind Madrid, far too many to catch up in four games. If they score, however, it will only be four. Ronaldinho gets the ball outside the area, spots Xavi running in front of him and loops the ball into his path. Xavi, in front of Casillas, his back half to the goal, gets a foot on the ball and directs it gently into the net. I look around at the fans, who are jumping up and down, arms in the air. Somebody is waving a half-litre glass of beer, which is slopping all over the people around him. No-one cares. The hymn comes on again, sung with even more gusto than before and directed by the woman, her arms windmills, a vast grin across her face.

'A valiant cry, we have a name that everyone knows,

Barça, Barça, Baaarça'

The music stays on, nobody needs the commentary now. But Barcelona have some defending to do. Four minutes of extra time are signalled. The heavy metal version of the hymn starts up. Real don't look like they have any gas left. Ronaldinho hits the ball just wide of the post. Will it matter? A grinning old busker, several teeth missing, is trying to cash in on the euphoria, playing his accordion under the TV set. You can't hear what he's playing for the noise. I look from the screen in front of me, to the joyful crowd behind, from screen to crowd, from screen to crowd, and realise I have a wide grin on my face, too. The referee raises his arms, there's another cheer. It's over! Barça have won!

Most everybody spills out on the street. I meet my landlord, Toni, at the door. He hugs me. In the confusion I don't recognise him. "We won, we won," he says. Then he reminds me that I was two weeks late with the rent last month.

## RESULTS JORNADA 34

| | | | |
|---|---|---|---|
| MÁLAGA | 1 | DEPORTIVO | 1 |
| ESPANYOL | 3 | ATLÉTICO | 1 |
| BETIS | 2 | REAL SOCIEDAD | 1 |
| CELTA | 1 | OSASUNA | 0 |
| RACING | 0 | ALBACETE | 2 |
| VALLADOLID | 1 | MALLORCA | 3 |
| ZARAGOZA | 4 | SEVILLA | 4 |
| VILLARREAL | 1 | MURCIA | 0 |
| **REAL MADRID** | **1** | **BARCELONA** | **2** |
| ATHLETIC | 1 | VALENCIA | 1 |

## LA CLASIFICACIÓN

| | P | W | D | L | F | A | Pts |
|---|---|---|---|---|---|---|---|
| VALENCIA | 34 | 21 | 8 | 5 | 66 | 24 | 69 |
| **REAL MADRID** | **34** | **21** | **7** | **6** | **68** | **43** | **68** |
| BARCELONA | 34 | 19 | 9 | 6 | 57 | 35 | 66 |
| DEPORTIVO | 34 | 18 | 8 | 8 | 54 | 32 | 62 |
| ATHLETIC | 34 | 14 | 10 | 10 | 47 | 41 | 52 |
| OSASUNA | 34 | 11 | 15 | 8 | 36 | 31 | 48 |
| ATLÉTICO | 34 | 13 | 9 | 12 | 41 | 44 | 48 |
| VILLARREAL | 34 | 13 | 8 | 13 | 42 | 43 | 47 |
| MÁLAGA | 34 | 14 | 5 | 15 | 45 | 49 | 47 |
| SEVILLA | 34 | 12 | 10 | 12 | 49 | 42 | 46 |
| BETIS | 34 | 11 | 13 | 11 | 42 | 38 | 46 |
| ALBACETE | 34 | 11 | 7 | 16 | 34 | 42 | 40 |
| REAL SOCIEDAD | 34 | 10 | 10 | 14 | 40 | 47 | 40 |
| MALLORCA | 34 | 11 | 6 | 17 | 43 | 60 | 39 |
| ZARAGOZA | 34 | 10 | 9 | 15 | 40 | 50 | 39 |
| RACING | 34 | 10 | 9 | 15 | 44 | 58 | 39 |
| VALLADOLID | 34 | 9 | 10 | 15 | 40 | 51 | 37 |
| ESPANYOL | 34 | 11 | 4 | 19 | 41 | 56 | 37 |
| CELTA | 34 | 8 | 12 | 13 | 44 | 60 | 36 |
| MURCIA | 34 | 3 | 11 | 20 | 25 | 52 | 20 |

GOLFO DE VIZCAYA

Deportivo
la Coruña

OCÉANO ATLÁNTICO

**Real Madrid**

MAR MEDITERRÁNEO

N
W
E
S

# TWENTY ONE
# LA CORUÑA

**FRIDAY APRIL 30TH**

I wake up in Galicia again, after spending the night half-sleeping in the middle bunk of a small six-man cell on the train from Barcelona. It's raining, of course. It's already light, and while I'm regaining full alertness with a café con leche in the cafeteria wagon, a number of sights through the window help me to acclimatise. Two horses drinking water from a wheelbarrow; rows of enormous cabbages in a field; a deer in the clearing of a pine forest freezing in fright then taking flight; two makeshift football goals next to a rich brown ploughed field; and, to prove we're not in Western Ireland, a stork making a poor landing in a bramble patch. I get a text message from Brenda, from Dublin.

'BIG NEWS,' it reads. 'BECKS COMING HOME'.

I send a message back to her to get more information (no asterisks included). She replies that it's all over the Irish and UK papers that Beckham's moving back to England next season, to play for Arsenal or Chelsea. It turns out just to be more speculation, from a 'close source'. But the Chelsea rumour is clearly gaining impetus.

When I arrive in La Coruña, at ten in the morning, I buy *Marca* to find out more over another coffee in a bar across from the station. There's nothing about Beckham. Another item of news dominates the front page. Real Madrid's appeal to the Referee's Federation against the Figo's yellow card (for his studs-up challenge on Puyol last weekend) has succeeded. The Portuguese winger will be allowed to play against Deportivo tomorrow. This seems scandalous, even for *Marca*, who have contacted a number of Valencia players and officials for their reaction.

"They've handed Real Madrid La Liga. They might as well just start celebrating it now," complains their captain, David Albelda.

"Why don't the Federation announce that we have to start 2–0 down against Betis (Valencia's opponents on Sunday)? adds Jesús Barradina, vice president. "They could have handicaps, like in golf. It was a red card, and they annulled it. They have no shame." It does seem scandalous. Whether he hit Puyol or not (something which has been debated all week in bars and workplaces all over the country) it was a dangerous, potentially career-ending challenge: a definite card.

Real are at full strength, with Ronaldo fit again and Beckham over a muscle-injury scare. They start as favourites, despite not having won at Dépor's Riazor stadium since 1991. Dépor are likely to be putting out what will virtually be their second team. They face one of the biggest matches of their history on Tuesday, a Champions League semi-final second leg against Porto in Riazor and it is taken for granted that their Basque manager Javier Irureta will only field players who are not in his starting line-up plans for the European game. For once Real Madrid are not the main attraction. I ring up Dépor's press officer, Rafael, to see if there's a training session this afternoon. He tells me to hop in a taxi, the last open session before the game is just about to finish, and there will be a press conference afterwards.

The taxi driver heads immediately for the motorway and drives me towards Lugo, where I've just come from. At a traffic light he winds down his window and asks another taxi driver directions. I ask him if it's far. "About 20 kms," he says, in that lovely Galician accent that sounds like an Italian speaking Spanish. "They say that it's a high-quality installation. They've only been using it for the last three years or so. I've never been." His round-about route proves this, as I sit in the back getting increasingly frustrated at the mounting price and the advancing hour as we stop three more times for directions and drive two kilometres past what eventually proves to be our turning. The final price is 28 euros. I think I might have missed the press conference. And as the cab drives off I realise that my mobile phone must have fallen out of my pocket onto the back seat.

Within a few minutes I'm more relaxed. The hilly, wooded countryside is lovely, the birds are singing their spring songs, the lush green training pitches are the best I've seen, and from the fifty-or-so journalists hanging round outside the square offices of the facility, I realise I haven't yet missed anything. What's more, mobile phones are the one object that you can ring up when you've lost them, to ask them where they are. And it's stopped raining.

Most of the journalists seem to be local, but I bump into Guillem Balaguer, the Sky Sports Spanish football expert I met in Málaga. He tells me that he is going to commentate on the Barcelona v Espanyol Catalan derby tomorrow for Sky.

"So you're going to be objective?" I ask, knowing which team he supports.

He laughs. "I'm going to be wearing my Espanyol shirt in the commentary box. You're the one who's supposed to be objective." His (jovially put) comment sends me into reflection. *Am* I being objective in what I'm doing? I started out my adventure with an objective viewpoint, but the more I've been sucked into the world of Spanish football, the more biased I've become. There's no doubt about it, I'm an anti-Madridista. I get a strong feeling of schadenfreude when they lose. Then I realise that every football fan I have met in Spain has either been a Madrid fan or an anti-Madridista. It's like a football civil war, which divides the country into two camps. I read in a recent survey done by *El Pais* newspaper that 38 per cent of football supporters in Spain are Real Madrid fans. But that leaves 62 per cent who aren't. Was it inevitable for me to fall this mindset, once I began to feel part of things in Spain?

Guillem is here to interview Dépor's defender Andrade. The Portuguese/Brazilian stopper is still waiting for the outcome of an appeal against his sending-off for play-kicking his best friend and ex-team-mate Deco during the first leg of the semi-final against Porto. "He is my friend," he said, rather sweetly, in English, to the referee Markus Merk, on seeing the red card. Unfortunately the German official didn't have a sense of humour. Nobody is holding out any hope of the appeal being successful. Still, this does mean that Andrade is likely to play the league game against El Real, alongside fellow Brazilians Mauro Silva, also suspended from the semi, and Djalminha, a hell-raising play-maker loved by the fans but considered too erratic to make the first-team with much regularity. Djalminha will always be remembered for one particular bit of skill which is often shown on the TV in Spain, a 'lambreta' (double-footed back flick over the head) on the edge of the box which nearly led to a goal against Real Madrid a couple of years ago. He's also remembered, according to my taxi driver, for his nights out on the town with friends like former Brazil striker 'O Animal' Edmundo, one of which, apparently, ended up in a fist-fight with an English tourist over a game of cards.

It's Djalminha who is first up for interview as I make my way to the second row of seats. I can just see him past the bottles of water that are always placed in front of players and managers in Spanish press conferences, with a big sign on top announcing their make, just in case you can't read the label. Unfortunately the Brazilian's conversation isn't as interesting as his style of play or sense of night-time fun, and he speaks with such a heavy accent the only thing that I can understand is that he's not saying much of any content.

Another player who will be facing Real Madrid is Lionel Scaloni, the Italian-Argentine who had a scuffle with Beckham in the Bernabéu earlier in the season, and who claimed that Beckham 'touched his (own) genitals' – a gesture he found so upsetting that he refused to shake his hand after the game, and has more recently said that he will refuse to shake it if it is proffered tomorrow. He's in his twenties, with jet-black spiky gelled hair and long sideburns. He is asked a couple of standard questions. I have one of my own. I've been building up to this moment all season. I've written the question down and checked with a nearby journalist if the Spanish is correct. There's a pause and Scaloni looks around for a final question. I pluck up courage.

"Is there still any morbo between you and Beckham?"

He looks at me, a little put out by the question. "No, there's nothing." It seems like he's going to stop there, but he carries on. "I've got nothing against Beckham, or anyone else. The match isn't Scaloni against Beckham, it's Deportivo against Real Madrid, and I want all three points. In the last match that was the talking point, but it should be left on the field. These things happen in the game of football." It's one of those non-answers designed to side-step the issue, but at least I've asked my first press conference question in Spanish.

The last of the three men up for interview is Javier Irureta, Deportivo de la Coruña's Basque manager, who sensibly shortens his surname from 'Iruretagoyena', and is one of my favourite characters in Spanish football. He's clearly an intelligent man, whose honest approach often leads to problems with his star players (such as Djalminha and the Sevillian striker Tristan). But he is a fine manager, architect of Dépor's only ever league championship in 2000, their only Copa del Rey win in 2002, and the inspiration behind the team's stunning recent 4–0 win over Milan in the quarter-finals of the Champions League. Dépor were 4–1 down from the first leg and Irureta promised that he would 'walk to Santiago on his knees' if the team got through, a promise he has yet to fulfil. (2004 is a 'Holy Year' for nearby Santiago: I've seen pilgrims with their wooden staffs and cockleshell hats all over the country, all year.)

Irureta has a good relationship with the journalists; there's none of the tension you feel when Queiroz gives press interviews (though to be fair, he's under a lot less pressure in provincial La Coruña). With a bright half-smile on his face, he fields questions about the Figo case ("everyone has a different opinion on these matters") and on rumours that Valencia have offered Deportivo players a win bonus ("how did I know that was going to be the next question? We need no extra motivation, we already get enough from our fans"). Then he's asked about his rotation system.

"What is this rotation you always ask about?" he says. "We know that the earth rotates around the sun. That is rotation. I have a squad and

I play a squad system. Nobody is anybody else's substitute. There are just two players for every position and I play the player who is in better form. If one player is tired, or needs to be saved for another game, then I will rest them. It's very simple."

Dépor have a player-signing policy which is the opposite of Madrid's. They tend to buy promising young players who've played a few seasons in Spain, Portugal, Argentina or Brazil. Irureta eases them into the team gently, allowing them time to grow within the squad. He has used the same formation as Real Madrid this season, but with a more defensive philosophy. Dépor rarely force the pace if they don't need to, preferring to sit back and attack on the counter, relying on the vision and skill of their play-maker, normally Valerón, to move things quickly up the field when their opponents lose the ball. It's a well-structured, tight and effective system, and so well-established that different players, trained in Irureta's ways, can be easily be inserted into it without disrupting its balance.

I get a lift back to town from Armando, a journalist on the local sports paper *Campeón Deportivo*. I ask whether Dépor will be up for the game tomorrow. "They'll be up for it, all right," he says. "The players who are playing know they won't be in the starting line-up on Tuesday, but they'll want to try to impress Irureta, so he gives them some minutes as substitutes. That's enough motivation. It won't be easy for El Real, especially as our squad is so strong. Even though we'll be missing our best players, there will probably be nine or ten internationals starting the game tomorrow." It's a far cry from Real Madrid's situation. When he drops me off, back at the train station, I phone my phone from a phone box. The taxi driver answers. Within five minutes he's found me and handed it back. I like this town.

I find a hotel and eat a cheap menu del día. It's the worst meal I've had in a long time, tasteless paella followed by cold and bony hake in breadcrumbs, and a bottle of poor red wine. With the coffee, without me asking, they bring a small, long-necked glass bottle with a metal spout in the cork. It's aguardiente (literally 'firewater'), the local grappa, to give the coffee a kick. The bottle is designed so that not much of the liquid can come out at a time. When the waitress isn't looking, I unstop the cork and pour in a slug. I realise the little fat eleven-year-old kid who's been in charge of lopsidedly putting the table cloth on and bringing me the wrong food, has seen me. I wink, conspiratorially, and he smiles back, shyly. Scaloni comes onto the TV, answering my question, then Irureta. They show Djalminha's 'lambreta' again.

I walk round La Coruña, which is rather more prosperous-looking and less industrial than its neighbour, Vigo, though smaller, with a population of just 320,000. The city is built on a mushroom-shaped peninsular with most of the shops and bars located in the stem. My walk starts on the curved sandy city beach, and immediately I'm rewarded by the sight of Riazor, Dépor's good-looking stadium, overlooking the far end of the sand. At the other end is the Hotel Meliá, where Real are to arrive that night. They'll be able to see the stadium from their hotel rooms. I find myself hoping that this puts fear into them: in the past few years they have lost 5–2, 4–0 twice and 3–0 twice there.

Beyond the hotel is the Torre de Hercules, a grim, Dickensian-looking lighthouse which I climb to get a view of the city. It's been built to withstand the elements, and has the beach on one side and the vast angular cranes of the dockyards on the other. I sit on the rocks at the edge of the peninsula. No-one else is around. It feels like the edge of the world. Soon I am completely overcome by the power of nature, as the waves crash below me, churning the moody blue sea white and coating me in fine spray.

I walk for four hours, ending up in the city's main square, just off the marina, Plaza María Pita. It's named after a local heroine, who saved La Coruña from invasion by the English in 1589. Sir Francis Drake (who the Spanish call 'that pirate Francis Drake') attempted an invasion of Portugal, taking advantage of free passage allowed by the damage done to the Spanish Armada after its disastrous attempt to invade England the previous year. An attack on La Coruña was the first stage of Drake's invasion. A fleet of 80 ships carrying 14,000 soldiers attacked the city, breached its walls, and a vicious hand-to-hand struggle ensued. The English looked to be winning the battle when local lady María Pita, her husband dead at her feet, took up his sword and killed an English standard bearer. This action rallied the Spanish, who went on to repulse the English attack. Pita is as big a heroine in Spain as Drake is a hero in England. In the centre of the square there's a bronze statue of her, her husband dead at her feet. She's holding a spear in the air, and a sword in her other hand. A flame burns 24 hours a day at her feet, above the legend 'Libertad'.

It's a story of the underdog triumphing against odds, one that the local team has taken on board. In the last ten years Dépor have turned themselves from a little-fancied provincial club, usually in the Segunda, into a team on the brink of a Champions League final. It is some achievement, mostly down to the brash, locally-born president César Augusto Lendoiro, a small man with big vision, who is extremely popular in town.

In the evening I go looking for Deportivo fans. This is the biggest week in their history, and there are blue-and-white scarves and flags all around town. The buses all have blue-and-white flags on their wing mirrors; even the wooden boards protecting roadworks are painted in the club colours.

I get chatting to José, the owner of a bar decked out in blue and white, the centre of the 'Peña Base'. José is about 50, and runs a peña which supports Dépor's 'equipo filial' (a cross between the reserve team and the youth team), currently in the Segunda B. I ask him how many young-sters have made it through to the first team.

"The only one is Fran," he says. Fran is the team captain, coming to the end of his career, a player who now relies more on guile than pace.

"How old is he?"

"34."

"There's no 'canterano' (former youth-teamer) younger than him in the first team squad?"

"No-one. It's terrible. The club have a policy of buying players and rarely give youth-teamers a chance. Galicia has never been a great place for producing young talent because there are few facilities for them to develop. Every player has been bought from another club. That's why we are in so much debt."

"How much debt?"

"140 million euros, at the last count."

I ask him if he prefers Madrid's system of Zidanes and Pavones, where at least the youngsters get a chance.

"I think that it is exaggerated. Young players need a chance but you can't throw too many of them in at the deep end at the same time, or the team won't work. Look at what happened to Rubén. (The Real Madrid defender, substituted after 24 minutes in Seville, was eventually packed off on loan to Borussia Moenchengladbach.) "You need to introduce them gradually, one at a time. Barcelona have done this well. They have a lot of canteranos in the team, but you never felt that there was too much pressure on them. I like the way Barcelona do things. They have a fantastic youth team set-up – La Masía – and you can see the products coming through. Iniesta, Valdés, Oleguer, Puyol. Each at their own pace."

The bars are starting to empty. I look in to one and see Rebecca Loos on the TV. So I walk in, their only customer. Loos, looking thin and nervous, is being interviewed by a panel of four journalists on the private Antena 3 channel. Every time they ask her a question, she does an inadvertent horsey laugh. They are giving her a much harder time than political correspondents give the Spanish politicians on the TV.

"What did you damage more, the marriage or the Beckham brand?" she is asked.

That laugh. "The marriage," she says. She talks about how she may become a TV presenter in Holland. Her Spanish is excellent, with a slight English accent.

"Which part of Beckham's body do you most like?"

"Everything."

"No, give us one part."

"Everything."

"Nothing in particular?"

"Everything."

There are text messages addressed to her at the bottom of the screen. They have received 5,343 messages. Some are insulting, some admiring. When the programme is over I leave, asking the barman on the way what he thinks of her.

"Good luck to her. She's earned herself a lot of money," he says.

I switch from Rebecca, to David, and have a beer in the Meliá Hotel. It is midnight. There is no sign of any of the players. I head for a bar where I have been told by Arximelo, from Vigo, that there is another peña. But I get lost, and ask a group of lads in their early thirties for directions.

"You're looking for Dépor fans? That's not difficult. Everyone in the town is a Dépor fan. We are all Dépor fans! Join us!"

So I do. We go from one bar to the next. To the next, to the next, to the next. The city's night-life centres around Calle San Andrés, the spine of the stem of the mushroom. Before midnight everybody goes to the east of the stem, to a series of streets popularly known as 'Calle de los Vinos' to drink wine and eat tapas. Then they cross to the west for late night 'copas': spirits and beer. It's a ball. We find ourselves in a bar where they're playing only English music from the '70s and '80s. The Clash, The Jam, David Bowie. There's a guy known as 'Rojo' (Red) who says he was part of the Dépor ultra group, Riazor Blues. It rings a bell, and I remember a story, which I ask him about. We are at the stage of the evening where you can be frank to strangers.

"Wasn't that the group where one member killed another this season?" It was. I get all the details.

In the first round of the Copa del Rey, in October, the Spanish FA makes Primera División clubs play against local clubs from the Segunda B in the lower division team's ground. This season Dépor were scheduled to play against Compostela, from Santiago, 70 kilometres down the road. It was a public holiday in La Coruña and 2,000 Deportivo fans went along to the game, 500 of them from the extreme left-wing ultra group, Riazor Blues. This was much more than expected – there were only 34 police present at the game. There isn't much of a history of violence between the two sets of fans – the teams have rarely played in the same division – but a number of the 'Compos' fans also support Vigo and some were wearing their light blue shirts to the game. Vigo and Dépor have a long-standing rivalry. As the match neared its end, with Dépor winning 2–0, it all kicked off. The Riazor Blues threw their seats at the Compos fans and there was a fight on the terraces. The police inside the ground – a group of only 12 officers – tried to charge the fans, to stop the violence, but were well outnumbered and had to retreat. The fighting spilled into the streets outside the stadium.

Manuel Ríos, a Dépor fan, was walking from the game with his girl-friend, Clara Castro, and another friend, and they came across a group of Riazor Blues attacking a 14-year-old Compos fan. According to reports, Manuel went in to try to stop the fight and was karate-kicked in the chest by one of the Riazor Blues. When it became evident that Manuel was a Dépor fan himself, his assailant apparently apologised and left the scene. But something was wrong. Manuel got a nosebleed, sat on a grassy bank and started vomiting blood. An ambulance was called: by the time it arrived at the local hospital, he was dead. A rib had been broken and punctured his liver. The case became a cause celebre in Spain, an example of how football hooliganism was getting out of hand. Several days later Manuel's attacker handed himself in to the police. The Riazor Blues had already announced, in a highly-articulate press release, that they would disband. That it had all gone too far: nobody should die for the sake of a football team.

"That was it for the Riazor Blues," says Rojo. "They'd been going since 1987. The leaders did the only thing they could. It had got too big. People were using the name of the group to cause trouble."

The lads and I end up queuing for a bar that opens at 7 o'clock in the morning, called El Run. I think it's going to be a sit-down breakfast café but it turns out to be a fully-blown heavy-metal disco bar. The others start dancing. After a while I slip off, walking back to my hotel in the early-morning sun. I need some sleep.


## SATURDAY MAY 1ST

I wake at three in the afternoon, which suits me, as there is less time to wait before tonight's game. I haven't been so excited for months about a match. I order a 'parradilla de carne' (huge plate of grilled chops, sausages and ribs) and absorb the sports pages. The local rag, *Campeón Deportivo*, has a picture of Roberto Carlos and Beckham arriving at the airport. 'Los Chinos' reads the headline (the China-men), presumably because they both have bald heads. Then: 'Chin Liga, Chin Copa, Chin Champions.' They are punning 'chin' with 'sin' (without), playing on the fact that Real Madrid risk winning nothing from a season in which they hoped to win the treble. *Marca* is rather more serious and announces that Beckham, having spoken with Florentino Pérez a few days ago, and with Valdano at Pérez' mother's funeral, is definitely to stay at least another year. Anyone wishing to buy him would have to pay his 180 million euro buy-out clause. Who would do that?

I study the table and the fixtures. An exciting end-of-season is in prospect, in contrast to England, where the championship and relegation issues have already been settled. With four games to play, nine clubs could still get relegated, from Celta on 37 points to Albacete on 43. One place above Albacete are Betis on 46 points, just two points off a UEFA Cup qualifying place. The four Champions League places are already decided, but three teams still have a chance of winning the title: Barcelona (66 points), El Real (70) and Valencia (71). I can't wait to see it all unfold. I pay my bill, leaving a plate of gnawed bones and an empty wine jug.

To kill time I walk into the old part of town. Up high, the home-reminding cry of seagulls. There are even more blue-and-white scarves and flags up than yesterday. I watch a wedding party gather in the square in front of a lovely medieval church, the women in foolishly-garish chiffon clothes, the men in black suits. How many of them are wondering why their friend should choose to marry on the day of Deportivo-Real? I ponder my own wedding plans, pencilled in for this coming September. It doesn't seem real, somehow. I've been observing all year, I can't see myself as the centre of attraction. But more than anything, I think of the game. Will Deportivo allow Real to win? I find myself back in María Pita square a bagpiper is standing in front of the statue, playing Galician tunes on his instrument (called the 'gaita' here) which is decorated with a blue-and-white scarf. He is wearing a Galician flag round his waist. He's not busking, just playing. His name, he says, is Loy. I wish him luck at the game. "I'm not going to the game," he says mournfully. "I haven't got enough pasta (dough)."

There are two hours till kick off but the stadium, right in the city centre, is already like a disturbed anthill. From afar I can see a convoy of trucks drive past it, beeping their horns. All the car-drivers beep their horns, too. Everybody, whether they are walking away from or towards the stadium, is wearing the club colours. A couple have attached a blue-and-white scarf around their baby's pram. There are flags hanging out of the windows of the office blocks around the stadium. There are Dépor-shirt-wearing groups of teenagers, sitting together on the beach that fronts the stadium, smoking joints and drinking spirits.

I pick up my ticket by the players' entrance, where hundreds are waiting for the Real Madrid coach to come in after its short journey from the Meliá Hotel. It arrives to an enormous cacophony of whistles; several eggs are thrown. The players get off, right in front of me. Beckham, looking smarter with his shaven head, hurries through. Figo is last off, and the whistling increases in volume and shrillness.

I go into the stadium and find my seat, halfway up, right in front of the corner flag. I am between a group of Dépor fans and some journalists from Portugal. On the big screen there is an advert, enticing people to buy shares in the club. The first part of the ad is set in 2000. An old guy in a crowded Bar Sport walks up to a porcelain saint and asks if he can arrange for Dépor to win La Liga. Tears miraculously run down the saint's face. That year they won their first league. It moves on to 2002. The old guy goes up to the saint again, asks him if Deportivo can win the Copa del Rey, against Real Madrid, in the Bernabéu, in Real's centenary year. Again tears. That year they won their first cup. We flash forward to 2004. The guy goes up to the saint again. "I want us to win . . . the Champions League." There is a pause. We expect more tears. But the saint's porcelain face bursts into laughter at the absurdity of the suggestion.

The players warm up, then go off again. A vast Galician flag (like the George cross, only with a blue cross on white) covers the bottom tier of the stand to my right. Covering the advertising hoarding below it is a banner reading 'Riazor Blues'. They must have reformed. Thousands of fans start jumping up and down, chanting the Triumphal March from Verdi's *Aida*. The players run on again, to the usual cheers, boos and whistles. The flag is unfurled to reveal a large banner underneath with the Real Madrid badge under a big red cross and the legend 'Anti Madridista'. The fans have been working hard, and however the Dépor players might perform, this isn't going to be an easy night for El Real. The 35,000 stadium is completely full; reventas (tickets tout) have been changing hands for 300 euros.

The match kicks off, Real attack and a Dépor player clears the ball into the crowd to my left. Beckham runs to the flag and stands waiting for someone to throw the ball back. The fan in possession keeps pretending to throw it then keeping hold of it, like a boy teasing a dog with a stick. Beckham flicks out a gesture of impatience. Another ball is thrown from the sidelines. "Puto Beckham, puto Real Madrid," chant the Riazor Blues. The corner is cleared.

The game settles into its pattern, with Real having more possession and Dépor sitting back and attacking on the break. Cambiasso hits the post, then Raúl goes close. You can see that Deportivo don't need a result. They are cooler, more relaxed – under pressure but not buckling, playing the ball out with skill and style when they get it. Just before the half hour, they produce a lightning quick move which completely slices through El Real's defence. Djalminha plays a lovely ball to Scaloni who has run into space. Scaloni shoots, Casillas can only parry the ball, and

Tristan hits it gleefully into the back of the net. When the crowd's celebrations have died down, a song goes round the ground, reminding the Real team of what they are likely to win this season if Dépor win:

"Ni Liga, ni Copa, ni Champions League! Ni Liga, ni Copa, ni Champions League!" I'm grinning like a fool.

Dépor start gaining a little more possession. Mauro Silva passes to Sergio. "Olé!" shout the crowd. Sergio to Djalminha. "Ooolé!" Djalminha to Capdevila. "Oooooolé!". Capdevila starts running down the left . . . "Oooooooooooo . . .." . . .and is brought down by Salgado. The second syllable is replaced by shouts of outrage. The Real Madrid players look angry, tired, unable to react.

"Ni Liga, ni Copa, ni Champions League," goes round the ground again. Zidane gets a yellow card for a needless foul in the centre circle. Beckham, annoyed by a tackle by Scaloni, chases after the similar-looking Capdevila and hacks him down. Yellow card. Djalminha stands in front of the Englishman, throwing several play punches which Beckham swats at, like an angry boy in the playground. Real win possession and Djalminha jumps on Beckham's back as the Englishman tries to shield the ball. Beckham goes down under his weight but, surprisingly, gives the Brazilian a friendly hug as they get up. He looks determined not to lose his cool. Then Zidane, who has hardly had a kick all game, delivers one straight into the heels of the Brazilian, again in the centre circle. The referee sends him off. He walks, dejected, to the corner in front of me where the telescopic red players' tunnel extends out for him, saving him from ten yards more of ridicule from the fans.

"Que baje Valdano!" (Valdano should come down) sing the crowd, in reference to the last time Zidane was sent off in the semi-final against Sevilla, when Real's Director Deportivo stormed into the referee's office at half-time to complain. There are dozens of Galician national flags waving in the Riazor Blues end. Using their extra man well, Dépor enjoy a spell of possession in their own half to another series of 'olés'. Beckham runs round like a bull amongst toreros. Then, too cocky by half, Andrade gives the ball to Raúl on the edge of the box. Raúl makes space and hits a shot straight at the crossbar. You can see from his expression that he knows it's going to be one of those days when the ball just won't go in. The referee blows for half-time, and, walking off the pitch, Djalminha and Roberto Carlos swap shirts.

It isn't over yet, though. Beckham starts the second half in great form, putting in a cross from the right, which Raúl heads straight at goalkeeper Molina. Then, from the centre of midfield, the Englishman hits a delicate diagonal pass into the path of Ronaldo. It is the sort of pass Ronaldo has been scoring from all season, but he's slow tonight and is tackled by Pablo Amo. Then Michel Salgado puts in a cross from the right, which Ronaldo heads just wide. Dépor are playing the game like a friendly, turning on the style when they get the ball. Djalminha does a back-heel nutmeg on Cambiasso, but loses the ball. Then Real get a free-kick on the edge of the Dépor box. Beckham and Roberto Carlos line up to take it. You can tell from his more determined body-language that it's going to be Beckham. This is his big chance to turn his season around. A goal now would change the game. It would keep el Real in the championship hunt and be a much-needed personal triumph for the Englishman. He needs it so badly. I want him to score, not because I want Real Madrid to equalise but because I want Beckham to have a bit of good fortune. He kicks the ball straight into the wall. From the breakaway, Dépor nearly score a second.

Five minutes later, on the hour, there's a flurry of activity around Queiroz' bench. Solari gets ready to go on. The board goes up . . . showing the number 23! Beckham, looking extremely put out, walks slowly to the touchline. On arriving at the bench, Beckham appears to makes an angry comment to Queiroz.

Real, knowing that a defeat would be disastrous for their title hopes, pour forward but get nowhere. Pablo Amo is having an excellent game. When Dépor get the ball, they try to keep possession, lapping up the 'olés' from the crowd. Then they get a free-kick outside the Real box: fairly central, about 25 metres from goal. Only two men stand in the wall. The ball is tapped to Capdevila, who thumps it left-footed into the goal off the post, Casillas well beaten. An eruption of blue and white joy. It's a great goal, and I sense the game is over as a contest.

Real Madrid don't give up – there are 20 minutes to go – but the crowd, the whole crowd, is celebrating a home victory. They sing 'the Aida' again, and there's a show of scarves from all four stands.

'Ni Liga, ni Copa, ni Champions League' is repeated over and over again. Clearly rattled, Real get desperate. Raúl and Roberto Carlos shoot over the top, Figo into the side netting. A Mexican wave starts up, goes round three times. I've never seen a Mexican wave in a Spanish ground before. Ronaldo gets taken off, replaced by young Portillo with his odd haircut, spiky at the back. Over the next ten minutes I don't see him touch the ball. Real finally give up hope. Roberto Carlos doesn't bother giving the ball back to Molina when it goes off for a goal-kick, as if he's trying to waste time. There's another show of scarves, and the final whistle is blown. A song comes onto the tannoy, with the word 'De-por-ti-vo' repeated faster and faster. Everyone chants along, showing their scarves: "De . . .por . . . ti . . .vo, De-por . . .ti-vo, Depor-tivo, Deportivo." All four stands are a sea of blue and white. "Ni Liga, ni Copa, ni Champions League," they sing again, as the Real Madrid players walk towards the red tunnel, heads down, hands on hips. In three days, the crowd will be back, hoping to see their side get into the Champions League final. This was just a starter. But what a starter.

Afterwards, down in the mixed zone, I meet the English journalists, waiting in case Beckham has a change of policy and wants to have a word with them. They know that it is futile but they have come all the way from Madrid. Beckham, however, just walks past.

"Happy birthday," shouts Eric from the *Sun*.

He turns round, smiles.

"Cheers," he says. Then he's onto the bus. We talk about what he said to Queiroz on being substituted. 'Why me?' is what they have decided.

Tension is high. Things are not going well for Beckham – or for Real Madrid. Their next game is at home to Mallorca and they know that, win or lose, their season's outcome is now in Valencia's hands.


### SUNDAY MAY 2ND

I spend the next day in La Coruña, waiting for a night-train back to Barcelona. I take another long walk around the city. There are even more flags up than yesterday. The port is waiting for the second leg of its first-ever European Cup semi-final. This provincial seaside town is enjoying its football miracle. Nobody can believe what's happening. One step from the European Cup final! With a win by their reserve team over mighty Real Madrid in the bag! The Real Madrid players will be back home, preparing for their forthcoming league match against Mallorca, a match they simply have to win to stay in with a chance of winning the league. Real Madrid being Real Madrid, they might still do it. But they look tired, dispirited, all played out. Queiroz looks like a dead man walking. The papers are already talking about his successor.

In the early evening I go walking near the pretty fishing port next to the town centre, summing up my thoughts. My adventure is nearly over. I feel drained, emotional, slightly tearful, lonely. I feel I am on the point of understanding what it's all meant to me, but I can't quite grasp it. I hear the sound of a bagpiper, and I am drawn to him, a portly fellow in a check shirt, on the edge of the quay, the gentle ocean slopping behind him. I spend half an hour sitting on an iron mooring mushroom, listening to the mournful sound of his pipes.

## RESULTS JORNADA 35

| | | | |
|---|---|---|---|
| ATLÉTICO | 3 | CELTA | 2 |
| **DEPORTIVO** | **2** | **REAL MADRID** | **0** |
| MURCIA | 2 | VALLADOLID | 1 |
| MALLORCA | 2 | MÁLAGA | 1 |
| ALBACETE | 3 | ZARAGOZA | 1 |
| SEVILLA | 2 | ATHLETIC | 0 |
| REAL SOCIEDAD | 2 | VILLARREAL | 2 |
| OSASUNA | 1 | RACING | 2 |
| VALENCIA | 2 | BETIS | 0 |
| BARCELONA | 4 | ESPANYOL | 1 |

## LA CLASIFICACIÓN

| | P | W | D | L | F | A | Pts |
|---|---|---|---|---|---|---|---|
| VALENCIA | 35 | 22 | 8 | 5 | 68 | 24 | 74 |
| **REAL MADRID** | **35** | **21** | **7** | **7** | **68** | **45** | **70** |
| BARCELONA | 35 | 20 | 9 | 6 | 61 | 36 | 69 |
| DEPORTIVO | 35 | 19 | 8 | 8 | 56 | 32 | 65 |
| ATHLETIC | 35 | 14 | 10 | 11 | 47 | 43 | 52 |
| ATLÉTICO | 35 | 14 | 9 | 12 | 56 | 32 | 51 |
| SEVILLA | 35 | 13 | 10 | 12 | 51 | 42 | 51 |
| OSASUNA | 35 | 11 | 15 | 9 | 37 | 33 | 48 |
| VILLARREAL | 35 | 13 | 9 | 13 | 44 | 45 | 48 |
| MÁLAGA | 35 | 14 | 5 | 16 | 46 | 51 | 47 |
| BETIS | 35 | 11 | 13 | 11 | 42 | 40 | 46 |
| ALBACETE | 35 | 12 | 7 | 16 | 37 | 43 | 46 |
| MALLORCA | 35 | 12 | 6 | 17 | 45 | 61 | 42 |
| REAL SOCIEDAD | 35 | 10 | 11 | 14 | 42 | 49 | 41 |
| RACING | 35 | 11 | 9 | 15 | 46 | 59 | 41 |
| ZARAGOZA | 35 | 10 | 9 | 16 | 41 | 53 | 39 |
| VALLADOLID | 35 | 9 | 10 | 16 | 41 | 53 | 37 |
| ESPANYOL | 35 | 11 | 4 | 20 | 42 | 60 | 37 |
| CELTA | 35 | 8 | 12 | 15 | 46 | 63 | 36 |
| MURCIA | 35 | 4 | 11 | 20 | 27 | 53 | 23 |

# TALE OF THREE CITIES

GOLFO DE VIZCAYA

OCÉANO ATLÁNTICO

**Barcelona** ○

**Real Madrid** ○

**Valencia** ○

MAR MEDITERRÁNEO

N
W E
S

# TWENTY TWO
# TALE OF THREE CITIES

**SATURDAY MAY 8TH**

The barman in the Madrid peña in L'Hospitalet, in the suburbs of Barcelona, looks pissed off. It's nine o'clock, an hour before kick-off of Real's penultimate home game of the season, against Mallorca. Three games to go, they're four points behind Valencia. I've asked him if I'll be allowed into the inner sanctuary of the club, the 'members only' section, for the match.

"No, that's for members only. That's why it says 'members only'. You can watch it in the bar, like all the other non-members." He points at a tiny TV in the corner of the room, next to the entrance.

I tell him about my project, that I was allowed there before, that I need to be where the atmosphere is thickest.

"There won't be much atmosphere tonight."

"Why not?"

"It is not a good time to be a Madrid fan."

"Please?"

"No!"

The league is reaching its climax and it doesn't look good for Real Madrid. If they lose today and Valencia win in Seville tomorrow, El Real won't be able to catch their rivals. If Barcelona also lose against Celta de Vigo in Balaídos tonight, a Valencia victory will bring them the title, for the second time in three years. I have booked a train ticket to Valencia tomorrow morning, just in case. They say the Valencianos know how to party.

Muttering curses about Franco under my breath, I walk down the road to another bar, to watch the last half of Barcelona's match against Celta de Vigo. There are about ten men there, who have, from the way they are shouting rather than talking to each other, been drinking all day. The atmosphere is dreadful. The old man behind me thinks it is funny to sneak behind the barmaid and shout in her ear to shock her. This encourages the other men in the bar to do the same to each other. I order some prawns and a glass of Rioja, and try to concentrate on the game. The atmosphere in Balaídos looks better. Celta are beating Barcelona 1–0. The stadium is full. They keep panning in on los Celtarras, behind the goal, who are singing and waving flags. I think I spot Marcopolo, the one who taught me the Celtarras' philosophy, his arms in the air. If Celta lose, they are more or less down. A win will give them a fighting chance of staying up.

Both teams have everything to play for, and the football is suffering as a result. Even Ronaldinho, usually the most graceful of players, is demonstrating more effort than style. Celta are awarded a penalty, which Luccin misses. Xavi beats Celta's keeper with a lob but full-back Juanfran somehow manages to head it off the line. The old men shout obscenities at the screen. The final whistle is blown. 1–0 to Celta. Juanfran is crying with the emotion of it all. He goes down on his knees and puts his face in the dirt. A journalist runs up with a microphone and grabs at his shoulder. The Celta fans start singing the Rianxeira. Barcelona's late and unexpected title challenge is, in effect, over. I finish my wine and leave.

Back to the Real Madrid peña. This is my third visit. Previously it has been packed, with up to 200 fans. This time, with a few minutes till kick off, there are only about 20: mostly men, aged between 50 and 70, but a couple of women, too. There's been a lot of drinking going on here as well. A raven-haired woman with a pointy face and glasses is balanced on a high stool nursing a large rum and coke, supporting her upper body on the bar. A well-dressed 50-something man looks at me, raises his hands in the air and roars "Whooooooah!" I don't quite know how to react. I order a glass of house red wine. With a couple of minutes till kick-off, half the group walk into the 'members only' section. As the players take their positions for kick-off I settle myself at a table in front of a large TV set by the curtains dividing the members-only bit from the main bar. 'This isn't too bad,' I think. Through the gap in the curtains I can see the big screen, and a flag of Spain with the black silhouette of a bull. The sort of thing you never see in Barcelona. One of the members comes out, turns the TV set off. "There's another TV over there," he says. He goes back into the forbidden zone, draws the curtains behind him. He means the tiny one at the entrance.

"What the . . ." I splutter, but I am not in a position to argue. My desire for Real Madrid to lose, and to lose humiliatingly, grows.

I find a place at the long bar and squint up at the tiny screen. The other ten are crowded in front of me. The match starts. I can hardly distinguish the players, they are so small. There is no sign of Beckham. After about ten minutes his name is mentioned, and I realise that up till then he hadn't touched the ball. There is a close up of his bony head. He looks unhappy. Soon after, Eto'o chases a ball into the box, controls it and shoots it past Casillas. Ten minutes gone, 1–0 to Mallorca. A guy with white brushed-back hair and a denim shirt starts shouting. He's looking at the barman, but he's directing the comment to the whole room.

"That whore Roberto Carlos is always up the wrong end of the whorish pitch trying to give the ball to that lazy-arsed Ronaldo instead of doing his job of defending. It's always the whoring same. Always down his side they score."

About five minutes later, Beckham hits one of those vicious outswinging corners of his onto the head of young Pavón, who forces it in from just outside the six yard box. 1–1.

"Who was that? Pavón? Ha!" says the denim guy. He's still angry. A statistic comes up: it is Beckham's tenth assist of the season. The camera focuses on him. He still doesn't look happy; more like he has just proved a personal point.

"He's good, Beckham," mutters the raven-haired woman.

"No he's not. He's a shit. We've got to get rid of him, too. Una mierda."

"No he's not," says the woman.

"You don't understand a whoring thing about football. Nothing. So shut your whorish mouth," shouts the guy in denim.

"And what are you, a trainer?" she says, softly.

On 36 minutes Eto'o scores a fantastic goal, running at the defence, beating Pavón and Raúl Bravo in the box and, with Beckham steaming in behind him, sidefooting it past Casillas. 2–1 to Mallorca. It's reminiscent of Maradona, and from a player that Real Madrid got rid of. I clench my fists, try to keep a smirk off my face. Just before half-time, Mallorca get a free-kick outside the Real box. Campano curls it into the top corner of the goal, with Casillas hardly moving. 3–1! 'Golgolgolgolgolgolgolgol!' shouts the excited commentator, perhaps betraying too much anti-Madridista glee. "This Madrid team makes me ashamed," says one of the guys.

The half-time whistle is blown.

"Still lads, think of all the years we've held our heads up high," says one man. "One year with your head hung low isn't too bad after all they've given us." This looks like being the first time Real Madrid haven't won a title for four years.

"Losing is one thing. Losing with shame is another," says denim shirt. The men from the forbidden zone walk back into the bar. A loud-voiced discussion ensues.

"We haven't got a whorish defence."

"Everybody a la calle (out). Get rid of the defence and get a new one."

"Get rid of the president." This is the first time I've heard a word said against Florentino Pérez by a Real Madrid fan.

"We need to buy some football players, not this bunch of maricones. Get rid of Ronaldo."

"It's the manager's fault."

"Well, at least he's out. Get rid of the president, too."

"Look, Barça have lost, we've lost. Valencia will lose tomorrow, too."

"No chance. We need a new president, a new regime. This one isn't working. And I'm ashamed to be watching it. I am ashamed of being a Real Madrid fan."

It's interesting to hear this anti-Pérez talk. Because the shambles I have witnessed over the last six weeks isn't all down to the players. It was Pérez who sent them on a lucrative but tiring Far East tour in August, instead of letting them concentrate on their vital pre-season fitness training. The result? Plenty of good publicity in China and Japan, plenty of shirts sold, and a team that is too tired to be able to play properly by the end of the season. On top of that, his policy of buying an expensive 'galáctico' every year, and having a star-studded team which increases the club's marketability at home and abroad, means that he can't afford to pay for any half-decent replacements for his stars when they are injured, suspended or simply tired, with the result that Queiroz has been unable to make the sort of squad-rotations necessary in top level, two-important-games-a-week modern football, further tiring out his men. There aren't even enough experienced top-level players to fill the team, let alone the squad. Which means that when Eto'o, the African Player of the Year in whom Real have a half-share but farmed out to Mallorca because they didn't want to shell out his wages, runs into the box, he is confronted not by a pair of world class defenders who might stop him but by Pavón and Raúl Bravo, who he can easily beat.

Pérez' experiment is leaving victims in its wake: Rubén, Mejia, Pavón and Raúl Bravo, for example, given too much responsibility too young, dragged straight from the Segunda B into the best league in the world and unable to cope, desperate doggy-paddlers drowning in the deep end. But it's not just the youngsters; the 'galácticos' are having a hard time, too. Zidane, recently voted by UEFA to be the best player Europe has ever seen, has publicly put his recent loss of form down to depression. Beckham, one of the best wide midfielders in the modern era, has been forced by the penny-pinching sale of Makelele into a position he'd never played before, and turned into a demoralised running-machine unable to get into positions where his penetrating passing game can flourish. Then there's the manager, Carlos Queiroz, dealt a losing hand and unable to rotate because he has nothing *to* rotate, the popular scapegoat for Real's dramatic end-of-season collapse, his reputation in tatters. And finally there's the fans, led at the beginning of the season to expect a wonder year, who were dreaming of a treble in March, but by May have had to suffer their team's embarrassing and spectacular collapse, turning their dream into a nightmare. Then I look at the guys crowded in front of the screen, waving their hands and shouting, bloated on a diet of success and petulant when none comes, angry and let down and turning on anyone they can turn on to let off steam. And I realise that I don't, after all, feel too sorry for the fans.

The referee gives Real Madrid a dubious penalty in the second minute of the second half. All 20 'merengues' are now standing in the same room, watching the small TV, the members having abandoned their big screen and flags so they can join the rest of their mates in their shouty post-mortem of Real's season. Figo scores it. There is ironic cheering. I get the feeling that they want Real to lose out of spite: their misery is giving them a kind of masochistic satisfaction. The referee makes Figo take the kick again, perhaps trying to atone for the fact that he shouldn't have given it in the first place. Figo scores again and the goal is allowed. It doesn't stop the moaning.

Raúl misses a chance from three yards out.

"This season Raúl is rubbish. He's already got old. We should sell him while he's still worth money."

"Yeah, sell him to Chelsea."

Then Ronaldo becomes the target.

"He's lazy, he doesn't track back, he doesn't know where the midfield is," says the guy that turned off my TV. "What's more he's fat. Look how fat he is!"

A right-wing cross comes over, which Ronaldo neatly volleys into the net. His detractor leaps into the air, arms outstretched. The referee disallows the goal for a hard-to-detect handball.

"I told you he was useless."

Real attack Mallorca throughout the second half but without much penetration, and fail to come close to scoring. The guys hardly watch the last quarter, conducting a heated debate about Pérez. One thinks that he should stay because he has got rid of Madrid's debt. The denim-shirted bloke is adamant that he should go. Pérez is up for re-election in July. There is talk of Lorenzo Sanz standing against him. "I can't put up with the shame any longer," he says. "And you know what? I hope whorish Valencia win tomorrow." The raven-haired woman, who has fallen asleep, topples off her stool.

## SUNDAY MAY 9TH

I arrive in Valencia at two in the afternoon, and as I leave the station I hear a series of loud explosions. Then I see fireworks sparking in the blue sky. I walk towards them: they are coming from the nearby Plaça del Ayuntament, the spiritual and administrative centre of Valencia, dissected by a busy main road and surrounded by grand-but-pompous Baroque and neo-classical buildings. There are a number of crashing booms and clouds of white smoke. Valencia is the firework capital of Spain, famous for its 'las Fallas' celebrations in March when vast effigies are burnt and the town indulges in an orgy of firecrackers and bonfires for a week to welcome in the spring. By the time I get to the edge of the watching crowd, the display is over. I ask a pair of sweet old ladies with identical hair-dos what the fireworks are for. Real lost the game 3–1 last night, but to win the title, Valencia still need to beat Sevilla in Seville tonight. It can't be for the football. Not yet.

"It's the Virgin's Day. The Day of the Mother of God. One of the biggest fiestas in Valencia."

"And the day that Valencia win the league, as well," I suggest, cheerfully.

"We hope so," says the one who seems to do the talking. "That really would be a complete day."

I have five or six hours to kill before the game, which I plan to watch in the square outside Manolo el del Bombo's bar. They are eventful hours. I rent a room in a pension next to the station. As I walk out the door, two fire engines turn up: the building next door has smoke billowing out of the top floor and an old lady is stranded on the balcony. I watch her being rescued, then walk into town. The centre is preparing for a procession: the streets are lined with wooden folding chairs and fine drapery has been hung from the balconies. I ask a passing man, and he tells me that a statue of the Virgin will be carried round town this evening. That many thousands will attend. I walk into a nearby church, adorned with a fifty-square-foot mosaic of dried flowers, and inspect the golden-haloed statue in question. It looks rather heavy. I enquire when the procession will be. Seven o'clock this evening – half an hour before the game. I love this sort of thing, but I'll have to miss it.

I eat a delicious plate of arroz negro, rice tinted black by the ink of the squid that it's cooked with. It's hot – 28 degrees. I walk back to my pension to pick up my camera. I find a guy slumped face down on the pavement in front of the door, his wallet lying beside him. I ask around in the bars if anyone knows him; they all say they do but they don't seem inclined to help him. 'He's always drunk,' says the woman in the bar next door. A policeman arrives on the scene. Relieved, I walk through the station forecourt to the bull-ring next to the station, which

is busy with excited, chattering people. There's a bull-fight at six. I estimate that I will be able to watch three bulls getting killed and still get to
Mestalla in time for the match, so I buy a ticket. A local lad named Juan
Ávila, making his debut, wins an ear, despite needing four sword-thrusts
to kill the third bull. It takes him so long that I have to get a taxi to the
square next to the ground.

I talk with the taxi driver about the game. He's a Valencia fan. After
my year of increasing obsession with Spanish football, the dozens of
games that I've seen, the hundreds of football conversations I've had all
over the country, the thousands of words I've written and the millions of
words that I've read on the subject, I am now fluent in conversing about
Spanish football in Spanish. I hold my own in the conversation. I tell him
how I admire his team, the way they have no 'galácticos' but thrive
because of their team spirit, good organisation and astute management.
How I love to see them play, they way they commit men to their attacks,
but then manage to get them quickly behind the ball when they lose
possession. How they are good at 'pressing' when they don't have the
ball, and how they attack in waves when they do. I say they are more
'team' than Real Madrid, tell him how much I am relieved that Pérez's
flash money-fuelled gamble has failed.

"We will win tonight," he says.

"No, you will draw. Sevilla are a good side, playing well. Julio Baptista
is in a good spell of form. What's more, they need the points to qualify
for the UEFA Cup." (I'm getting a bit pompous, I know.)

"No, we will win," he says.

Mestalla stadium looms into view, and the taxi is stopped from entering
the road leading to it by two policemen who have barricaded the entrance.
I hear a great hubbub of singing, shouting and plastic-horn tooting as
I pay my man, and when I walk round the corner I can't believe it. My
hopes of finding a seat were ridiculously over-optimistic. There are about
five thousand fans in the square, all wearing scarves and shirts, waving
flags. They look like they've been there for hours. There are fans teetering
precariously on the top of the large statue that dominates the plaza.
There are fans balanced on telephone boxes. The fans stretch back so
far that most of them won't have a hope of distinguishing what's
happening on any of the ten TV sets that have been set up for them.
It doesn't look like they're going to mind. They're here to party.

There's non-stop singing. 'A por ellos!' (get into them) 'campeones, campeones, oé oé oé.' I get some beers in 'El Pequeño Mestalla' (the bar next
door to Manolo's) and find a place right next to the door of the bar where,
if I look up, I can see three quarters of the television screen. I reckon it's
about the best I can do. I'm blocking no-one's view, and if I turn around,

I can see the all the fans facing me, too. There's a good mix of girls and blokes. Four girls wrapped in flags in front of me are painting people's faces with the Valencia colours (orange, black and white), asking people who their favourite player is and writing it on their forehead.

About 10 per cent of the fans are wearing curly orange wigs; many have scarves wrapped round their heads, pirate-style, and there are thousands with flags. I feel self-conscious, one of the very few without even a scarf. Even more so when scores of fans start pointing in my direction and singing 'este es maricon' (that one's a pansy). Then I spot a guy to my right with long blond hair and a Viking beard, who waves his hands in the air as if to conduct the singing, laughing, taking it well.

I hear some raw shouting and look round to a particularly rowdy group standing next to the statue. A clearing suddenly forms in the middle of them as they try to get away from something on the floor. They all turn their backs to whatever it is and hunch. Then there's a loud series of explosions and a thick cloud of smoke. The fans all cheer, turn round, jump into the smoke and start dancing around, singing:

"Madridista el que no bote, oe! oe!" (whoever doesn't jump is a Madrid fan).

The match starts, the singing continues. I try to concentrate on the game but the fans are just as interesting. After about ten minutes Manolo, wearing a pizza-shaped (and pizza-sized) red beret, comes out from his bar with his big drum and starts banging it, making the fans sing even more.

'Campeones, campeones, oé, oé, oé.'

As if rallied by the singing, Valencia start an attack. The ball is passed to Vicente on the left, who controls it, dribbles it into the box and hits it past the keeper into the net. Total mayhem erupts around me. I get an involuntary vicarious surge of thrill, and jump up and down myself. What other occasion in life can make you spontaneously jump with joy? More firecrackers, as the replay affirms the goal.

"Ni Liga, ni Copa, ni Champions League," chant the fans, revealing that at least part of their joy comes from the fact that it is Real Madrid that they are going to take the title from.

The Valencia team becomes tense as Sevilla mount a number of dangerous attacks but it doesn't seem to rub off on the crowd, who are acting as if victory is assured. A lad comes up to me, asks me where I'm from.

"My mate David is a Madrid fan," he shouts, pointing at a young man draped in a Valencia scarf, with 'Mista' written on his forehead.

"Hijo de puta!" shouts David, and cuffs his friend round the head quite hard. He looks genuinely upset but is soon cajoled out of his mood. They're not watching the game, they are trying to start up songs, with some success. To the tune of OMD's *Enola Gay*:

'Lololo, Valencia Club de Football . . ."

A few rows back stands a woman of about 50, one of the few people in the whole crowd not wearing any colours.

"Qué bote la abuela," sings one of the lads (jump up and down granny) and the crowd around her takes up the song. She doesn't look amused or jump, staring intently at the screen. As well she might. Valencia right-winger Jorge López controls a cross on his chest and hits the ball past the Sevilla keeper. More mayhem, but there's something wrong. López is holding his head in his hands. It's been disallowed for offside. It takes a while for the crowd to realise. A replay shows that he wasn't offside. A thin guy standing at the other side of the doorway kicks a plastic bin-bag of empty beer cans, making its contents fly into the air. Nobody else seems to mind; it doesn't affect their mood, just spurs them on to more singing.

Soon after Sevilla launch their own attack and the little scurrying Carlitos, who has been looking dangerous all half, heads the ball past a rooted-to-the-spot Cañizares. There's a moment of shock until this, too, is ruled offside and the singing continues. Thousands of fingers are prodded upwards, knuckles to the screen. The half-time whistle is blown. I head into the bar for a second-half supply of beers.

The second half is torture, though most of the Valencia fans don't seem to feel the tension as Sevilla besiege the Valencia area.

"Are you not worried?" I ask one of the lads next to me, 'Albelda' written on his forehead. He's singing and joking, hardly bothering with the football.

"If we don't win it tonight, we'll win it next Sunday," he says. "And if not then, then the one after. It'll just mean more parties." Ayala, desperate to make tonight the night, is a monster in defence, winning every header, every tackle, a real central defender who might have made all the difference to Real Madrid if they had managed to sign him in the summer. The fans around me aren't so much watching the football, as waiting for the final whistle. Aimar starts warming up, to tremendous acclaim. The little Argentinian playmaker has missed most of the last two months through injury and although the team's results suggest that he hasn't been missed – they have won eight and drawn two of their last ten fixtures – the sight of him brings a loud cheer. And when he comes on, he brings relief as Valencia at last have an outlet for their clearances from defence. A superb Cruyff turn that wins space and time in the Sevilla half draws a mass 'olé'. I've worked out that the Spaniards' love of flamboyant skills, and their nicknames for them (la vaselina, la chilena', la ruleta) stems from their love of bullfighting moves and produces the same response.

Sevilla continue pressing forward, their fans in the stadium willing them on. They need points to get into the UEFA Cup. There are five minutes left. A shot by Darío Silva, now with hair and 'tache, looks for a second as if it's gone in when it ripples the netting behind the goal. It hasn't worried the fans, who are singing 'Sí,sí,sí, la Liga está aquí' (we've won the league) and 'Madrid cabrón, saluda al campeón' (Madrid, you cuckolds, salute the champions). Valencia's strength in depth is shown by the players on the bench. Baraja, their vice captain and arguably their best player, has been rested from the starting line-up this game, only introduced on the hour to replace Oliveira. With a minute on the clock, he plays a one-two with Xisco, receiving the ball back in the area, and calmly kicking it past the keeper. 2–0! Firecrackers, dancing, hugging, flag-waving. Euphoria. More euphoria than I've ever seen. I hug and am hugged. The guy standing on the telephone box sprays a shaken-up can of beer all over the fans in front of him. My shoulder gets covered. They don't care, I don't care, we don't care. We welcome the beer-spray like madmen enjoying the rain. That's it. That's the league. A conga goes past, singing 'Esto es afición, Valencia campeón' ('we are true fans, and Valencia are the champions').

I shove through the crowd to Manolo's bar. He is too busy selling beer to talk much. He has given up using the till; there is a pile of notes and coins on a shelf behind the bar. On the TV I see the Valencia chairman, Jaime Ortí, give an interview, wearing an orange curly wig. I buy a beer and head for the crowd which has developed in the road in front of Mestalla. I pass a stall, selling scarves as fast as Manolo was selling beer. I pick out an orange and black one with 'Valencia CF' on it. Ten euros. Then I see someone buying one which says 'Anti Madridista' over the Valencia bat symbol. I go back to the woman.

"Can I change my scarf for an Anti-Madridista one?"

"No, you've already bought that one."

"Please."

"Why do you want a different one?"

"I just prefer the Anti-Madridista one."

She relents and I tie my new scarf round my neck the way I used to, when I really did wear a football scarf like I meant it, in a knot like a big tie.

I push my way into the middle of the crowd. 'Madrid cabrón, saluda al campeón,' they are singing. I get as far in as I can, jumping along with everyone else. There are about ten songs, being sung over and over again. About a third of them are Anti-Madridista in tone. I'm starting to learn the words, and singing along.

'Madridista el que no bote, oé, oé!'

'Puto Madrid, puta capital.'

'Madrid cabrón, saluda al campeón.'

I see someone lay down a string, tying together 20 or so fireworks, on the ground. I move with the crowd away from it, turning my back. There is a machine-gun series of deafening bangs, then we turn around again, run back into the space. Everyone is slam-dancing in the cloud of smoke. 'Madrid cabrón, saluda al campeón!'

After an hour of this I walk off and sit on the same bench I sat on after the Valencia v Madrid game, where I met the tramp and then Sid Lowe. There is a bank of geraniums behind me; I pick one and put it in the front pocket of my jacket. Cars are driving past, the drivers beeping their horns, the passengers hanging precariously out of the windows, waving flags. In front, in the dried-up river, there is a fair with a bouncy castle, shaking with the impact of its temporary inhabitants. Groups of fans walk past me in both directions, waving their scarves when they see mine, shouting, singing.

But after the euphoria, the hiatus. I gradually start to feel like a charlatan. What have I been doing? I am not a Valencia fan. I wanted them to do well in the league, at first because I didn't want Real Madrid to run away with it, then because I developed a strong dislike for Florentino Pérez' club and everything it stood for, and I started supporting any force that stood against it. Then I became obsessed with the issues involved. I didn't want El Real to win, and every week I started looking forward to their games for the chance that I might see them lose, for the chance that I might see Pérez' capitalist-dream empire collapse. I based my whole year on this growing obsession, filling my head with statistics and facts about Spanish football, watching as many games as I could, becoming boring to anyone that wasn't a football bore themselves. I stopped buying the serious Spanish newspapers, filling myself with football trivia from *Marca*, and *As*. My girlfriend, my *fiancee*, left our dream in Spain, bored to tears with my obsession with Beckham, with football, my odd lifestyle of charging round the country following Real Madrid, only to want them to lose. When did we last speak of our wedding plans? And me approaching 40. Behind me klaxons and horns are still beeping, and flags are still flying as fans from Valencia celebrate their victory. But my thoughts muffle the noise. In front of me, the fair over, the bouncy castle deflates.

I walk back towards my pension, trying to hitch a lift in a klaxon-tooting flag-waving car to raise my spirits. None of them stop. Then, approaching the Plaza de Ayuntament, another crowd of several thousand people waving flags. In the middle of the crowd, I stop my journey home, infected with the enthusiasm of these Valencianos. One is wearing a traffic cone as a hat. Another has found a paint can, and is bashing it like a drum. A pair of real drummers with genuine drums are encouraging the crowd to sing, though they don't need much encouragement. Somebody is playing a trumpet; several girls get given the bumps. My spirits pick up. I stick around, singing and occasionally jumping, and waving my scarf around my head. For twenty years I have supported two teams, Newcastle and Brighton, and I have never felt the joy of my team winning a trophy. I will celebrate here, even if 'I' haven't deserved it.

An old-fashioned white leather football is kicked up in the air, the crowd becomes obsessed with its progress, yelling 'olé' when it is kicked skywards or caught, and 'ooh' when it falls to ground. I am desperate for it to come my way and suddenly it does. I jump like a keeper to catch it and for a precious split second it is in my hands. Then it slips though, someone behind grabs it, and kicks it into the air. "Olé!" shout the crowd, but not for me. It is time to leave.

## RESULTS JORNADA 36

| | | | |
|---|---|---|---|
| ATHLETIC | 1 | ALBACETE | 1 |
| ZARAGOZA | 1 | OSASUNA | 0 |
| RACING | 2 | ATLÉTICO | 2 |
| CELTA | 1 | BARCELONA | 0 |
| ESPANYOL | 2 | DEPORTIVO | 0 |
| **REAL MADRID** | **2** | **MALLORCA** | **3** |
| MÁLAGA | 1 | MURCIA | 0 |
| VALLADOLID | 2 | REAL SOCIEDAD | 2 |
| VILLARREAL | 1 | BETIS | 0 |
| SEVILLA | 0 | VALENCIA | 2 |

## LA CLASIFICACIÓN

|  | P | W | D | L | F | A | Pts |
|---|---|---|---|---|---|---|---|
| VALENCIA | 36 | 23 | 8 | 5 | 70 | 24 | 77 |
| **REAL MADRID** | **36** | **21** | **7** | **8** | **70** | **48** | **70** |
| BARCELONA | 36 | 20 | 9 | 7 | 61 | 37 | 69 |
| DEPORTIVO | 36 | 19 | 8 | 9 | 55 | 34 | 65 |
| ATHLETIC | 36 | 14 | 11 | 11 | 48 | 44 | 53 |
| ATLÉTICO | 36 | 14 | 10 | 12 | 46 | 48 | 52 |
| VILLARREAL | 36 | 14 | 9 | 13 | 45 | 45 | 51 |
| MÁLAGA | 36 | 15 | 5 | 16 | 47 | 51 | 50 |
| SEVILLA | 36 | 13 | 10 | 13 | 51 | 44 | 49 |
| OSASUNA | 36 | 11 | 15 | 10 | 37 | 33 | 48 |
| BETIS | 36 | 11 | 13 | 12 | 42 | 41 | 46 |
| MALLORCA | 36 | 13 | 6 | 17 | 48 | 63 | 45 |
| ALBACETE | 36 | 12 | 8 | 16 | 38 | 44 | 44 |
| REAL SOCIEDAD | 36 | 10 | 12 | 14 | 44 | 51 | 42 |
| ZARAGOZA | 36 | 11 | 9 | 16 | 42 | 53 | 42 |
| RACING | 36 | 11 | 10 | 15 | 48 | 61 | 42 |
| ESPANYOL | 36 | 12 | 4 | 20 | 44 | 60 | 40 |
| CELTA | 36 | 9 | 12 | 15 | 47 | 63 | 39 |
| VALLADOLID | 36 | 9 | 11 | 16 | 43 | 55 | 38 |
| MURCIA | 36 | 4 | 11 | 21 | 27 | 54 | 23 |

# MURCIA

GOLFO DE VIZCAYA

OCÉANO ATLÁNTICO

**Real Madrid**
○

Murcia ○

MAR MEDITERRÁNEO

N
W E
S

# TWENTY THREE
# MURCIA

## THURSDAY MAY 13TH

Impressions of a new city are often coloured by what happens when you first arrive. Murcia starts well. It's already dark when I walk out of the train station, but it's warm enough not to have to wear a jacket. I get given pleasant directions from a pretty girl, walk through a park full of enormous rubber trees, and carry on across an iron bridge over a flowing river full of illuminated ducks. I head past the beautiful Baroque façade of the cathedral, find my pension and in a hassle-free transaction get a cheap but very large and clean room in the centre of town. Then, five minutes later, I walk towards the music I can hear in the distance, and watch the last half an hour of an Algerian group playing for free in front of a large and enthusiastic open-air crowd. It's part of a festival to celebrate the three different cultures, Muslim, Jewish and Christian, that figure in the city's history. 'Nice place,' I think.

A strange place, though. Murcia is in the south-east of Spain, but is situated in the fertile river valley of the Río Segura. It's protected from the arid semi-desert around it by two low mountain ranges, and so enjoys its own microclimate. A thousand-odd years ago the area was a swamp, but the Moors, who founded the city in AD 825, put their sophisticated irrigation techniques to use and it soon became a fine place for growing fruit and vegetables. And, despite the last 'Moros' being kicked out in the 17th century, it still is. 'La Huerta de Europa' they call the valley around Murcia (the market garden of Europe): it produces peppers, onions, tomatoes, aubergines, courgettes, lettuce, peaches, you name it, for the rest of the country. The produce is tinned and shipped round the world, too.

The city, then, has a prosperous look about it that you don't normally get so far south in this dry country. You can see it from the architecture, you can see it from the cars, you can see it from the clothes and look of the people walking round. They're obviously well-fed: I walk into a bar near the cathedral and have a salad of fresh anchovies, plump olives and the most succulent tomatoes I've ever tasted, as well as a plate of serrano and ibérico ham. The latter – the expensive stuff – melts in your mouth. Murcia is reputed to be one of the best places in Spain for food.

But not for football. Despite Murcia being a regional capital, Real Murcia, the city's main football club, have only managed to spend 16 years in the Primera División in their history. It's not for lack of trying. They have been promoted to the top flight a total of eight times since the war. Their eighth relegation has already been decided: they went down in March. They are quite obviously the worst team in the division, having won only four games all season. Their manager, John Toshack, twice sacked from Real Madrid, was brought in this February to try and achieve a miracle, but barely managed to slow their plummet down the relegation 'well'. He did manage, though, his habitual trick of translating non-transferable English idioms literally into Spanish along the way. 'We were like chickens running around with no heads,' for example. And, to the bemusement of the pressmen at the conference 'there could be pigs that fly in the air'. The press have got their own back by transcribing his eccentric comments literally into their newspapers. Real Madrid need a win in Murcia to stay in the driving seat in the race for second place (and the automatic Champions League place that comes with it). It looks like they can expect to get it.

They need the points. Barcelona, a point behind but with a slightly better goal difference, will play Racing de Santander an hour and a half before Real's kick-off on Sunday, and will go two points ahead if they win. The papers are calling this race for second place 'the sub-Champions League' (you get awarded the title of 'subcampeones' if you finish second, considered an honour for most clubs). The way of deciding which team finishes ahead if their points are level is different in Spain. First you look at the aggregate score of the two games played between the teams (in Barça and Real's case 3–3). If that's even you look at the goal differ-ence (which the Spanish call 'goal average', a misnomer). Barça have a two-goal advantage before this, the penultimate game of the season. If goal difference ends up even, you look at goals scored. Real win out on this factor. It's tight just off the top.

Finishing second is particularly important for Real Madrid. Assuming that first or second place was already assured, Florentino Pérez has already arranged a series of lucrative friendlies in the Far East and the United States to be played in August 2004. If Real fail to finish second, they will have to cancel much of the tour at great cost (they tend to earn up to £3 million per friendly) to prepare instead for the home-and-away Champions League pre-qualifiers in the same month. This would be highly ironic. Many think that one of the reasons the team has collapsed so dramatically in the last quarter of the season is their participation in one such tour in August 2003, instead of concentrating on pre-season fitness training. If they fail even to come second due to the tiredness caused by this money-over-all-else approach, at least they will be able to train fully for the forthcoming season.

## FRIDAY MAY 14TH

After all the travelling I've done myself this season, I know how they feel. I'm tired. I've travelled a long way. But have I done what I set out to do? Have I learnt what makes this country tick? I find a restaurant displaying 50 or 60 different tapas behind the bar. A weaselly guy serves me. Eight o'clock shadow, a Bobby Charlton haircut with gel. He's not used to foreigners: when I don't understand the bar's way of serving tapas, two or three together on a plate, he adopts a disdainful look which he repeats whenever he glances my way. After my meal I ask for an 'orujo' with herbs. On the way back from the fridge, he drops the whole bottle. He's obviously drunk. The others all have a go at him; he's not even capable of cleaning it up. Just before leaving I ask him if he is going to the football. He puts that face on.

"I don't like football," he says. "I like fighting cocks and fighting dogs."

"What, you mean illegal stuff?"

He nods his head as if to indicate that such indulgences make him more of a man. I press for more information, he is not forthcoming. Perhaps he is lying. I leave.

In the evening I meet two of my best friends, who have come over for the weekend. Johnny is 40 tomorrow. I am 40 in a month. Rick is 40 in August. When we first met, at school in Sussex, all the football players were older than us. Now they are all younger. In the evening, celebrating our shift into middle age, we end up in the sort of neon-lit Spanish-disco-music-orientated bar/night-club that get packed full on Fridays with people in their twenties. It's the best possible place to be to drum the reality of our age into our heads. I'm on the edge of things, on a different agenda to the others. They are both single. Rick, in pigeon Spanish, starts making a group of five girls hoot with laughter. Johnny, who speaks good Spanish, bulldozes in on the group. They are no longer amused. We obviously don't fit into this environment.

## SATURDAY MAY 15TH

We walk round town, stopping in several of Murcia's lovely silver-chaired squares, drinking beer, talking the talk of three grown men who've known each other for 25 years. We try to analyse where it all went wrong. Why I'm the only one with a steady relationship, and that with a woman currently living in a different country. We are very different but we can see similar problems in ourselves. We have all ended up living unsteady adult lives. We yearn to be abroad, to live an adventure, to shy away from commitment. It has not made any of us particularly happy. There have been ups and downs. But what ups! And what downs.

Johnny lived in Spain for ten years, got married to a Spanish girl. Now he lives on his own in London. We get talking about the difficulty of fitting into Spanish life as a foreigner. Spain is a country in which you see the generations mix, where family life is all important, where kids tend to stay at home until they're into their thirties. If you're not part of a family, you're not fully part of life in Spain. Friends tend to go out in the same close knit groups ('cuadrillas') for years. It is difficult to break into one of these groups. The only people I know who have really settled into Spain and don't behave like an ex-pat on an extended working holiday, are those who have married into the country and, in effect, have Spanish kids. But even they are considered an oddity. I've had conversations with people all over Spain this year, and I've noticed a very common response to my strange accent and idiosyncratic grammar. "Tu eres forastero," people say. 'Forastero' means 'foreigner', but also means 'outsider', 'stranger', 'alien'. I get the feeling that however long I stay in Spain, however much I try to improve my Spanish, however fluently I learn to express my virulent Anti-Madridismo, I will always remain a 'forastero' in this country.

Beckham is one of the most famous men in Spain, but he is very much a forastero himself. The three of us, who have all lived abroad, get talking about Beckham's rise and fall this season in Spain. We know that living abroad is a difficult thing, but there are many compensations for the difficulties you face. It is fascinating to absorb a new culture, to get to know the language, the food, the art, the customs, the politics. Beckham doesn't seem to have made any effort to do this. He doesn't seem to have much of the intellectual curiosity necessary to enjoy the differences around him. When he was living in the hotel, he went to great expense having English food specially prepared for him. Apart from the words 'Hala Madrid' he uttered when he first signed for the club in July, I haven't seen him publicly use a single word of Spanish. Of course he's going to find it hard to fit in.

It's not all his fault. When Beckham goes out, he needs body-guard protection. If he goes for a meal, special security arrangements have to be made. He has worked on his image and achieved a superstardom which earns him millions of pounds a year, simply from his image rights. But this has stopped him from living an ordinary existence, especially in Spain, where people respect your privacy and personal space less than they do in England. Beckham is so famous here (and he has been from the day he signed for Real Madrid) that he can't just stroll around. He can't pop into a bar, have some prawns and a glass of Rioja, maybe chat to the waiter a little, watch the football. He can't nip round the market, get some tomatoes and chicken, make himself a quick lunch.

I get the feeling, now the season has nearly ended, that David Beckham's move to Real Madrid has not been great for Real Madrid or for Beckham. That he tried hard, but he was given a job that was too difficult for him to pull off. After a great start he struggled, but perhaps he was bound to. He was asked to play in a position he wasn't used to. To make matters worse, for whatever reason he was forced to spend much of the season away from his family, his wife and two young children. A difficult time for a family man. So what happens? He gets accused of having an affair with the only female English-speaker around him. His performances on the pitch decline along with his prestige off it. His team collapses around him at the same time: a double disaster. Babel is falling down around his head, and he hasn't even learnt the language. And, you've got to ask yourself, how much has Real Madrid's snowballing decline been down to that of their English midfielder? It's a factor, but there are so many more. Listing the reasons for Real's decline has become a national past-time over the last few weeks. The tiring but lucrative pre-season tour. The 'short' squad, and the need to give the established (shirt-selling) players too many 'minutes', like the old Hollywood principle of keeping the star on-screen as much as possible. The whole 'Zidanes and Pavones' policy, which pushes young players into the deep end and expects them to do the butterfly. The (necessary) lack of rotation. The continued reliance on trusted favourites even when off-form or unfit. The choice of a relatively inexperienced manager, whose hands were tied from the start of the season by a top-heavy decision-making process. Too many stars in the same dressing room. The heightening believe-the-dream arrogance of the club and its fans until March, and the hysteria that resulted when that arrogance was discovered to be unfounded. A dream gone wrong, the romantic experiment of a vain rich man, pushed too far. Pérez, Pérez, Pérez. It all boils down to Pérez.

**SUNDAY MAY 16TH**

Matchday. In the daytime we take a drive up to a national park in the mountains that overlook Murcia. We take a long walk in the hot sun. Pine forests, the odd bird, blue skies. In front of us the river valley is flat, flat, flat. The combination of the familiar (my oldest friends) and the unfamiliar (it's an alien environment, it'll always be an alien environment) makes me yearn for home.

I've been to most of the major cities in Spain now, but I haven't found anywhere I'd like to settle. I love Barcelona but I don't feel part of it. I admire Madrid for many reasons but I don't feel any affinity for the place and I couldn't live in the middle of all this land-mass. I can't see myself in the south (too rough, too raw). The dry central meseta towns are provincial in the way only a town surrounded by virtual desert can be provincial. The Basque country? Too self obsessed. Galicia? Well, there's always Galicia. Good old rainy Galicia with its pubs, its green countryside, its quirky sense of humour. I might as well go home.

The lads drop me off in the town centre: they're going to the airport and back home. I get to the stadium with about two and a half hours till kick-off. The place is already packed. The large concourse in front of the stadium is full of fans waiting for the team buses, and touts selling tickets – for over 200 euros. The stadium, all concrete and girders, looks like something from England in the '70s. It's called La Condomina and it's been sold out, for the first time this season, for days. Murcia might be down but Real Madrid haven't played here since 1988 and nobody wants to miss it. Not that there's much room. The capacity of the stadium is just 16,000.

A black Mercedes pulls into the concourse and drives slowly to the official entrance to the ground. The good-natured mood turns ugly and 20 or so fans follow the car. Out steps a well-dressed man with slicked back grey hair. Jesús Samper, the Murcia president. The fans start shouting at him. Security guards form a cordon around him. He doesn't hurry into the stadium, kisses a girl on the cheek, has a little chat. "Ruso, ruso," shout the fans (Russian, ie corrupt). Then some Real Madrid fans start joining in. 'Directivo de tercera,' they chant, suggesting the club's board of directors is of Third Division standard. He walks into the building. The ugly mood passes.

I get talking to a casually dressed grey-haired man as I queue for my press ticket. He's a friend of Iker Casillas and has been promised a ticket by him. We talk about Beckham. He talks in analogy, like Spaniards often do. "I can try to mend my pipes, if there is a problem with my plumbing. I might even have all the right tools. But I won't be able to do the job properly because I am not a plumber. You need experience, you need practice. Beckham was a painter, and they told him to do the plumbing. There's no wonder the house is falling down."

I walk around the ground, taking in all the pre-match atmosphere. To complete my circuit I have to walk round the city bull-ring, too. The Real

Madrid bus passes by at the end of the road. An enormous girl is shouting 'venga, venga, las pipas y el agua para el fútbol' (sunflower seeds and water for the football). A carload of girls stops and the driver chats with a man on the pavement.

"We saw Beckham!" she says.

"Did he have any hair?" replies the guy.

"No, but he was gorgeous."

"Did he have any hair?" He seems to think this comment is hilarious. There is a traffic jam of cars on the road and people on the pavement patiently waiting for the conversation to finish. But no tooting of horns or tutting of impatience. There's none of the sort of tension round the stadium that you normally get before a football match. Murcia are long relegated. People are just looking forward to the game, to a crack at 'los galácticos'. If Murcia manage to beat Madrid today it will be El Real's fourth defeat on the trot, the worst sequence of results in the club's history.

I find my press 'cabin' right in the corner of the ground. There's a Japanese journalist there, then another Japanese guy arrives, then Simon Cass of the *Daily Mail*. They've stuck all the 'forasteros' together and put us in the place with the worst view.

"I'm the only one here tonight," says Simon, meaning the only British journalist. Only three foreign journalists in total, and me. It's a far cry from earlier on in the season.

I read the free match programme, which gives details of the Murcia players. They are a collection of cast-offs from other clubs and second-rate foreigners, by the look of things. Their best player, Luis García, is a Real Madrid reject, a right-sided midfielder who has scored nine league goals, six more than Beckham. The ground fills up, and so do the balconies of the flats to my left. There seems to be an unobstructed view of the ground from about 20 balconies and the flat-owners have all invited friends round. I have a quick conversation with Simon Cass, who asks me the title of the book.

"You should call it *El Becks: Don't Blame it on the Sunshine*," he says. I'm still holding out for a happy ending, of sorts. For Beckham to score a couple of cracking goals, preferably from free-kicks. I still want him to do well, to win over the mounting criticism he has been facing. Simon uses the internet to find out how Barça are doing. They're beating Racing 1–0, with 78 minutes gone. *Under Pressure*, by Queen, comes on over the tannoy.

The Real Madrid team news is interesting. There's no Ronaldo or Roberto Carlos (both suspended), that much I knew. No Raúl Bravo or Cambiasso, either, both out injured. Poor Mejía, roasted when played out of position at right back against Santander, is in at left back. He's right-footed.

Guti, who complained about the manager in midweek, has been dropped, replaced by young Borja. The players start their warm-up routines. The Murcia players are followed onto the pitch by a mascot with a radish head. The announcement of Beckham's name on the tannoy causes a high-pitched squeal of delight.

There is a minute's silence for Jesús Gil y Gil, Atlético's former president, who died in the week after suffering a brain tumour. Gil was a construction multi-millionaire and the former mayor of Marbella, a man who was, when he fell ill, facing a possible jail sentence for alleged fraud in his dealings with Atlético. An old-fashioned Fascist responsible in the '60s for the death of scores of people when one of his buildings fell down, the sort of man who was terrible for the image of the Spanish game. But he was nevertheless much loved by the Spanish public for his larger-than-life personality and his blunt manner of saying what he thought. And his virulent strain of anti-Madridismo. The minute's silence is well-kept, with only a couple of shouting dissenters.

The game kicks off and within a couple of minutes young Mejía is in trouble, forced to give away a throw-in. The ball is hurled into the box, Casillas seems to drop it and Luis García, the Real Madrid reject, kicks it into the net. Goal! The crowd, who have been quiet, look too surprised to react very much. They wave their hands around, and a chant of 'Murcia' goes round. You get the feeling they've forgotten how to celebrate. The goal, however, seems to liven everyone up. Murcia start moving the ball around with some confidence and there's an 'olé!' every time a pass finds its man. Then the crowd hushes as an out-of-position Casillas is lobbed. Another goal? No. Helguera, somehow, manages to clear off the line. The atmosphere livens up a notch more. Murcia get a free kick. Beckham organises the wall. I wonder, with his lack of Spanish, if he is the best man to be communicating with Casillas. The wall does its job.

Soon after Beckham runs onto a loose ball in midfield and sprints towards the goal, hitting a thumping drive that the goalkeeper somehow manages to flamboyantly keep out of the top corner. Beckham takes the corner himself, right below me. He can't get a proper run up because of all the cameras and puts on a 'what *is* this?' face. The cameras move, he hits in a vicious in-swinger. It's cleared. He starts pulling the strings for Madrid in midfield, mixing long balls with short, rarely losing possession, always available, always wanting the ball. Murcia are not pressurising the man on the ball; he has more space than normal and he obviously likes it. Real improve. Raúl heads wide. Solari runs through the defence and whacks a shot against the crossbar. A Raúl shot on the turn is tipped over. Then a Zidane shot is tipped over. 'It's only a matter of time,' I think.

Then, disaster for Madrid. The ball hits Helguera's hand in the box. The referee awards a penalty. The Real players crowd round him. They're indignant, angry, bullying. Can't they see they won't be able to make him change his mind? Beckham is to the fore. I wonder what he's saying. The referee shoos off the angry whites. Luis García thumps the ball into the top right corner of the net, and performs three cartwheels. Now the crowd *do* know how to celebrate. I look beyond the stadium at the balconies and the fans there are jumping up and down, too.

Murcia, relaxed, with nothing to lose, play the ball around in little triangles, making the Real Madrid players run around after it. The crowd sing 'olé' at every pass. It's like a large game of piggy in the middle, with Zinedine Zidane, world footballer of the year, and Figo, the proud Portuguese, as piggies. And this against Murcia, quite easily the worst team in the Primera. A Mexican wave starts up, with the accompanying cheering. 2–0 up against Real Madrid! The people on the balcony join in the wave. Real's collection of Zidanes and Pavones are being taunted. The little kid has turned the tables on the playground bully. I'm really enjoying myself. I consider joining in the wave.

Murcia attack down the right. Beckham does a great sliding tackle that puts the ball into touch. The referee signals a foul, free-kick to Murcia. There's another melee of white shirts round the black. More intimidation. The referee goes up to the linesman, then flashes a red card. But who for? White shirts surround the linesman. What's going on? It's down the other corner, I can't see. A familiar figure jogs up the touchline, clapping sarcastically at the linesman. The fans are cheering like another goal has been scored. I look at Simon. He looks at me. It can't be? It is. Beckham off! David Beckham has been sent off! A straight red card! But what the hell for?

Simon gets on the phone to Eric, of the *Sun*, who's watching on the TV in Madrid. He's off the phone quite quickly. "Apparently he said 'hijo de puta' to the linesman," he says. 'Hijo de puta' means 'son of a whore' and is the most common insult made in Spain. But it's not something that you say to a linesman. I can't believe the irony of it. Beckham, who hasn't spoken Spanish all season and who has given up on his language lessons, getting sent off for delivering a perfectly executed insult in Spanish to the referee's assistant.

Suddenly Simon's a busy man as his 'watching brief' turns into a full-blown match report. It takes me a while to realise that the card was a straight red. That Beckham's going to miss the next game. The last game of the season. His season in the sun is now over, in the most disastrous manner. As the match continues, with more Mexican waves, more 'olés' from the home crowd and more and more frustration for

Real Madrid, I wonder whether this spells the end of his career as a Real Madrid player, too. Will he get blamed for this humiliation and in turn, for the debacle of a season Real Madrid have had? 2003/4 started out as 'Beckham's season', with everybody talking about the glamour and ability of the young Englishman. It will be remembered as the most disappointing season ever in Real Madrid's history, one which promised so much yet delivered nothing but shame and humiliation. Will the humiliation be offloaded onto him?

The second half doesn't get much better for Real Madrid. It is punctuated by more 'olés' and Mexican waves as the on-pitch humiliation of ten tired men continues. Real get a late consolation goal through Guti, on as sub, but they can't muster another and the players trudge off the pitch, disconsolate, pissed off, funeral-faced. I wonder how they will greet Beckham in the dressing room. I feel sorry for him, a man whose world seems to be turning to dust in his hands, as Real Madrid's season goes from bad to worse. Barcelona go second, two points ahead. Now there is a chance of Deportivo pushing Real Madrid into *fourth* place next week. And this is the first time in the club's 102-year history that they have lost four games on the trot.

### SUNDAY MAY 23RD

I wake up not knowing where – or even whether – to watch El Real's last game of the season, at home to Real Sociedad. They are still in with a chance of coming second and saving their lucrative pre-season tour, but could, if results go against them, finish fourth. This would mean a place in the Champions League qualifiers, but would be the final humiliation. If Dépor win (in the Sardinero, away to Racing de Santander) and El Real lose, this will be the case whatever Barcelona do in Zaragoza.

During the week the Madrid-based sporting press turned against Beckham. He got another '0' in *Marca*, with the comment 'bocazas' (bigmouth). Míchel, the paper's star columnist and a former Real hero, took the mickey, talking about 'evidence of Beckham's linguistic progress coming at the most inopportune moment'. As the week went on, the clamour for Beckham's head grew stronger. After the Murcia game he flew directly from Madrid to London, where he played the first few minutes of Martin Keown's testimonial at Highbury. The next day there was an unflattering picture of him in an incongruous navy blue kit on the front cover of *Marca* with the headline 'What's Beckham playing at?' and the bye-line 'the club is starting to get tired of him'. There were suggestions that he might be swapped for Lampard, of Chelsea. On the back page Roberto Palomar, the paper's chief reporter, stated 'he tricked us into thinking he's good at free-kicks (he isn't), he tricked us about playing on the right (he doesn't know *where* he's playing) and he tricked us by using an interpreter when he knows Spanish well enough to swear like a trooper.' Palomar went on to suggest that Beckham signed for an athletics club rather than a football club, because he knows how to run, but that's about all. It read like an epitaph. It was looking more and more like Beckham's 'season in the sun' would be his first and last in Spain.

Later in the week, the paper changed its tune, suggesting that Beckham was likely to stay. The Englishman had given his first press conference for two months, stating that he wanted to play for Real Madrid for at least another year. Victoria Beckham had said that she was going to move to the country. The 'sources' that *Marca* use changed their tune, suggesting that the club, after all, wanted to keep him. It would, reading between the lines, not look good for the regime if he went, at least not in this early stage of the summer. Florentino Pérez, facing a re-election battle on July 11th, has been trying desperately to mount a damage limitation campaign. It now looks like José Antonio Camacho, an old Real Madrid hero from his playing days, will become the new coach next season – a dictatorial, headstrong manager who will be able to get the dressing room in order. Pérez has also announced the signing of Walter Samuel, a top quality Argentinian international centre-back, from Roma, a transfer agreed with lightning speed after the end of the Italian season to signal Pérez' intentions of hardening up the defence. He has also laid the first stone of the city's latest training ground, talking about a 'new era' for the club. He's realised how damaging to his cause the last two months have been, and wants to do his utmost to convince the fans he can get things back on track. Selling off the club's most famous player, its most marketable icon, its biggest shirt-shifter, a player who was signed amid such hype and hope, would not be a vote-winning move a few weeks before such an important poll.

Returning to England might not be the best thing for Beckham either. He came to prove himself in Spain and after a good start, ended up being ridiculed. If he left after such a professional and personal disaster of a season, he would always be remembered in Spain as a failure, rather like Ian Rush after his year at Juventus in the '80s. Would he want that? Or would he prefer to fight back, to try to win trophies with Real Madrid in 2004/5 (and beyond) in order to prove to the Spanish public that he *is* after all, worthy of all the hype that surrounds him?

Beckham, of course, will not be playing the last game of the season, will not be displaying the new tattoo on the back of his neck to his home fans (a sword with wings, above the line of his collar, a radical and very evident mark). He will be at the game, though, along with his family and a number of other absentees from the team. The high number of cards and injuries Real have suffered in their dramatic end-of-season collapse means that there will be no Zidane, no Guti, no Roberto Carlos, no Cambiasso, no Raúl Bravo. This will leave Real Madrid playing for second place with Jordi and Borja in central midfield.

For the first time in the season, all the weekend's matches are to be played on the same day, today, Sunday, to lessen the chances of bribery and corruption. Half the teams playing have nothing to play for and there has been much talk of 'maletines' (suitcases full of money passing from club to club as incentive to win, rather than just lay down and die, an institution in the Spanish newspaper rumour mill). So the Spanish FA want to avoid the possibility of teams knowing the result they need before they kick-off.

I've asked around and the only place I can go to see Real Madrid playing Real Sociedad is the peña in L'Hospitalet. Everywhere else is showing El Barça. And I really don't want to go back to that sordid place: all those long faces, all the shouting, disappointment and meanness. What's more, I have little desire to watch Real Madrid at all without Beckham. Just to inwardly cheer for the opposition and enjoy the disappointment of the old drunk merengues, to indulge in the joy of defeat rather than the glow of victory.

I've been thinking about my anti-Madridismo, about what it entails. I have a soft spot for a few teams in the Primera, mainly down to liking the people I've met who support them. Celta de Vigo, Real Sociedad, Albacete. I like Athletic de Bilbao for their stubborn policy of playing 11 Basques in their team. I have funny mixed feelings for Barcelona, that symbol of the Catalan nationalism that I have felt alienated by for the last two years. I admire Valencia and Deportivo for their organisation and team-work. But there is no team in Spain I could actually say I 'support'. No team that makes me jump in the air when they score, that makes me unhappy when they lose, that makes me tensely hopeful when they attack, nervous when they other team has possession. It's like falling in love: you can't just make it happen. Instead, over the year, I have nurtured an anti-support for Real Madrid, and have had the inverse feelings of an ordinary supporter. A completely negative set of responses. Joy after defeat, disappointment after victory. What's more I have become an anti-Madridista de lujo (deluxe), going to every away game they play, sitting with the home fans when I have been able to, willing on the opposition, hoping for their defeat, their humiliation if possible, the increasing fervour of my feelings tempered only by the presence of David Beckham in the team.

Is this healthy? Of course it's not. It is incredibly unhealthy nurturing a negative obsession all year. And now that the season is nearly over I want to cast off this obsession, move on with my life. It is representative of the fact that I haven't acclimatised to the 'country' that I have been living in for a total of two years (and the more I've travelled, the more I've realised that it's more a collection of communities than a country, tied together by a political system, a dodgy TV network, and – a big and, this – a football league).

A royal family, too. There was a royal wedding yesterday. Prince Felipe de Borbón married Doña Leticia Ortiz, a former national newsreader. It was an enormously popular match throughout Spain's diverse regions. The media went big on the event, the streets were curiously empty all day, even in Barcelona, as millions stayed in on a lovely afternoon to watch it. I didn't witness a single minute of the coverage. I watched Manchester United beat Millwall in the FA Cup final in a pub called the Michael Collins near the Sagrada Familia cathedral.

It's my own fault, this alienation. I'm not blaming the Spanish. All year I have been surprised by the openness, friendliness and spontaneous generosity of the people I have met on my adventure following Beckham around Spain. I have been given valuable insight into the character of the country. I have enjoyed the food, the wine, the hospitality, the weather, the architecture. But I have never felt 'part' of the country (least of all in Barcelona). I have always felt like a foreigner, an outsider looking through a window at the most amazing things going on. I have had privileged insight but I will never get inside. And I don't know if I want to. I have my own language, my own culture, my own form of humour. I have lived in different countries for nearly half of my adult life, and I love how doing so stimulates my curiosity. But it's time for me to go home. It's time for me to settle down. I am grateful that, unlike in the case of my compatriot David Beckham, my decision whether to stay or go hasn't been the subject of intense media scrutiny.

In the end I decide to go to watch Espanyol play Murcia at the Olympic Stadium in Montjuic, a half-hour walk from my flat. They're practically giving away tickets to garner support during their fight against relegation: a friend of a friend has a spare one. Espanyol need to win, to definitely avoid going down. They are one point above Celta de Vigo, two above Valladolid. Only one of the three will stay up, and all three are playing the last match, simultaneously, in their home stadiums. My friends are late, we miss the first ten minutes. The stadium is just about full: there are over 50,000 people here, more than twice the normal number. The atmosphere is cracking when the place is this full, when there is such tension in the air. Our seats have been taken when we get there: no matter, we get a good view standing. About one in five fans has ear-phones in: they are listening to radio commentaries of the other games and telling the scores to their friends. Espanyol attack and attack, but they just can't score. Little Iván de la Peña, 'lo pelat', the bald one, is orchestrating the team in a way that Beckham was expected to do at Real Madrid. But the ball just won't go in. At half time I get the other scores from an old fellow with a big moustache. Valladolid are winning 1–0, Celta are drawing 0–0. If it stays like this, Valladolid will stay up, Espanyol go down. I ask another, younger man what's happening at the top. Barça are drawing. Real Madrid are losing 3–1 in the Bernabéu. It was 3–0, but Figo scored a penalty.

"And Dépor?"

"Dépor won 1–0." (Their match kicked off earlier as the result didn't determine a relegation or European qualification issue.)

"That means?"

"It looks like Real Madrid are going to finish fourth."

That horrible feeling of glee.

Espanyol start the second half poorly and people are nervous. There's a lot of smoking going on. Even the 'Brigadas Blanquiazules', the far-right hard-core with their Spanish flags, have gone quiet. A guy to my right has his head in his hands. His eyes are closed. Murcia are trying hard. With 20 minutes to go they launch a couple of dangerous attacks. Luis García hits the post. Then, a minute later, Espanyol launch their own attack. Raúl Tamudo hits the crossbar. Hands go in heads. It's not looking good. Iván de la Peña picks up the ball in midfield, runs to the edge of the Murcia box and passes a ball into the area, where Tamudo is running in. He hits a narrow-angled shot inside the near post. That tell-tale ripple. Goooooooooooool! Everyone's on their feet. Luis Fernández, Espanyol's manager slides along his knees onto the pitch. Flares go off in the Brigadas Blanquiazules end. The unrestrained joy of relief. I clap three or four times. I'd have preferred Celta to stay up.

Espanyol score a second goal shortly after and the celebrations begin in earnest. Singing, dancing, flares. The Brigadas Blanquiazules throw seats and fireworks at the police. An Espanyol player gets sent off. It doesn't matter. The final whistle blows. People are crying with relief. "Espanyol, Espanyol, Espanyol!" is chanted. My friends leave; I want to stay and watch. Some fans jump over the fences, over the moats, and onto the pitch where the entire squad is celebrating. Several are caught by security guards and hauled off. But the guards have no chance. More and more jump the fences to reach the pitch. Pretty soon the security guards give up and thousands stream onto the turf. They congregate in the goals, pull down the crossbar nearest me. Soon much of the pitch is full of blue and white shirts. Occasionally a player emerges, and staggers into the tunnel, stripped to his underpants by trophy-hunters. I look down and see a route to the pitch that is relatively easy to negotiate. Then I think again. I've had too many vicarious thrills this season, I don't need any more.

I leave the stadium and take the marvellous route down the hill to La Plaza de España, the best exit from a football ground I've ever made. Past the magnificent two-towered Palau Nacional building, past the shimmering, dancing, coloured fountains, walking down the many steps with fans too exhausted with relief to sing or even talk. I don't care so much about Espanyol but I'm emotional, too. The season is over. I think about my journey. Beckham got to see the airports, the plush hotels, the inside of the stadiums. I've been more privileged. I think about all the places I've been, the people I've met, the food I've eaten, the drinks I've drunk. What makes this country tick? It's the fucking football. What makes all these fans and teams from different regions more motivated than anything else? Their games against the establishment team from the capital, Real Madrid. I think of all the clubs I've supported against Real. All the excitement, the joy, the sorrow.

I realise that I've forgotten to ask about their final result. I look for someone with a radio. Everybody's put them away. Then I spot a short old man, rotund, in a black jacket, who still has his ear-plugs in. He's a few yards in front. If Madrid lost their fifth consecutive match, they finish fourth. Poor Beckham's season will have been a disaster. Pérez' vain dream will have had the worst possible ending. I catch him up, tap him on the shoulder.

"What did El Real do in the end?"

"Huh?"

"EL REAL MADRID. WHAT DID THEY DO?"

"El Real? They lost. 4–1."

Again, that horrible feeling of glee.

## RESULTS JORNADA 37

| | | | |
|---|---|---|---|
| OSASUNA | 1 | ATHLETIC | 2 |
| DEPORTIVO | 3 | CELTA | 0 |
| MALLORCA | 4 | ESPANYOL | 2 |
| REAL SOCIEDAD | 1 | MÁLAGA | 1 |
| **MURCIA** | **2** | **REAL MADRID** | **1** |
| BARCELONA | 1 | RACING | 0 |
| ALBACETE | 1 | SEVILLA | 4 |
| VILLARREAL | 2 | VALENCIA | 1 |
| BETIS | 1 | VALLADOLID | 0 |
| ATLÉTICO | 1 | ZARAGOZA | 2 |

## RESULTS JORNADA 38

| | | | |
|---|---|---|---|
| RACING | 0 | DEPORTIVO | 1 |
| MÁLAGA | 2 | BETIS | 3 |
| VALENCIA | 0 | ALBACETE | 1 |
| VALLADOLID | 3 | VILLARREAL | 0 |
| ESPANYOL | 2 | MURCIA | 0 |
| CELTA | 1 | MALLORCA | 2 |
| ZARAGOZA | 2 | BARCELONA | 1 |
| ATHLETIC | 3 | ATLÉTICO | 4 |
| SEVILLA | 1 | OSASUNA | 0 |
| **REAL MADRID** | **1** | **REAL SOCIEDAD** | **4** |

## LA CLASIFICACIÓN

|  | P | W | D | L | F | A | Pts |
|---|---|---|---|---|---|---|---|
| VALENCIA | 38 | 23 | 8 | 7 | 71 | 27 | 77 |
| BARCELONA | 38 | 21 | 9 | 8 | 63 | 39 | 72 |
| DEPORTIVO | 38 | 21 | 8 | 9 | 60 | 34 | 71 |
| **REAL MADRID** | **38** | **21** | **7** | **10** | **72** | **54** | **70** |
| ATHLETIC | 38 | 15 | 11 | 12 | 53 | 49 | 56 |
| SEVILLE | 38 | 15 | 10 | 13 | 56 | 45 | 55 |
| ATLÉTICO | 38 | 15 | 10 | 13 | 51 | 53 | 55 |
| VILLARREAL | 38 | 15 | 9 | 14 | 47 | 49 | 54 |
| BETIS | 38 | 13 | 13 | 12 | 46 | 43 | 52 |
| MÁLAGA | 38 | 15 | 6 | 17 | 50 | 55 | 51 |
| MALLORCA | 38 | 15 | 6 | 17 | 54 | 66 | 51 |
| ZARAGOZA | 38 | 13 | 9 | 16 | 46 | 55 | 48 |
| OSASUNA | 38 | 11 | 15 | 12 | 38 | 37 | 48 |
| ALBACETE | 38 | 13 | 8 | 17 | 40 | 48 | 47 |
| REAL SOCIEDAD | 38 | 11 | 13 | 14 | 49 | 53 | 46 |
| ESPANYOL | 38 | 13 | 4 | 21 | 48 | 64 | 43 |
| RACING | 38 | 11 | 10 | 17 | 48 | 63 | 42 |
| VALLADOLID | 38 | 10 | 11 | 17 | 46 | 56 | 41 |
| CELTA | 38 | 9 | 12 | 17 | 48 | 68 | 39 |
| MURCIA | 38 | 5 | 11 | 22 | 29 | 57 | 26 |